Issues and Actors in the Global Political Economy

Also by André Broome

The Currency of Power: The IMF and Monetary Reform in Central Asia

Issues and Actors in the Global Political Economy

André Broome

First published 2014 by
PALGRAVE MACMILLAN

Palgrave Macmillan in the UK is an imprint of Macmillan Publishers Limited,
registered in England, company number 785998, of Houndmills, Basingstoke,
Hampshire RG21 6XS.

Palgrave Macmillan in the US is a division of St Martin's Press LLC,
175 Fifth Avenue, New York, NY 10010.

Palgrave Macmillan is the global academic imprint of the above companies
and has companies and representatives throughout the world.

Palgrave® and Macmillan® are registered trademarks in the United States,
the United Kingdom, Europe and other countries

ISBN 978–0–230–28915–4 hardback
ISBN 978–0–230–28916–1 paperback

This book is printed on paper suitable for recycling and made from fully
managed and sustained forest sources. Logging, pulping and manufacturing
processes are expected to conform to the environmental regulations of the
country of origin.

A catalogue record for this book is available from the British Library.

A catalog record for this book is available from the Library of Congress.

Typeset by Cambrian Typesetters, Camberley, Surrey

Printed in China

For Zoë

Contents

PART I   ACTORS IN THE GLOBAL POLITICAL ECONOMY

List of Boxes

List of Figures

List of Tables

Acknowledgements

This book emerged from discussions with Len Seabrooke from the Copenhagen Business School and Steven Kennedy from Palgrave Macmillan at the British International Studies Association annual conference in Leicester in December 2009. Originally conceived as a co-edited collection on contemporary actors and issues in the global political economy, the project gradually evolved into a sole-authored volume. My grateful thanks go to Mark Beeson for the initial suggestion to develop a new IPE textbook. Throughout the course of the project Len Seabrooke provided invaluable support as an intellectual sounding board, while Steven Kennedy was consistent in his editorial support, encouragement and patience. I am grateful to the reviewers for the publisher who provided insightful feedback and suggestions on the draft proposal, sample chapters and the full manuscript. Undergraduate and graduate students at the University of Birmingham and later at the University of Warwick helped to provide inspiration for the contents and scope of the book, and prompted me to reflect on how to organize the text for IPE novices. A large number of colleagues provided valuable feedback on specific chapters. A particular note of thanks goes to Mark Beeson, James Brassett, Shaun Breslin, Chris Clarke, Michel Goyer, John Hobson, Caroline Kuzemko, Jiesheng Li, Sam McPhilemy, Jens Mortensen, Lena Rethel, Ben Richardson, Amin Samman, Alex Sutton, Lisa Tilley, Lauren Tooker, Eleni Tsingou and Matthew Watson. Above all, I am indebted to Alexandra Homolar for her sound intellectual advice on this project from its initial conception to eventual completion.

ANDRÉ BROOME
University of Warwick

List of Abbreviations

APEC	Asia-Pacific Economic Cooperation
ASEAN	Association of Southeast Asian Nations
BIS	Bank for International Settlements
BRICs	Brazil, Russia, India, China
CFCs	chlorofluorocarbons
DSB	Dispute Settlement Body
EC	European Commission
ECB	European Central Bank
EME	emerging market economy
ERM	Exchange Rate Mechanism
EU	European Union
Eurodad	European Network on Debt and Development
FDI	foreign direct investment
FSB	Financial Stability Board
FTA	free trade agreement
G5	Group of Five
G6	Group of Six
G7	Group of Seven
G8	Group of Eight
G10	Group of Ten
G20	Group of 20
G30	Group of 30
GATT	General Agreement on Tariffs and Trade
GDP	gross domestic product
GEF	Global Environment Facility
GHG	greenhouse gas
GST	Goods and Services Tax
HDI	Human Development Index
HDR	Human Development Report
HIPC	heavily indebted poor countries
IBRD	International Bank for Reconstruction and Development
IDA	International Development Association
IEA	International Energy Agency
IFI	international financial institution
IFT	informal fund transfer
ILO	International Labour Organization
IMF	International Monetary Fund

IOs	international organizations
IOSCO	International Organization of Securities Commissions
IPCC	Intergovernmental Panel on Climate Change
IPE	International Political Economy
IR	International Relations
ISI	import-substitution industrialization
ITO	International Trade Organization
JVI	Joint Vienna Institute
MDGs	Millennium Development Goals
MDRI	Multilateral Debt Relief Initiative
MFN	most-favoured nation
MNCs	multinational corporations
NAFTA	North American Free Trade Agreement
NGOs	non-governmental organizations
NIEs	newly industrialized economies
ODA	Official Development Assistance
OECD	Organisation for Economic Cooperation and Development
OPEC	Organization of the Petroleum Exporting Countries
PRSPs	Poverty Reduction Strategy Papers
SDR	Special Drawing Rights
TNCs	transnational corporations
UN	United Nations
UNCED	United Nations Conference on Environment and Development
UNCTAD	United Nations Conference on Trade and Development
UNDP	United Nations Development Programme
UNEP	United Nations Environment Programme
UNFCCC	United Nations Framework Convention on Climate Change
UNODC	United Nations Office on Drugs and Crime
VAT	Value-Added Tax
WDR	World Development Report
WIPO	World Intellectual Property Organization
WTO	World Trade Organization

Chapter 1

Introduction to International Political Economy

Introduction

On Black Tuesday in October 1929 the Wall Street stock market crashed, wiping out the enormous stock gains of the Roaring 20s and leading to the Great Depression of the 1930s. The global economic and political instability that ensued fostered the political conditions for World War II. At the same time, policy experiments from the Great Depression era subsequently shaped the construction of a new postwar international economic order. In September 2008, 79 years after the Wall Street crash of 1929, the investment bank Lehman Brothers Holding Inc. filed for bankruptcy protection in the USA, with record debts exceeding US$600 billion. The collapse of Lehman Brothers, later satirized in the animated children's film *Despicable Me* as the 'Bank of Evil', is widely credited with being one of the critical events that led to the world economic crisis of 2008–09, which saw the global financial system brought to its knees.

Understanding these events, explaining the global dynamics that helped to produce them and analysing their long-term political, economic and social consequences are fundamental issues for the study of the global political economy. This book gives students a solid foundation in what this entails, how and why the study of the global political economy has continued to evolve and the ways in which to go about the business of analysing different issues and actors in the field. Through exploring the critical issues and actors in the global political economy, it equips those students who are engaging with the field for the first time and those who are brushing up on their knowledge with the key tools of the trade.

The global political economy as an evolving subject matter

The global political economy has changed dramatically since the Industrial Revolution of the late eighteenth and early nineteenth centuries, and maintaining a historically grounded view of the global political economy as an evolving subject matter is essential. This means that the study of the global political economy involves thinking reflexively about how and why changes in one dimension of the global political economy interconnect and overlap with others. Through the lens of the past, we can gain a better and more dynamic understanding of the evolution of the present in terms of changing forms of governance, authority, relationships and outcomes in the global political economy. Landmark events in three key areas – money, trade and crises – serve to illustrate the scope of changes in the global political economy.

During the last 140 years the structure of the international monetary system has been transformed on several occasions. From the 1870s until World War I, states such as Britain, France and Germany operated under the Gold Standard, and maintained the convertibility of their currencies at a fixed price in gold in the absence of controls on capital movements. International liquidity was maintained by cooperation between central banks, via loans and gold shipments. After the end of World War I this system was briefly re-established in a modified form as the Gold Exchange Standard from the mid-1920s until the mid-1930s (Oliver 2006: 109). Following the political and economic chaos associated with the breakdown of the interwar Gold Standard and the Great Depression of the 30s, a new international monetary system was created at the end of World War II with the 1944 Bretton Woods agreement, termed the Bretton Woods system. The post-World War II international monetary system incorporated the general acceptance of national controls on capital flows in order to support a fixed but adjustable exchange rate system, while maintaining the commitment to an open international trade system (Helleiner 1994: 25). The Bretton Woods agreement established the International Monetary Fund (IMF) as the institutional linchpin of the new international monetary system. The IMF was charged with overseeing multilateral monetary cooperation between countries based on a fixed rate at which the US dollar was convertible into gold, with the 'par values' of other currencies linked to the US dollar and periodically readjusted as economic conditions altered. The Bretton Woods era came to an end following the 1971 Nixon Shocks, which suspended the convertibility of the dollar into gold at a fixed rate of exchange. Many countries subsequently adopted 'floating' market-determined exchange rate regimes. Others fixed their exchange rates or managed their currency values through exchange rate intervention against major currencies such as the dollar, the deutschmark, sterling, the franc, or the yen. The dollar and the euro are now the most common 'anchor' currencies in the international monetary system. In contrast to the restrictive currency practices of the 1930s and the early decades after the end of World War II, few countries today maintain permanent restrictions on access to foreign exchange for trade in goods and services.

Since 1870 world economic output has grown on average by around 3 per cent annually. Merchandise trade in 1960 trade was over 12 times greater than it had been in 1900 (Statistical Office of the United Nations 1962). World merchandise exports have continued to increase substantially in percentage terms since 1964, with the most notable exception being a major contraction of international trade in 2009 in response to the global financial crisis, when global trade in goods decreased by 23 per cent (WTO 2011a). Growth in trade in goods and services has gone hand-in-hand with the greater legalization of global trade rules, as multilateral trade principles negotiated through the General Agreement on Tariffs and Trade (GATT, created in 1947) gradually gained authority through successive rounds of trade talks and international agreements. This led to the establishment of the World Trade Organization (WTO) after the eighth round of the GATT negotiations was concluded in 1994. The legalization of international trade has increased the stability of actors' expectations in how cross-border trade in goods and services are transacted, what procedures govern how imports and exports are taxed and paid for, and what principles and rules should limit local and central government support for domestic industries in relation to competition from foreign firms. As a result, the development of the post-World War II liberal multilateral trade system greatly expanded the volume of cross-border economic transactions, which served to integrate national markets for production and trade in goods and services.

The world economy has experienced at least eight major international financial crises since the late nineteenth century. The first four of these were: (1) the Great Depression of the 1870s; (2) the Panic of 1890; (3) the 1907 Bankers' Panic; and (4) the Great Depression of the 1930s. The Great Depression of the 1870s was driven by the collapse of German and Austrian stock markets, which led to declining capital flows and crises in European and American economies. In the Panic of 1890, sovereign debt crises in Latin America following the end of a credit boom nearly caused the collapse of the London-based Baring Brothers bank, which was heavily exposed through lending to Argentina and Uruguay. This prompted the Bank of England Governor, William Lidderdale, to form an international consortium of banks that guaranteed Baring's debts in order to avert a wider depression. The 1907 Bankers' Panic in the USA resulted in the New York Stock Exchange losing close to half its value from the previous year, prompting a loss of confidence among bank depositors, widespread bank runs, and a sharp spike in bankruptcies. Financier J.P. Morgan and other New York bankers used their own financial resources to inject liquidity into the banking system to prevent a systemic collapse, in a series of events that eventually led to the establishment of the US Federal Reserve System in 1913 (Rethel and Sinclair 2012: 12). At the end of the Roaring 20s, the Great Crash of 1929 on Wall Street contributed to the onset of the Great Depression of the 1930s. This led to a worldwide depression and sharp declines in international trade and capital flows throughout the decade preceding World War II (IMF 2009b: 128).

Since the breakdown of the Bretton Woods international monetary system in the early 70s, the world economy has experienced four further international financial crises, while individual countries have experienced a far greater number of national economic and financial crises. Credit problems in Latin American countries in 1981–82 produced a series of debt crises that lasted for most of the decade, and contributed to the long-running debt crises in a group of low-income economies that are now termed heavily indebted poor countries (HIPCs). The collapse of real estate and equity price bubbles in 1991–92 caused a severe banking crisis in Scandinavian countries, and led to a sustained recession in Japan, where the Nikkei stock market index fell by over 60 per cent between 1989 and 1992 and real estate prices dropped sharply between 1991 and 1998. These international financial problems also contributed to the European exchange rate mechanism (ERM) crisis in 1992, when the British pound was forced to withdraw from the ERM on Black Wednesday, on 16 September 1992, in response to strong pressure from currency speculation. Half a decade later, the Asian financial crisis of 1997–98 and the Russian financial crisis of 1998 prompted large outflows of capital from emerging economies, causing dramatic falls in the exchange rates of national currencies. The Russian crisis resulted in the government defaulting on its domestic debt after the stock market lost three-quarters of its value between January and August 1998. Most recently, after the expansion of residential property booms around the world over the course of the 2000s, the 2007 US subprime crisis and the 2008–09 global financial crisis were driven by the bursting of asset price bubbles and a crunch in retail and wholesale credit markets (see Chapter 13).

This brief sketch of some of the key markers of change in the global political economy since the end of the nineteenth century previews many of the evolving issues and dynamics that are discussed in greater depth throughout the chapters in this book. It highlights that the study of particular phenomena in the global political economy involves the development of both issue-specific knowledge and systematic knowledge of the global political economy in historical context. To fully grasp how the different pieces of the puzzle fit together, students of the global political economy must aim to develop in-depth knowledge of key features of the global political economy at the same time as gradually building a broad base of subject knowledge that cuts across specific issue areas.

Studying the global political economy

International Political Economy (IPE) is an interdisciplinary field of enquiry within the social sciences that is concerned with the study of the past, present and future dynamics of the global political economy. The precise definition of IPE as an academic discipline, which areas of the global political economy should be its core research focus and how they should be studied have remained contested. Like other disciplinary fields within the social sciences, IPE scholars tend to take different standpoints when it comes to questions of what there is to know, what can be known and how it can be known. Using the vocabulary of the philosophy of science, this means that they disagree in terms of *ontology* (the study of the nature of being, centred on questions about what there is to know about particular objects of study), *epistemology* (the study of what the nature of knowledge is, how it is acquired and to what extent a given subject or phenomena can be known) and *methodology* (how one goes about the business of knowing – the procedures and principles for investigating a particular subject or issue).

The parameters of IPE thus stretch to include different types of scholarship that ask starkly different questions about the global political economy. Such academic distinctions and disagreements orient the focus of IPE research towards investigating some issues more than others, and towards examining the roles played by some actors in the world economy more than others. IPE initially emerged as a sub-discipline of Political Science and International Relations (IR) in North American, European and Australasian universities in the early 1970s. During this period the global political economy underwent a process of prolonged turmoil and structural change, which produced sweeping changes in key economic sectors and in the role of states as economic governors. This involved transformations in the nature of international economic cooperation, international economic governance, the distribution of wealth stocks and resource flows between and within different countries and the balance of authority between state actors and market actors.

The importance of differences in how the field of IPE is typically understood by scholars can be illustrated by looking briefly at how it is defined in three well-thumbed texts. Robert O'Brien and Marc Williams

(2013: 24) describe IPE in broad terms as an open field of study that encompasses both the national and the international, an interdisciplinary endeavour that 'crosses the boundaries between the study of politics and economics', which may also draw on a range of other social science fields such as history and geography. John Ravenhill (2011: 19), in contrast, offers a more parsimonious and perhaps easier to grasp definition of IPE as 'a subject matter whose central focus is the interrelationship between public and private power in the allocation of scarce resources'. A further definition from Ronen Palan (2012: 1) does not see IPE as an academic discipline in its own right, but rather as a research agenda that brings together a range of social science disciplines that address two key concerns. The first is that a substantive and critical difference exists between a world economy that is understood as operating 'in an environment that is divided among sovereign states of various power and size' compared with the imagined seamless global economy that exists in the abstract in conventional economics textbooks. The second key concern for Palan is that political action in an environment of increasing international economic integration differs markedly from the understanding of political action that is the starting point within conventional studies of Political Science and IR.

In addition to competing conceptions of how the subject matter of the field is defined, scholars also differ over the appropriate historical starting point in IPE. The majority of IPE textbooks concentrate for the most part on the changing dynamics of the global political economy in the period after the end of World War II, and especially on changes that have occurred since the breakdown of the Bretton Woods international monetary system in the 1970s (see Chapter 11). Here the stress is on understanding the contemporary era of economic globalization. This era dates from the early 70s, and is associated with global dynamics of change in trade, production, monetary relations and finance. Today's globalization was preceded by an earlier era of international economic integration in the nineteenth century and early twentieth century. At this time, the world economy was dominated by colonial imperialism and was fuelled by technological changes in international transportation, a period which ended with the start of World War I in 1914 (Schwartz 2010: 165). Taking a longer-term historical view in the study of IPE helps to show how the features and dynamics of the world economy have changed over time – as well as revealing important sources of continuity across time periods that are often assumed to be historically unique. Excellent texts that skilfully explore the origins of the contemporary global political economy by combining current IPE trends with a broad historical coverage include those by O'Brien and Williams (2013) and Herman Schwartz (2010), among others.

This book does not seek to erect firm borders around an exclusive idea of the field of IPE and shares the openness of O'Brien and Williams (2013) to drawing from multiple social science disciplines for studying issues and actors in the global political economy. Crucially, IPE is conceived here as an evolving field of enquiry. This is essential in order for students and teachers in IPE to ensure that the parameters of the field keep pace with changing developments in its subject matter. For example, until the global financial crisis in 2008–09 made a mockery of such disciplinary limits, issues related to housing finance systems were largely seen as peripheral 'domestic' issues for IPE scholars (see Schwartz and Seabrooke 2009).

Contentious terminologies

Concepts and terms in the social sciences, as in all academic disciplines, comprise a language of their own that straddles the ideas and words that are commonly used in everyday conversations. The language used in the study of IPE is sometimes intimidating for novices because such terms are usually unfamiliar, but there is nothing intrinsically difficult to master about the concepts themselves. In particular, these 'contentious terminologies' can sometimes trip students up because specialized concepts from other social science disciplines often have a distinct meaning in the study of IPE. One example that helps to illustrate this point from IR is the concept of 'securitization'. Within IR, this refers to Copenhagen School approaches that study how traditionally non-security issues become 'securitized' in particular societal and political contexts at different points in time (McDonald 2008). In contrast, within IPE securitization refers instead to the economic process by which various types of financial assets are 'pooled' by financial institutions, enabling non-tradable assets such as mortgages to be repackaged and sold on to new investors (see Chapters 7 and 13). A further example is the contentious term 'globalization'. Definitions of globalization abound, and may include a more expansive emphasis that encompasses changes in cultural, technological and population mobility processes at the global level that foster interconnectedness and reduce the importance of territorial borders between many societies (Scholte 2008). Within IPE, however, economic globalization is usually defined more narrowly as the 'international integration of markets in goods, services, and capital' (Garrett 2000: 942), processes which have contributed to increasing relations of interdependence between different categories of actors in the global political economy.

Methodology is another key term used in the study of the global political economy, which refers to the set of principles and procedures that are used to investigate a specific subject or issue. There is, however, widespread contention about what techniques should be employed. Methodological debates in IPE tend to centre on the relative advantages of quantitative techniques of statistical analysis compared with qualitative analysis, and whether research designs based on large numbers of cases or small numbers of cases (or single case studies) are better for producing robust knowledge about how the global political economy works. Whereas qualitative methods aim to gain an in-depth understanding of action and behaviour, and the reasons that produce particular actions and behaviour, quantitative methods aim to systematically investigate social, economic and political phenomena through measurement. As the following brief look at the use of statistics shows, choosing a methodological 'side' is not a simple or straightforward matter.

Numbers are powerful tools in the study of the global political economy. They enable the uncovering of economic trends and comparative analysis across different countries and regions, which provide snapshots of economic change between countries and within the same country over time. The chapters in this book draw upon a wide range of descriptive statistical data to show national, regional and global trends. Like all international statistics, the statistical information that is presented here provides useful indicators of past, present and possible future trajectories in the world economy. Yet it is important to exercise caution when engaging with quantitative analyses as they often implicitly assume that 'statistics represent reality', and thus accept such data as 'a neutral, sanitized, and objective expression of an unseen truth' (Ward 2004: 25). As Robert Wade (2012) points out, 'National and international statistics offices always operate in the tension between professional standards of objectivity and political insistence on certain results.' This does not mean that all statistics are politically biased, but helps to highlight that processes and techniques of measurement – and the aggregate statistical indices they produce – can serve as a potent means of political persuasion and influence. From another perspective, statistics are fundamentally interpretive, because numbers 'embody theoretical assumptions about what should be counted, how one should understand material reality, and how quantification contributes to systematic knowledge about the world' (Poovey 1998: xii).

Like all methodological choices in the social sciences, the tools that are used to analyse, understand and explain different issues in the field shape both the types of research questions that can be asked and the quality of the answers that empirical research can provide. The choice of method should thus be based on 'a clear understanding of the comparative strengths and limits of various methods, and how they complement each other' (George and Bennett 2005: 5). For example, methodological choices influence how different types of cases are analysed and under-stood. A case is 'an instance of a class of events' such as economic crises, types of institutional change and policy reform, or bureaucratic cultures within international organizations, which 'the investigator chooses to study with the aim of developing theory (or "generic knowledge") regarding the causes of similarities or differences among instances (cases) of that class of events' (George and Bennett 2005: 17–18). To stay with the example of quantitative techniques, reliance on statistical methods orients analysis towards some subjects rather than others, and shapes what issues are identified as policy problems for authorities at different levels of economic governance. The use of statistics in macro-level analy-sis of a large number of cases (large-N studies) can potentially obscure how dynamics and processes of change actually operate at the micro- and meso-levels (Jerven 2013). In a reversal of this methodological problem, substituting qualitative approaches for quantitative statistical analysis can potentially generate greater understanding of how causal mecha-nisms work in a smaller number of cases or a single case (small-n studies), but the general applicability of these insights in other contexts may be harder to demonstrate.

The key point to note here is that it is important to understand and reflect upon how, when and why particular empirical methods are used to study different types of phenomena. Too often students of IPE fall into an ontological trap by assuming that either the global political economy is based on material properties that can only be studied as objective facts through the use of a quantitative methodology; or it is based on ideational properties that can only be studied through processes of inter-subjective construction in a qualitative analysis. To avoid this trap, it is helpful to recognize there 'is a very wide range of useful knowledge between mathematical certainty on the one hand and romantic fiction or superstition on the other' (Stretton 1999: 26).

Expanding IPE

Issue areas that have traditionally received the most sustained attention within the study of IPE, such as international trade, production, money and finance, have been transformed as the world economy has evolved during the twentieth and twenty-first centuries. Compared with a world economy dominated by colonial empires and economic imperialism at the start of the twentieth century, the world economy of the twenty-first century is populated by a far greater variety of global actors whose behaviour is consequential for how the global political economy works, and for who gets what, when and why from global economic processes.

As a result of these changes, the common portrayal of states managing domestic economies with a high degree of national policy autonomy during the 1950s and 60s has been replaced by processes of international economic integration and economic interdependence that have intensified in the last four decades.

When IPE emerged as a distinct field of enquiry in the 1970s, much of the early literature in the field was primarily concerned with studying relations between a small number of the world's largest economies, and how these changing relations were reshaping structures of authority and economic processes in the global political economy. Notwithstanding the differences that exist both within and across research cultures (Cohen 2008), non-state actors and smaller or weaker states initially received little attention from IPE scholars. While the predominant focus of attention during the 1970s in the study of IR was on East–West relations in the Cold War, within IPE the primary country focus was usually on major West European economies, the USA and Japan, and how these countries were affected by structural changes in international monetary relations, international trade and global energy production.

Contemporary IPE research has challenged the eurocentric bias of the field (Hobson 2012), and scholars have made a strong case for 'globalizing' IPE in order to transcend the analytical limits of a preoccupation with studying advanced industrialized economies at the expense of investigating all of the 'constituent regions and processes' of the global political economy (Phillips 2005: 2). Theoretical approaches in IPE have developed in recent years to encompass new perspectives on cultural political economy (Best and Paterson 2009), everyday political economy (Hobson and Seabrooke 2007), constructivist IPE (Abdelal *et al.* 2010) and poststructuralist IPE (de Goede 2006), among others. Meanwhile, the geographical focus of scholarship has expanded to examine a broader variety of political-economic systems and different forms of economic practices across a wider range of social environments. Examples include the emergence and rapid growth of Islamic finance and banking practices in the last four decades (Rethel 2011), economic identity and national economic strategies in post-Soviet states (Abdelal 2001) and economic development processes in non-democratic political systems (Tsai 2007), to name only a few. A common theme among recent contributions to IPE scholarship has been the attempt to 'combine disciplinary knowledge that begins with Politics and Economics in ways that transcend or go beyond the specific approach of both' (Hobson 2012: 23). These scholarly developments in the field have opened up the range of issues and actors that constitute important subjects of enquiry, and have helped to expand the theoretical approaches available to formulate research questions and address empirical puzzles in new ways.

This book incorporates many of the traditional issues that have preoccupied the field as well as discussing a range of issues that have gained traction more recently. In particular, the book aims to expand how students conceive of the types and roles of actors in the global political economy, and how different categories of action are consequential in shaping and transforming global economic processes. Six categories of actors are examined in individual chapters in Part I: state actors; international organizations (IOs); club forums; market actors; non-governmental organizations (NGOs); and everyday actors. These actors cross traditional understandings of the boundaries between public and private domains of action, on the one hand, and economic and social domains of action on the other. As Figure 1.1 illustrates, these analytical boundaries are not hard-and-fast real-world distinctions in the global political economy, even though different categories of actors are often situated more in one sphere than in others.

A common way of defining the subject matter of IPE is to say that it is concerned with asking questions that fall into one of two main areas of enquiry. The first is 'how politics constrains economic choices'; the second is 'how economic forces motivate and constrain political choices' (Walter and Sen 2009: 1). Here politics is understood as comprising the public domain, while economics is located in the private domain. A similar distinction is often found between market actors (such as commercial banks and firms) and social actors (such as NGOs), whose activities are separated between the 'for-profit' economic sphere and the voluntary/non-profit 'third sector'.

These traditional distinctions are a useful way to grasp some of the core differences in actors' roles, but they can also lead students of IPE to adopt problematic assumptions about what different categories of actors do in the global political economy, and the dynamic interactions between them. State actors do not just regulate market activities and govern the 'rules of the game' that constitute how economies work. They are also major market players as employers, consumers of market goods and services, and property owners and managers. Private market players act purposively in areas that go beyond commercial transactions. This may include organized political lobbying, and funding think-tanks that aim to shape public opinion and political discourse about economic policy (Hacker and Pierson 2010). Their economic actions have enormous effects for society as a whole. NGOs, while typically understood as social actors, may also play important economic roles such as the delivery of development services.

Because of these blurred distinctions, the maintenance of strict divisions between economic and social or public and private domains is seldom possible in IPE research, even if it may sometimes serve a useful

Figure 1.1   *Domains of action in the global political economy*

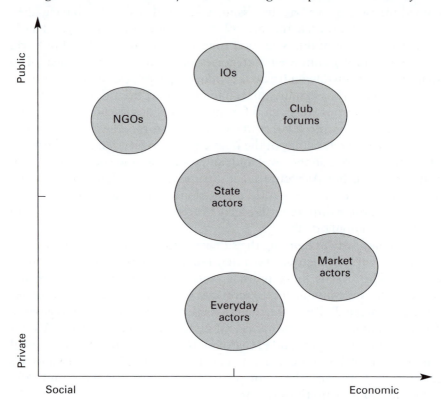

heuristic purpose. As Figure 1.1 suggests, different actors tend to operate more in some domains than others, and specific categories of action may be more commercially or more politically sensitive. Yet understanding the range of factors that shape political-economic processes and outcomes requires a multidimensional analysis.

As other IPE scholars such as Geoffrey Underhill (2005) have high-lighted, systems of political authority and market systems of wealth production and distribution form 'part of the same, integrated ensemble of governance' rather than distinct realms of action. The dynamics of political interaction therefore constitute '*the means by which economic structures, in particular the structures of the market, are established and in turn transformed*' (Underhill 2005: 4, emphasis original). In short, market systems and political systems are co-constitutive: states both create economic structures of production and distribution, and in turn are shaped by, and through, these market processes. The co-constitutive relationship between states and markets also cuts across the analytic distinction that is typically drawn between domestic economic processes and international economic processes. Specific institutional arrangements may be organized at the national, regional, or global level (Underhill 2005: 6), such as national trade policies, regional free trade arrangements and multilateral trade rules enforced by the WTO. For the purposes of explaining and understanding how these institutional configurations are created, which actors exercise the most influence over them, what outcomes they produce and how and why they evolve over time, a strict separation of 'international' political economy and 'domestic' political economy into separate spheres is artificial.

The focus of the book

International Political Economy is not a homogeneous academic discipline with clear agreed parameters on the limits that constitute the field. Students and scholars of IPE working in different research cultures, as well as different intellectual traditions of IPE within the same country or the same institution, define the field in various ways. These differences have consequences for what content is studied in undergraduate and graduate courses in IPE, how issues are examined, which actors are given the most attention, how dynamics of change are understood and what constitutes the historical subject matter of IPE. This book aims to provide a pluralist introduction to the global political economy, which provides students with the essential toolkit that allows them to effectively address three fundamental questions:

1. How does the contemporary global political economy work, and for whose benefit?
2. How has the global political economy changed over time, and why?
3. How do different actors shape processes of change in the global political economy, and with what effects?

While the book explains theoretical approaches and empirical concerns that relate to these three questions, it does not provide straightforward answers to the wide range of normative 'right' or 'wrong' questions that often guide the ways in which the contemporary global economy is portrayed and studied. Rather, it seeks to foster students' own critical engagement with the subject matter by showing that the ways in which *who*, *what*, *when* and *how* questions are answered can lead to radically different evaluations of the nature and purpose of the global political economy. Examples of normative questions are: (a) How should the global political economy be organized? (b) How should the architecture of global economic governance be reformed? (c) How should the goals of global economic justice be defined and pursued? The focus of the book on *who*, *what*, *when* and *how* questions offers students an essential step to navigate and effectively address normative positions in IPE, while discouraging them from accepting pre-fabricated answers from the outset.

Overall, the book departs significantly from how IPE has traditionally been taught. Inspired by the pioneering work of Susan Strange (1994), who identified four channels of power in IPE – security, production, finance and knowledge – many undergraduate and graduate courses have traditionally put their main emphasis on the specific power structures that are assumed to shape the global political economy. This book takes a distinctive approach: while being sensitive to how power structures operate across a range of issue areas, it begins with the importance of understanding how different actors exercise agency in the global political economy and centres on the core contemporary issues with which they engage.

In contrast to other introductory texts, the book does not privilege one set of actors (such as states, club forums, or big business) as inherently more important subjects of study than others (such as NGOs, IOs, or everyday actors). It also seeks to avoid presenting one set of relational dynamics (such as inter-state rivalries, market competition, or global governance) as more consequential across-the-board for determining causal mechanisms and shaping outcomes in the global political economy. The book identifies as core concerns for the study of IPE questions relating to the distribution of wealth within and across national, regional and global contexts, and questions over the nature and evolution of different sets of power relations. This approach aims to provide students with the tools to understand and to explain how different categories of action and relational dynamics operate in contingent ways across domains, through the development of both issue-specific and systematic knowledge of the global political economy.

The next two chapters provide a basic grounding in the theoretical approaches and concepts that are used to understand current and historical developments in the field, and discuss several major debates that have dominated IPE in recent years. Following these primer chapters, Parts I and II of the book introduce the key actors and issues that comprise the contemporary study of the global political economy, beginning with the different types of actors that perform meaningful roles in global economic processes. Part I aims in particular to broaden how students of IPE understand the question of *who acts* in the global political economy, and the equally important question of *whose actions matter*. As well as introducing how the roles of different categories of actors can be understood, the chapters in Part I illustrate the importance of understanding differences between actors within the same analytic category, such as the distinctions between varieties of states, IOs, clubs, private market actors, NGOs and everyday actors. The nine chapters in Part II extend the discussion of different categories of actors by examining key topics in IPE, drawing particular attention to the evolution of different issues, contemporary developments, and future challenges and trends. The book does not contain a separate chapter on what is perhaps the paramount concern within contemporary IPE – economic globalization. The chapters in Part II instead illustrate how changing dynamics across a range of issue areas have contributed to globalizing processes in IPE, in order to provide a multidimensional understanding of the sources and challenges of international economic integration.

No single book can comprehensively include all the relevant issues and actors in the global political economy; this requires reading widely from other texts to supplement the introduction this book provides. Contemporary issues that are not examined here in chapters of their own include the changing global dynamics of economic diplomacy (Pigman 2010), health (Harman 2012), migration (Phillips 2011a), financial crime (Sharman 2011) and work (Amoore 2002). Meanwhile, actors that feature in the book but which are not the focus of individual chapters include regional institutions (Katzenstein 2005) and national agencies such as ministries of finance and central banks (Baker 2006; Hall 2008). Many of these issues and actors are discussed across different chapters, but this text is intended to be a useful point of departure for studying IPE, not the end of the journey.

Further reading

Eichengreen, Barry. 2008. *Globalizing Capital: A History of the International Monetary System*, 2nd edn. Princeton, NJ: Princeton University Press.

O'Brien, Robert and Marc Williams. 2013. *Global Political Economy: Evolution and Dynamics*, 4th edn. Basingstoke: Palgrave Macmillan.

Phillips, Nicola (ed.). 2005. *Globalizing International Political Economy*. Basingstoke: Palgrave Macmillan.

Ravenhill, John (ed.). 2011. *Global Political Economy*, 3rd edn. Oxford: Oxford University Press.

Schwartz, Herman M. 2010. *States versus Markets: The Emergence of a Global Economy*, 3rd edn. Basingstoke: Palgrave Macmillan.

Walter, Andrew and Gautam Sen. 2009. *Analyzing the Global Political Economy*. Princeton, NJ: Princeton University Press.

Chapter 2

Theoretical Perspectives in International Political Economy

Introduction

This chapter introduces the main perspectives used in the field of International Political Economy (IPE) to understand the workings and dynamics that drive the global political economy by discussing the principal elements within each theoretical cluster, which share a common ontology, epistemology and primary unit of analysis. Theories are abstract constructs that comprise ideas about what the world is, how it works and how it can be studied. In particular, theory aids the creation of information shortcuts that simplify the process of comprehending complex phenomena, identifying causal mechanisms and establishing causal effects. Theory helps us to understand the subject matter of IPE by providing an analytical toolkit for analysing both contemporary and historical empirical research puzzles. Different theories make it possible to show alternative scenarios of the dynamics of change and continuity in the global political economy, and they can stimulate new ways of thinking about who can shape agendas, ideas and outcomes, why and what difference it makes.

The process of deciding how to apply an existing theoretical framework to a specific research question, how to develop new conceptual insights through theory-building, or how to recombine elements of different theories in new ways is a critical part of IPE research. Theories are unlikely to yield new insights if they are simply taken 'off-the-shelf' as static frameworks to investigate any empirical problem, regardless of context. The best use of theory in IPE is able to produce new knowledge through the careful tailoring of theoretical frameworks, rather than a cookie-cutter approach. This enables theory to be operationalized in a way that is both context-sensitive and directly addresses specific research questions.

Overview

What were the causes of the global financial crisis? Was fiscal austerity a necessary policy response? In the aftermath of the crisis, how can we think about alternative economic models? While theories of IPE provide different ways of systematically addressing these types of empirical questions, they do not provide answers on their own. Rather, they offer an abstract lens for explanation and understanding, which orients the user towards a particular way of understanding their object of analysis and prioritizes some answers over others (Cox 1981). Different sets of these analytical tools do not perform equivalent tasks, nor are they equally useful for understanding and explaining the same empirical puzzles and issues. As economic historian William Barber (1967: 14) noted, 'Tools useful for dealing with certain problems often fail to provide the leverage needed for others.'

All theories in IPE incorporate foundational assumptions about how the world works and what there is to know about it, for without such assumptions they would be empty of both content and explanatory value. The goal for students of IPE is not simply to recognize what these foundational assumptions are with respect to different theoretical perspectives. It also involves the more challenging job of assessing the explanatory or normative value of different theoretical perspectives in relation to empirical evidence, while avoiding the problem of selection bias.

The seven theoretical clusters discussed in this chapter consist of related but analytically distinct perspectives. Each cluster differs in terms of its respective unit of analysis (the actors, structures, or processes it primarily focuses on), how it understands conditions of change in the global political economy and the evidential standards used for assessing

---

Box 2.1   Selection bias

Selection bias occurs when errors in the process of data collection distort research results. Selection bias may occur in quantitative research through selecting a non-random sample of a population for analysis. In qualitative research, selection bias can occur if researchers inadvertently 'cherry pick' their evidence to fit preconceived conclusions, by discounting relevant factors that are necessary for reaching a valid conclusion for a specific research question, or by weighting the role of one factor or series of factors too strongly. One way to overcome the potential for selection bias is to use 'triangulation' to double (or triple) check the validity of research results by employing more than two methods of enquiry.

Table 2.1 *Theoretical clusters in IPE*

Theoretical perspectives	Ontology	Epistemology	Unit of analysis
Classical political economy	Economic relations are co-constituted with other social relations	Economic knowledge combines empirical observation and abstract theory	Economic and social processes and problems
Constructivism	Ideas constitute actors' identities, interests and institutional forms	Ideas are essential for understanding motivations for action	Social communities
Feminism	Authority operates through gendered power structures	Gender situates how knowledge is sought and constructed	Gender relations
Liberalism	Actors bargain in order to maximize their self-interests	Outcomes result from bargaining, cooperation and competition	Individual actors and interest groups
Marxism	National/transnational elites exploit subordinate actors	Change is a result of class conflict and intra-elite struggles	Social class dynamics
Realism	The economy is subordinate to the needs of the state	State interests drive international cooperation/conflict	Nation-states
Poststructuralism	Objects of study are produced through discursive practices	The emergence of new discursive formations shapes global practices	Discursive practices

the strength of competing causal claims and arguments. As Table 2.1 illustrates, theoretical perspectives in IPE employ different epistemological positions on how knowledge about the global political economy is produced, and begin from different ontological starting points about what there is to know about the global political economy. Ontology is concerned with the nature of being, and centres on questions about what there is to know about particular objects of study. Epistemology refers to the nature of knowledge, how it is acquired, and to what extent a subject or phenomena can be known (see Chapter 1). Each theoretical cluster is also organized around a primary unit of analysis. This serves to highlight that clusters tend to concentrate analytical attention on a specific category of actors or a specific type of process, a focal point each perspective considers to be critical for understanding the workings of the global political economy.

Two caveats should be noted before proceeding. The first is that students who wish to develop an in-depth knowledge of the differences in focus, points of intellectual disagreement and conditions of change within each theoretical cluster must also engage in extensive further reading of the seminal texts in the field. The second is that every theoretical cluster incorporates both analytic and normative elements. This means that while each theoretical approach comprises an analytical toolkit for understanding the global political economy it is also built around normative beliefs about how the global political economy works (or how it ought to work). This latter point highlights the need to differentiate the processes of analysis that are incorporated within a given theoretical perspective from its underlying normative assumptions. When engaging with theories of IPE and empirical investigations that are guided by a particular theoretical perspective, it is important to recognize when theory is used as an analytical tool to enhance our understanding of an issue, and when it is used to promote particular conclusions through rejecting alternative explanations out of hand.

Realist International Political Economy

Realist approaches understand the global political economy as centred on the roles and activities of states and the dynamics of inter-state competition. From a realist perspective the study of IPE centres on three key assumptions. First, the state is the central actor in the international system, and should therefore comprise the primary unit of analysis. Second, international dynamics are shaped by the calculated (rational) pursuit by states of their national interests. Third, the international environment is an anarchic system, in which states interact and compete to maximize their interests in the absence of an overarching authority which could constrain, regulate and sanction state behaviour (Kirshner 2009: 36). An important difference exists, however, between state-centric realism, which sees the nature of states as the key driver of their behaviour, and system-centric realism, which focuses on the distribution of material capabilities among states as the key driver of state behaviour and international political outcomes (Gilpin 2000: 16–17). In the state-centric variant, national political and economic elites are the main determinants of state interests whereas the systemic-perspective concentrates on how state interests shift in response to changes in the international distribution of material capabilities among other states (Gilpin 2000: 18). Although realist IPE sees states as the primary actors, this perspective does not exclude from analysis the potential significance of IOs like the IMF and the World Bank, regional organizations like the European Union, NGOs, or global commercial entities such as banks or firms as relevant actors, but rather emphasizes that the role of the state is primary to understanding processes and outcomes in the global political economy.

There are three main approaches that are commonly grouped together as a cluster under the realist label in IPE: economic nationalism, mercantilism and statism. Economic nationalist and mercantilist approaches are significantly older than the academic disciplines of IPE and IR. They have their respective roots in the seventeenth century (mercantilism) and the nineteenth century (economic nationalism) (Helleiner 2002). These perspectives concentrate on the role of the state in governing domestic economic activity and how a state's domestic economic capabilities impact upon its external role and influence in relation to other states in the global political economy. A less state-centric variant of economic nationalism in contemporary IPE is 'economic patriotism'. This is defined as 'economic choices which seek to discriminate in favour of particular social groups, firms, or sectors' based on their territorial status. Rather than economic partiality in favour of national economic entities or for the purposes of building national material capabilities, economic patriotism can also be based on supranational or subnational conceptions of citizenship (Clift and Woll 2012: 308). In contrast to economic nationalism and mercantilism, statist approaches to IPE emerged from the discipline of IR during the 1970s. These perspectives focus on the interactions and rivalries between states, and why certain tools of economic statecraft are more or less effective as instruments of power in a given situation (Drezner 1999). They have tended to be concerned primarily with questions about the consequences of interdependence in the global political economy and the possibilities for international cooperation (Kirshner 2009: 39). Statist approaches are the predominant perspective within the realist cluster. In studying the behaviour of states in the global political economy and interactions between them, they emphasize that the way in which states project economic power internationally is premised upon states' national interests defined in narrow terms as achieving 'military security and political independence' (Gilpin 2000: 17), thereby placing the state ontologically prior to the market. The objective of national economic policy is to enhance a state's relative power in the international realm in pursuit of these national interests, which means that economic relations simultaneously are shaped by and impact upon state power. As states compete to maximize their gains in relation to other states, realist approaches understand international economic interactions as constituting a zero-sum game where one actor's gain is another's loss.

In realist IPE, states are therefore suspicious of international cooperation and do not assign an independent role to IOs. Rather, IOs and international regimes are regarded as structures that have been created by hegemonic and major power states in order to suit their own national economic interests, which constrain the autonomy of weaker states while enhancing the material capabilities of major powers. This assumption forms the basis of 'hegemonic stability theory'. From this perspective, the character of the global political economy is primarily determined by the distribution of power capabilities among leading states, and an open international economic system is most likely when a single state has a predominant position of power (Webb and Krasner 1989).

Liberal International Political Economy

Liberal approaches in contemporary IPE differ from realist perspectives in four key respects. First, the international system is defined as characterized by interdependence and cooperation rather than anarchy. Second, in addition to states, individual actors and interest groups are primary units of analysis. Third, bargaining and competition between actors can result in positive-sum rather than zero-sum outcomes where all participants can gain benefits, although some may benefit relatively more than others. Finally, states are likely to cooperate through IOs and favour the formation of international regimes in order to achieve mutual benefits, even if major powers benefit relatively more than weaker states.

Most liberal approaches to the study of IPE incorporate a normative commitment to open capitalist markets and international economic integration. The principles of economic liberalism are considered to benefit all states through reducing the motivation for international economic disputes to spill over into inter-state conflict, because interdependent states have more to lose from damaging their relationships with other countries. Yet liberal approaches to IPE do not reflect the one-size-fits-all caricature of neoliberalism that is sometimes uncritically repeated in the field. For example, rational institutionalist approaches focus on how international institutions can facilitate cooperation between national governments through 'the mutual coordination or adjustment of state policies' (Cooley 2009: 50). Under the Bretton Woods system, for instance, the principles of 'embedded liberalism' legitimated international economic openness and cooperation in terms of trade and monetary relations in order to preserve domestic policy autonomy (see Chapter 11). Social liberal approaches to political economy also have a long intellectual tradition of their own, such as the work of John A. Hobson in the late nineteenth century and twentieth century, which centred on the potential for state intervention in the economy to conform to moral categories for economic action that might improve the domestic distribution of wealth while encouraging international economic prosperity (Seabrooke 2004).

As a broad cluster of theoretical perspectives that ranges from classical liberalism to social liberalism to neoliberalism, different liberal approaches within the study of IPE maintain a greater degree of heterogeneity between their main premises than most other theoretical clusters. These distinctions include competing conceptions of economic rationality, as well as whether economic policy should be used to shelter actors from market-based processes of distribution or, more narrowly, to alleviate the consequences of those processes after the fact (Watson 2011). Today, most liberal approaches share the basic premise that markets work best as mechanisms for allocating resources (both domestically and internationally) if state intervention in market processes is kept to a minimum. Key state functions include the provision and regulation of critical economic infrastructure (such as transportation), maintaining the rule of law as a means to settle economic disputes and to protect property rights, and correcting for 'market failure', where the allocation of resources through market processes is inefficient and states should step in to provide essential public goods.

It is commonly assumed that liberal ideas in favour of limited state intervention in market processes have been institutionalized at the global level through the mandates, decision-making rules and operational practices of IOs such as the IMF, the World Bank and the WTO. This view was strengthened by the prominence given to the idea of the 'Washington consensus' during the 1990s (see Chapter 16). Nevertheless, substantive differences exist between variants of liberal perspectives, as well as between the practices of the IOs that are commonly seen as champions of economic liberalism. From a neoliberal perspective, the role of IOs in bailing out sovereign states that run into economic difficulties potentially creates a 'moral hazard' problem by encouraging risky behaviour by private market actors and reducing the incentives for state actors to adjust policies to adapt to changes in market conditions before they reach a crisis point, although the evidence for this *ex ante* effect of IMF and World Bank lending is mixed (Dreher and Gassebner 2012). Compared with this more extreme version of liberalism, most liberal approaches see IOs as essential agents of international cooperation that provide an important check on the unilateral exercise of power by one state over another, as well as helping both public and private actors to solve collective action problems and reduce information asymmetries through the collation and transmission of economic data and policy surveillance.

Marxist International Political Economy

Like liberal approaches in IPE, Marxist approaches encompass a variety of different theoretical strands. The theoretical cluster of Marxist approaches in IPE share three main assumptions. First, historical processes of change in societies and at the global level reflect different modes of economic development and wealth accumulation. Second, capitalism is the main driving force in the global political economy. Third, capitalist processes induce class conflict between the owners and managers of economic wealth who form the ruling elite and workers who are a subordinate and exploited class. From these three premises, Marxist approaches to IPE share a common focus on understanding the social dynamics of exploitation in global wealth-making processes. However, Marxist perspectives range from those which primarily stress the importance of material dynamics, to those which have a greater focus on understanding ideational dynamics of identity construction and intellectual domination. Marxist perspectives also differ in conceptions of the scope for subordinate actors to exercise agency in the global political economy.

Varieties of Marxist perspectives in IPE include open Marxism (Burnham 1994), historical materialism (Bruff 2010), neo-Gramscian (Bieler and Morton 2008) and new Marxist approaches (Germain 2011), among others, some of which overlap in their conceptual orientation while using different theoretical labels. One of the most common variants of a Marxist approach in contemporary IPE is transnational historical materialism, which differs from liberal and realist approaches to the field in two main ways. First, transnational historical materialism elevates the dynamics of social relations above the primacy of the state as the principal actor in IPE, whereby state formation and inter-state relations are conceived as expressions of the 'transnational dynamics of capital accumulation and class formation'. Instead of social relations being subordinate to the state and relegated to the domestic sphere of politics, from a transnational historical materialist perspective the state and inter-state relations remain 'subordinate to the dynamics of social relations'. Second, in contrast to IPE perspectives that privilege the causal role of either structures or actors, transnational historical materialism concentrates on understanding what is termed the '*dialectic totality* of structure and agency' (Overbeek 2012: 163, emphasis original).

Four of the key research themes in Marxist approaches to IPE include: (1) commodification in capitalist social relations; (2) the articulation of class interests; (3) state–society relations; and (4) transnational hegemony. The first involves studying the mechanisms through which goods, ideas, services, or practices that are not usually deemed to be economic goods are transformed through market practices into commodities. The second centres on how class interests are politically articulated and inscribed in concepts of the national interest, and how these become accepted across different social classes. The third examines changing dynamics in state–society relations, while the fourth focuses on the construction of transnational hegemony as a form of class rule, rather than as a feature of national material capabilities (Overbeek 2012: 165–70). In contrast to both realist and liberal approaches to IPE, the national interests that states pursue in their external relations with other states are seen as primarily reflecting the interests of the ruling economic class. Another key theme for Marxist approaches to IPE is the concept of 'new constitutionalism'. This refers to the political processes through which the economic policy discretion of states is constitutionally constrained through legislation or by transferring authority for operationalizing policy to formally independent agencies, such as granting central banks control over official interest rate decisions (Overbeek 2012: 171–2). Recent work has also focused on 'counter-hegemonic' social movements by subordinate actors, which have challenged the acceptance of neoliberal principles and practices through processes of resistance (Morton 2011).

Constructivist International Political Economy

Constructivist IPE aims to understand the dynamic roles played by ideas, norms, values and identities in processes and outcomes in the global political economy. Ideas are understood as an essential ingredient in the social construction of both: (1) who an actor thinks he or she is within a particular context (their identity); and (2) what he or she seeks to gain through the performance of their social role (their interests) (Blyth 2003). By shaping actors' identities and their interests, economic ideas can influence how actors view the world, what values they consider are important and which strategic goals they select to pursue. In elite debates over economic policy options, for example, the politics of ideas not only shapes which policy initiatives may gain currency and receive broad support across different communities of actors, but also shapes the choice-set of options that are able to be discussed within the range of 'thinkable' policy alternatives.

The chief assumption common to different strands of constructivism is that the intersubjective bases of everyday social reality shape political processes, practices and outcomes (Hopf 1998: 182). Constructivist approaches differ most from rationalist approaches such as realism and liberalism because of the specific role they assign to ideational factors in the process of institutional change, policy reform and political contests, which constitute political practices and political power (Checkel 1998). While constructivist approaches have emphasized the constitutive role of shared ideas for actors' identities and for constructing norms that define socially legitimate actions, shared ideas and norms do not necessarily perform this role in every political contest. Norms can also drive behaviour without actors necessarily believing them to be legitimate, based on an actor's expectation that they will incur material costs if the social norms of a particular community are not adhered to, or based on a calculation that they stand to gain material benefits from norm compliance. Rather than actors responding instrumentally to a 'logic of consequences' which links specific actions to material costs, regulative norms embody a 'logic of appropriateness' which defines 'socially acceptable rather than selfishly optimizing behavior' (Sharman 2006: 52).

Much of the disagreement between constructivist IPE and other theoretical perspectives such as liberalism, realism, or Marxism centres on how much causal significance is attached to the role of norms, identities, or ideas in shaping actions and outcomes. For example, other theoretical perspectives might understand norms or ideas as simply 'congealed rational responses to an objectively present material or organizational obstacle course'. Rather than by-products of strategic calculation by rational actors, from a constructivist perspective social mechanisms are understood to have a constitutive effect on norms, ideas and identities (Abdelal *et al.* 2009: 18–19). In this view, norms 'saturate the determination of material interests' rather than competing against interests as alternative motivations for actors' behaviour (Seabrooke 2006: 7).

While liberal and realist approaches to IPE conceive of theories as mental maps that reflect material reality, constructivist approaches highlight the ways in which theory can also shape how state and societal interests are articulated and defined by constituting social reality (Widmaier 2004). Economic theory is therefore not simply an 'instruction sheet' that details how the economy works, but, further, is causally important in the process of constructing the economy by influencing choices over 'which rules to pick, which policies to follow, and how to design different institutions'. However, because economic theories only map 'incompletely ... onto the world they strive to describe', this leads to significant blind spots in how the dynamics of the global political economy are understood (Blyth 2013: 38–9).

Feminist International Political Economy

Feminist IPE scholarship both articulates a critique of 'mainstream economic theory and policy ... [and] suggests alternative modes of analysis that put centre stage both productive and reproductive economies' (Rai 2013: 264). From this perspective gender is understood to be 'constitutive of the global political economy' (Elias 2011: 100). All topics in the field from trade, to money, to labour, to the environment can be analysed through examining how gender relations matter for the constitution and causal dynamics of economic practices and concepts. In particular, feminist research has concentrated on understanding issues of production and reproduction, as well as changing dynamics of governance. In contrast to conventional approaches that focus on problems related to economic production, distribution and consumption in the global political economy, feminist scholarship highlights how global markets operate through structures of gendered social relations. Prominent examples include the connection of women's labour with household work, and the ways in which gendered social relations intersect with other forms of hierarchical division and unequal power relations between different actors and social groups, such as race, class and nationality (Elias 2011: 105).

Feminist scholarship in IPE has challenged how key concepts in the field are understood, as well as emphasizing the importance of behaviour, processes and actors which tend to be left out of conventional IPE studies or are deemed to be of marginal relevance to them. For instance, feminist research has shown how traditional concepts of income, wealth, property and development are based upon gendered definitions of labour, productivity, ownership and social progress. These concepts are problematic because they refer to power relations in the global political economy that cannot be understood without focusing on how gender relations are embedded in, and reproduced through, practices of defining what does and does not count as income and paid work, who owns and manages wealth and property, and how the agents, processes and goals of development are defined. The conventional understanding of the public–private divide in the study of IPE is therefore problematic because household work and labour are relegated to the private realm, while markets are conceived as gender-neutral processes for the allocation of economic resources. The study of gender relations within IPE aims to broaden understanding of issues related to resource allocation, as well as demonstrating the methodological problems with, and hidden power relations within, existing techniques for measuring economic growth, development, poverty and well-being (Griffin 2007).

Incorporating the analysis of gender relations within the study of IPE is not simply about the redefinition of existing economic concepts and processes, nor is it just about highlighting the importance of studying female actors in the global political economy. Instead, feminist approaches to IPE make a strong case for the incorporation of gender relations in the field to encompass the production and reproduction of female roles and identities, as well as male roles and identities through studying processes of constructing masculinity (Hooper 1999). To do so effectively requires both the redefinition of many of the key concepts that are used for description and analysis in IPE, as well as expanding the horizons of the subject matter to encompass a broader range of issues that have tended to receive scant attention. Examples include the commercial sex trade (including both the female and male sex trade) and the international political economy of violence against women (Smith 2011; True 2012).

Feminist scholarship has also illustrated how gendered political practices operate at national, regional and global levels of economic governance. For example, critique has focused on how IOs and other global governance actors have reproduced simplistic representations of the role that women play in the economy and in development processes, as well as highlighting the connections between gendered structures of economic inequality and the dynamics of economic globalization (Elias 2013). In the field of IPE as a whole, the study of gender relations helps to increase understanding of 'how the world is structured such that individuals are enabled (or not) to act in certain ways and to certain ends' (Griffin 2009: 1).

Poststructuralist International Political Economy

Poststructuralist perspectives in IPE examine the role that economic discourses play in constraining how the global political economy is understood and how the economic realm is constituted. They look, in particular, at how discursive practices produce disciplinary effects on the identity of individuals as economic subjects. Poststructuralist approaches to the economy emerged as a non-conventional strand of economics in the late 1980s and early 90s as scholars began to emphasize the power relations that are embedded in economic language and concepts, which have constitutive effects in shaping what the economy is and how it is understood. For example, the day-to-day work of economic policy officials involves the use of concepts, forms of language and knowledge practices to describe economic activity as though these are neutral tools. However, the ability to make authoritative statements about economic phenomena also represents the power to define common sense through discursive practices. From a poststructuralist perspective, the use of a foundational theoretical approach such as liberalism, Marxism, or realism entails the imposition of certain values, norms and standards on objects of study, which limits and distorts how the social world is understood. The ideas and policy prescriptions of neoliberalism, for example, form part of 'a large discursive struggle over meaning and interpretation' about what the economy is, how markets work and what the role of the state should be in governing economic activity (Bleiker 2001). Economic discourses are therefore conceived by poststructuralist scholars as systems of knowledge which restrict what can be known, while representing reality as a static object that is independent of the particular knowing practices that are being employed in order to see, interpret and construct what there is to know.

From a poststructuralist perspective, knowledge strategies are analysed as a form of power relations. The relationship between power and knowledge is twofold. On the one hand, power relations always constitute a field of knowledge; on the other hand, the formation of knowledge simultaneously presupposes and constitutes particular relations of power (Foucault 1991: 27). Strategies of power and knowledge are therefore integrally related and co-constitutive. Economic knowledge is understood as information that is 'produced within specific discursive conditions' which are 'culturally inscribed and socially constructed' (Brown 1993: 64). In the study of economic phenomena 'Facts do not speak for themselves', but are mediated by social products such as a specific culture, paradigm and experience, which shape processes of description and interpretation (Samuels 1990: 6–7). The authority to explain economic events and to interpret and measure economic activity therefore involves a range of complex power relations which serve certain agendas rather than others. When actors use a particular discourse to identify and explain objects of study, this limits the scope of understanding through discursively constructed rules regarding 'who has legitimate control over what' (Shapiro 1981: 63).

An example of the power of economic discourse can be drawn from the study of financial practices. For Marieke de Goede (2003: 81), financial activities 'do not exist prior to, or independently from, ideas and beliefs about them'. Instead, de Goede emphasizes how financial discourses '*in themselves* exercise a particular power' (2003: 96, emphasis original), which is hidden under a cloak of objectivity and neutrality. Financial discourses can nonetheless channel access to credit and influence the creation and distribution of wealth, via power–knowledge dynamics which poststructuralist approaches in IPE have sought to (re)politicize (Langley 2009: 136). Therefore, rather than defining neoliberalism solely as an ideology, a policy agenda, a state form, or a mode of governance, from a poststructuralist perspective neoliberalism is an economic discourse that may combine each of these forms and processes in variegated ways across different environments (Springer 2012). At the heart of this critique is the idea that the economy cannot be understood 'as a direct or brute fact of existence' independent of the discursive practices that construct it and render it visible as an object of analysis. Instead of assuming the economy exists as an objective fact, 'economic concepts, modes of analysis, statistical estimates, econometric methods and policy debates' are seen as artefacts established through economic discourses, which constrain alternative ways of understanding, defining, measuring and producing economic activities (Brown 1993: 70).

Classical political economy and IPE

A further cluster of theoretical perspectives in IPE has been inspired by classical political economy thinkers of the seventeenth, eighteenth and nineteenth centuries. The historical emergence of political economy as a diverse area of enquiry preceded the division of the social sciences into specialized academic disciplines (Krätke and Underhill 2005: 26). From the emergence of IPE as a modern field of study in the 1970s onwards, scholars have drawn intellectual inspiration and theoretical concepts from this far older tradition of classical political economy, which existed prior to the splitting off of economics and political science following the 'marginalist revolution' in the 1870s (Underhill 2000; Watson 2010: 58–9). In the late 1960s and early 70s, for example, work by Richard N. Cooper and Raymond Vernon in the field of economics drew from classical political economy to examine the changing dynamics of state–market relations, which provided an important source of inspiration for the subsequent development of IPE (Germain 2009: 81; Krätke and Underhill 2005: 30). While Marxist and neo-Marxist work is perhaps the most easily recognized body of IPE literature that has been inspired by pre-twentieth-century thinkers, contemporary scholars have also drawn on a far broader range of concepts and perspectives contained in classical political economy thought.

Thinkers whose ideas have been used by contemporary scholars include classical political economists such as Adam Smith (1772–1823), David Ricardo (1772–1823), Thomas Robert Malthus (1766–1834), John S. Mill (1806–1873) and Karl Marx (1818–1883), as well as later thinkers such as Thorsten Veblen (1857–1929), Gunnar Myrdal (1898–1987), Karl Polanyi (1886–1964) and John Maynard Keynes (1883–1946), whose works share 'many of the intentions of their classical predecessors' (Watson 2005: 47–8). These earlier political economy thinkers did not represent a unified theoretical tradition, but rather shared a common goal of investigating 'economic and social problems from the broadest possible perspective' (Watson 2005: 70). The 'ecumenism' of classical political economy has been embraced by contemporary scholars, who have made the case for intellectual diversity in how the dynamics of the global political economy are investigated and understood (Krätke and Underhill 2005: 32). In particular, scholars have drawn upon classical political economy approaches to IPE to argue against the rising popularity of neoclassical economic assumptions within the field, and in order to contest the intellectual lineage that is often drawn from contemporary versions of economic liberalism to the eighteenth-century thought of Adam Smith, whereby Smith's ideas are seen as the precursor to current economic models based on rational expectations and public choice theories.

A common thread that extends throughout much of the contemporary IPE scholarship that draws on classical political economy approaches is a concern with understanding the moral underpinnings of modern markets, which knit individuals together into a social order that cannot be reduced to atomized individual agents rationally pursuing their own self-interests without regard for concerns over moral and ethical issues or social justice (Archer and Fritsche 2010; Watson 2011, 2012). Classical political economy scholars have shown how, when read closely, Adam Smith is less the champion of unfettered markets and limited government that is the common caricature found in modern economics, and instead his work represents a far more critical perspective on how 'commercial society' operates (Tribe 1999). In addition to classical political economy approaches in contemporary IPE that have drawn on eighteenth- and nineteenth-century thinkers, recent scholarship has also drawn on canonical thinkers from the early twentieth century to challenge contemporary assumptions that markets can – and should – be 'self-regulating' (Gammon 2008; Holmes 2012). Rather than reproducing the neat division of specialized academic disciplines into economics, on the one hand, and political science, on the other, classical political economy approaches start from the assumption that 'We are all political and economic agents at one and the same time, whatever the historical context' (Krätke and Underhill 2005: 35).

A distinction can be drawn between two strands of classical political economy scholarship in contemporary IPE. On the one hand, scholars have closely examined the complex twists and turns that constituted the history of economic ideas and economic discourse among pre-twentieth-century political economy thinkers, which shaped contemporary understandings of the economy (Walter 2010). On the other hand, another strand of work has explicitly aimed at recovering the insights of these earlier thinkers for contemporary empirical research, by applying a classical political economy lens to understanding current developments and dynamics in the global political economy (Watson 2005). The boundary between these approaches is often porous: examining the theoretical antecedents of IPE also contributes to understanding how earlier thinkers' ideas and insights can be applied to study contemporary empirical puzzles, and vice versa. Both varieties of classical political economy scholarship aim to contribute to the study of IPE by expanding knowledge of how contemporary ways of thinking about states, markets and societies have been shaped by earlier intellectual traditions.

Summary

International Political Economy incorporates a wide variety of theoretical perspectives, which orient the study of the global political economy in different directions and structure the key concerns of the field in particular ways. This chapter has briefly summarized the principal common elements within realist, liberal, Marxist, constructivist, feminist, poststructuralist and classical approaches to IPE. These theoretical clusters ask different types of research questions and have distinct methods of enquiry and standards for assessing the validity of causal claims. In the chapters that follow in Parts I and II, a range of these theoretical perspectives are drawn upon to inform the articulation of IPE issues and to illustrate how key challenges and puzzles in the field might be understood.

Further reading

Realist International Political Economy

Drezner, Daniel W. 2007. *All Politics is Global: Explaining International Regulatory Regimes*. Princeton, NJ: Princeton University Press.
Gilpin, Robert. 2000. *The Challenge of Global Capitalism: The World Economy in the 21st Century*. Princeton, NJ: Princeton University Press.

Liberal International Political Economy

Frieden, Jeffrey A. 2007. *Global Capitalism: Its Fall and Rise in the Twentieth Century*. New York: W.W. Norton.

Keohane, Robert O. 2005. *After Hegemony: Cooperation and Discord in the World Political Economy*. Princeton, NJ: Princeton University Press.

Marxist International Political Economy

Morton, Adam David. 2011. *Revolution and the State in Modern Mexico: The Political Economy of Uneven Development*. Plymouth: Rowman & Littlefield.

Panitch, Leo and Sam Gindin. 2012. *The Making of Global Capitalism: The Political Economy of American Empire*. London: Verso.

Constructivist International Political Economy

Abdelal, Rawi, Mark Blyth and Craig Parsons (eds). 2010. *Constructing the International Economy*. Ithaca, NY: Cornell University Press.

Blyth, Mark. 2002. *Great Transformations: Economic Ideas and Institutional Change in the Twentieth Century*. Cambridge: Cambridge University Press.

Feminist International Political Economy

Griffin, Penny. 2009. *Gendering the World Bank: Neoliberalism and the Gendered Foundations of Global Governance*. Basingtoke: Palgrave Macmillan.

Rai, Shirin M. and Georgina Waylen (eds). 2008. *Global Governance: Feminist Perspectives*. Basingstoke: Palgrave Macmillan.

Poststructuralist International Political Economy

de Goede, Marieke (ed.). 2006. *International Political Economy and Poststructural Politics*. Basingstoke: Palgrave Macmillan.

Langley, Paul. 2008. *The Everyday Life of Global Finance: Saving and Borrowing in Anglo-America*. Oxford: Oxford University Press.

Classical Political Economy

Watson, Matthew. 2005. *Foundations of International Political Economy*. Basingstoke: Palgrave Macmillan.

Clift, Ben. 2014. *Comparative Political Economy: States, Markets and Global Capitalism*. Basingstoke: Palgrave Macmillan.

Chapter 3

Contemporary Debates in International Political Economy

Introduction

Scholarly debates serve as intellectual foils that help to highlight the qualities and characteristics which constitute the subject matter of a field and how its disciplinary limits are defined. They also operate as arenas of contention in which to thrash out scholarly disagreements over the relative merits of alternative theoretical perspectives and methodological approaches. When seen in the rear-view mirror with the benefit of hindsight, major scholarly debates can lead to the creation of 'disciplinary ortho-doxy' over how a particular field has developed (Quirk and Vigneswaran 2005). Like other fields of enquiry, the study of IPE is characterized by a range of scholarly debates over what should constitute the parameters of the field, which actors are most signif-icant for understanding the global political economy and what factors matter most in determining outcomes.

This chapter examines the main features and summarizes the key points of contention across three debates in contemporary IPE: (1) the debate over interests and ideas in understanding the dynamics of action in the global political economy; (2) the respective merits of analytic eclecticism compared with theoretical parsimony; and (3) the 'transatlantic divide' between British and American schools of IPE. Other contem-porary debates that are not examined in this chapter but which are discussed in the chapters in Part I and Part II include debates over the changing dynamics of hegemony, alternative models of economic development, and the sources of power in the global political economy.

Ideas versus interests in IPE

Many of the theoretical differences that characterize contemporary IPE scholarship result in part from whether 'interests' or 'ideas' are deemed to be paramount in shaping actors' behaviour, institutional processes and outcomes in the global political economy. The debate over ideas versus interests in IPE during the 1990s and 2000s grew largely out of earlier debates in IR between constructivist scholars and rationalist scholars. More recently this debate has moved on from the question of whether ideas or interests matter more as competing explanatory variables, to a greater focus on how interests and ideas intersect in shaping behaviour and dynamics of change in the global political economy. Recent research has focused on assigning causal weight in order to demonstrate how much ideas matter in shaping political-economic outcomes (Chwieroth 2009), as well as how concepts such as 'identity' can be operationalized as a variable that can be measured empirically in order to explain how an actor's identity translates into particular types of action or behaviour (Abdelal *et al.* 2009).

The concept of 'interests' in IPE is typically used to refer to either the self-interest of individual actors, institutions, or specific groups of actors, or the national interests of a country or state. In its simplest form, behaviour that conforms to an actor's interests is action that is deemed to be utility maximizing, with the conscious aim of gaining certain rewards, achieving preferences that match a given actor's favoured outcomes, or avoiding costs, based on a clearly conceived ranking of preferences. Interest-driven behaviour is conceived to be rational to the extent that it is based on an actor's calculation of the potential costs and benefits from alternative possible courses of action. In pursuing their interests, actors are therefore deemed to undertake purposive action that is calculated to achieve certain ends they will derive benefits from.

At the most basic level, the concept of the 'national interest' refers to the fundamental interest states have in their own survival. For realist scholars, the national interest centres on the protection of a state's 'physical, political, and cultural identity against encroachments by other nations' in a world comprised of states competing with each other for power (Morgenthau 1952: 972). In contrast, liberal scholars view self-interested states as actors that will often seek 'to realize their interests collectively' through mutual agreements and international cooperation, especially when they lack the capacity to effectively control events in a given issue area on their own (Keohane 1983: 170–1).

A series of foundational assumptions underlie how actors' interests are typically understood within different rationalist approaches to the study of IPE, which mirrors how they are conceived in the field of IR. The defining characteristic of rationalist theories of IPE is a conception of interests as facts which – while variable – are inherently material in nature. From this perspective self-interested actors comprise the primary unit of analysis for understanding processes of global political and economic change. Compared with the realist focus on how states pursue their national interests, liberal theorists tend to focus on self-interested individuals, groups and firms who are conceived as 'rational and risk-averse' and who seek to promote their interests 'under constraints imposed by material scarcity, conflicting values, and variations in societal influence' (Moravcsik 1997: 516). Despite these differences in levels of analysis, interests are conceived in both liberal and realist approaches as behavioural incentives that motivate actors to seek material gains or to avoid material costs.

Examining how actors' differentiated material interests informs their behaviour provides a powerful tool for explaining both processes and outcomes in the global political economy. Many scholars nonetheless disagree with primarily focusing on how actors respond rationally in a given situation based on their material interests. For example, this approach may ignore the social mechanisms that produce the rules, norms, ideas and identities that influence how actors conceive of their interests (Abdelal *et al.* 2010: 18). One of the main challenges to the conception of actors' behaviour as essentially interest-driven is the problem of uncertainty in situations where actors may be unable to 'anticipate the outcome of a decision and cannot assign probabilities to the outcome' (Beckert 1996: 804). To overcome the problem of how actors reason through uncertainty, a number of IPE scholars have turned to the role of ideas as critical factors shaping actors' behaviour in order to explain processes of change and outcomes in the global political economy.

Ideas are developed mental constructs that are shared within a particular community or across different communities of actors. They come in various forms and may perform different political, social and economic functions depending on how they are used by particular actors. In relation to economic policy and institutional change, the role of ideas can be differentiated in four main ways based on a typology set out by John Campbell (1998: 385). First, ideas may form 'cognitive programmes' which serve a prescriptive function to guide decision-making and courses of action among national, regional, or global policy-makers. For instance, prescriptions for 'best practice' policy reforms and institutional change that are diffused by IOs such as the IMF, the World Bank, the OECD and other bodies provide policy-makers with clearly defined blueprints for altering their national policy settings and the structure or functions of domestic economic institutions. A selection of prominent examples of cognitive programmes that have been promoted by IOs in recent years include economic ideas such as inflation-targeting, balanced budget rules, capital account liberalization, macro-prudential regulation and poverty reduction strategies. These policy prescriptions represent explicit articulations of economic ideas that 'operate in the foreground of policy debate' (Campbell 1998: 384).

Second, ideas may constitute 'cognitive paradigms' which comprise background assumptions that constrain the range of 'thinkable' policy options and solutions for decision-makers. In this respect, economic ideas can perform an agenda-setting role that delimits the policy choice-set decision-makers have at hand to select from. The emergence of the 'Washington consensus' during the late 1980s and 90s was an example of a new cognitive paradigm in the global political economy (see Chapter 16). In comparison to economic theories, policy paradigms such as the Washington consensus potentially exercise an enduring coercive power over decision-making processes because they are 'embedded in the practices of bureaucratic organizations' such as states, regional organizations, IOs and private firms (Babb 2012: 4). Rather than the promotion of concrete policy proposals such as inflation-targeting or balanced budget rules, therefore, policy paradigms constitute a set of 'background assumptions' that orient decision-making and economic governance in a particular policy direction (Campbell 1998: 389). Conceived as a cognitive paradigm, the economic ideas embedded in the Washington consensus might prompt national decision-makers to prefer forms of economic governance that are rule-based and which limit the scope for policy discretion – such as inflation-targeting and balanced budget rules – rather than eliciting support for specific policy proposals.

Third, ideas may perform the role of 'normative frames' that enable the legitimation of proposals for change and policy solutions to a specific problem, or which constitute normative standards that form the basis for determining the appropriateness of a given set of policies. In the period leading up to the subprime mortgage crisis in the USA in 2007, for example, complex processes of financial innovation were framed as socially legitimate because they enabled greater credit access for low-income groups to expand home ownership and asset-based financial security (Seabrooke 2010b). Like cognitive programmes, ideational frames operate in the foreground of political debates and may provide a means for elite actors to mobilize public opinion to support or oppose specific policy initiatives (Campbell 1998: 394).

Finally, ideas may act as 'public sentiments' which serve as normative constraints on the scope for political action. Broadly shared conventions and economic and social norms exercise a constraint on what economic policies a government considers socially acceptable to adopt, and may lead to policy failure when economic changes meet with entrenched public resistance (Broome 2009a). At the same time, public sentiments serve to focus political attention through popular pressure for policy reform in a specific issue area (Thirkell-White 2009), and can provide political 'impulses' for governments to respond to changing societal expectations about the role of the state as an economic manager (Seabrooke 2007).

While they often serve normative functions, ideas should be distinguished from norms in the study of IPE. Norms refer to a set of ideas that are socially accepted 'as a standard of appropriate behaviour for actors with a given identity' (Finnemore and Sikkink 1998: 891). Ideas may be shared among some of the actors within a community (such as a particular social group, a national institution such as a central bank, a deliberative forum such as the G20, or an international organization such as the World Bank), but may not be socially accepted as constituting a legitimate norm. While norms are sometimes institutionalized within bureaucratic agencies, they should not be conflated with the institutions they are associated with and are seldom 'controlled' by institutional actors. Ideas are therefore developed mental concepts that are shared by a particular community of actors or some of the actors in a community, while norms are ideas about a particular way of acting or performing a given function that are widely deemed by others to be legitimate.

Analytic eclecticism versus theoretical parsimony in IPE

Controversy over analytic eclecticism versus theoretical parsimony centres on how different variables or causal logics can and ought to be incorporated in the study of IPE in order to reach an adequate level of understanding and explanation of a given issue. This debate is about what level of complexity conceptual frameworks must attain in order to form meaningful and credible statements of explanation about the global political economy. Theoretical parsimony typically refers to 'Highly general and abstract theories ... which set aside intervening processes and focus on correlations between the "start" and the "finish" of a phenomenon'. Such theories aim to 'describe independent, stable causal mechanisms that under certain conditions link causes to effects'. They may be less effective, however, when it comes to understanding and explaining the contingent conditions in which a nuanced set of factors will lead to a given outcome and those in which they are overridden by other mechanisms (George and Bennett 2005: 7–8). An approach to IPE based on analytic eclecticism, in comparison, 'begins with research questions that are framed so as to capture, not bracket, the complexity of interesting political phenomena' (Sil and Katzenstein 2011: 483). This aims to expand understanding of the multiple pathways through which different social mechanisms lead to diverse political, economic and social results.

For Sil and Katzenstein (2010: 2) analytic eclecticism refers to investigating 'substantive relationships and revealing hidden connections among elements of seemingly incommensurable paradigm-bound theories, with an eye to generating novel insights that bear on policy debates and practical dilemmas'. This is not a claim that 'anything goes' in conceptual approaches to the study of IPE and IR, or that all social science research should strive to be (more) policy relevant. Rather, the focus is on 'making intellectually and practically useful connections among clusters of analyses that are substantively related but normally formulated in separate paradigms'. Sil and Katzenstein (2010) argue that most analytic divisions between competing clusters of theories are based upon their foundational assumptions about how claims about the world should be developed and supported. The emphasis here is on overcoming the ingrained exclusivity of different research traditions, in order to develop more robust and useful understanding through the careful amalgamation of theoretical constructs and conceptual tools drawn from distinct theoretical approaches.

In contrast to an approach based on analytic eclecticism, proponents of theoretical parsimony claim that knowledge in the study of IPE and other social sciences is best developed through discrete research programmes that maintain a common standard for assessing the validity and credibility of competing claims. Theoretical parsimony is often associated with 'orthodox' IPE scholarship that utilizes a positivist epistemology. This style of scholarship proceeds on the basis of 'incommensurable' theoretical perspectives which 'represent different ideologies of political economy' (Tooze and Murphy 1996: 682). Analytic eclecticism concentrates on the development of research through a puzzle-driven approach, in which a range of theoretical tools may be drawn upon to address the core question being investigated. In comparison, theoretical parsimony involves the accumulation of knowledge through research that is situated within clear and explicit ontological foundations.

One of the main arguments against analytic eclecticism in IPE is that adding complexity to a programme of research may obscure – but cannot transcend – ontological limits on what is being studied, how it is understood and how causal statements about the object of study are constructed (Bruff 2011: 81). This line of critique is dodged rather than resolved by proponents of analytic eclecticism through elevating the prospective empirical benefits of analytic flexibility above the need to respect ontological boundaries. One of the aims of an eclectic approach is therefore 'to temporarily bypass or suspend irresolvable metaphysical debates for the purpose of exploring substantively important problems' (Sil and Katzenstein 2011: 484). From this competing perspective, however, foundational assumptions are not only useful for IPE scholarship but are critically important for recognizing the limits such assumptions introduce on understanding, as well as for prompting reflection about the concepts that are based upon them.

Intellectual bridge-building is at the heart of attempts to operationalize analytic eclecticism in the study of IPE. Through combining the conceptual insights of more than one theoretical approach to empirical research, such cross-fertilization can help to develop greater analytic purchase on specific issues as well as to illustrate dimensions of a problem that may not be easily recognized using a single perspective (Nielson *et al.* 2006). Analytic eclecticism is also motivated by an attempt to move away from research programmes that centre on various 'isms', which can lead to the production of intellectual monocultures. Rather than relying on 'high theories' of IPE that are organized around ontological and epistemological distinctiveness, analytic eclecticism aims to facilitate mid-level theorizing that links contingent 'purpose-built' conceptual frameworks to practical outcomes. What is at issue here is not the question of 'which approach is inherently superior, but which yields greater insights under what circumstances' (Lake 2011: 466). The eclecticism twist on this statement is that it is not which approach on its own, but which combination of conceptual tools across approaches can yield greater insights in understanding and explaining how a particular set of conditions has contingent causal effects.

In the contemporary study of IPE one influential example of theoretical parsimony is the 'open economy politics' (OEP) approach. OEP uses economic theory to deduce actors' interests within specific economic groups based on how individuals expect different policies and outcomes to impact upon their future incomes. As an analytical perspective the OEP approach is a textbook case of theoretical parsimony in practice, but it achieves parsimony at the cost of bracketing out the dynamics of social interaction, the constitutive effects of institutions on actors' identities and the relevance of different social and cultural environments in shaping how actors' individual interests are produced (Sil and Katzenstein 2010: 107; Hobson 2012: 4–5). As the example of the OEP framework suggests, the debate over analytic eclecticism versus theoretical parsimony centres on competing models of causation in the study of world politics. An emphasis on achieving theoretical parsimony typically goes hand-in-hand with the research objective of uncovering regularities in behaviour, processes and outcomes that are broadly generalizable across different social and institutional environments. In contrast, analytic eclecticism can potentially provide scholars with a better-equipped conceptual toolkit that can complement the search for general causal patterns with 'the investigation of ruptures ... that undermine existing regularities and the understandings of the actors on which they are often based' (Lebow 2010: 5). In terms of understanding and explaining contemporary dynamics in the global political economy, these differences between analytical frameworks influence how processes and outcomes are conceptualized in a specific issue area within short-term time horizons, as well as how larger macro-level changes unfold gradually over time.

The transatlantic divide in IPE

Scholarly debates over the nature of the field have characterized many of the intellectual divisions that exist within IPE as the differences between a 'British School' and an 'American School' of International Political Economy (Murphy and Nelson 2001). Most recently, the debate over a 'transatlantic divide' in the study of IPE gained greater attention following the publication of an article in *Review of International Political Economy* by Benjamin J. Cohen (2007), which was the prelude to his book on the subject (Cohen 2008). In Cohen's articulation of the divide between British and American IPE, these two schools differ on fundamental questions about the scope of the subject matter of IPE, which actors, processes and dynamics of change are the proper object of study, and what constitute valid and credible methods of enquiry in the field. While recognizing that the distinction between British and American IPE is not necessarily a geographic one, for Cohen (2007) the two schools are distinguished by their varying conceptions of ontology and epistemology in IPE research.

Cohen (2007: 199–200) views the American school of IPE as primarily state-centric, concerned with explaining the behaviour of states and governance issues in the global political economy. In contrast, his depiction of the British school of IPE includes a more heterogeneous range of actors besides states, as well as more openly embracing normative issues and ethical research questions in contrast to the objectivist goals of American IPE. Similarly, the American school is identified with mid-level theorizing compared with the British school's aims 'for grander visions of systemic transformation'. There are echoes here of the analytic eclecticism versus theoretical parsimony debate discussed above. For example, Cohen (2007: 207, 215) notes the attractiveness for the American school of IPE of a reductionist style based on formal economic methodologies, whereas in Britain, he argues, 'Professional status did not require sacrificing detail for parsimony.'

Cohen's (2007, 2008) work prompted a wave of responses on the 'state of the art' in different traditions of IPE scholarship. Subsequent publications on the transatlantic divide took aim at his characterization of British IPE and, to a lesser extent, American IPE, as not being rooted in an authentic representation of either presumed 'school'. Higgott and Watson (2008: 16), for example, criticize Cohen's oppositional logic in demarcating the field of IPE between a British and an American school, a caricature which they view as having the potential to produce self-fulfilling categories as future students and scholars in IPE erroneously position their work explicitly in opposition to one or the other camp. They argue that recent work in IPE has attempted to transcend methodological and ontological divides between agency and structure, ideas and interests, and state power versus market power, a category of IPE scholarship that is wholly absent from Cohen's depiction of the field (Higgott and Watson 2008: 12).

Other IPE scholars have criticized Cohen's division between a British school and an American school as either missing out 'the rest' of IPE (from Europe, Latin America, East Asia and so on) or for lumping all non-American IPE into the unsatisfactory category of a 'British' school (Phillips and Weaver 2010). Meanwhile, Ravenhill (2008: 27) takes aim at Cohen's depiction of the American and British schools of IPE as 'represented by "hard" rational choice analysis on the one hand and "Critical Theory" on the other'. Ravenhill (2008: 27) suggests instead that neither of these categorizations is an accurate representation of 'the richness of approaches to the study of IPE on both sides of the Atlantic', and ignores what he terms the 'missing middle' of IPE scholarship which crosses – and connects – both American and British IPE research communities.

There are obvious perils for students of IPE in uncritically accepting this carving up of the field of IPE into American and British schools. In particular, Cohen's 'great scholars make intellectual traditions' technique for unpacking the intellectual history of the field misrepresents the diversity of IPE scholarship in both the USA and in the UK (Clift and Rosamond 2009: 97). A dichotomous understanding of IPE also discounts the contributions made to the field's development both by scholars who are geographically based outside the USA and the UK, and by those whose work is intellectually distinct from Cohen's characterization of American and British scholarly traditions in IPE. Meanwhile, for some observers the key divide is not so much between British and American traditions of IPE, but rather IPE scholarship that is closely connected with the field of International Relations (IR/IPE), versus IPE scholarship that draws more on the classical tradition of political economy (PE) or comparative political economy (CPE) (see Phillips 2009; Underhill 2000).

Cohen's depiction of American IPE as dominated by neo-utilitarian rationalism and British IPE as dominated by neo-Gramscian scholarship

inspired by the work of Robert Cox implicitly erects disciplinary boundaries that limit the scope for interdisciplinary engagement between IPE
and other fields of social sciences (apart from economics). Here, the critical problem that Cohen (2008: 174–5) identifies is a new 'dialogue of
the deaf' between state-centric and rationalist American IPE scholarship
and normative British IPE scholarship that he suggests is preoccupied
with critical theory. While noting that the British school of IPE is more
interdisciplinary in orientation, a clear preference is expressed for greater
intra-disciplinary engagement between American school rationalism and
British school cognitivism. This leaves to one side the potential benefits
that IPE scholars as a *transnational* community can gain from engagement with diverse fields such as economic geography, sociology, anthropology and cultural studies, an engagement which many IPE scholars are
already undertaking (see, for example, Best and Paterson 2009; Hobson
and Seabrooke 2007; Langley 2008; Weaver 2008). Cohen's intellectual
history of IPE provides interesting and accessible discussions of several
great scholars that have made important contributions to its development. In light of the shortcomings that numerous scholars have identified
with the notion of a transatlantic divide as a definitive marker in the field,
however, it should not be treated as representative of the diversity of
scholarship traditions in contemporary IPE.

Summary

Scholarly debates perform a range of important disciplinary functions. Debates
over contentious issues can help to drive intellectual development and open up
new avenues of enquiry, and provide a stimulus to greater theoretical sophistica-
tion and conceptual refinement. However, major scholarly debates can sometimes
obscure relevant issues and points of contention in the field of IPE at the same time
as they might illuminate others. Debates can also play an influential role over time
in maintaining or altering the parameters of a discipline's subject matter by
constructing a narrative that 'tells stories about its evolution' (Clift and Rosamond
2009: 95). For these reasons it is important to remain alert to what questions and
issues are not being asked and addressed within particular debates, as well as carefully examining the competing claims and areas of contention that are explicitly
presented.

Further reading

Blyth, Mark (ed.). 2009. *Handbook of International Political Economy (IPE):
IPE as a Global Conversation*. London: Routledge.

Campbell, John L. and Ove K. Pedersen (eds). 2001. *The Rise of Neoliberalism and Institutional Analysis*. Princeton, NJ: Princeton University Press.

Frieden, Jeffrey A., David A. Lake and Kenneth A. Schultz. 2013. *World Politics: Interests, Interactions, Institutions*, 2nd edn. New York: W.W. Norton.

Phillips, Nicola and Catherine E. Weaver (eds). 2011. *International Political Economy: Debating the Past, Present, and Future*. London: Routledge.

Shields, Stuart, Ian Bruff and Huw Macartney (eds). 2011. *Critical International Political Economy: Dialogue, Debate and Dissensus*. Basingstoke: Palgrave Macmillan.

Sil, Rudra and Peter J. Katzenstein. 2010. *Beyond Paradigms: Analytic Eclecticism in the Study of World Politics*. Basingstoke: Palgrave Macmillan.

Actors in the Global Political Economy

Chapter 4

State Actors

Introduction

States have traditionally constituted the main actor focus in International Political Economy. More specifically, a small number of 'major power' states dominate the attention of IPE students and scholars. Yet substantial differences exist in how states engage in the global political economy, what levels of influence and agency they are able to exercise across different issue areas, and especially whether they are able to shape processes and outcomes in global economic governance or must accommodate the effects of international regimes that are created by others. The powers available to different types of states encompass a broad range of instruments and tactics. Theoretical perspectives in IPE hold different starting assumptions of what states are and what they do in the global political economy, as well as what are the main drivers of change in state roles and activities.

This chapter provides an introduction to states as actors in the global political economy, while emphasizing the range of actor roles that different types of states play and the conceptual frameworks used within IPE for understanding these roles. This includes discussion of the differences between states as actors based on: economic size; population size; geography; institutional capacities; and organizational memberships in the global political economy. The chapter looks at how the domestic attributes of states inform their international status and roles in the global political economy, but does not examine states' domestic agential powers. Instead, it focuses on providing an overview of states' varying degrees of international agential power, defined as their ability 'to determine policy and shape the international realm' (Hobson 2000: 6).

Background

Based on international law in the 1933 Montevideo Convention, which was signed during the Seventh International Conference of American States in Montevideo, Uruguay, states are entities which have: '(a) a permanent population; (b) a defined territory; (c) a government; and (d) a capacity to enter into relations with other states' (Dixon 2007: 115). In standard conceptions of the modern international society of states, sovereignty forms one of the foundational institutions that 'define[s] legitimate statehood and rightful state action' (Reus-Smit 1997: 558). States are legally equal actors in terms of their juridical sovereignty, despite enormous differences in their substantive resources, purposive capacities, functional responsibilities, international roles and degrees of independence as sovereign actors. There is nothing inevitable or natural about an international system that is composed of states as the main political units. While they may be legally equal, states are not fixed, unchanging entities, but are 'always in the process of formation, change, and potential decay' (Cerny 1990: 4).

Contemporary debates over the changing role of the state in an era of economic globalization often focus on national variations in institutional capacities and organizational power as a key determinant of how international economic integration influences the policy options that different governments face. For example, 'Organisationally strong states' are potentially able 'both to internalise and to resist the pressures of economic, social, and political globalisation'. In contrast, 'Organisationally weak states' are more likely to be 'undermined by globalisation'. For these countries crisis may become 'endemic' (Cerny 2010: 18). Variations in state structures and capabilities therefore mediate the consequences of globalization in different ways across countries.

With respect to their engagement in and openness to the global political economy, states of different sizes clearly 'differ in their basic condition' (Katzenstein 2003: 10). This may include differences in the size of the territory they control, the size of their populations and the size of their economies. For example, Kazakhstan is the ninth largest country in the world, with a territory that is larger than Western Europe but a population around the same size as the Netherlands, a country whose geographic territory is equal to less than 2 per cent of Kazakhstan's. In addition to territorial size, further geographic differences between states that may have important economic consequences include whether the territories they control are landlocked or have sea access, whether they share land borders with other states and how close or distant they are in relation to key markets for their goods and services.

Many of the main differences between various types of states, including their different levels of resources and international roles, can be illustrated through looking at how small states engage in the global political economy. For small states both the geographical size of the territory under their jurisdiction and the scale of their activities represent significant indicators of different qualities of statehood compared with larger states. Yet what may matter more is the construction of their identities as 'small states', based on perceptions of relatively greater vulnerability in the global political economy (Katzenstein 2003: 11). How the constraints and opportunities of their size is interpreted by small state actors can therefore be as much a function of processes of identity construction as it is about relative resource constraints (Browning 2006). If perceptions of greater relative vulnerability are shared among small state actors this may make them more open to rapid processes of learning, policy adaption and institutional change in order to carve out a competitive advantage over the more cumbersome state bureaucracies of larger states and the potential for economic governance in larger states to be more constrained by the market power of domestic private actors. In New Zealand, for example, the comparative smallness of the country's economy, population, political system and governmental apparatus enabled the state to 'turn on a dime' in a radical new policy direction after 1984. Economic reforms under successive New Zealand governments from 1984–99 reoriented the entire basis of the country's economic policy-making from a protectionist policy orientation to neoliberal structural reforms and policy experiments, which were held up as a model for other states to follow by IOs such as the IMF and the World Bank (Broome and Seabrooke 2007).

State power and international hierarchy

State agency refers to the agential power of a state to purposively exercise influence in a specific realm of action. State agency in the global political economy refers to the power 'to determine policy and shape the international realm' (Hobson 2000: 6). In contrast to perceptions of vulnerability among small states, larger states are more accustomed to being able to shape global economic rules and processes through their dominant position as regulators of large domestic markets (Drezner 2007). They are also more likely to have a seat at the table in negotiations over global economic rules and international regimes. According to much of the conventional wisdom in the field, therefore, small states usually serve as 'policy-takers' in the global political economy, and are unable to exercise much agency over global rules, norms, principles and market processes

Figure 4.1   *Hierarchy of state influence in the global political economy*

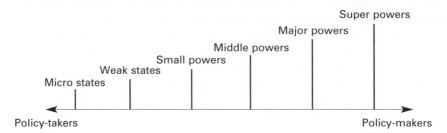

that are exogenously determined. In comparison the largest states are assumed to be 'policy-makers'. The resources and dominant economic position of these states allow them to write the rules of international regimes in different policy areas, to dominate representation and decision-making in both formal IOs and informal governance forums and to discipline global market forces through their actions and decisions.

These differences in states' relative positions in the global political economy are illustrated in a 'hierarchy ladder' of state influence in Figure 4.1. Adapted from Handel's (1990: 10) five gradations of state power, this provides a snapshot of traditional distinctions in state power and influence. At the top of the food chain, based on this hierarchy of influence, are superpowers such as the USA (and the Soviet Union during the Cold War), followed by major powers which have substantial capacities to shape dynamics of change in the global political economy, such the states represented in the Group of Eight (G8, see Chapter 6). Other states have constructed international identities as middle powers that can exercise substantive influence through multilateral forums and organizations but lack the capacity for unilateral action. One such example is Australia (Ravenhill 1998), whose middle power identity is both a reflection of, and serves to justify, its strategic aid priorities as well as its international military commitments alongside the USA. Despite being ranked 51st in the world in 2009 in terms of population size, Australia has developed capacities to play an important role in the global political economy through its strategic alliances and bilateral economic agreements, institutional representation in regional groupings such as the Asia-Pacific Economic Cooperation (APEC) forum and global governance forums such as the Group of 20, and its capacity to punch above its weight in terms of economic size (in 2009 Australia ranked 15th in the world in total GDP). States may belong to the category of middle powers if, like Australia, they have small populations but are highly developed with relatively large economies. Alternatively, this group of states may include those that have large populations but have less economic weight (Handel 1990: 23).

Small powers, in contrast, are able to exercise some degree of leverage in the global political economy, though this usually falls far short of that of major powers and middle powers. Their influence may be more likely to be found in specific issue areas where they are deemed by others to have legitimate strategic interests, moral authority and niche expertise or experience, such as New Zealand and nuclear testing in the South Pacific or Iceland and fisheries. Small states may also gain influence as 'honest brokers' that do not share major power interests in mediating between parties in international disputes. Alternatively, they may be able to punch above their weight through membership of regional institutions, such as Luxembourg's role in the EU (Hearl 2006) or Singapore's role within the Association of Southeast Asian Nations (ASEAN) (Daquila and Huy 2003).

The category of weak states depicted in Figure 4.1 refers to those that are relatively 'powerless' to exercise influence in the global political economy. Greater resource constraints and fewer direct means of exercising leverage can still be mediated by tactical skill and economic diplomacy to enhance the impact of weak states in the world economy (Lee and Smith 2008). Weak states are both the largest group of state actors in the global political economy and the hardest group to define with any degree of analytical precision. This is because attributes of power and weakness are a continuum rather than fixed properties. Power also comes in different forms, and states can be powerful in some areas and weak in others (Handel 1990: 257). All states have varying levels of 'state capacity' in different areas. This refers to the organizational, material and social resources a state has access to, and how well it is able to order and deploy those resources in terms of both efficiency and effectiveness. State capacity can be disaggregated into four main components: (1) ideational state capacity; (2) political state capacity; (3) technical state capacity; and (4) implementation state capacity (see Nørgaard and Cummings 2004).

Microstates and small island developing states are typically assumed to be the weakest state actors in the global political economy. This is due primarily to their population size, which may be smaller than a medium-sized city in countries with larger populations. Even here substantial differences exist between the fortunes and potential international influence of microstates, especially if the classification of a microstate is taken at the upper limit of a population of 2 million from the range of microstate definitions that are commonly used (Imam 2010). The United Nations *Barbados Programme of Action* defines small island developing states as those which are 'limited in size, have vulnerable economies and are dependent both upon narrow resource bases and on international trade, without the means of influencing the terms of that trade' (United Nations General Assembly 1994). Many small island developing states have far lower per capita income levels than larger countries. During the global financial crisis of 2008–09, many small island developing states suffered disproportionately from a sharp reduction in global demand, tourism and private capital flows, as well as greater competition for bilateral aid. The Maldives, for example, experienced a current account deficit equal to half of GDP in 2008, which was followed by a budget deficit of almost one third of GDP in 2009.

A number of microstates have nonetheless taken advantage of their juridical status as sovereign entities by using sovereignty as a 'commercial asset' to attract business from both corporations and individuals by offering greater anonymity, a lack of corporate regulation, and the ability to either evade or greatly reduce tax obligations in their home states (Palan 2003a). By enabling the rapid expansion of cross-border economic transactions, the dynamics of international economic integration over the course of the last four decades has impacted upon the capacity of states to control financial flows, to monitor the overseas activities of domestic businesses and to control where corporate profits are located for tax purposes (see Chapter 15). This has provided weak states with a means of attracting capital flows and generating revenue in a globalized world economy – regardless of their size or institutional capacities – by offering tax concessions and financial anonymity to foreign corporations and high net worth individuals. As these examples from the 'policy-taker' end of the spectrum in Figure 4.1 illustrate, 'powerlessness' among states in the global political economy is a matter of degree, not an absolute category, and in specific areas or on certain issues weak states are capable of exercising important forms of agency.

The role of the state in the global political economy

One way to illustrate the differences in policy autonomy, policy options and economic and social outcomes in states of different sizes is to look at how they fare when faced with a global economic crisis. Here, small states generally face many of the same constraints as most other states during a period of systemic crisis, with the exception of the largest and most powerful economies (such as the G8, see Chapter 6). However, the sovereignty, political and credibility costs are potentially higher in the case of small states that are forced to seek financial bailouts from IOs in comparison with larger states. This may be especially the case if small states have developed scale economies in niche industries that depend upon an exogenous growth model for expansion, such as the banking sector in Iceland prior to 2008 (Broome 2011).

In terms of their capacity to weather global financial storms, small states are perhaps best defined on the basis of population rather than employing other potential indicators of smallness, such as gross domestic product or geographical territory (Maass 2009). One reason for preferring this definition is that, even when small states have large economies or control a large territory, their low population size limits the effectiveness of the range of policy tools they have at their disposal when faced with financial disaster. Such limitations are again relative rather than absolute. For example, increasing taxes on a workforce of 300,000 to tackle a blowout in external debt obligations caused by a banking crisis in a small state where the financial sector is internationalized and far outstrips the size of the domestic economy can be expected to be relatively less effective (or at least more likely to involve a steeper tax hike) compared with a state that has a workforce of 30,000,000. In the latter case, the fiscal cost can be spread more lightly across the population through changes in income, consumption, property and corporate tax rates.

In a similar vein, states with smaller populations can find it difficult to build a broad manufacturing base in the absence of economies of scale. While their small size can sometimes belie scale economies in specialized industries (Herbertsson and Zoega 2003), the significant challenges faced by small states often constrain efforts to diversify their economies in order to mitigate vulnerability to terms of trade shocks (Payne 2008). Even comparatively wealthy small states with high per capita incomes usually lack the consumption power derived from large domestic markets to shape international regimes in the global political economy (Drezner 2007), and are less likely to gain a seat at the table in key governance forums (with some exceptions; see Thorhallsson and Wivel 2006).

Compared with larger countries, therefore, the governments of small states that are dependent upon external drivers of growth have less room to manoeuvre through economic policy adjustment during a systemic crisis episode. Small states have reduced scope for enacting significant changes in fiscal and monetary policies that can effectively combat exogenous shocks without severe domestic contraction. In particular, states with small populations are likely to find it more difficult to stimulate demand to prop up economic growth or to soften the effects of a recession during a balance of payments crisis, especially in the context of significant capital outflows.

The properties of statehood that define a state as a 'major power' are no less difficult to pin down and clearly define than what constitutes other states as 'small' or 'weak'. Much of the academic literature both in IPE and in the study of IR more broadly has focused on the domestic attributes of states from which their international role might be extrapolated. As discussed above, obvious starting points here include a state's

Figure 4.2   *Top-ten countries in population size, 2009*

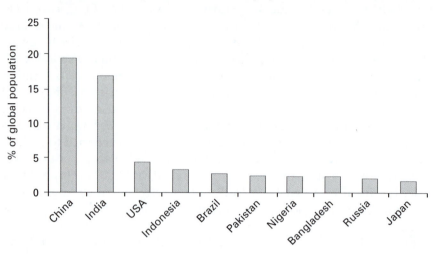

Source: World Bank (2011) *World Development Indicators Database* (http://site resources.worldbank.org/DATASTATISTICS/Resources/POP.pdf).

Figure 4.3   *GDP of top-ten countries in population size, 2009*

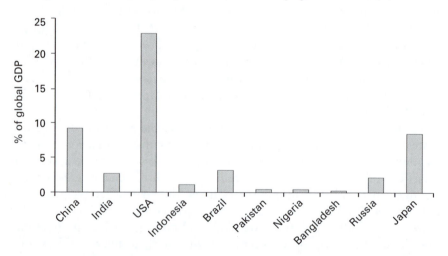

Source: World Bank (2011) *World Development Indicators Database* (http://site resources.worldbank.org/DATASTATISTICS/Resources/GDP.pdf).

population size and its GDP. From these criteria it is relatively straightforward to identify which states constitute large countries in population size (Figure 4.2) and in economic size (Figure 4.3). Less straightforward is: (a) which criterion should count more for classifying states' roles in the global political economy; and (b) what is the relationship between domestic attributes, such as size of population or economy, and a state's international role and influence.

As a comparison between Figures 4.2 and 4.3 makes clear, the top-ten countries by population size differ markedly in the size of their economies. Despite having under 2 per cent of the world's population, for example, Japan accounts for close to 9 per cent of global GDP, while the USA has 5 per cent of the world's population and accounts for 23 per cent of global GDP. India, meanwhile, has 17 per cent of the world's population, but only accounts for 3 per cent of global GDP. Such differences make it problematic to draw a clear causal connection between the domestic attributes of states and their respective roles and influence in the global political economy.

Having substantial material resources may indicate the potential for states to exercise a high degree of leverage in the global political economy and to perform the role of a major power, but does not mean that such states actually do so in practice. Potentially powerful states may opt to limit their unilateral use of power for a range of reasons. One example of voluntary restraint on the use of state power in international security was the strong reluctance of Germany to engage its armed forces in international military commitments after World War II. This was based on the German state's post-World War II conception of its role as a 'civilian power' (*Zivilmacht*) which maintained tight legal restrictions on the overseas military operations of the *Bundeswehr* until the early 1990s. Within IPE, examples might include states that have large material capabilities and unilateral forms of leverage at their disposal but opt to bind themselves to abiding by multilateral rules (such as trade rules in the WTO) rather than engaging in bilateral economic coercion, which constrains their autonomy of action even if they still wield significant influence within a multilateral system of rules.

Similar conceptual problems exist with attempts to use military capabilities as a proxy for state power, especially if these are based on a state's military expenditures rather than a measure of their actual capacity to deploy military resources overseas. While military resources are commonly understood as an international security issue rather than an IPE issue, this represents a false dichotomy between academic sub-disciplines which overlap in terms of issues, actors, problems and research puzzles. The study of international security and IPE are therefore 'two sides of the same coin', not least because it is difficult for states to wage wars against other states without first having substantial economic resources to pay for them (including the capacity to access credit on favourable terms) (Homolar 2010).

As Figure 4.4 illustrates, the USA maintains a position far ahead of all other states in terms of the volume of its annual military expenditures.

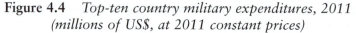

Figure 4.4   *Top-ten country military expenditures, 2011 (millions of US$, at 2011 constant prices)*

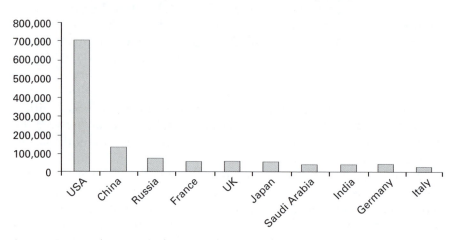

Source: SPIRI Military Expenditure Database (2012) (http://milexdata.sipri.org/).

Nevertheless, it is difficult to draw clear causal links between spending on military goods and services – or, indeed, actual military capabilities – and a state's role in the global political economy. Where military spending does perhaps correlate with differences in status between states is between those that are commonly classed as middle, major, or superpowers taken as a group and the small states, weaker states and microstates that make up the rest. For example, each of the world's top-ten consumers of military goods included in Figure 4.4, whose combined military expenditures in 2011 equated to over 74 per cent of estimated global military spending, would be classed in the former category, while most states, whose military expenditures fall far below the global top-ten, would fall into the latter camp.

Different theoretical perspectives in the study of IPE present contrasting understandings of what type of actor states are and how they operate in the global political economy (see Chapter 2). The concept of the state is variously defined as: (1) government; (2) public bureaucracy and institutionalized legal order; (3) ruling class; and (4) normative order (Krasner 1984: 224). For example, from a strategic-relational perspective the state is neither a unified subject that consistently performs a given set of functions, nor is it a simple instrument of power used by a select group of actors to pursue their interests. Rather than conceiving the state as a fixed entity, it is instead defined from a strategic-relational perspective as a form of social relation (Jessop 2008: 1, 3).

Theories of how states operate in their external relations diverge between conceptions of the state as: (1) a unified rational actor, which

Table 4.1 *The role of the state in the global political economy*

Theoretical perspectives	Ontology of the state	Sources of change	International role of the state
Constructivist	Ideas constitute state identities, interests and institutions	Crises and shocks create uncertainty, which leads to changes in ideas	States draw on ideas to construct international normative orders
Feminist	The state mediates gendered economic relations	Changing conceptions of 'public' and 'private' spheres of action	States tend to reproduce gendered economic relations at the global level
Liberal	Institutionalized bargaining arena for competing interests	Interest-based struggles and bargaining	International cooperation helps to solve collective action problems
Marxist	The state is an instrument of class domination by the ruling elite	Conflict between social classes, and intra-elite struggles	States seek new markets and common rules in the interests of corporate elites
Realist	The economy is subordinate to the needs of the state	Changes in the international distribution of capabilities lead either to inter-state cooperation or conflict	Inter-state relations are anarchic, and states must engage in zero-sum games
Poststructuralist	States are not fixed entities, but are produced by discursive practices	The emergence of new discursive formations shapes global practices	Discourses of power shape the formation of actors' subject positions

makes calculated choices in order to realize strategic objectives; (2) an organizational process, with political acts and choices resulting from patterns of bureaucratic behaviour and organizational routines; and (3) an arena for bargaining games between the principal political players in government (Allison 1971: 4–6). These analytical distinctions influence whether states are conceived as more or less strategic actors in the global political economy, which exhibit a high degree of unity and clear preference rankings, or whether they are conceived instead as 'splintered' political units, characterized by bureaucratic turf wars and conflicts between officials that may pull national policies in multiple directions at different points in time (Cerny 1990: 168). A basic typology of how the role of the state in the global political economy is seen through different theoretical lenses is illustrated in Table 4.1. This represents three important distinctions in how states can be understood, based on: (1) different concepts of the ontology of the state; (2) what conditions and processes shape changes in state practices; and (3) what international roles and functions states perform.

Contemporary challenges and sources of change

One of the most commonly identified challenges for the contemporary international society of states is the rise of new powers in the system. The label 'rising power' is commonly ascribed to states that are deemed to be rapidly increasing either their material capabilities or their influence in the global political economy, or both. The term is often used but is less-often concisely defined, although it usually refers to the increasing economic weight (and assumed growing political muscle) of states such as Brazil, Russia, India and China (collectively referred to as the BRICs). A problem with the rising powers label is that it is mostly used to refer to the rapidly increasing size of the economies of states that are categorized as 'on the rise', with less attention paid to examining changes in these states' political leverage in the global political economy, or what can be called their 'diplomatic GDP' (Cooper 2010a: 64).

This problem of definition also applies to other categories of states such as major powers, middle powers and small powers. In essence, the question boils down to whether the status that is ascribed to a particular state in the global political economy simply reflects its domestic attributes in terms of population size, economic output and growth rates, or military capabilities. An alternative basis for differentiating their status and international roles is state behaviour, and specifically the extent to which a state is able to exercise leadership behaviour. Rather than solely being a function of state capacities, for example, their willingness to engage in international activism is sometimes seen as an important marker of 'middle power' status for states such as Australia and Canada (Ravenhill 1998).

External behaviour in the global political economy is perhaps a more useful focus for understanding the changing international status of 'rising powers' in particular. For these countries, rising power status is not derived solely from economic or military capabilities, but also 'depends on how power is exercised, in relation to whom, the motivations that underpin this exercise, and ... how action and reaction are interpreted or misinterpreted' (Narlikar 2013: 561). Studying external behaviour can help to shed light on whether a state with increasing economic weight and political muscle is oriented towards acting as a 'regime-conforming' status quo power which plays an active role in but does not seek to fundamentally challenge or change existing international regimes, or whether it is a 'revisionist' power which is more likely to seek to use growing leverage to restructure or replace existing international regimes and global economic governance processes (Narlikar 2010a: 452). If leadership is defined not simply as state capacities but in terms of attributes which include 'a willingness to bear the costs of agenda-setting and free-riding' at the international level (Narlikar 2010a: 454), the states most often identified as rising powers – China and India – may meet this leadership threshold in some issue areas but not (yet) in most (Breslin 2013; Narlikar 2010b). In their attempt to move up the 'hierarchy ladder' of states depicted in Figure 4.1, rising powers that are not willing to assume a greater share of costs in the global political economy may risk becoming stuck at the level of middle powers.

Rising power states do not need to act in accordance with a 'revisionist' definition of their role in order to be recognized as attaining major power status, however. State actors may assume there is more to gain in the long run from gaining a seat at the top table in key governance forums and achieving greater formal representation in IOs. This could allow rising powers to push gradually for incremental 'revisions' while accommodating existing international regimes, without having to foot the lion's share of the bill in exchange for achieving more substantial immediate influence over the dynamics of change in global economic governance. Such a stance may enable rising powers to exercise a form of veto power over changes in rules and principles they deem unsuited to their interests, even if it does not in the short term translate into the capacity to set policy agendas and achieve their preferred outcomes (Narlikar 2007).

Summary

Achieving a certain status in the global political economy is a quality that is informed by a state's domestic attributes – and especially by economic size and growth trajectory – but is not determined by them. Instead, state capacities must be matched by a willingness to deploy organizational resources effectively in order to exercise substantive influence over global economic agenda-setting processes. At the same time, indicators point to the fact that a relative decline in the capabilities of existing powers does not automatically translate into a loss of international status and systemic privileges (Norrlof 2010). Gaining the status of middle or major power – let alone a superpower – depends in large part on how a state behaves in its external economic relations and diplomatic activities. Crucially, it is a quality that must be conferred by other state actors in the global political economy through granting membership and representation rights to 'newcomers', as well as the recognition by others of a state's right to exercise leadership in shaping global agendas.

Despite possessing equal rights in terms of their juridical sovereignty, states are not created equal in their resources, their capacities, their autonomy of action, or their international roles. The contemporary global political economy includes states of radically different economic, geographic and population sizes. Different states perform a broad spectrum of roles, not all of which fit neatly into fixed categories of 'policy-makers' versus 'policy-takers'. For example, states which are classed as rising powers in the global political economy may be in a long-term process of changing, haphazardly, from being global policy-takers to policy-makers. Among weaker states, common perceptions of vulnerability and powerlessness do not capture the complete picture of the international role and influence of state actors. The tax haven strategies adopted by some of the world's smallest microstates remains an intractable problem for many major power states, despite the enormity of their differences in material capabilities and resources. Moreover, in a globalized economy small states may be faster at learning how to adapt and innovate in their economies and institutional structures to gain a competitive edge over larger states which face less immediate pressures to adjust to changing global economic conditions due to their larger domestic markets. In short, individual states cannot be assumed from the start to be constantly either 'powerful' or 'powerless' actors across different issues or over time in the same issue area. Instead, a state's influence must be carefully identified in specific cases using multiple variables, while also being considered in connection with the potential influence of other state and non-state actors in the global political economy.

Discussion questions

1. What key factors inform states' varying levels of influence in the global political economy?
2. Are small states always 'policy-takers'? If so, why? If not, why not?
3. How do the military capabilities of states relate to their roles in the global political economy?
4. Should all states have equal juridical status as sovereign actors despite their varying size and capabilities?
5. Which is more important for international status, the size of a state's population or its economy?
6. What examples show how 'weak' states can exercise agency in the global political economy?

Further reading

Alexandroff, Alan S. and Andrew F. Cooper (eds). 2010. *Rising States, Rising Institutions: Challenges for Global Governance*. Washington, DC, and Waterloo: Brookings Institution Press and Centre for International Governance Innovation.

Drezner, Daniel W. 2007. *All Politics is Global: Explaining International Regulatory Regimes*. Princeton, NJ: Princeton University Press.

Hobson, John M. 2000. *The State and International Relations*. Cambridge: Cambridge University Press.

Lake, David A. 2009. *Hierarchy in International Relations*. Ithaca, NY: Cornell University Press.

Narlikar, Amrita. 2010b. *New Powers: How to Become One and How to Manage Them*. London: Hurst & Co.

Weiss, Linda (ed.). 2003. *States in the Global Political Economy: Bringing Domestic Institutions Back In*. Cambridge: Cambridge University Press.

International Organizations

Introduction

International organizations (IOs) have been a major focus of academic research and controversy in IPE since the field emerged. Like most topics in IPE, how much attention IOs receive at a given point tends to rise and fall depending on the hot-button topics of the day and scholarship trends. During much of the 2000s, for example, mature IOs such as the IMF were widely viewed as institutional relics from an earlier era, their machinery and resources designed for the postwar international economic order and unsuited to the fast-paced, globalized economy of the twenty-first century. At the same time, the more recently established WTO became a target of intense public criticism and social activism from critics of contemporary models of economic globalization. Meanwhile, the difficulties associated with negotiating multilateral environmental agreements for action on climate change have prompted calls for the creation of a new World Environment Organization (WEO) within the United Nations system. With the onset of the global financial crisis in 2008–09 and subsequent sovereign debt crises among Eurozone economies, interest in the contemporary roles of IOs has expanded in recent years. Previously settled assumptions about the balance of private and public authority in the global political economy and the aims of global economic governance are also being rethought. This chapter provides a basic introduction to IOs, the instruments they use to shape other actors' behaviour and the roles they play in the global political economy, as well as how IOs may be retooled or redesigned in the future.

Background

The contemporary global political economy is populated by a host of IOs. Today, IOs have assumed at least partial responsibilities for issues that range from international crisis management to economic development and poverty reduction, from policy training to global labour market standards, and from global export credit and investment insurance to the protection of intellectual property, areas which may be characterized by 'collective action problems' for states. Examples of IOs that perform these different functions include: the IMF; the World Bank; the Joint Vienna Institute (JVI); the International Labour Organization (ILO); the Berne Union; and the World Intellectual Property Organization (WIPO). Collective action problems in the global political economy refer to situations where a group of actors all stand to gain from a certain action, but the costs involved make it unlikely that any one actor can or will undertake it on their own. IOs can help to solve collective action problems by facilitating burden-sharing between states, and through the creation of specialist bureaucratic expertise at the global level. Yet the importance and consequences of the roles of IOs in the global political economy is hotly contested. For some observers IOs are seen simply as tools of economic statecraft for major powers, while for others they are viewed as 'institutional Frankensteins' that have gained too much independence from member states and infringe greatly on their economic sovereignty, leading to pathological outcomes in global economic governance (Hawkins *et al.* 2006: 4). As with most binary oppositions in the study of IPE, the reality is more complicated than a simple dichotomy between IOs as all-powerful 'world police', accountable to no one, and IOs as the foreign policy instruments of Western developed countries.

International institutions are defined as 'relatively stable sets of related constitutive, regulative, and procedural norms and rules that pertain to the international system, the actors in the system (including states as well as nonstate entities), and their activities' (Duffield 2007: 7–8). From this broader definition, IOs are intergovernmental organizations established by formal rules that constitute their mandated purpose and the scope of their activities, which grants them an international legal personality that is distinct from club forums or coalitions of states (see Chapter 6). Following Duffield (2007: 12–14), the functions of IOs can be classified into three categories: (1) constitutive functions, such as a codified institutional mandate that establishes an IO as an actor; (2) regulative functions, such as making, monitoring and enforcing rules and norms that regulate actors' behaviour; and (3) procedural functions, such as the governance structures within an IO that formalize decision-making

Figure 5.1   *Levels of hierarchy in the global political economy*

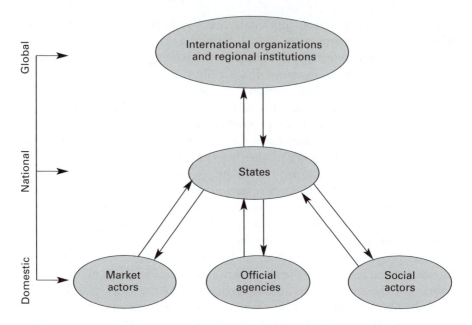

processes and arrangements that govern interaction between member states. An important analytical distinction can also be drawn between whether the legal framework within which an IO may have delegated authority for prescribing, proscribing, or authorizing certain kinds of behaviour is characterized by 'hard law' that incorporates precise legally binding obligations, or less precise obligations and principles that constitute 'soft law' (Abbott and Snidal 2000: 421–2).

The hierarchy of authority in the global political economy is often depicted as a straightforward, top-down set of relations running from IOs and regional institutions, as actors operating 'above' the state, to states, as the pre-eminent actors that make rules governing economic activity in their domestic markets and which negotiate international economic agreements to govern cross-border activities. At a subordinate level are the actors that are both governed by states and that lobby states for their own policy preferences, including market actors as well as NGOs, workers and consumers, trade unions and professional associations, and official agencies, among others (Figure 5.1). This depiction of levels of hierarchy in the global political economy captures the traditional understanding of the business of IOs, but presents an overly static conception of the types of roles that actors play, how they interact and the dynamics of operationalizing international economic cooperation. It also suffers from the implication that non-state actors such as firms, commercial banks, industry lobby groups and NGOs are by definition sub-state actors that can only influence processes in the global political economy through states. Non-state actors are often 'global' actors in their own right, and may engage with IOs directly rather than via national governments (see Chapters 7 and 8). This view of hierarchy as organized from top to bottom in a formal legal conception of authority fails to incorporate the dynamic ways in which authority in the global political economy can be conceived as being 'divided among different levels of governance and different rulers' (Lake 2009: 3).

A different conception of hierarchy based on the functions of actors in the global political economy is depicted in Figure 5.2. This illustrates how connections between different categories of actors are not always the arms-length relationships that are assumed in a formal legal conception of levels of hierarchy. There is significant overlap in functional responsibilities and organizational representation across governance forums, especially when it comes to international economic cooperation and negotiations. This also highlights how the roles of market and social actors – as well as official agencies – are critical to the implementation of rules and principles negotiated at the global level. With respect to negotiations over international economic rules between parties with different objectives, IOs are both incubators of deliberation through their own

Figure 5.2   *Functions of hierarchy in the global political economy*

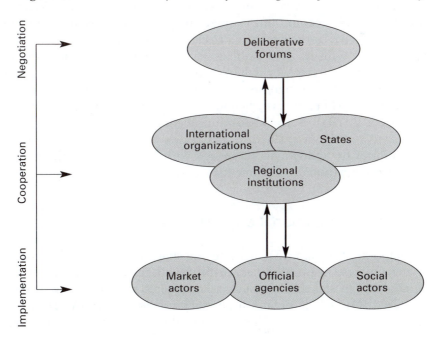

governing boards, summits, annual meetings, working groups and issue-specific negotiations, as well as participants in external deliberative forums. For example, the IMF managing director and the World Bank president participate in Group of 20 (G20) leaders' meetings, while each organization has representatives who attend formal meetings of the other's governing board as observers (see Box 5.1). In terms of regional institutions, the European Central Bank has observer status to attend IMF Executive Board meetings on topics broadly relating to Eurozone issues, while a number of IOs participate as observers in Paris Club meetings of official creditors (see Chapter 14). As Figure 5.2 suggests, authority in the global political economy is not only divided across governance levels and political actors, but the same actor(s) may exercise authority vertically across different levels as well as horizontally in multiple governance forums.

Engagement with IOs is not limited to official actors and non-state organizations. Academic and policy experts are regularly brought in by IOs as outside consultants to provide expertise on particular issues, while individual officials are commonly seconded from other IOs as well as national governments. In particular, independent experts sometimes play a critical role in the quasi-autonomous review functions of IOs. Examples include the IMF's Independent Evaluation Office and the World Bank's Independent Evaluation Group, which produce formal reviews of policies and procedures that have resulted in substantive organizational and operational changes within IOs. In some cases IOs have also developed accountability mechanisms which enable people adversely affected by their activities to challenge whether an organization has complied with its own policies and guidelines. One high-profile example of this is the World Bank's Inspection Panel, which enables people – rather than formal organizations or states – to seek a review of whether the World Bank has acted in a specific case according to its own rules (Park 2010a). Such bottom-up accountability mechanisms, in contrast to top-down evaluation and review bodies, provide (limited) opportunities for individuals to engage with IOs directly without first going through national governments.

Power and international organizations

Contemporary IOs come in many different shapes and sizes. They possess varying powers, responsibilities, institutional capacities and forms of autonomy from stakeholders such as member states. The most widely recognized IOs include organizations such as the IMF, the World Bank and the WTO, which are seen as being at the forefront of international

economic integration as champions of globalization and economic liberalization (Woods 2006). Both the IMF and the World Bank possess large
and highly trained bureaucracies, control substantial financial resources
for multilateral lending, technical assistance and policy training, and
represent a common target of public protest by anti- or alterglobalization
activists. IOs that are multilateral lenders can perform a lender of last
resort function by extending financial assistance when other official or
private creditors will not. In contrast, multilateral technical assistance
focuses on transferring economic knowledge and information to recipients, as well as processes for managing and utilizing information and
knowledge, rather than financial resources. In the universe of IOs, the
IMF and the World Bank are unusual in the size of their bureaucracies
and the volume of financial resources they control. Others are remark-
ably small in terms of the staff size of their secretariat, such as the
Financial Action Task Force whose small staff is housed in the OECD
headquarters in Paris and draws substantially on OECD resources
(Sharman 2006: 32).

A common stumbling block for students of IPE is the question of how
to understand the power of actors such as IOs in the global political
economy (Barnett and Duvall 2005). Unlike states, most IOs seldom
have sufficient direct relational power over the behaviour of other actors
to be able to compel them to do something they would not otherwise
wish to do. The power of IOs more often rests in their capacity to shape
institutional arrangements in the global political economy that serve to
influence processes of agenda-setting, and which may limit the choice-set
of options that is available in deliberative governance forums on specific
issues. Further sources of power available to some IOs include both
structural and productive forms of power. Their privileged position in
structures of global economic governance, combined with their
economic expertise and stock of comparative policy knowledge, may
grant IOs the authority to shape ideas about how policy problems are
diagnosed and understood, and which potential solutions are 'thinkable'
in relation to other actors' identities and interests. This constitutes a form
of structural power that is comparable to how the UN Security Council
has the unique authority in the international system to sanction the 'legitimate' use of force – even if an agreement to use force is the result of inter-
state bargaining and backroom deals (Reus-Smit 2005). In a similar
fashion, some IOs enjoy privileged resources and capacities by virtue of
their position in the global political economy in relation to other actors.

The structural benefits some IOs can access are closely connected to
productive forms of power. These include more diffuse social processes
of knowledge production, the construction of global policy standards
and 'best practice' economic governance norms, and the systematization

of techniques of economic measurement, economic forecasting, economic performance benchmarks and cross-country comparisons. IOs can potentially exercise a productive form of power through the construction of 'cognitive authority' (Broome and Seabrooke 2012). An actor has cognitive authority when it is recognized as having authoritative knowledge in an issue area as a result of its expertise, position and experience (Wilson 1983: 13). Some IOs are deemed to 'know what they are talking about' on a given issue by virtue of their expertise, their stock of comparative policy knowledge and institutional memory and their first-hand experience in dealing with particular policy challenges, such as systemic financial crises. The formal status of IOs such as the IMF and the World Bank as 'apolitical' actors can also allow them to present proposals for national economic policy solutions and changes to international regimes as based on 'sound economics' rather than national or sectoral interests (Barnett and Finnemore 2004: 68–9), which provides an additional source of discursive power.

While IOs can sometimes operate through recourse to relational, structural and productive forms of power, organizations vary greatly in their ability to wield instruments of power in the global political economy. In practice, the powers of IOs vary enormously and encompass both material and nonmaterial levers of influence. This may range from the capacity to exert economic coercion by withholding financial assistance (such as multilateral lending from the IMF and the World Bank) to the power to adjudicate on international economic disputes and to sanction retaliatory measures against rule-violators (such as the WTO's Dispute Settlement Body, DSB). Nonmaterial instruments of power may include peer pressure, shaming and surveillance, as well as nonmaterial sanctions that generate material consequences. When IOs use nonmaterial sanctions such as blacklisting to generate pressure for compliance, targeted actors may suffer actual material costs or may anticipate future material costs as a result of reputational damage (Sharman 2009: 574). The instruments of power available to different IOs to change behaviour among a particular category of actors therefore include those that cause direct material costs, nonmaterial instruments that generate behavioural change through social processes including dialogue and monitoring, and instruments that indirectly threaten to cause material costs for target actors.

The roles of international organizations

In addition to the range of instruments that IOs may possess to exercise leverage over other actors in the global political economy, wide variation exists in the extent to which different IOs operate with institutional autonomy from their member states in performing their various roles (Table 5.1). IOs that are able to exercise a high degree of operational autonomy can create a 'principal–agent' problem for their member states. This refers to the difficulties of motivating one party – the agent – to act in accordance with the wishes of another – the principal. Here member states collectively represent the 'principal', with an IO as the 'agent'. The degree of an IO's autonomy from its membership often depends upon the following criteria:

1.   The nature and political sensitivity of specific policy areas.
2.   How an issue is expected to impact upon the interests of key stake-holders.
3.   The number of external negotiating parties whose consent is essential for effective action.
4.   Whether a decision on specific issues is linked to states' other foreign policy objectives.
5.   An IO's funding model and its current/future level of budgetary autonomy.
6.   The scope of the constitutional rules that provide an IO with its institutional mandate.

Despite mandated areas of independent action and decision-making the degree of an international organization's autonomy is often negotiated in practice issue-by-issue, and may not remain constant in the same issue area in different contexts. After an IO is created it may undergo a process of 'autonomization' as the organization's bureaucratic resources and institutional capacities develop. This can result in an IO gradually gaining greater sources of independence from its member states over time (Koch 2009). At a certain point, member states may make a concerted effort to rein in an IO's autonomy of action through reducing the scope for 'agency slack'. This is defined as independent action by an IO which is not intended by member state principals.

The determinants of an IO's performance are typically assumed to be either external material dynamics (in principal–agent models) or internal social and cultural dynamics (in constructivist approaches). Principal–agent models of IO behaviour are useful for understanding how powerful states structure the incentive environments of IOs, which are designed to maintain a degree of control over the activities of international bureaucracies. They help to shine a spotlight on the delegation of authority from states to international organizations, and provide a clear typology of the types of 'agency slack' and discretion IOs potentially enjoy (Hawkins *et al.* 2006). However, such theories tend to assume that organizational behaviour which deviates from the outcomes

Table 5.1   *The contemporary roles of international organizations*

International cooperation	Policy transmission	Policy learning	Decision-making	Crisis management
Economic statecraft	Policy advice	Economic surveillance	Deliberative forums	Policy coordination
Agenda setting	Policy diffusion	Comparative statistics	Policy innovation	Lender of last resort
Standard setting	Norm advocacy	Policy training	Policy implementation	Policy signalling
Inter-forum cooperation	Policy enforcement	Technical assistance	Rule interpretation	Dispute settlement

intended by state principals is a result of bureaucratic self-interest on the part of the IO. This restricts consideration of other external factors that might shape an IO's level of performance, such as domestic contextual variables (Gutner and Thompson 2010: 238).

From a constructivist approach, principal–agent models of IO behaviour ignore the importance of internal bureaucratic culture and social dynamics in shaping patterns of organizational action and outcomes. As well as responding to external stimuli such as state interests and financial incentives, organizational behaviour is also guided 'by culturally conditioned rules which manifest themselves in certain routines for action and which give meaning to those actions' (Brunsson and Olsen 1993: 4). Rather than IO behaviour that deviates from the intentions of state principals representing a clear-cut case of deliberate 'agency slack' by an organization, an IO can be driven to engage in 'dysfunctional' behaviour by a series of cultural factors. These include both the external normative and cultural environment in which an IO operates and the internal bureaucratic culture of an IO (Barnett and Finnemore 2004: 37). For example, the institutionalized routines and cognitive processes that are used by a particular international organization to 'see' the environment in which it seeks to act create 'tunnel vision' effects. As a consequence, internal bureaucratic processes may exclude local knowledge and practical experience in favour of an excessive reliance on abstract models and generic policy solutions for a given problem (Broome and Seabrooke 2012). While their internal cultural dynamics may often result in pathological outcomes, IOs can also exploit the discretion that is granted by their member states to pursue broader 'public interest' concerns that cut across national preferences (Baker 2012).

As Table 5.1 illustrates, contemporary IOs perform a wide variety of roles in the global political economy. The Bretton Woods institutions (see

Box 5.1) and the WTO perform many of these roles under their broad mandates and responsibilities. Other IOs only perform a small selection of these functions. The OECD, for example, performs most of the roles in the 'international cooperation' and 'policy transmission' columns (with the notable exception of policy enforcement), and operates within a framework of 'soft law'. Member states have nonetheless used the OECD as an instrument of economic statecraft in order to exert pressure on countries that are deemed to encourage tax evasion (Sharman 2006, 2009). In contrast, the main activities of the International Labour Organization (ILO) include norm advocacy, standard setting and policy advice, as well as producing comparative labour statistics, engaging in policy training through the International Training Centre of the ILO and providing technical assistance to developing countries (Standing 2010). The ILO is one of the world's oldest IOs, founded in 1919 following World War I with a unique tripartite organizational structure including state, employer and worker representatives. The ILO lacks a framework of 'hard law' for enforcing members' obligations, however. It has more limited decision-making responsibilities for determining the global governance of labour issues in comparison to the WTO's responsibilities for global trade governance or the IMF's responsibilities for global monetary governance.

Other IOs are more specialized. The JVI also has an innovative structure, with most of its primary and contributing members being other IOs rather than states. JVI members include the IMF, the International Bank for Reconstruction and Development, the OECD and the WTO, as well as the Austrian central bank and ministry of finance. The JVI's primary activity is policy training, although its role may also include policy diffusion and norm advocacy among JVI course participants (Broome 2010b). Originally established with a 'sunset clause' in 1992 as an international training organization for post-communist policy-makers, the JVI provides a useful example of the staying power of IOs once they are created. After deciding to extend the JVI's operations until 2004, the primary members of the organization agreed to make it a permanent feature of the IO landscape in 2001. These examples from the large number of IOs that operate in the contemporary global political economy help to illustrate the differences between the largest IOs that perform most of the roles listed in Table 5.1 and more specialized organizations, as well as those with weaker forms of leverage over other actors. They also indicate the range of organizational structures, institutional mandates and memberships that different IOs comprise.

How effective IOs are at performing their respective roles in the global political economy – and how much autonomy they can maintain from their members – depends in large part on their institutional legitimacy.

Several of the most high-profile IOs have seen the sources of their legitimacy subject to sustained challenge from their member states, as well as from market actors and social actors. In response to perceived shortcomings in the institutional legitimacy and effectiveness of IOs, the location of key decision-making processes has tended to migrate away from formal international organizations in recent decades towards more ad-hoc and informal deliberative governance forums. These include the various 'G' summit meetings such as the Group of Seven and the Group of 20, as well as technocratic forums such as the Basel Committee on Banking Supervision (see Chapters 6 and 7).

Institutional legitimacy is an intersubjective quality that can only be conferred on IOs by other actors. The institutional legitimacy of contemporary IOs is comprised of three main elements, which relate to their expertise (technical legitimacy), governance (procedural legitimacy) and performance (practical legitimacy). How much legitimacy is conferred on an IO by its member states and other actors in the global political economy depends upon the technical expertise and bureaucratic capacities of its staff, its fairness and effectiveness as a multilateral governance forum that provides a buffer against the pursuit of national interests by individual states and its track record in fulfilling mandated objectives such as coordinating multilateral solutions to global economic problems. Each of these three potential sources of institutional legitimacy depends on how an IO is viewed by different audiences. This includes whether an IO's staff is perceived as technically proficient by national officials, and potentially also by market and social actors; whether an IO follows rule-bound procedures that are broadly deemed to be fair and responsive to the needs and interests of its membership as a whole; and whether an IO's actions are deemed to be appropriate and effective responses to the challenges and problems they are designed to tackle (Buchanen and Keohane 2006).

Contemporary challenges and sources of change

The most high-profile current challenge for IOs in the global political economy relates to the effectiveness of their respective roles as crisis managers. This incorporates three core functions: (1) crisis prevention; (2) crisis management; and (3) post-crisis solutions. As the financial crisis of the late 2000s starkly demonstrated, the various actors which make up the architecture of global economic governance struggle to prevent crises from emerging. The reasons for this are manifold, and include many factors that are out of the control of IOs, such as inter-state rivalries and economic competition, insufficient resources and authority to tackle transnational problems in private sector markets, as well as the constraining role of domestic politics in shaping the art of the possible in international economic cooperation. Other explanations for the inability to prevent crises may include a status quo bias, as well as a segmented analysis of the nature and drivers of emerging economic problems. Both of these factors make it difficult for IOs charged with preventing economic crises at a global level to 'connect the dots' in time.

Organizations such as the IMF and the World Bank are often assumed to exercise more influence over the dynamics of crisis management than crisis prevention, through their ability to persuade national officials to choose one policy strategy over another. This is often reinforced by the opportunity to use loan policy conditions (or 'prior actions' that must be implemented before loans will be approved) as leverage for shaping national policy agendas. At least three factors might reduce their influence even during crisis episodes, however. The first is the continuing ability of states to ignore the policy preferences and advice of IOs, even if such a course of action comes with a high material cost. The second is the persistent question of whether the IMF and the World Bank offer national officials the right advice for managing an economic crisis, or whether following their advice may in some cases make a bad situation worse, as is widely recognized was the case with the IMF in the 1997–98 Asian financial crisis. The third is that IOs seldom have a free hand in their dealings with national governments, due to the interests of other parties as well as their own limited resources. In negotiating bailouts for Eurozone economies, for example, the IMF must negotiate with the European Commission, the European Central Bank and borrower governments, while the bilateral influence of creditor states such as Germany also shapes bargaining dynamics over Eurozone bailouts.

When it comes to the gradual development of post-crisis regulatory and policy solutions aimed at structural changes that might help to prevent future global economic crises, the jury so far remains out on how effective IOs will be in proposing new ideas for global economic governance reforms. On the one hand, there is a potential conflict of interest in asking an organization to propose designs for its own reforms, as resulting reforms may be tilted towards the bureaucratic interests of the organization itself rather the needs of its members. On the other hand, existing IOs have a unique advantage over many national governments in terms of their technocratic expertise, institutional memory and comparative policy knowledge when it comes to the design of new international regimes and policy solutions.

With each of these three crisis-related functions contemporary IOs face the issue of resource constraints. In the case of a systemic crisis, the resource constraints within which IOs operate shape the range of policy

Box 5.1 The International Monetary Fund and the World Bank

Created at the same time following complex negotiations at the 1944 United Nations Monetary and Financial Conference held in Bretton Woods, New Hampshire, in the USA, the IMF and the World Bank formed the heart of the postwar compromise of 'embedded liberalism'. The new international economic order agreed at Bretton Woods centred on achieving the difficult task of balancing multilateralism and international openness with sufficient domestic policy autonomy to enable states to establish, rebuild, or expand national welfare states. This was to be realized through international cooperation to reduce national tariff levels and foreign exchange restrictions on trade in goods and services, combined with national controls on capital flows to guard against financial speculation and instability, while supplying external sources of credit to support postwar reconstruction and economic development.

Until the 1970s the postwar era was characterized by national capital controls to allow for variation in domestic policy settings, combined with open current accounts and exchange rate coordination through the IMF to provide a hospitable international environment for the expansion of world trade and economic growth. After a period of growing economic pressure on the USA, US President Richard Nixon unilaterally suspended the convertibility of the US dollar into gold at the official exchange rate in 1971. Despite a series of subsequent efforts to re-establish a rule-based system of semi-fixed exchange rates during the early 1970s, the 1971 'Nixon Shocks' effectively ended this component of the postwar international economic order, which quickly led to the emergence of 'floating' exchange rates among the major industrial economies and a shift towards capital mobility.

With the onset of severe sovereign debt crises in the early 1980s the IMF gained a new international crisis management role as an enforcer of policy reforms in borrowing member states, and as a mediator between debtor governments and their external creditors. The expansion of IMF 'conditionality' (explicit policy reforms agreed between member states and the IMF in exchange for access to IMF loans) generated heated controversy about the organization's crisis management role for two main reasons. First, conditionality necessarily infringes upon national economic sovereignty, thereby diminishing the policy discretion available to governments to chart their own developmental trajectories. Second, 'Washington consensus'-style loan conditions were directed towards the liberalization and international integration of national economies. This involved structural reforms that were often associated with negative economic and social consequences, including increasing income inequality and slower economic growth.

The main business of decision-making in the IMF is conducted through the Executive Board, which is chaired by the IMF managing director and consists of 24 directors who represent either individual countries or groups of countries. The IMF's system of representation has been a growing source of controversy in recent years, in particular because the IMF managing director is traditionally chosen by European governments, while the distribution of voting rights concentrates influence in the hands of a small number of large developed economies. For example,

→

→

eight executive directors currently represent individual countries: the USA, Japan, the UK, Germany, France, Saudi Arabia, the People's Republic of China and Russia. The remaining 180 member states of the IMF are organized into country groups that are represented on the Executive Board by 16 executive directors, diluting the collective influence that developing countries are able to wield in the IMF.

To complement the IMF's role in fostering global economic stability, the World Bank was designed to provide support for countries undergoing post-conflict reconstruction and economic development through the promotion of trade, private investment and equilibrium in national flows of trade and finance. With the inter-war international organizations widely perceived as failed experiments in international cooperation, the new organizations set up in the aftermath of World War II were intended to remedy the design flaws of earlier schemes. The World Bank's two lending arms are the International Bank for Reconstruction and Development (IBRD), which opened its doors in 1945 and now lends to middle-income developing economies, and the International Development Association (IDA), established in 1960, which provides concessional interest-free loans and grants to the world's poorest 82 economies. The IMF is funded by member states' 'quotas', interest earned from loan repayments and bilateral official financing, and is not permitted to borrow on capital markets. The World Bank's loans through the IBRD to governments and public enterprises are funded through top-rated World Bank bonds issued on international capital markets, backed by sovereign guarantees. Following postwar reconstruction in Europe and Japan, the World Bank's lending became concentrated in developing countries (and later the 'transition' economies of East and Central Europe and the former Soviet Union), with World Bank credit comparatively cheaper for developing countries than private sources of credit because of the World Bank's top credit rating. In contrast, the World Bank's IDA lending is financed through the income earned from IBRD loan repayments and periodical contributions from donor states.

The World Bank's internal accountability mechanisms are more complicated than those of the IMF due to the larger size of the organization, as well as the institutional differences between the five component parts of the World Bank Group in contrast to the more centralized hierarchy of the IMF. In addition to the IBRD and the IDA, the World Bank Group also includes three additional bodies: the International Finance Corporation (IFC); the Multilateral Investment Guarantee Agency (MIGA); and the International Centre for Settlement of Investment Disputes (ICSID). Most of the day-to-day decision-making in the World Bank takes place through the organization's Board of Directors, which has 24 executive directors. Like the IMF, member state influence in the World Bank is also concentrated in the hands of developed economies. Five executive directors represent individual countries that are the World Bank's largest shareholders: Germany, France, Japan, the UK and the USA. The remaining 183 members are represented in multiple-country constituencies by 19 executive directors, while the Board of Directors is chaired by the World Bank president, who is traditionally nominated by the USA. The overall governance structure of the two Bretton Woods institutions is therefore heavily weighted towards developed economies with respect to both state representation and leadership selection.

options on the table, and may determine the effectiveness of responses. The decline of the IMF's own financial resources relative to world trade and capital flows and international currency reserves has been a continuing problem for the organization over many years. The IMF on its own has lacked the volume of funds required to support developed or middle-income developing economies experiencing a financial crisis. When faced with major financial crises such as the 'Tequila crisis' in Mexico in 1994 or the Asian financial crisis of 1997–98, the organization has been forced to depend more heavily upon 'supplementary finance' provided by major bilateral donors, other multilateral donors such as the World Bank, regional development banks or the EU, and large commercial banks. This has weakened the IMF's institutional legitimacy, due to widespread claims that the IMF's policy conditions in its rescue packages have been geared towards the interests of creditors such as the US Treasury or commercial banks rather than the interests of country borrowers (Wade and Veneroso 1998). Unlike the cataclysmic effects of the Great Depression in the 1930s and World War II, the recent global financial crisis has not swept away previous institutional forms of international policy coordination, which in some cases have been strongly reinforced, such as the recent boost to the IMF's lending resources (see Chapter 13). However, many conventional assumptions about 'best practice' economic governance have been severely challenged. In the continuing crises that have followed the peak of the global financial crisis three main dynamics can be identified that point to likely trends in the future evolution of global economic governance. These dynamics centre on the renewed importance of and relations between: (1) national institutions and club forums; (2) regional economic agreements and institutions; and (3) IOs.

The global financial crisis has shown that the nature, effectiveness and respective roles of national economic institutions remain crucially important. For example, the 'light touch' financial regulation models of the UK and the USA have been discredited by both the emergence of the crisis and the way it has been managed at a national level, while current policy debates in many developed countries are prompting a rethink of the respective roles of central banks, finance ministries and other national regulatory institutions to achieve a better balance between growth and stability. In addition, the role of intergovernmental 'G' summit meetings of a select group of national leaders and policy officials are likely to continue to remain the principal forums for proposing, approving, or vetoing major changes in the architecture of global economic governance (Baker 2006).

With regulatory authority in the global political economy split unevenly between multiple levels of governance, the evolving relationship between regional institutions and IOs is likely to prove an important motor of long-term change in global economic governance across the board. For example, some observers have suggested that the proliferation of regional and bilateral preferential trade agreements might weaken the effectiveness of the WTO as the global arbiter of international trade rules. At the same time, others have pointed out that the strengthening of regional trade ties could provide an important stepping stone for the WTO to move forward through further increasing the density of international trade legalization at a level where it is more politically feasible for governments to achieve multilateral agreement.

The global financial crisis has also reaffirmed the importance of the main IOs. This is most obvious in the case of the IMF, with a large number of countries drawing on the organization's financial resources to plug severe balance of payments shortfalls compared with the stigma many countries associated with borrowing from the IMF in the decade following the Asian financial crisis. In addition, formal IOs remain more suited than informal governance forums to the task of filling in the concrete technical details, definitions and procedures of international regimes. They are also better able to effectively diffuse, monitor and enforce compliance with new rules, standards and norms.

This suggests that for the foreseeable future IOs will continue to play the following major roles with respect to global economic governance. Lending organizations such as the Bretton Woods institutions will continue to be important sources of credit for many developing countries, especially the HIPCs that have little recourse to alternative sources of external finance, as well as middle-income developing and developed countries facing sovereign debt problems. Despite the stronger spotlight that is now focused on finalizing long-overdue reforms to IMF and World Bank lending practices, both organizations will continue to apply some form of policy conditionality before agreeing to extend credit, which means that they will have an ongoing role in domestic processes of policy reform and institutional change in borrowing countries.

IOs will continue to play a major role in global policy surveillance and economic forecasting. In the wake of the global financial crisis, the need for more comprehensive oversight of the world economy and policy surveillance to monitor the prospect of future financial crises has become more urgent. This led G20 leaders in April 2009 to call for increased collaboration between the IMF and the new Financial Stability Board (FSB, the successor to the Financial Stability Forum set up in 1999 in the aftermath of the Asian financial crisis) to report on macroeconomic risks and the potential actions needed to address them.

Moreover, the continued existence of formal IOs can help to diminish the potential for economic disagreements to spill over into strategic conflicts. In this respect, the formal mechanisms of the Bretton Woods institutions and the WTO's dispute settlement procedures remain important. While major states can choose to violate these international rules and principles, the existence of codified principles for governing international cooperation and economic interactions helps to stabilize other actors' expectations of a state's behaviour, which raises the political and economic costs associated with unilaterally breaking the rules of the status quo. On the other side of the coin, the Bretton Woods institutions and the WTO continue to provide useful mechanisms for achieving compliance with global policy norms, which can potentially serve to reduce the more blatant unilateral exercise of economic power by one government over another.

The above roles suggest that IOs will continue to perform a series of important intellectual tasks with respect to global economic governance. Among other things, these are likely to include collectively supplying national governments with the following functions:

1. Templates for crisis management options and short-term policy solutions to restore stability in fragile economies.
2. A source of new ideas for changes to international regimes.
3. A source of comparative policy knowledge on national economic reforms.
4. The capacity to model the effects of both national and international policy changes, as well as to monitor spill-over effects between economies.
5. The promotion of global compliance with agreed rules, norms and principles.
6. A source of comparable cross-country economic data and economic forecasting.
7. A storing house for institutional memory of what has worked, and what has not worked, with respect to global economic governance in the past.

Taken together, these functions can help to resolve collective problems at the global level that both national governments and market actors would struggle to address effectively in the absence of a formal architecture for global economic governance.

Summary

Many of the familiar features of global economic governance in the contemporary era are unlikely to disappear any time soon, and the future of global economic governance remains in large part a story of continuity in the principles, policy norms and rules that guide the functions of IOs. The roles that mature IOs play in the global political economy have nonetheless changed markedly since their creation, and are continuing to do so in the wake of the global financial crisis. In addition, a plethora of new governance forums have been established in recent years at the regional and global level to tackle issues that may be beyond the remit of traditional organizations, or because national governments have wished to retain a greater degree of direct influence over the development and implementation of new regulatory solutions. This has contributed to increasing both the complexity and the diversity of contemporary processes of global economic governance. Whether these changes are sufficient to address the ongoing policy challenges of economic globalization, as well as the persistent political challenges of improving the institutional legitimacy of IOs in the aftermath of the world's worst financial crisis for more than 70 years, remains an open question.

Discussion questions

1. How have the contemporary responsibilities of IOs evolved over time?
2. Who drives processes of change in IOs?
3. Why do some IOs suffer from a crisis of legitimacy?
4. How should the IMF and the World Bank be reformed, and why?
5. What are the sources of influence available to different types of IOs?
6. How should the crisis management roles of IOs be reformed, and why?

Further reading

Avant, Deborah D., Martha Finnemore, and Susan K. Sell (eds). 2010. *Who Governs the Globe?*. Cambridge: Cambridge University Press.

Barnett, Michael and Martha Finnemore. 2004. *Rules for the World: International Organizations in Global Politics*. Ithaca, NY: Cornell University Press.

Hawkins, Darren G., David A. Lake, Daniel L. Nielson and Michael J. Tierney (eds). 2006. *Delegation and Agency in International Organizations*. Cambridge: Cambridge University Press.

Park, Susan and Antje Vetterlein (eds). 2010. *Owning Development: Creating Policy Norms in the IMF and the World Bank*. Cambridge: Cambridge University Press.

Stone, Randall W. 2011. *Controlling Institutions: International Organizations and the Global Economy*. Cambridge: Cambridge University Press.

Woods, Ngaire. 2006. *The Globalizers: The IMF, the World Bank, and Their Borrowers*. Ithaca, NY: Cornell University Press.

Club Forums

Introduction

The role of club-based models of governance in the global political economy has become an important topic of study in its own right. While students are usually familiar with the most high-profile club forums, such as leaders' summits of the Group of Eight (G8) or the Group of 20 (G20), club-based models of governance incorporate a variety of club types. The membership of different club forums may include public actors or private actors, or they may represent hybrid models that incorporate a range of public and private actors. Most clubs in the global political economy operate outside the spotlight of the global media, and are poorly understood because their functions and influence are exercised behind the scenes. Meanwhile, the club forums that most often make the headlines are seen as elite governance forums that lack legitimacy precisely as a result of their closed and selective memberships. In general, club forums enable more flexible, ad-hoc deliberations and negotiations over policy coordination and international regime changes between members. Intergovernmental club forums may also serve to diffuse the hegemony of a dominant state through multilateral processes, which can offer a range of advantages to other club members in comparison to bilateral negotiations characterized by asymmetric power relations. This chapter provides an overview of the emergence of club forums in contemporary global economic governance, focusing in particular on clubs that are formed between state actors, and how the dynamics of club-based models of governance can be understood in IPE.

Background

Formal IOs are commonly identified as the most prominent global governance mechanisms that operate 'above the state' in the global political economy, which provide their member states with collective benefits that range from crisis management expertise to the regularization of state interactions in specific issue areas in line with common rules and principles (see Chapter 5). Global government can be defined as 'a cohesive institutional system of fully global scope that exercises, at minimum, formal supremacy in decision making over states or other political subunits on a significant range of legislative and juridical activities'. In contrast, global governance is defined as 'purposive and continuing coordination among actors in the global system to address specific problems' (Cabrera 2011: 1–2). Despite their uneven track record, the centralized bureaucratic capacities and autonomy of IOs has traditionally been seen as the key to their potential to accomplish governance goals that individual states could not achieve on their own (Abbott and Snidal 1998). However, contemporary processes of global economic governance have become increasingly fragmented and diffuse, and now incorporate a far greater variety of public and private actors than in the past (Stone 2008).

In the last four decades, club-based models of multilateral governance have grown both in number and prominence as elite deliberative forums – and are sometimes seen as compensating for procedural or efficiency shortcomings that have emerged in formal IOs. One of the ironies of the contemporary global political economy is that many of the most prominent formal IOs have suffered from a crisis of legitimacy even as their memberships have become more universal in the aftermath of the Cold War and they have adopted more transparent decision-making procedures in response to external criticism. This weakening of the legitimacy of formal organizations has prompted some states to engage in 'forum shopping' to increase their leverage over governance outcomes. Forum shopping refers to the practice whereby an actor or group of actors seek to shift deliberation or decision-making in an issue area from one forum to another that is likely to be more favourable to their interests. In global economic governance, forum shopping may also refer to situations where actors create new purpose-built forums for the governance of specific issues, rather than operating through existing IOs. This has helped to create space for the rising influence of exclusive club-based models of governance that operate without the constitutional procedures and representation systems that function within IOs, and whose decision-making is almost exclusively conducted behind closed doors. The practice of forum shopping potentially enables clubs of actors with high material capabilities or high levels of cognitive authority the means to evade the formal constraints of IOs, and to take decisions or form collective positions among themselves that are then presented to international organizations as a done deal.

The club-based model of global governance refers to actor groupings that are defined by their exclusive membership and less-formalized institutional presence in the global political economy. Clubs, in contrast to many IOs, are not open to all. While this may be viewed as a weakness in terms of their broader legitimacy, retaining a more limited membership can potentially lead to more effective processes of negotiation and international cooperation (Drezner 2007: 67). Rather than seeking to be inclusive, club members deliberately restrict '*the range of actors involved in the making of policy and define what type of actor is relevant with high entry rules based on prestige and position*' (Tsingou 2012: 18, emphasis original). Club-based models of governance include the following activities: (1) elite decision-making forums, which are linked to negotiating specific regime changes within formal international organizations (Keohane and Nye 2002); (2) deliberative governance forums that agree broad policy principles between leaders or key economic officials such as finance ministers and central bank governors (Baker 2006); and (3) transnational policy networks and hybrid public–private groupings that gain extensive influence over specialized issue areas, some of which may be outside the remit of formal IOs (Tsingou 2012).

Club forums are an example of global governance networks. Such networks comprise 'a non-hierarchical governance structure in which relations among actors are repeated and enduring, but where no one has the power to arbitrate and resolve disputes among the members' (Martinez-Diaz and Woods 2009: 1–2). Because club forums retain a limited membership compared with IOs that have a universal representation such as the IMF, the World Bank and the WTO, their leaner structure enables a flexible approach to multilateral decision-making that can potentially complement the role of formal IOs, as well as serving to constrain IOs' autonomy of action. Among other things, club forums can foster ad-hoc and informal deliberation among major power states on global economic governance issues, propose new policy initiatives and cooperate to shape international regime changes. Rather than adhering to formal decision-making and enforcement procedures, such forums rely principally upon encouraging voluntary compliance among members and the establishment of broad principles for governing international cooperation. While club forums lack collective enforcement powers, they can potentially provide a more flexible platform for the negotiation of controversial issues that require multilateral policy coordination between members in order to achieve effective solutions (Beeson and Broome 2010).

Multilateralism and hegemony in the global political economy

Most conventional understandings of governance forms in the global political economy view formal IOs as preferable to informal multilateral forums due to the former's rule-governed processes and clearly defined membership obligations. In a similar fashion, less-formal multilateral forums between groups of states are seen as superior to bilateral negotiations and interactions between pairs of states, because the latter type of relations have a higher probability of being characterized by economic coercion and dominance. This point is especially salient for bilateral relations between state actors with varying powers and capabilities. As Friedrich Kratochwil (2006: 150) suggests, 'Bilateralism tends to reinforce the differentials of power' between a hegemonic state and others, whereas multilateral organizational forms serve to create 'a new "strength in numbers" and commits the *hegemon* prima facie (if not necessarily in actual practice) to exercise much of its power through multilateral channels'. Hegemony can be defined as 'the predominance of one state that is militarily, economically, politically or culturally superior to other states' when other states confer legitimacy on a predominant state's right to exercise leadership (Homolar 2012: 106–7). In comparison, multilateralism is defined as 'an institutional form that coordinates relations among three or more states on the basis of generalised principles of conduct' (Ruggie 1993: 11). For many scholars in IPE the crucial differences between multilateralism, bilateralism and unilateralism are the formal and informal obligations that multilateral processes place on a hegemonic state. This raises the question of what characteristics can be used to define a state as 'hegemonic', as well as how the exercise of hegemony through multilateralism can be differentiated from the more direct exercise of economic coercion and dominance in the global political economy.

In its simplest form, economic power refers to a state having 'Dominance in the distribution of international economic capabilities' (Mastanduno 2009: 153). From this perspective, in the post-World War II era the USA has not simply been an international policy-maker (see Chapter 4), but has performed the additional roles of a 'system-maker' and 'privilege-taker' through its structural advantages in the global political economy, although its relative economic advantages over other states have declined since the end of the Cold War. To understand a powerful state's international role the concept of dominance should be differentiated from hegemony. Hegemony does not refer solely to a state's material capabilities and resources, but is 'a qualitative attribute which is conferred on a dominant state by others through social relations' (Homolar 2012: 108).

Table 6.1   *Hegemony versus dominance*

	Hegemony	*Dominance*
Power	Self-restrained	Unrestrained
Relationship	Consent–acceptance	Coercion–submission
Strategy	Multilateralism	Imperialism
Means	Leadership: • Attract support • Provide incentives to comply • Involve • Cultural/ideational power	Oppression: • Coerce support • Punish non-compliance • Dictate • Military power/ economic sanctions

Source: Homolar (2012).

The exercise of hegemony through multilateral forms of governance involves a degree of self-restraint on the part of a dominant state, as well as consent and acceptance of a state's leadership role by others. As Table 6.1 illustrates, the concept of hegemony can be differentiated from the concept of dominance in terms of the nature of a state's use of power, the form of a state's relations with other states, its strategy of international engagement and the means through which a state pursues its international goals. This does not mean multilateral processes that are established through one state's hegemonic influence are necessarily benign, or that the benefits of multilateral coordination are distributed equally among states. Rather, hegemony exists when a state's international leadership role is accepted by (some) other states as legitimate, which grants a dominant state a unique position within multilateral forums while also potentially constraining its behaviour (Finnemore 2009: 84).

The G7, the G8 and the G20

The most prominent types of club-based governance today are global governance forums that include the most powerful states in the global political economy, and which negotiate common principles and values that are translated into international regimes (see Table 6.2). Until recently the global governance forum that gained the most attention was the G8, which includes most of the world's largest economies. The G8 grew out of the Group of Ten (G10), which was created in 1961 to negotiate solutions to global liquidity problems in the international monetary system, and the Group of Five (G5) meetings of ministers of finance and central bank governors that developed in the mid-1970s in the aftermath of the breakdown of the Bretton Woods system. The G5 included finance ministers and central bank governors from the USA, the UK, Germany, France and Japan, and expanded to become the G7 in 1986 with the inclusion of finance ministers and central bank governors from Italy and Canada (Baker 2008: 104).

The G7 meetings of finance ministers and central bank governors are distinct from the G7 leaders' summits of heads of state or government, which began in 1975 as the Group of Six (G6) and originally included political leaders from France, Germany, Italy, Japan, the UK and the USA, with Canada joining the following year. While G7 leaders' meetings expanded in 1998 with the inclusion of Russia to become the Group of Eight (G8), Russia is not a full member of the meetings of G7 ministers of finance and central bank governors. Contemporary examples of the influence of the G7 group of finance ministers and central bank governors in processes of global economic governance include the negotiation of common positions on IMF and World Bank lending processes and governance mechanisms, as well as the G7 veto of the IMF's proposal for a new sovereign debt restructuring mechanism (SDRM) in 2003 (Baker 2008: 105). G8 leaders' summits have played an important role in agreeing changes to the international sovereign debt regime for HIPCs, such as the agreement at the Gleneagles G8 Summit in 2005 to accept 100 per cent cancellation of HIPC debts owed to the IMF and the World Bank, which subsequently led to the establishment of the Multilateral Debt Relief Initiative (Baker 2006: 223; see Chapter 14). Despite the influence of both the G7 group of finance ministers and central bank governors and the G8 leaders' summits in the global political economy, unlike formal IOs both club forums lack a permanent bureaucracy or headquarters and do not have a codified mandate or formal powers to take binding decisions (Gstöhl 2007).

One of the most significant changes that was prompted by the global financial crisis in 2008–09 was the substitution of the G20 for the G8 as the primary club forum in global economic governance. This was made official at the G20 leaders' summit in Pittsburgh in September 2009, where participants agreed to establish the G20 as 'the premier forum ... for international economic cooperation' in order to foster concerted action among members (Group of Twenty 2009). Compared with the G8, the G20 can credibly claim to be a more representative forum for achieving informal international economic cooperation because it better reflects the shifting balance of economic power away from Europe and North America towards major emerging economies. Collectively, G20 members represent approximately two-thirds of the world's population, and account for 85 per cent of the world's gross domestic product as well as 80 per cent of global trade (Beeson and Bell 2009).

The G20 was first established in 1999, following the Asian financial crisis, as a deliberative governance forum that was based on the G7 model but with ministerial representation from both developed economies and major developing countries. Unlike the G7/8 forums which comprise politically 'like-minded' states, the composition of the G20 is viewed as 'more representative of the global diversity of power, wealth, and values' (Cooper and Thakur 2013: 12). Developing country members include Argentina, Brazil, China, India, Indonesia, Mexico, Saudi Arabia, South Africa, South Korea and Turkey. Other members include the G8 countries plus Australia and the European Union. Despite having a numerical advantage in developing-country representation in the G20, the consensus-based format of the G20 potentially undermines the capacity for developing-country participation to be translated into political influence. G7 members also maintain a strong advantage in their influence over other IOs that are linked to the G20, including the IMF, the World Bank, the FSB and the BIS (Martinez-Diaz 2009: 43–4).

The first leaders' summit of the G20 took place in the midst of the global financial crisis in Washington, DC, in November 2008, and the G20 quickly gained a global profile as the key forum for negotiating changes in international regimes. However, the key changes that have been agreed through G20 leaders' summits have primarily aimed to reinforce or reform existing IOs and institutional processes, rather than introducing more fundamental changes in the architecture of global economic governance (Helleiner and Pagliari 2009). For example, the second G20 leaders' summit in London in April 2009 agreed to reinforce the crisis management role of the IMF by tripling the size of its financial resources for sovereign bailouts. Subsequent summits in Cannes in November 2011 and Los Cabos in June 2012 resulted in stalemate and disagreements over proposals for structural reforms, such the introduction of a global tax on financial institutions, financial activities, or financial transactions, which the 2010 G20 summit in Toronto ruled off the table.

Despite the shifting locus of international economic cooperation from the G7/8 to the G20 it is not yet apparent whether the G20 will function over time along similar lines as an expanded G8, or whether a new form of club-based global economic governance is in the process of emerging. As Cooper and Thakur (2013: 123) note, 'The G20 could be the vehicle through which key global issues could be addressed and resolved, but leaders do not solve complex problems among and by themselves at summits.' Despite the lack of grand designs for a new Bretton Woods-style refashioning of the architecture of global economic governance, the

G20 forum has been credited with being instrumental in coordinating national policies during the global financial crisis, which helped to avoid a return to the more extreme forms of economic protectionism that characterized the Great Depression of the 1930s (Cooper 2010b).

As a club forum the G20 offers members some of the same benefits as the G8, as well as new advantages. For example, the G20 potentially enables the diffusion of hegemonic influence among a wider group of states in order to enhance the legitimacy of the agreements that result from inter-state bargaining, by including major emerging economies as full partners rather than observers. At the same time, informal governance through the G20 is likely to preserve the prerogative of major powers to decide core principles and international regime changes among themselves rather than acting through formal IOs, which may grant G7 members more scope for achieving national policy preferences. These potential benefits do not come cheap, with the security and organizational costs of hosting the 2010 Toronto G20 summit reaching approximately US$679 million (Kirton *et al.* 2010), while the budget estimate for the 2014 G20 summit in Brisbane is approximately US$380 million. As the price tag for summits lasting only a few days, these figures compare unfavourably with the administrative budgets for running the secretariat costs of IOs, with the IMF's gross budget in 2012 totalling US$1,013 million for the entire year (IMF 2012: 55). Meanwhile, a tension continues to exist between 'the need for standing official machinery in the form of a new [G20] secretariat and the strong antipathy toward any more international bureaucracy' (Cooper and Thakur 2013: 127). This has left the G20 dependent on outsourcing bureaucratic expertise from IOs such as the IMF.

Varieties of club-based governance in the global political economy

Club forums take a variety of different forms, use different criteria for membership and have varying scope in terms of the issue areas they cover and their level of influence over the governance of those issues in the global political economy (see Table 6.2). *Policy coordination forums* between state actors aim to achieve similar objectives to *global governance forums*, such as the negotiation of common principles and values for international economic cooperation, but do not include the state actors that comprise the main policy-makers in the global political economy. Membership in policy coordination forums may instead centre on rising or middle powers, such as the growing weight of the BRICs, or may include weaker state actors that seek greater influence through participation in forums with

Table 6.2 *Varieties of club forums in global economic governance*

Forum types	Membership	Role	Scope of influence	Examples
Global governance forums	Major/rising power state actors	Negotiating common principles and values for international cooperation	Determining agendas and regimes within and outside the remits of formal IOs	Group of Eight; Group of 20
Policy coordination forums	Rising/middle powers and weaker state actors	Negotiating common principles and values for international cooperation	Potential for exercising veto power in formal IOs and shaping agendas	BRIC summits; ASEAN Plus Three
Issue-specific governance forums	State actors with dominant positions related to the issue area	Decision-making and multilateral agreements in specific issue areas	Cooperation to solve collective action problems in a specific issue area	Paris Club; Basel Committee on Banking Supervision
Multi-stakeholder forums	State, market and civil society actors with high prestige	A platform for discussion and networking across multiple categories of actors	Implicit role in shaping global policy agendas across multiple issue areas	World Economic Forum; International Economic Forum
Transnational policy forums	A range of elite actors deemed to have high levels of cognitive authority	Policy innovation and advocacy based on the expertise of participants	Agenda-setting influence and cognitive authority in specific issue areas	Group of 30

rising powers, such as the ASEAN Plus Three process, which incorporates the members of ASEAN as well as China, Japan and South Korea (Nesadurai 2009). While policy coordination forums among relatively weaker state actors may not be able to determine agendas for the negotiation of international regimes and policy changes within formal IOs, they can potentially exercise an agenda-setting role through forming a collective position to restrain or veto proposals by major powers.

Issue-specific governance forums may involve all the dominant state actors (as well as private actors) in an exclusive grouping to discuss governance arrangements in a defined policy area. This can enable regular issue-specific forms of international cooperation in order to solve collective action problems that individual states may face in acting alone on a particular policy challenge, such as how to handle debt problems among borrower countries or cross-border issues related to financial supervision. While issue-specific governance forums lack the broader scope of global governance forums, they may be more likely to develop mechanisms of international cooperation which become institutionalized over time due to their limited focus.

Clubs also take the form of *multi-stakeholder forums*, which comprise both groups with a broad scope and those which have a more specific focus. While still relying on exclusive membership criteria, such forums may include large memberships. One example of an exclusive club forum with a large membership is the annual World Economic Forum meetings in Davos, Switzerland, which bring together over 2,000 actors who have high prestige from business, government, academia, civil society and IOs. Despite its large size, the World Economic Forum has a potential advantage over intergovernmental clubs because meetings do not need to result in identifiable outcomes such as new international agreements or communiqués, thereby allowing greater exchange of ideas between participants as well as networking opportunities (Pigman 2006b). Multi-stakeholder forums thus create a platform for discussion and knowledge exchange across multiple categories of actors in the global political economy, which can play an indirect role in shaping the evolution of global policy agendas across different issue areas.

A further category of club forums are *transnational policy forums*, which include a select group of elite actors from both the public and private spheres who are deemed to have high levels of cognitive authority through their expertise and professional roles. The category of transnational policy forums encompasses a variety of different sub-types, ranging from those that more closely resemble some of the characteristics of large multi-stakeholder forums to those that are smaller and more limited in membership (Stone 2008). One example of a small transnational policy forum that has had a substantive influence on the development of global financial governance since it was established in 1978 is the Group of 30 (G30). The G30 comprises a select group of private financial actors and public actors who hold or have held key roles in national and global economic governance, as well as high-profile academic economists. The membership is limited to 30 individuals who do not act as representatives of their respective institutions or businesses, and do not engage in horse-trading over policy coordination. The G30 has nonetheless played a critical role in policy innovation and shaping the parameters of policy debates at the national and global level in the 1980s and 90s through the expertise of its members (Tsingou 2012: 72–6).

As this basic typology of a selection of club forums in the global political economy illustrates, clubs vary greatly in their respective size, scope, membership, role and influence. Critically, clubs need not involve major power states – or need not include states at all – in order to exercise a substantive influence over the dynamics of change in global economic governance. Despite most club forums lacking the bureaucratic and material resources that are available to many formal IOs, their more flexible design, lack of codified procedures and absence of entrenched bureaucratic interests can enable them to be more effective at policy innovation, policy coordination and global agenda-setting. While some high-profile clubs such as the G8 or the G20 are commonly seen as vehicles to diffuse the hegemonic power of the USA in multilateral processes, such forums can also serve to restrain or alter how the structural power of dominant states in the global policy economy is used. Meanwhile, club forums that have been created among relatively weaker actors may act as a check on the agenda-setting powers of those states that have traditionally been seen as the principal policy-makers in global economic governance.

Summary

Not all club forums involve states, and not all clubs are powerful actors in their own right. Club forums in global economic governance may supplement, substitute for, or compete with the authority and responsibilities of formal IOs. While club-based models of governance in the global political economy are not new they have now become a staple of international economic cooperation. The reasons why states and other actors in the global political economy have turned to club forums for deliberation and international cooperation are manifold, but some of the key motivations include: (1) the perception of a decline in the efficiency and legitimacy of formal international organizations; (2) the emergence of new policy challenges that fall outside the remits of existing IOs; (3) a desire for smaller closed-door negotiations between groups of actors that share common values and policy norms, or which face specific common problems; and (4) a desire to exercise greater control over the agendas of international negotiations in contrast to the agenda-setting influence that IO bureaucracies may be able to wield. The rise of club forums presents a complex challenge for students of IPE wishing to understand the powers and roles of different categories of actors in the global political economy. Club-based models of governance can be sometimes seen as a more efficient form of governance deliberation and decision-making, but their exclusive membership criteria and non-transparent processes also raise numerous questions about accountability, representation and legitimacy in global economic governance.

Discussion questions

1. Why have club forums gained prominence in recent years?
2. How do the activities of clubs impact upon the functions of IOs?
3. Is the G20 more legitimate as a governance forum than the G8? If so, why? If not, why not?
4. How might hegemony be exercised through club-based models of governance?
5. Are G20 leaders' summits worth the organizational costs? If so, why? If not, why not?
6. How might club forums be reformed to make them both more effective and more legitimate?

Further reading

Baker, Andrew. 2006. *The Group of Seven: Finance Ministries, Central Banks and Global Financial Governance*. London: Routledge.

Beeson, Mark. 2008. *Institutions of the Asia-Pacific: ASEAN, APEC, and Beyond*. London: Routledge.

Cooper, Andrew F. and Ramesh Thakur. 2013. *The Group of Twenty*. London: Routledge.

Dobson, Hugo. 2006. *The Group of 7/8*. London: Routledge.

Martinez-Diaz, Leonardo and Ngaire Woods (eds). 2009. *Networks of Influence? Developing Countries in a Networked Global Order*. Oxford: Oxford University Press.

Newman, Edward, Ramesh Thakur and John Tirman (eds). 2006. *Multilateralism under Challenge: Power, International Order and Structural Change*. Tokyo: United Nations University Press.

Chapter 7

Market Actors

Introduction

The roles of private market actors in the global political economy have changed markedly over the course of recent decades. The changing dynamics of economic globalization have enabled market actors to dramatically expand the size and distribution of their activities across different countries in terms of sales, production processes, labour tasks, information management systems and customer service functions. Stimulated by government actions to eliminate or reduce restrictions on cross-border economic activities, the international integration of national markets for trade in goods, services and capital has revolutionized how large businesses operate in the twenty-first century compared with the Bretton Woods era of the 1950s and 60s. At the 'big end of town', large banks and firms control enormous volumes of capital, while their production, investment, lending and speculative activities shape the economic fortunes of major powers and small states alike. Critically, the actions of major commercial banks, transnational corporations (TNCs) and credit rating agencies now have systemic effects on global macroeconomic stability. Their combined influence constitutes material and ideational constraints on what states can and cannot do in economic policy, while their decisions can both drive economic prosperity and precipitate economic crises. Focusing on the activities of firms, banks and rating agencies, this chapter introduces students to the dynamic changes that have underpinned the evolving roles that market actors play in the global political economy, as well as how different theories of IPE account for the causes and consequences of economic globalization.

Background

The increased material influence of market actors in the post-World War II era, and especially since the breakdown of the Bretton Woods system in the 1970s and the intensification of processes of international economic integration, has led to a shift in the balance of authority in the global political economy. The capacity to effectively exercise authority over economic processes and outcomes is commonly assumed to have significantly drained away from public actors such as states, IOs and other official agencies – replaced by an expansion in private authority, defined as 'institutionalized forms or expressions of [private] power' (Hall and Biersteker 2002: 4). This has been buttressed by an increased concentration of market power in the hands of firms, banks and rating agencies whose operations can have a global impact.

The consequences of successive policy actions to enable market integration have altered the material capacities of states, as well as how policy-makers and publics conceive of the appropriate role of the state in governing national economies. In short, economic globalization has altered both the material and ideational circumstances that inform what governments can do to shape economic processes and outcomes, and what they are expected to do as economic managers by different audiences. The dynamics of how these constraints operate differ across economic policy areas as well as in different national contexts. Globalized markets do not determine governments' policy autonomy in uniform ways, although they do generate similar types of policy challenges for states.

Theories of IPE account for contemporary processes of economic globalization in a variety of ways. Neoliberal accounts of globalization tend to privilege the role of markets and market actors as a globalizing force (Peck 2010). According to this view, while national policy-makers have played a role in furthering market integration by relaxing outdated regulatory restrictions, they did so because they possessed few alternatives to liberalization in the face of growing market power. This represents a conception of markets as ontologically prior to states – whereby state-based restrictions on flows of trade, capital and money are artificial constructions that have been eroded by the inevitable progress of economic development.

In contrast, realist accounts of globalization emphasize how major power governments have intentionally enabled international economic integration through the coercive exercise of state power in pursuit of their national interests. Even under conditions of economic globalization, realist perspectives point to the continuing ability of major powers to shape global economic processes through the dominant size of their internal

Table 7.1   *Five concepts of the sources of globalization*

Unit of analysis	Key drivers	Key dynamics
Markets	Economic development	Market competition
States	National interests	State coercion
Social classes	Capitalist expansion	Economic exploitation
Ideas	Paradigm change	Discursive contests
Institutions	Policy experiments	Institutional learning

markets and associated material capabilities (Drezner 2007). Neo-Marxist perspectives have focused on how processes of international economic integration are bound up with modern state formation, uneven processes of development and class-based contests (Morton 2011). Further accounts of globalization in IPE include economic constructivism, which has focused on how the politics of ideas has shaped changing conceptions of the appropriate role and capacities of the state and the nature of market processes across different governance contexts (Blyth 2002; Chwieroth 2009), and institutional perspectives that examine how market integration has been shaped by processes of institutional change, experimentation and policy-learning (Campbell 2004).

As a field of study, IPE is therefore characterized by a series of competing conceptions of the key drivers and dynamics of economic globalization (see Table 7.1). Regardless of which theoretical lens is applied to understand the dynamics of market integration, however, most observers agree that governments have not been passive observers of these processes (Stopford and Strange 1991), and that IOs have been instrumental in encouraging economic liberalization in many countries (Woods 2006). At the very least, governments are recognized as having made strategic decisions that led to the reduction of national restrictions on cross-border economic activities, as well as affecting how domestic rules and institutions create incentive structures which shape processes of production, corporate competition and ownership, investment, income and employment, and consumption within their borders. In other areas governments have intentionally acted as 'market-makers', strategically changing the policy environment to create markets in sectors as varied as education, healthcare, housing, public transportation, infrastructural development, energy, telecommunications and broadcasting. In the recent past many of these sectors were subject to little or no market competition in many countries, or competitive pressures were tightly regulated in order to achieve social purposes that overrode commercial interests in maximizing profits.

These broad processes of economic change are bound up with shifting conceptions of the social purpose of market actors, and the nature and limits of their obligations to the societies in which they operate and where they generate commercial profits. Neoliberal conceptions of the role that firms should play in national economies have suggested that the only 'social responsibility of business is to increase its profits' (Friedman 1970, cited in Scherer *et al*. 2006: 509). Most governments and their populations – as well as many firms – have tended to take a more expansive view of the responsibilities market actors have to society as a whole. In particular, contemporary debates have focused on alternative conceptions of 'corporate social responsibility' (Scherer *et al*. 2006) and 'corporate citizenship' (Matten and Crane 2005).

At a governance level, the legally defined obligations that market actors must fulfil have altered significantly over the course of the past four decades. In some areas the social obligations on private actors that governments enforce have been rolled back, while in other areas they have been significantly expanded. A number of governments have expanded the scope of legislation and regulation with respect to firms' environmental responsibilities and consumer rights. In France and Germany, for example, governments responded to pressures from consumer groups and market producers in the 1970s and early 80s by substantially expanding national consumer protection policies, which established new domestic consumption regimes that have shaped the commercial strategies and practices of domestic market actors at the same time as reconstituting the rights and responsibilities of individuals as economic citizens (Trumbull 2006). In other areas popular understandings of the social purpose of market actors – as well as their legally defined social obligations – have become more narrowly circumscribed. A case in point is how some governments have permitted market actors to structure their business activities in ways that reduce their contribution to public revenue through tax liabilities (see Chapter 15).

The nature of economic governance and the effectiveness of compliance mechanisms have also changed in recent years. A common way to evaluate the qualities of economic governance is to analyze how closely the regulatory framework for a particular sector aligns with industry preferences, or whether regulation is designed on the basis of a wider set of public interest concerns. Conflicts of interest occur when an actor is faced with multiple interests, one of which might corrupt the motivation for acting in accordance with another. In the case of the former regulation may 'do little more than entrench narrow interests', while in the latter situation regulation is intended to 'fulfil broader public purposes' (Mattli and Woods 2009: 4). National policy-makers in many countries have also encouraged different sets of private market actors to voluntarily 'self-regulate' their practices in line with the public interest, rather than be regulated 'from above' by state agencies and rules. The expansion of self-regulation regimes for some industries can be viewed as an efficient means to govern market actors that is sensitive to changing economic conditions and market practices. However, self-regulation may also lead to conflicts of interest between the profit-oriented goals of market actors and broader public interests such as macroeconomic stability and economic fairness, the outcomes of which can potentially be catastrophic.

Global production

Contemporary changes in the dynamics of global production processes have been strongly influenced by the liberalization in many countries of restrictions on cross-border economic activities such as trade in goods and services (see Chapter 10), currency speculation and exchange rate regimes (see Chapter 11) and investment flows (see Chapter 12). Companies with substantial international production and investment activities have long been an important feature of the world economy. During the colonial era, for example, the international operations, shipping capacities and capital resources of the Dutch East India Company in the seventeenth century enabled it to exercise monopoly power in determining the price and quantities of goods in the international spice trade (Schwartz 2010: 38). While international production processes and international investment are not new phenomena, the size, intensity and scope of private companies' production and investment activities has markedly expanded in the last six decades following World War II. Most international investment flows take place between OECD economies, or between OECD economies and a select group of rapidly growing emerging market economies. However, the global operations of internationally oriented companies and commercial banks have assumed greater significance for the economic prospects of all countries in the contemporary global political economy, with the exception of a dwindling number of autarkic economies such as North Korea, which prioritize economic 'self-sufficiency' over international integration.

While global production and foreign investment fell sharply during the global financial crisis of 2008–09, recent indicators suggest that the crisis represented a temporary setback rather than a turning point in contemporary trends. By 2011, for example, global foreign direct investment (FDI) flows had rebounded to US$1.5 trillion. While 23 per cent lower than the pre-crisis peak in 2007, this figure exceeds average global investment flows in the years preceding the crisis. From total FDI flows in 2011, flows to developed countries accounted for US$748 billion, while inward FDI flows to developing countries rose to a record figure of US$684 billion. Combined investment flows to developing countries and post-communist transition countries accounted for slightly over half of global FDI in 2011, most of which was concentrated in a small group of high-growth developing countries (see Chapter 12). Meanwhile, the business activities of non-financial global companies generated US$28 trillion in sales in 2011, with these firms employing some 69 million workers around the globe (UNCTAD 2012: 1–2).

The increased size, intensity, and scope of global production processes and investment flows has had an important impact on the policies developing countries have adopted in order to improve national economic performance and to reduce poverty by increasing living standards (Kaplinsky 2005). Changing global production dynamics have also shaped continuing debates over competing models of economic development (see Chapter 16). Advocates of neoliberal market-based models of development have used the globalization of production to argue that developing countries which integrate their domestic economies within global market processes will achieve superior economic performance, greater increases in per capita income and higher living standards than countries which maintain restrictions on inward investment flows and controls on the business activities of foreign firms. The short version of this argument sees countries competing to attract the wealth-creating business of highly mobile firms and capital investors – a scenario in which the maintenance of policy restrictions on foreign investment flows and the rights of foreign firms will deter market actors who may opt for a more investment-friendly climate elsewhere.

Economic globalization has also prompted the development of new analytic categories and vocabulary for studying the contemporary dynamics of production and investment. For example, a wealth of research in the past two decades has focused on the development and characteristics of 'global production networks' or 'global value chains' (Gereffi *et al.* 2005). A global production network refers to 'the nexus of interconnected functions, operations and transactions through which a specific product or service is produced, distributed, and consumed' (Coe *et al.* 2008: 272). A production network can be termed global to the extent that it 'is one whose interconnected nodes and links extend spatially across national boundaries and, in so doing, integrates parts of disparate national and subnational territories' (Coe *et al.* 2008: 274).

The concept of global production networks has become a distinct analytic category for understanding how major firms operate across national borders, which helps to orient the focus of analysis away from studying a particular firm and its foreign affiliates as discrete actors in different economies, and towards gaining a more comprehensive

Figure 7.1   *Top-ten non-financial TNCs, 2011 (ranked by foreign assets)*

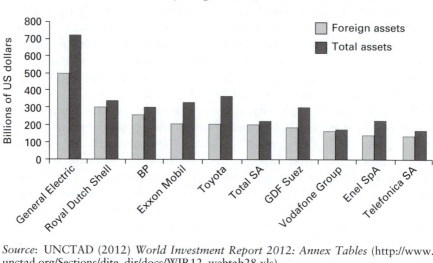

Source: UNCTAD (2012) *World Investment Report 2012: Annex Tables* (http://www.unctad.org/Sections/dite_dir/docs/WIR12_webtab28.xls).

understanding of how global business practices can integrate geographically distant markets in dynamic ways. In particular, IPE scholars have applied the concept of global production networks to the challenge of understanding how firms' activities shape regional political economy dynamics (Bernard and Ravenhill 1996), and how globalized production networks have generated structural changes in labour practices and processes of economic inclusion and exclusion (Phillips 2011).

A further example of how processes of economic globalization have led to the development of a new vocabulary for discussing contemporary market actors in the global political economy is the concept of the 'transnational corporation' (TNC). The 'transnationality' of TNCs 'refers to the geographic spread of firms and implies the existence of a home country and one or more host countries' (UNCTAD 2007: 1). TNCs can be distinguished from the older concept of multinational corporations (MNCs), although the two terms are frequently used interchangeably. While MNCs are national firms with foreign subsidiaries, the activities of TNCs are geographically dispersed across many countries. In recent decades both the overall number of TNCs in the world and the volume of their assets have substantially increased. Based on data from the United Nations Conference on Trade and Development (UNCTAD 2007: 3), the number of TNCs increased from 37,000 in the early 1990s (with 170,000 foreign affiliates) to 77,000 in the mid-2000s (with 770,000 foreign affiliates). Where TNCs choose to invest their

Figure 7.2 *Ten largest economies, 2011 (GDP in current prices)*

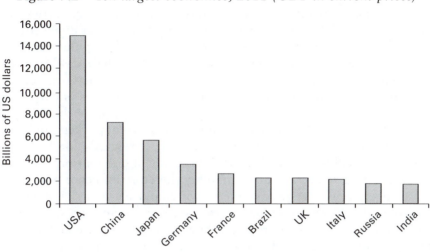

Source: IMF (2012) *World Economic Outlook Database: October 2012* (http://www.imf.org/external/pubs/ft/weo/2012/02/weodata/index.aspx).

resources and reinvest their profits has great importance for national economic performance and GDP growth. As Figure 7.1 shows, the total assets controlled by just ten of the world's largest TNCs represent enormous economic resources, even when compared against the GDP of the world's ten largest economies (see Figure 7.2). When these amounts are combined, the total assets of the top-ten TNCs in 2011 accounted for nearly US$3.2 trillion, or more than the individual GDP of six of the ten largest economies in the world, with the exception of the USA, China, Japan and Germany.

The size and scale of the business activities of the world's top TNCs dwarfs the national GDP of the majority of the world's countries, and their combined economic transactions and operations are enormous even when measured against the yardstick of the very largest economies. The rapid growth in the 'transnationality' of big business has prompted new questions about how firms can and should be governed in a globalized economy. Major corporate scandals in the last two decades, including examples such as Enron and WorldCom among many others, gave these concerns greater urgency well before the near-collapse of the international financial system in 2008. How large domestic firms and TNCs ought to be regulated has therefore become a prominent concern of policy-makers as well as IPE scholars.

At the heart of such issues is a general concern with corporate accountability and governance. While international economic integration has shaped the policy choice-set that national governments face, political choices over alternative policy settings still matter. Although the degree of national economic policy discretion in many countries has narrowed, 'Global capital flows are not an automatic straitjacket that forces states to submit to rules set by blind markets' (Tiberghien 2007: 8). As Peter Gourevitch and James Shinn (2005: 1) emphasize, 'Corporate governance is about power and responsibility.' While national policy settings and regulations shape the design of firms' systems of corporate governance, it is the internal 'authority structure of a firm' that 'shapes the creation of wealth and its distribution into different pockets' and may create both 'temptations for cheating and ... rewards for honesty' (Gourevitch and Shinn 2005: 2–3). The effects of different processes of corporate governance and accountability therefore influence how businesses operate with respect to their own employees and shareholders, how they shape and are shaped by the political systems and societies in which they are headquartered, and how they regulate the activities of foreign affiliates around the globe. In seeking to understand the dynamics of how firms behave in different contexts, IPE scholars often concentrate on one set of factors over others. Examples include how different rationalities for economic action are socially constructed and mediated by the politics of ideas (Woll 2008), and how material incentives shape policy formation and actors' responses through the politics of interests (Gourevitch and Shinn 2005: 93).

Despite the large volume of academic research and popular writing on how processes of economic globalization have stimulated greater convergence between national economic dynamics and national systems of economic governance, the notion that globalization has shaped national economies and policy settings in uniform ways should be treated with scepticism due to the lack of compelling evidence to support such assertions. While indicators of cross-border economic transactions show substantial increases in capital movements, trade flows and production networks, it is less straightforward to demonstrate that these dynamics are producing the degree of convergence in national policy settings and national policy autonomy that is sometimes claimed. As Berger (1996: 7) suggests, 'Although statistics abound to illustrate magnitudes of capital on the move in the world today, it is considerably more difficult to determine the significance of these facts.' Some observers have predicted an inevitable 'race to the bottom' as governments choose – or are forced – to adopt policy reforms in order to accommodate the pressures generated by the rise of global production networks, TNCs, global capital mobility and increased market sensitivities to the judgements of credit rating agencies. Others have argued that distinctive 'varieties of capitalism' around the globe not only persist, but are likely to remain a prevalent feature of a globalized economy. Scholars working within a 'varieties of capitalism' framework have suggested that national economies continue to exhibit a high degree of institutional distinctiveness in how problems of coordination are managed in the areas of industrial relations, vocational training and education, corporate governance, inter-firm relations and how firms manage their human resources (Hall and Soskice 2001: 7).

Global banking

Like non-financial TNCs, internationally active commercial banks have grown in scope, scale and systemic importance in recent decades. These changes have presented new policy dilemmas for political decision-makers and financial regulators at the same time as the societal risks from global banking activities have greatly increased. The challenges associated with regulating global banking practices and financial markets more broadly were demonstrated with devastating consequences during the global financial crisis of 2008–09. International bank lending (new cross-border loans minus repayments) reached a high of US$4.3 trillion in 2007 across 184 countries before the crisis hit. In 2008, in contrast, net international bank lending fell to almost negative US$1 trillion – over a US$5 trillion drop in the space of a year (Minoiu and Reyes 2011: 4). Despite the plummeting rate of cross-border bank lending during the global financial crisis, since then the financial resources controlled by global banks have continued to rise, with the total assets of the world's 1,000 largest banks reaching a new record in 2010–11 of an estimated US$101.6 trillion, a 6.4 per cent increase on the previous year. These enormous financial assets are unevenly distributed across different countries. Figure 7.3 illustrates that global banking assets are concentrated in a select number of countries which host international financial centres, with the combined banking assets held in the USA, the UK, Japan, China and France accounting for over half of global bank assets in 2010.

As the recent crisis showed, when financial institutions go bust and market relations between financial institutions break down the social and economic costs of market failure in banking are enormous. At their core, banks are financial intermediaries whose operations 'allocate investment and savings across time and space', functions which 'help economies to grow by mobilising savings so that consumption can be higher in the future as a result of investments made today' (Warwick Commission on International Financial Reform 2009: 9). In theory, banks are like financial bridges that connect customers with savings to those with deficits. How banking works within a society and across different societies, and for whose benefit, are fundamental questions that

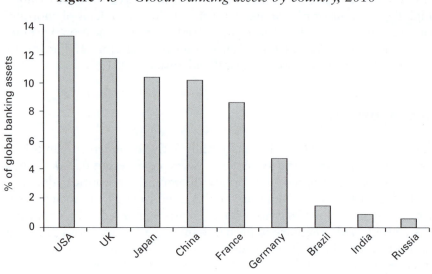

Figure 7.3   *Global banking assets by country, 2010*

Source: Burggraf (2012).

are bound up with the goals and instruments of financial regulation, as well as the degree of social legitimacy a financial system enjoys. How policy-makers govern banking activities – and how responsive the banking sector is to the needs of the broader population – determine who has access to credit, on what terms and who carries the cost when banking systems fail (Seabrooke 2006).

A critical issue for contemporary global banking activities is the importance of size, and in particular how the financial size of internationally active banks has complicated the question of how they can and ought to be regulated at the national, regional and global levels (Germain 2012). Contemporary growth in global banking activities has enabled banks to engage in processes of 'regulatory arbitrage', whereby financial institutions structure their activities in order to exploit opportunities for lighter regulatory compliance costs either within or across national jurisdictions. While cross-border regulatory arbitrage is sometimes presented as an inevitable consequence of economic globalization and increased capital mobility, it is better conceived as a 'socio-political construct' that has been made possible by the changes in the legislative framework and policy settings of national governments (Rethel 2014). Yet while many banks experienced exponential growth in the global scope and scale of their financial activities, banking practices have also become more complicated as a result of what is termed 'financial disintermediation'. Rather than banks continuing to play a pivotal role as financial intermediaries allocating financial assets from savers to borrowers, much of the 'middleman' role played by banks has been cut out as both savers and borrowers have switched to other sources of investment or credit access such as financial markets (Rethel and Sinclair 2012: 58–9).

When capital markets expanded and deepened over the course of the 1990s and 2000s, the cost of 'direct financing' through capital markets became cheaper compared with intermediated lending from commercial banks, a development which prompted major banks to lobby the governments of international financial centres to repeal legislation and rules such as the US Glass–Steagall Act of 1933, which had maintained regulatory constraints on investment banking activities prior to its repeal in 1999 (Smith *et al.* 2012: 27). Legislative deregulation of banks' financial activities (which in the USA had already been loosened through the Federal Reserve's reinterpretation of existing rules in 1988) enabled a boom in financial speculation and 'securitization' of non-tradable debt, such as mortgage-backed securities. Securitization of mortgage loans transforms a non-tradable asset – the income-stream from mortgage interest payments – into a tradable asset that can be sold on to other investors. Securitization allowed banks to shift mortgages and other loans off their balance sheets, thereby boosting their capacity for new lending by reducing the amount of capital a bank must put aside to hedge against credit risks, and increasing revenue from transaction fees associated with structuring and issuing asset-backed securities.

Processes of 'financial engineering' in asset-backed securities during the 2000s involved structuring contractual debt into different risk categories and pooling these together in order to make securitized financial assets more attractive for institutional investors such as pension and insurance funds (Best 2010). Among other things, complex processes of financial engineering prior to the global financial crisis made it harder for investors to effectively monitor the level of risk associated with asset-backed securities. This generated information asymmetry and moral hazard problems for banks and other financial institutions that had 'procyclical' effects which contributed to the further expansion of asset bubbles, especially in the USA (Schwartz 2009) (see Chapter 13). Moral hazard is a situation where risk-taking is encouraged because the costs of risky behaviour are borne by others, while information asymmetry is a situation where an imbalance of power exists between two parties when one has access to more or better-quality information.

The changing dynamics of both domestic and cross-border banking activities during the last four decades increased the pressure for national policy-makers to negotiate common financial governance rules and standards to mitigate the systemic risks associated with international financial integration. While a number of forums and institutions exercise various responsibilities in the area of global financial governance, such as the IMF and the Financial Stability Board (Moschella 2010b, 2013), the pre-eminent forum for governing banking activities and setting regulatory standards is the Basel Committee on Banking Supervision (Basel Committee). The Basel Committee was established in 1974 as a forum for international cooperation among a select group of banking supervisory authorities, which frames guidelines and standards for participating authorities in different areas of financial supervision that have been adopted by a large number of non-participating countries. Until recently, membership of the Basel Committee was limited to 13 countries: Belgium, Canada, France, Germany, Italy, Japan, Luxembourg, the Netherlands, Spain, Sweden, Switzerland, the UK and the USA. Since 2009 all major economies of the Group of 20 are now represented in the Basel Committee, as well as Hong Kong and Singapore. Based at the Bank for International Settlements in Basel, Switzerland, the Basel Committee has issued three influential sets of rules and principles on banking supervision that resulted from negotiations between national authorities, known as the Basel Accords.

The background conditions for the first Basel Accord included a rapid expansion of international banking activities during the 1970s and 80s, as well as more frequent bank failures and associated financial instability in several of the world's largest economies. Over the period from 1964 to 1980, for example, international banking activities grew at a compounded rate of over 30 per cent each year (Singer 2007: 38). Faced with growing financial instability and systemic risks, policy-makers in major financial centres became increasingly concerned with the problem of how to enhance banking regulations without causing their financial institutions to lose market share to less-tightly regulated foreign competitors.

The first Basel Accord was published by the Basel Committee in 1988, and focused primarily on how to regulate credit risk in commercial banks. The Accord developed through bilateral policy discussions between the chairman of the US Federal Reserve, Paul Volcker, and the Bank of England Governor, Robin Leigh-Pemberton, during 1986 and 1987. The process was a response to the strategic interests both central banks had in creating a stronger regulatory framework to safeguard financial stability and manage risks in the banking sector, at the same time as establishing a 'level playing field' between major economies so that tighter regulations did not put individual countries at a competitive disadvantage in international financial markets (Kapstein 1994: 113–14). Over 100 countries subsequently implemented the key regulatory elements of the Accord during the 1990s and 2000s. The Basel I

Accord established five categories of credit risk for banks' financial assets, based on 'risk-weighted capital adequacy ratios', which define how much capital banks must hold in reserve against different risk categories of lending. Internationally active banks were required to hold capital equal to 8 per cent of their risk-weighted assets.

The Basel Accords have been criticized for emerging through transnational policy processes that were largely insulated from democratic accountability, transparency mechanisms, or wider consultation. Industry pressure groups such as the Institute of International Finance and other elite actors including the finance and monetary officials, academic economists and financial sector representatives who comprise the Group of 30 played an important role behind the scenes in shaping the terms of debate for the Basel Committee process (Tsingou 2012). When it was published by the Basel Committee in 2004, the second Accord was subject to greater political contestation and a lower rate of implementation compared with Basel I, at least prior to the onset of the global financial crisis in 2008. The main focus of Basel II centred on enhancing the role of 'market discipline' as a key supervisory tool in global financial governance. The second Accord established regulatory principles based on 'three pillars' of banking supervision: (1) *minimum capital requirements* to address credit risk, operational risk and market risk; (2) expanded processes of *supervisory review*; and (3) new financial information disclosure requirements to institute greater *market discipline*. In contrast to Basel I and II, Basel III has shifted the focus of regulatory principles towards measures to manage systemic stability. Agreed by Basel Committee members in 2010–11, the third Accord was developed in response to the global financial crisis in order to improve the capacity of the banking sector to absorb financial shocks, and is scheduled to be introduced gradually from 2013 to 2018. To guard against systemic financial risks, Basel III is intended to raise the quality, consistency and transparency of banks' capital base; expand the range of risks covered by the regulatory framework; control financial leverage through a leverage ratio requirement; reduce pro-cyclical market dynamics by building up 'capital buffers' during periods of strong growth; and introduce a global minimum liquidity standard for internationally active banks.

With the pivotal role that it has come to play in shaping global financial governance, the Basel Committee process has attracted increasing controversy in recent years. In particular, the Basel Committee has been strongly criticized for being unduly influenced by private sector lobbying from the banking industry. This has been characterized as producing a process of 'regulatory capture' whereby 'the content of regulation is actively designed by, and in the interests of, the regulated industry itself', although research also suggests that private sector lobbying has in some cases resulted in the development of more stringent rather than weaker regulatory principles through the Basel process (Young 2012: 664). In addition to regulatory capture that might result from private sector lobbying on the content of specific banking proposals, observers have also criticized financial policy-makers for exhibiting a broader form of 'cognitive capture' in the period leading up to the global financial crisis, whereby officials came to internalize the general policy preferences of the financial actors they were responsible for regulating (McPhilemy 2013).

In terms of policy effectiveness, the Basel I and Basel II Accords were criticized for an exclusive concentration on limiting financial risks to individual institutions, which produced a blind spot over how to manage the emergence of financial risks to the banking system as a whole. The earlier Basel Accords largely ignored issues related to 'macro-prudential' regulation, which is oriented towards restraining pro-cyclical dynamics in financial markets and systemic risks. In addition, the regulatory principles contained in Basel I and II inadvertently encouraged pro-cyclical market dynamics that exacerbated the growth of financial asset bubbles prior to 2008 (Baker 2012). The focus on micro-prudential tools of regulation that were process-driven rather than results-oriented also increased the regulatory costs that were borne by small banks. This granted larger, internationally active banks a competitive advantage through effectively raising the barrier against new banking sector entrants (Warwick Commission on International Financial Reform 2009: 6). While the Basel III framework has moved more firmly towards embracing macro-prudential regulation to guard against systemic risks in the banking sector, critics have highlighted the tendency for financial governance reforms to be based on the assumption that future banking crises can be prevented simply 'by regulating against a repeat of the most recent crisis' (Rethel and Sinclair 2012: 97), an assumption that in recent decades has been proven wrong on numerous occasions.

Global creditworthiness

In contrast to both TNCs and global banks, credit rating agencies do not directly control substantial material resources of their own. Yet the judgements issued by rating agencies on the creditworthiness of the different actors they rate generate significant material consequences. Credit ratings are evaluations of a debtor's ability to repay a loan and the probability of default. Rating agencies are private actors that assign credit ratings for a range of public and private actors that issue debt, as well as for specific debt instruments. Rating judgements affect the creditworthiness of national and local governments, firms, banks and other private companies, and in theory function to reduce uncertainty and information asymmetry problems for investors (IOSCO 2003). While rating agencies are private actors, in the contemporary era their role has become embedded in public policy through regulatory and legislative changes in many countries as well as the evolving principles of global financial governance. Under the Basel II framework, for example, rating agency judgements of an actor's creditworthiness are used by regulators to assess banks' capital reserve requirements. In the USA the Securities and Exchange Commission enables investment banks and financial brokers to use ratings issued by recognized credit rating agencies for similar purposes. As a result of these changes in financial governance and regulatory tools, rating agencies have been characterized as 'nominally private makers of a global public policy' (Sinclair 2005: 177).

How rating agencies construct credit ratings and the subsequent market effects of their ratings remain highly controversial issues. Within the economic literature on credit rating, for instance, it remains a point of contention whether the creditworthiness assessments issued by rating agencies anticipate changes in market conditions or simply react to them (Kiff *et al.* 2012). As Timothy Sinclair (2005: 176) points out, the process of constructing credit ratings is not 'rocket science', and the variables that inform an agency's creditworthiness assessments comprise both quantitative and qualitative elements. The main credit rating agencies typically form rating committees in order to initiate, withdraw, or alter a credit rating. Rating committees are composed of a mix of market analysts and managing directors or supervisors, who make rating decisions by a simple majority vote to decide whether an issuer of debt securities can be expected to make timely repayments on its loans. These votes are informed by information that has been provided by the debtor as well as additional research conducted by the rating agency's analysts (IOSCO 2003: 5).

In the last two decades credit rating agencies have frequently been blamed for missing the warning signs that precipitated a series of financial crises. In a number of cases they have been accused of acting in ways that had pro-cyclical effects that fuelled asset bubbles through overly favourable ratings, and then exacerbating periods of financial distress via sharp rating downgrades. Recent examples where rating agencies have attracted political controversy and blame range from the Eurozone debt crisis that emerged in 2010 to the US subprime crisis in 2007 (see Box 7.1), the Asian financial crisis in 1997–98 and the Mexican crisis of 1994–95 (Kiff *et al.* 2012). For both public and private borrowers alike, credit rating agencies can affect a debtor's access to financial markets as well as their funding costs. The possibility of significant material effects

---

Box 7.1 Rating agencies and the US subprime property bubble

In the period leading up to the US 'subprime' crisis in 2007 credit rating agencies assigned high ratings to mortgage-backed securities and collateralized debt obligations, which provided a 'seal of approval' investors relied on when purchasing securitized assets. Credit rating practices consequently enabled mortgage-backed securities to further inflate the US property bubble during the 2000s, especially after 2003 when total subprime mortgage lending – residential property loans that do not meet the criteria for 'prime' mortgages – outstripped prime mortgage loans. The subprime market expanded from around US$160 billion in new subprime mortgages in 2001 to US$700 billion in mid-2007, while the combined value of outstanding mortgage-backed securities rose from a total of US$1 trillion in the late 1990s to over US$5 trillion in 2008. Through rapid growth in the market for securitized debt products rating agencies received fees in exchange for rating the risk of securitized assets (Seabrooke 2010b). The faster the subprime market in mortgage-backed securities expanded, the higher the fee income credit rating agencies received from assigning new ratings.

---

flowing from a credit rating downgrade imbues rating agencies with a potent source of symbolic power in the contemporary global political economy. Because their ratings are market-sensitive and consequential for a range of other actors, both national and local government policy-makers may face strong incentives to internalize the preferences of credit rating agencies in setting fiscal and other economic policies. National policy-makers sometimes disclose prospective fiscal policy changes with rating agency representatives before they are publicly announced or presented to national legislatures, especially if they anticipate that their sovereign rating might be downgraded in response to the proposed changes, while ministers of finance in countries with top credit ratings commonly use them to claim external validation of a government's economic policy strategy.

Rating agencies are not new market actors. The three largest and most influential rating agencies are Standard and Poor's, Moody's Investors Service and Fitch Ratings, companies which date back to the late nineteenth and early twentieth centuries. Ratings issued by the three major agencies constitute a rank ordering of credit risk. Long-term ratings, for example, are distinguished between different ranks of 'investment grade' ratings (ranging from the top AAA rating, issued by Standard & Poor's and Fitch Ratings, to the BBB rating) and 'non-investment grade' or 'speculative grade' ratings (BB ratings and below.)

Ratings below investment grade are considered to have a moderate to high credit risk of non-repayment.

The symbolic power rating agencies exercise over public and private actors comes primarily from their role as 'reputational intermediaries', based on their public image as independent, authoritative actors that are capable of making accurate expert assessments of the creditworthiness of the institutions and products they assign ratings to (Sinclair 2005: 176–7). The reputational authority of rating agencies can sometimes be observed in how markets respond to a government's annual spending plans or announcements of longer-term changes to fiscal policy settings. More broadly, their practices may have a systemic effect when governments and private companies adopt financial and economic norms that are implicitly promoted through the assessment mechanisms that rating agencies employ, or what Sinclair (2005: 17) terms 'the mental framework of rating orthodoxy'. The contemporary practices of credit rating agencies can influence the social context that informs how governments decide their economic policies and which shapes the range of alternative choices that are considered, at least for those countries which either hold or seek to obtain an investment grade sovereign rating.

Market actors can potentially exercise relational power over policymakers, either indirectly in the case of rating agencies or directly via the decisions by large firms and banks over where their business activities are located, how their production, investment and financial operations are structured and how commercial profits are distributed. Like credit rating agencies, TNCs and internationally active banks can also exercise various forms of symbolic power in the global political economy. Through corporate lobbying, transnational and national policy networks and informal consultation processes, market actors can promote policy choices and governance norms that reflect their underlying preferences as 'best practice' solutions to contemporary policy dilemmas. In addition to feeding ideas for specific reforms into economic policy-making processes, the exercise of symbolic power by private actors may also reflect a broader agenda to limit how governments regulate domestic and cross-border economic activities, in order – to paraphrase Albert Hirschman (1982: 1473) – to endow imperfect market systems with political legitimacy.

Summary

From the perspective of many large firms and commercial banks, the contemporary global political economy is no longer composed of territorially bound national economies, but in recent decades has come closer to resembling a global marketplace where flows of goods, services and capital can cross national borders with ease, subject to far fewer restrictions than at any point in the past century. Many companies and banks now structure their activities across different national jurisdictions in order to take advantage of local opportunities for maximizing returns. Such opportunities may come in the form of an abundant supply of cheap labour or highly skilled workers, geographical proximity to large markets, preferential treatment for specific forms of investment or the ability to shelter income from higher taxes in other countries, fewer environmental protections and other forms of regulatory arbitrage. Despite directly controlling no material resources of their own, rating agencies exercise substantial symbolic power over the products and actors whose creditworthiness they rate, by providing judgements that are consequential for the responses of other market actors. For the overwhelming majority of the world's population, however, territorial borders and structural processes and outcomes within national economies remain critically important in shaping trends in income, employment and welfare. For most people the rules that govern economic processes within national borders continue to shape their economic 'life chances' in important ways, despite national economic performance being increasingly subject to both positive and negative spill-over effects generated by changing economic dynamics in other countries or in global market processes.

Discussion questions

1. What factors explain the shifting balance of authority between public and private actors?
2. How has the globalization of production impacted upon corporate governance?
3. How did the behaviour of private actors create the conditions for the global financial crisis?
4. How have processes of financial governance been reformed in the aftermath of the crisis?
5. In what ways can credit rating agencies constrain governments' policy autonomy?
6. Is private market authority legitimate?

Further reading

Campbell, John L. 2004. *Institutional Change and Globalization*. Princeton, NJ: Princeton University Press.

Gourevitch, Peter A. and James Shinn. 2005. *Political Power and Corporate Control: The New Global Politics of Corporate Governance*. Princeton, NJ: Princeton University Press.

Kaplinsky, Raphael. 2005. *Globalization, Poverty and Inequality: Between a Rock and a Hard Place*. Cambridge: Polity.

Rethel, Lena and Timothy J. Sinclair. 2012. *The Problem with Banks*. London: Zed.

Sinclair, Timothy J. 2005. *The New Masters of Capital: American Bond Rating Agencies and the Politics of Creditworthiness*. Ithaca, NY: Cornell University Press.

Woll, Cornelia. 2008. *Firm Interests: How Governments Shape Business Lobbying on Global Trade*. Ithaca, NY: Cornell University Press.

Chapter 8

Non-Governmental Organizations

Introduction

International Political Economy has traditionally focused on a narrow range of elite actors as the principal institutions or groups of individuals capable of influencing processes of change in the global political economy. For much of its disciplinary history, the analysis of political and economic change in the field of IPE has concentrated on the activities of major states and IOs and changes occurring in financial markets, trade and production. Broader social mechanisms – such as the pressures generated by non-elite actors and public campaigns – have until recently tended to play a marginal role in most accounts of change in IPE. Most scholars have concentrated on adding to what we know about the behaviour of a limited range of actors – and the reasons why their actions achieve or fail to achieve change. Yet understanding the role of non-governmental organizations (NGOs) is often a more complex task compared with the roles of other actors such as states and IOs, which typically have legally defined responsibilities and procedures, a clear organizational hierarchy and a public mandate that empowers their right to act in specific issue areas. This chapter brings the role of NGOs into the main focus of the field of IPE, and shows how NGOs perform a variety of distinct functions that impact upon the behaviour, ideas and interests of other actors in the global political economy, as well as highlighting the characteristics of different types of NGOs as actors in their own right.

Background

Although organizations which would today be described as NGOs have existed since the first half of the nineteenth century, the term 'non-governmental organization' was introduced in Article 71 of the United Nations Charter, but was initially left undefined (Willetts 2011: 7). Unlike many other actors, NGOs typically do not decide public policy, nor are they usually directly responsible for policy implementation. Their activities may involve a consultation, lobbying, or public campaigning role with respect to national and global policies, while the functions of some NGOs impact upon how international regimes and policies are implemented in different local contexts. On the one hand, a growing volume of IPE research suggests that NGOs are now major players at all levels in the global political economy, with authority flowing away from states as well as formal IOs to non-state social and market actors. On the other hand, a contrasting body of research suggests that the contemporary role of NGOs in IPE has been exaggerated. NGOs lack most of the formal levers of power that are associated with public institutions, which can enforce compliance among subordinate actors, and do not have the legal responsibility to design, implement and monitor economic policies. Understanding the roles NGOs now play in the global political economy can be differentiated between two related lines of enquiry. First, questions about how effective and legitimate existing forms of global economic governance are, and how the practices associated with international regimes are implemented. Second, questions about who drives change in the global political economy and how the dynamics of change are understood.

As a distinct category of actors in the global political economy, NGOs differ markedly from states and the various club forums and IOs that states have created. In particular, NGOs are seen as having a set of preferences over possible strategies of action and ideal outcomes that are independent from official actors. In contrast to national governments and IOs, therefore, 'NGOs are the creation of like-minded private individuals who share a founding idea' (Drezner 2007: 68). NGOs are most commonly defined as legally constituted organizations that operate independently from official public entities, even if part of their funding may be derived from government sources, and which are not profit-seeking enterprises such as businesses organizations. NGOs constitute one category of actors within civil society, despite the term 'NGO' often being used as a synonym for civil society (Van Rooy 2004: 7). Civil society can be understood as '*a political space where associations of citizens seek, from outside political parties, to shape societal rules*' (Scholte 2011: 34, emphasis original). The normative definition of NGOs' activities also excludes criminal behaviour and the use of political violence to achieve objectives, although the conceptual distinction between non-violent civil society groups and social groups that use armed force to achieve their ends is sometimes difficult to maintain in practice (Henry 2011).

In comparison to official actors in the global political economy, NGOs are far greater in number. For example, a recent edition of the Union of International Associations' (2012) *Yearbook of International Organizations* includes entries on 65,736 civil society organizations. Following Drezner (2007: 69), the main functions of NGOs can be grouped into two main categories: (1) advocacy functions; and (2) service functions. The advocacy functions of an NGO refers to deliberate strategies that are aimed at changing existing governance practices, processes and policies at a national, regional, or global level, in line with the preferred processes or outcomes of a specific NGO. The service functions of NGOs, meanwhile, can be defined as practices that compensate for, challenge, or supplement the practices of other actors in the global political economy such as states, market actors and IOs. For example, the service functions of NGOs may involve monitoring the enforcement of international regimes, agreements and rules to track the level and quality of compliance among the actors that are party to them.

Some of the activities of NGOs overlap between advocacy and service functions. NGO networks such as the European Network on Debt and Development (Eurodad), which includes 58 individual NGO members, have published numerous reports on the implementation of international agreements to improve the 'debt sustainability' of HIPCs through the various debt relief initiatives that operate under the auspices of the IMF and the World Bank (see Chapter 14). By identifying problems with the effectiveness of IMF and World Bank policies on debt relief, such reports both perform an advocacy role in generating pressure for changes in IO policies, as well as potentially providing a service to other actors, such as both creditor and borrower states who may lack the capacity or willingness to monitor the actions of IOs on debt issues themselves. The potential for NGOs to provide rival expertise on a given issue can therefore involve an NGO playing an advocacy role in a campaign to change existing global policies, as well as a service function through creating an alternate source of cognitive authority that state actors can draw upon to monitor 'agency slack' in IOs themselves.

Accountability and legitimacy in global economic governance

In terms of global economic governance, the activities of many NGOs have specifically focused on improving accountability mechanisms with respect to IOs and major club forums such as the G8 and G20. Accountability, defined as a mechanism whereby a particular actor must account for its practices to those actors who are affected by them, can be disaggregated into four main features. These include: (1) the level of transparency with respect to an actor's behaviour; (2) the degree of consultation with affected parties over decision-making processes and outcomes; (3) independent evaluation of an actor's behaviour that assesses how it has impacted upon affected parties; and (4) the possibility of correction when policies and practices have had negative unintended consequences or resulted in policy failures (Scholte 2011: 16–17).

Mechanisms of accountability are closely related to the degree to which an actor can be said to command legitimacy in terms of its decisions and actions. Legitimacy is an intersubjective quality that is conferred on an actor's decisions and behaviour by others when it is recognized as conforming to socially sanctioned norms, rules and principles (Reus-Smit 2007). In seeking reforms to the practices and processes of existing IOs, one of the hurdles NGOs face can be termed the 'efficiency and legitimacy trade-off' in global economic governance. This refers to the problem that measures to increase an organization's legitimacy – through enhanced accountability mechanisms and new rules that constrain that scope of its actions – might diminish the organization's 'operational efficiency'. This is defined as an IO's 'ability to achieve its goals without wasting resources' (Cottarelli 2005: 3). With respect to the accountability of IOs to their member states, one challenge here is that part of the core objectives of organizations such as the IMF, the World Bank and the WTO is precisely to ensure that members comply with agreed rules, norms and principles that form their common obligations of membership. In this sense, while accountability and legitimacy is critical to the ability of an international organization to perform its roles effectively, by diminishing the independence of an organization accountability mechanisms may prove counterproductive if they result in greater scope for member states to limit the extent to which they comply with their formal obligations, provide opportunities for watering down the terms of their multilateral commitments, or if they allow a bending of the rules (such as policy conditions attached to IMF and World Bank loans) when these are applied to states that are allied with major powers.

With respect to the surveillance activities of IOs, greater transparency in decision-making may include costs associated with the public dissemination of market-sensitive information. While these costs accrue more to member states rather than an IO itself, this negative feedback effect points to the difficulties involved when greater transparency might result in adverse reactions by market actors, which may also reduce the opportunities for an IO to persuade state actors to adopt policy changes that

might avoid future economic problems (Cottarelli 2005: 15). One example that illustrates some of these potential problems is provided by the
case of Thailand during the Asian financial crisis in 1997–98, when the
IMF insisted that the Thai government release sensitive financial details
of the low level of the central bank's remaining foreign exchange
reserves, information which quickly prompted a greater outflow of capital from the country (IMF 2000). In this example, secrecy rather than
transparency might have proven to be a more effective strategy. A further
potential problem that can arise from greater accountability in IOs is the
idea of a trade-off between transparency and candour in policy dialogue
between an organization's staff and other actors in the global political
economy. This could result from IO actors knowing in advance that their
written reports will be made publicly available, which might lead to a
watering down of policy advice and criticism of existing government
policies (Cottarelli 2005: 18). These possible problems with strengthening the accountability mechanisms of IOs have been highlighted by
actors within the organizations themselves. The point for many NGOs,
however, is that accountability reforms are not intended to increase the
opportunities for member states to shirk their multilateral obligations,
but rather to redistribute political power and membership rights within
organizations such as the IMF and the World Bank in order to reduce the
organizations' perceived bias towards the interests of large developed
countries.

While many NGOs have pushed formal international organizations to
improve their accountability mechanisms in recent years, and IOs have
sometimes proved receptive to certain elements of the criticisms levied at
their actions by NGOs and other actors, the main motivation for IOs in
reforming or expanding their accountability processes has been a loosely
defined goal of improving their institutional legitimacy. Most IOs recognize that improving their legitimacy can enhance their effectiveness, as
well as the capacity to gain acceptance from other actors that they should
comply with an IO's norms, rules and procedures. In this sense, 'legitimacy is the glue that links authority and power' (Bernstein 2011: 20).
However, legitimacy should be conceived as a 'legitimization spectrum'
rather than a fixed property that an actor either has or does not have
(Brassett and Tsingou 2011). An organization may reach a point where it
can be described as suffering from a crisis of legitimacy 'when it experiences a decline in the level of social recognition that its identity, interests,
practices, norms, or procedures are rightful' to such an extent that the
organization is faced with a stark choice between either adapting or
losing credibility and influence as an effective actor (Reus-Smit 2007:
157). Apart from this type of ultimate crisis point, the legitimacy of an
international organization at a certain point in time can seldom be

described as 'legitimate' or 'illegitimate' in absolute terms, because concepts of legitimacy are contingent upon the particular organization in question, the discursive framework in which the appropriateness and effectiveness of its actions are evaluated and understood, and its interactions with a range of other actors in the global political economy, including both state and non-state actors (Brassett and Tsingou 2011).

The existing literature in IPE encompasses a wide range of perspectives on how accountability can be identified and measured, as well as differences over how the accountability of IOs can be improved. Two important differences in how the accountability of IOs is conceived include whether this is defined in narrow or broad terms. From a state-centric perspective, IOs such as the IMF, the World Bank and the WTO may be seen as directly accountable only to their member states, which in turn are accountable to their own populations. This conception of accountability limits the relationship of IOs to non-state actors as a form of indirect accountability through states. Even this narrow application of the concept can prove problematic as a means of assessing accountability because IOs may not be able to be accountable to all their member states all the time. For organizations such as the IMF and the World Bank where representation and voting rights are based upon economic factors rather than the principle of sovereign equality (in comparison to the WTO and the UN General Assembly), accountability might be defined even more narrowly as answering for their conduct to the large shareholder states who contribute the most to the organizations' financial resources. From a different perspective, borrowers might be deemed the most important state actors to whom the IMF and the World Bank should be accountable, as they are most affected by the organizations' policies, and in the case of the IMF most of the organization's operational costs and administrative budget are financed through interest and charges on IMF loans that are paid by borrowers, although creditor states put up the initial capital.

Taken at face value as the need for an actor to be accountable 'to those whom it affects' (Scholte 2011: 16), IOs may instead be expected to be more broadly accountable to the people, social groups, businesses and legislative bodies within countries who are affected by an IO's actions in addition to the executive branch of national governments and national economic institutions. This complicates the job of identifying clear requirements for legitimacy when the communities that are deemed important for an actor's legitimacy lack coherence or are characterized by a high degree of normative contestation between different groups (Bernstein 2011: 21). While mechanisms to achieve this form of accountability exist within some IOs, on the whole most fail to reach this expanded standard of accountability (as do many states with respect to their own populations). Notwithstanding the difficulties involved with establishing and maintaining broader mechanisms of accountability in IOs (Cabrera 2011; Park 2010a), in recent years a number of IOs have expanded their accountability mechanisms with respect to transparency and evaluation. Most IOs have been less effective at broadening the scope of accountability mechanisms with respect to consultation and correction over policies, governance procedures and decision-making.

Private authority and global economic governance

Aside from market actors, non-state actors have traditionally been understudied in IPE. As discussed above, the majority of IPE research continues to focus on interactions between state, intergovernmental and market actors in the global political economy. The most obvious exception to the continued focus on states and markets in IPE is the increased attention many scholars have given to examining the changing roles that NGOs now play in an increasing number of issue areas within IPE, and especially the role of NGOs in processes of global economic governance. For example, many scholars have begun to focus more closely on the interactions between NGOs and the IMF (Thirkell-White 2004), the World Bank Group (Park 2005) and the WTO (Scholte *et al.* 1999). This has been driven in part by the changing practices of the organizations themselves. In an effort to improve their public image, and thereby ameliorate perceived legitimacy crises, several of the major IOs have turned to increased civil society participation as a catch-all solution in response to the trenchant criticisms they have recently faced. In addition, some scholars have sought to build an explicitly normative case for expanding the international role of NGOs and 'global civil society' more broadly. From a cosmopolitan perspective, for example, progressive goals might be achieved through incorporating NGOs within the formal decision-making structures of IOs, as a means to achieve greater democratization. In contrast, critical perspectives envisage NGOs remaining outside formal structures of public authority, as independent actors that might help to increase public deliberation and awareness on global governance issues (Smith and Brassett 2008).

The primary characteristics of individual NGOs can be differentiated based on their goal orientation, including both advocacy and service objectives such as welfare, development, education, research and networking (Vakil 1997: 2063). Other distinguishing features include the scale of their operations, which may range from a local sub-state focus to national, regional and global activities, as well as their memberships (including size, type, level of participation and whether they comprise coalitions or networks of other NGOs). In addition to the problems that persist in classifying different types and functions of NGOs, even greater care is needed in efforts to establish their collective influence in the global political economy.

In some areas the influence of NGOs may be readily apparent in changing practices and discourses within both major power states and IOs themselves. During the 1990s and 2000s the sustained pressure from NGOs and other actors for IOs to increase the transparency of their decision-making processes and actions gained some significant results. Despite a long history of secrecy regarding its negotiations and policy dialogue with member states, for example, the IMF gradually became more open to publishing details or summaries of its surveillance activities with member states as well as the summaries of Executive Board meetings and loan negotiations with borrowing governments (Cottarelli 2005: 17). A vast amount of information that was kept confidential for the first five decades of the IMF's existence is now readily accessible from publications on the organization's website. While NGOs have generated sustained public pressure for changes in the accountability mechanisms and policies of IOs, tracing the processes through which their advocacy efforts have directly influenced changes in the decision-making processes and actions of IOs remains challenging, due to the multiple causal factors and different motivations that play a role in such changes.

Today, NGOs are commonly viewed as being able to exercise an important form of authority in the international system. If authority is defined as 'institutionalized forms or expressions of power' that are recognized and accepted as socially legitimate, then authority necessarily involves 'both a social relationship between author and subject, and a definable domain of action' (Hall and Biersteker 2002: 4, 6). More simply, authority can be defined as 'the ability to induce deference in others' (Avant *et al.* 2010: 9). As actors in the global political economy, NGOs are conceived as being capable of exercising one of several forms of 'moral authority' that can potentially influence the preferences and behaviour of other actors. The recognition of a specific actor as having authority 'does not mean that one always agrees with or likes the authority' (Avant *et al.* 2010: 10). Similarly, being recognized as having moral authority does not mean that an actor is intrinsically 'good'. Thomas Biersteker and Rodney Bruce Hall (2002: 218) define three bases of moral authority that NGOs can develop and use to achieve their goals. These include: (1) the capacity to provide alternative expertise; (2) the capacity to act as a referee; and (3) the capacity to promote normative positions.

When NGOs are perceived to be competent knowledge producers, they can potentially exercise moral authority as agenda-setters by reordering the preferences of other actors. They might also exercise a transformative influence through the creation of issues that were not previously recognized as problems, or through defining existing issues in new ways (Carpenter 2010). Like IOs, NGOs that are able to competently draw on their own stock of expertise to provide policy advice, to monitor behaviour and to evaluate the policies and decisions of other actors can develop their own source of cognitive authority. This may be consequential if their cognitive authority is recognized by the actors that are the target of their activities or by other institutions that shape public debate, such as media organizations. NGOs are also recognized as having moral authority as a result of their normative commitments and their unique institutional characteristics in comparison with state actors, IOs and market actors. Because they are not driven by profit motives or by national interests, NGOs are assumed to be capable of operating as more neutral actors that do not represent vested interests. They may also be viewed as more representative actors if they attract public support that transcends territorial boundaries and is oriented towards normative goals rather than material rewards (Hall and Biersteker 2002: 14).

In terms of global economic governance, NGOs can be categorized into different groups based on the nature of their relations with IOs such as the IMF and the World Bank, as well as how they interact with global governance forums such as the G8 and the G20 (Cooper 2013). These groups can be broadly termed 'insiders', 'reformists' and 'abolitionists'. The first group includes NGOs such as think-tanks and economic research institutes that broadly agree with IMF and World Bank objectives, but may disagree over issues such as policy priorities and the sequencing of economic reforms. The second group are NGOs that seek major reforms of IMF and World Bank policies and operating procedures. In the third group are NGOs that more strongly criticize the mandates and practices of the IMF and World Bank in global economic governance, and are more likely to seek their abolition than reform (Dawson and Bhatt 2001). While most IOs seldom engage with the third group of NGOs, the first group of NGOs have regular access through joint seminars, conferences and workshops that bring together IO staff and external policy experts. In recent years, both the IMF and the World Bank have engaged in more extensive consultation with the second group of 'reformist' NGOs. Such engagement has involved direct contact between the management of IOs and select NGO representatives, contact between members of the IMF and the World Bank's Executive Boards and NGOs, as well as NGO briefings by IO staff and an expansion of the activities of IOs' public relations departments. At a national level, the country representatives of IOs have also begun liaising on a more regular basis with local and national NGOs (Dawson and Bhatt 2001).

In some respects this deliberate move by IOs to engage in greater 'outreach' activities illustrates a significant degree of success in the efforts by NGOs to pressure IOs to expand their accountability mechanisms beyond member states. It also indicates the recognition within IOs that their legitimacy now depends in part on engagement with a greater range of non-state actors. These forms of engagement often remain modest, however. On the one hand, IOs such as the IMF may seek primarily to exchange information with NGOs, and to justify their own policies and practices as a public relations strategy. On the other hand, an IO's outreach activities may be aimed simply at 'reading off' opinions from select civil society actors, rather than engaging in more substantive consultation that could alter the policy direction, governance and procedures of the organization itself (Thirkell-White 2004).

In addition to the expansion of direct forms of contact between IOs and NGOs, a role for civil society organizations has been formally incorporated within the IMF and the World Bank's Poverty Reduction Strategy Papers (PRSPs). Adopted in 1999, countries must complete a PRSP in order to be eligible for debt relief through the HIPC Initiative. NGOs are specifically included as surrogates for societal participation in the formulation of a country's Poverty Reduction Strategy, which is intended to broaden social consensus around the goals of poverty reduction while simultaneously expanding local stakeholder influence in policy design. This change has been welcomed by some NGOs, which had long criticized the exclusion of societal actors from IO and member state negotiations over policy reforms. Nevertheless, the PRSP process also raises critical issues regarding the legitimacy of NGOs and 'mission creep' in the roles of the IMF and the World Bank. Both the IMF's and the World Bank's mandates include a commitment to remain 'apolitical' organizations. This rests on a very narrow conception of what is defined as 'political', which excludes dialogue and negotiations over economic policy settings as a political process. The requirement to involve domestic societal actors in PRSPs can be criticized as an expansion of interference in state–society relations for IMF and World Bank members. Furthermore, PRSPs have imposed substantial administrative and opportunity costs on HIPC governments, and the PRSP process has been criticized for promoting the inclusion of a select group of NGOs as authoritative actors in development processes, while marginalizing the involvement of other societal actors (Craig and Porter 2003).

Like all actors who gain authority, NGOs can also lose it. Despite the advocacy roles that NGOs have played in attempting to reshape the accountability, processes and effectiveness of global governance actors, NGOs themselves have also been subject to sustained criticism regarding their own accountability mechanisms, their representativeness and the effectiveness of their activities. The legitimacy of some NGOs has been challenged when a mismatch has emerged between 'an organization's methods and message', which can lead to the decline of an NGO's perceived moral authority (Van Rooy 2004: 103). Further challenges for NGOs include the perception that many of the most prominent, professionalized and influential NGOs at the global level narrowly promote liberal ideals of how societies and governance systems should be organized (Davies 2008: 14–15). From this perspective, rather than being part of the solution to deficiencies in contemporary processes of global economic governance, large NGOs with transnational operations are sometimes seen as part of the problem of a political bias in global economic governance towards 'Western' concepts of development, good governance, capacity building and accountability (Goldman 2005).

Summary

NGOs now perform a variety of roles in the global political economy, most of which can be categorized as either advocacy or service roles. NGOs have been instrumental in promoting changes in the policies and practices of international organizations through providing an alternative source of cognitive authority, organizing public campaigns to generate political pressure for institutional reforms and through challenging the objectives and operational procedures of IOs on normative grounds. In the last two decades, these efforts have been influential in motivating global governance actors to expand and reform their accountability mechanisms, as well as to engage in greater 'outreach' activities with NGOs. Many IOs have enacted reforms that increased the transparency of their decision-making, as well as promoting mechanisms for independent evaluation and review of the effectiveness of their practices. At least partly as a result of the activities of NGOs, IOs such as the IMF now publicly disseminate a wide range of information and internal reports and documents that were previously kept confidential, while both the IMF and the World Bank involve select NGOs, to varying degrees, in consultations over governance reforms and major changes to their policies. At the same time, questions remain over the accountability, representativeness and effectiveness of NGOs themselves as legitimate actors in the global political economy.

Discussion questions

1. What roles do NGOs play in global economic governance?
2. What are the sources of legitimacy for NGOs?
3. How might NGOs exercise influence in the global political economy?
4. How might IOs enhance their accountability through engagement with NGOs?
5. How can the effectiveness of different NGOs be assessed?
6. How is the growing prominence of NGOs changing the practice of global governance?

Further reading

Cabrera, Luis. 2010. *The Practice of Global Citizenship*. Cambridge: Cambridge University Press.

Keck, Margaret E. and Kathryn Sikkink. 1998. *Activists Beyond Borders*. Ithaca, NY: Cornell University Press.

O'Brien, Robert, Anne Marie Goetz, Jan Aart Scholte and Marc Williams. 2000. *Contesting Global Governance: Multilateral Economic Institutions and Global Social Movements*. Cambridge: Cambridge University Press.

Scholte, Jan Aart (ed.). 2011. *Building Global Democracy? Civil Society and Accountable Global Governance*. Cambridge: Cambridge University Press.

Van Rooy, Alison. 2004. *The Global Legitimacy Game: Civil Society, Globalization, and Protest*. Basingstoke: Palgrave Macmillan.

Willetts, Peter. 2011. *Non-Governmental Organisations in World Politics: The Construction of Global Governance*. London: Routledge.

Chapter 9

Everyday Actors

Introduction

Most studies of actors in International Political Economy concentrate on how global processes and dynamics of change are shaped by the behaviour of public and private elites. In particular, a primary focus is on understanding and explaining the question of 'who governs' in the global political economy. A growing body of literature is now also concerned with the distinct question of 'who acts' in the global political economy, and how their actions are consequential for the possibilities of economic governance and its effectiveness (Hobson and Seabrooke 2007: 12). While the agential power of elite actors is assumed across many if not most areas of enquiry in IPE, non-elites are typically understood as actors that are characteristically lacking in agency, without sufficient material and ideational capacities to influence global political economy dynamics. To complement the discussion of the roles played by actors with high organizational capacities and institutionalized forms of power such as states, IOs, club forums, market actors and NGOs, this chapter examines the role of 'everyday actors' in the global political economy. The emphasis is on how non-elite actors are capable of exercising diverse forms of agency, which can be easily missed when the focus is on formal power structures and the behaviour of actors with high material capabilities. Reorienting the focus of analysis from elite to non-elite actors can help to provide a corrective to overly structural understandings of power in IPE, and emphasizes the importance of understanding how the sources of change in the world economy can be bottom-up processes shaped by everyday actors as well as top-down processes driven by public and private elites.

Background

Everyday actors are by definition *non-elite* actors in the global political economy. Collectively, non-elite actors form the population of the global political economy, whose everyday behaviour, choices, expectations and responses shape the economic fortunes of different countries, the economic and political capacities of states and how wealth is accumulated by business actors. The first step in the incorporation of everyday actors in contemporary studies of the global political economy is to move beyond a concern with understanding the relative degrees of 'agential power' exercised by state actors, defined as the ability to make policy and shape the domestic or international realm without being constrained by structural requirements or the interests of other actors (Hobson 2000: 5, 7). Both elite and non-elite actors can potentially exercise various forms of agency in their everyday experiences. Rather than exploring the everyday action of elites (Slaughter 2004), the focus on everyday actors in IPE is a deliberate attempt to expand the focus of analysis away from an exclusive concentration on powerful elite actors and power structures towards non-elites.

The conception of power resources commonly used in the field of IPE is often disaggregated into analytic categories that mirror older definitions found in other disciplines of social research. These categories include: (1) the ability to alter material rewards; (2) the ability to 'punish' through the exercise of coercive power; (3) the right to prescribe appropriate behaviour through the exercise of legitimate power; (4) the power of attraction, or 'referent power'; and (5) informational forms of power based on expertise and cognitive authority (French and Raven 1959: 156–63). For example, prominent IPE scholar Susan Strange (1994) identified four channels of power in the global political economy based on structures of security, production, finance and knowledge. Rather than focusing on the properties of structural power, research on everyday actors in the global political economy is more concerned with understanding how non-elite actors exercise agency. This conception of agency can be understood as the degree to which non-elite actions have both productive effects and limiting effects on the legitimate exercise of public and private authority in the global political economy.

The analytic category of 'everyday actions' can be defined as *'acts by those who are subordinate within a broader power relationship but, whether through negotiation, resistance or non-resistance, either incrementally or suddenly, shape, constitute and transform the political and economic environment around and beyond them'* (Hobson and Seabrooke 2007: 15–16, emphasis original). Effectively studying how everyday actors matter in the global political economy involves exploring the complex and dynamic relationship between actors' beliefs, norms and values and their material interests, policy preferences and public opinion. People's beliefs can be a challenging subject to study because they are more difficult to observe and to measure, but are highly consequential in shaping how economies work. To effectively study how everyday actions matter in the global political economy it is therefore important to exercise analytic flexibility in investigating how processes and dynamics of change are constituted, contested and transformed through social mechanisms that may not be amenable to generalizable models of cause-and-effect. While much of the scholarship within IPE concentrates on establishing positive facts about cause-and-effect relationships in the global political economy, facts do not 'choose themselves'. Rather, economic 'theory and information is shaped throughout by the social assumptions and values' which guide how they are selected (Stretton 1999: 12–13). At the other end of the spectrum of work in IPE are scholars who concentrate on studying causal dynamics and outcomes in the global political economy as 'social facts' that are intersubjectively produced rather than representing objective truths about the world. This analytic distinction between the materiality of the global political economy and how it is interpreted lies at the heart of several contemporary debates in the field (see Chapter 3).

From elite-centric to everyday international political economy

Contemporary understandings of the global political economy often reproduce common assumptions about the differences between hierarchy 'above the state' in the world economy and the nature of hierarchy in domestic contexts. A standard starting point is to note that national governments typically exercise far greater powers of coercion and persuasion over their own populations than can be found at the global level due to the absence of a world government that could monopolize the use of material and symbolic power to govern global economic activities. Even between states of vastly different capabilities, the agential powers of major states are understood to be far less decisive at the global level compared with the domestic sphere. As Lake (2009: 178) observes, 'Dominant states typically exercise less authority over subordinate states ... than states themselves do over their own citizens.' This open question of 'who governs' at the global level is thus usually assumed to be settled when it comes to domestic political economies. One important consequence of this way of conceiving hierarchies of power is how the assumption that states largely dominate within their own borders limits the scope for conceiving of non-elite actors within states as being capable of influencing, let alone transforming, the global political economy, at least outside of formal political processes and the aggregation of everyday preferences through pressure groups and political parties in democracies. The focus of everyday IPE approaches, in contrast, tends to start from the assumption that even subordinate non-elite actors 'have some capacity to change their political, economic and social environment' (Hobson and Seabrooke 2007: 13).

Two varieties of 'everyday IPE' have emerged in recent years. The first is an *everyday life* approach, which focuses on understanding how the 'disciplinary logics' embedded within structural power relations in the global political economy operate at the everyday level. The second is an *everyday politics* approach, which takes an 'actions-based' focus (Hobson and Seabrooke 2009). The latter emphasizes the mechanisms through which everyday actions might transform the global political economy, rather than non-elites responding passively to stimuli from economic incentives, formal rules and structural processes. Both variants of everyday IPE have been inspired by insights from a range of other social science fields, including anthropology, cultural studies and economic sociology. Everyday IPE approaches have also built on efforts within the fields of IPE and IR to move beyond bounded research programmes by developing eclectic methodological toolkits, which enable researchers to answer new questions about empirical puzzles that are not amenable to elite-centric explanations on their own (Sil and Katzenstein 2010). Where the study of everyday actors in IPE has perhaps gained the most inspiration from other fields of enquiry is in how the qualities and expressions of 'agency' have been reconceptualized in order to overcome the limitation of assuming that only those actors already recognized as 'powerful', or those situated at the top level of powerful structures, are capable of exercising agency in the world economy. This has extended into the study of IPE the insights of work by anthropologists and others that have challenged conventional assumptions of political strength and weakness in different societies, and have shown that the 'weapons of the weak' can be effective in transforming how larger structures of power and influence operate even in non-democratic political systems (Scott 1985; Kerkvliet 2005).

The shift from elite actors to everyday actors represents an effort to expand the field of enquiry to encompass different dimensions of traditional issues in IPE, new types of issues, new categories and sites of action and variegated dynamics of change across alternate time horizons. As Charles Tilly (1989: 145) suggests, 'Historically grounded huge comparisons of big structures and large processes help establish what must be explained, attach the possible explanations to their context in time and

space, and sometimes actually improve our understanding of those structures and processes.' Recent scholarship has examined how the study of
globalized financial markets can be enhanced by tracing how financial
dynamics at the national level and the global level shape – and are in turn
shaped by – changes in the economic and social beliefs, behaviour and
preferences of everyday actors. This has involved exploring how contemporary changes in global financial practices have reconstituted the qualities of social relations for everyday actors, driving changes in everyday
life with respect to saving and borrowing that have had important rami-
fications for the dynamics of financial inclusion and exclusion, the nature
of financial power, and the construction of everyday financial identities
(Langley 2008). Moreover, scholars have also examined how the evolution of distinct varieties of housing finance systems not only produce
differences in property rights and levels of home ownership, but influence the constitution of political preferences regarding appropriate levels
and forms of public spending, taxation and inflation (Schwartz and
Seabrooke 2009).

By moving analysis beyond the dynamics of how financial markets
have been globalized and what systemic effects this has had on national
policy capacities, IPE approaches that focus on everyday actors have
developed an expanded understanding of how global financial processes
shape local financial practices and vice versa. In addition, broadening
the dimensions of financial market practices that are studied in IPE
helps to illustrate how changes in the behaviour, beliefs and preferences
of everyday actors not only shape the limits and possibilities of state
action, but can also stimulate generational processes of change in
domestic savings, asset ownership and inequalities of wealth. Exploring
how everyday actors respond in different ways to broader processes of
economic change, and how their responses also shape the evolution and
effectiveness of economic governance and policy frameworks, provides
important insights into the sequencing effects of processes of economic
globalization. As Tilly (1989: 14, emphasis original) suggests, '*when*
things happen within a sequence affects *how* they happen', because
'Outcomes at a given point in time constrain possible outcomes at later
points in time.' In the case of financial globalization, therefore, a focus
on everyday action illustrates how the policy decisions governments
make at one choice point shapes non-elite actors' behaviour, beliefs and
preferences in ways that constrain the range of policy choices – and the
types of policy problems – governments may face in the future. This
point is critical for how students of IPE understand the nature and
dynamics of globalizing processes, but is one that can easily be missed if
the focus remains on global–regional–national interactions and cause-
and-effect sequences between states and global markets rather than

incorporating domestic political economy dynamics into studies of the global political economy.

In addition to expanding how traditional topics and problems within IPE are understood, a focus on everyday actors also helps to incorporate different types of issues and sites of action that have been understudied in the field. For instance, a greater focus on the evolution of everyday actors' economic identities can serve to reveal the social processes that inform a state's policy choices and national economic strategies. As Rawi Abdelal (2001: 1) suggests, 'What societies want depends on who they think they are.' This enables alternative choices for national economic strategies to be understood as not simply resulting from either domestic material interests that feed into national policy processes or from the exogenous economic conditions states face, but from domestic political contestation over national identities that constitutes how those interests are defined. This underlines the importance of how societies generate new normative conceptions of the state's role in managing the domestic consequences of economic globalization. These normative shifts in how non-elite actors should be protected from adverse economic changes cannot be explained solely by examining differences in institutional capacity, economic conditions, or formal political structures (Trumbull 2006: 172–3).

Once the categories of relevant actors in IPE are expanded beyond the elite actors that are assumed to call the shots within states, markets and other non-state forums and organizations, it quickly becomes clear that non-elite everyday actors exercise important forms of agency that can be influential not only in a local community context but also for broader structures of power and dynamics of change in the global political economy. Everyday agency is not the preserve of citizens who live within affluent developed economies. Across subject areas as varied as global remittances and informal money transfers, fair trade social movements and cooperatives, microfinance credit practices and local capacity-building development efforts it is readily apparent that non-elite actors in less-affluent countries potentially exercise important forms of agency that can transform their political and economic environments despite occupying subordinate positions within broader sets of power relations (Cabrera 2010: 174–8).

A fundamental subject area whose importance has been brought into studies of traditional issues in IPE by everyday approaches revolves around how gender relations have been contested and transformed through large-scale processes of economic change. A growing body of literature has concentrated on exploring how globalized production processes and changing workplace regimes have stimulated new forms of political contestation and defiance over gendered labour practices (Elias

2010: 607), and how scholarship on gender and IPE can 'demonstrate the importance of social reproduction' to local, national and global market processes (Rai 2013). The focus on everyday actors and gender relations has challenged conventional assumptions about the subordinate position of women in broader economic structures and power relations, such as portrayals of female migrant workers as 'having little or no agency in the world economy' (Ford and Piper 2007: 63). Instead of conceiving of the economic activities of female migrant workers in less-affluent countries who have low social status or economic rights as inherently 'powerless', a focus on 'southern sites of female agency' is able to demonstrate how everyday actions to engage in hidden or informal acts of defiance can challenge how gender relations are practised in the workplace (Ford and Piper 2007).

In addition to expanding the dimensions of traditional issues in IPE and introducing new categories and sites of action, a focus on everyday actors can also help to broaden our understanding of how variegated dynamics of change in the global political economy operate across a range of different time horizons. This provides a useful corrective against the continuing dominance of 'punctuated equilibrium' models of change in IPE. Such models view structural processes of change in economic policy and governance systems as typically characterized by extended periods of stasis that are 'punctuated' by periods of radical change stimulated by exogenous shocks. In contrast, everyday approaches in IPE highlight how non-elite actors can provide political 'impulses' for change through shifting 'conventions among the mass public and ... their expectations about economic and social life' (Seabrooke 2007: 800). Changing expectations among everyday actors about the appropriate role and social purpose of the state as an economic manager might be easier to observe and find stronger expression in elite ideas for economic policy change during periods of major crises and economic uncertainty, but the dynamic interplay between the policy preferences of elite decision-makers and the beliefs of non-elite actors represents a continuous process of political contestation that also occurs during periods of 'institutional equilibrium'.

To gain a comprehensive understanding of the rapid inflation of residential property bubbles during the previous decade in countries such as the USA, the UK, Australia and New Zealand, it is necessary to look beyond a narrow focus on how governments' economic policies enabled and encouraged house price inflation over the five- or ten-year period before the emergence of the subprime crisis in the USA in 2007. These policy actions – as well as policy inaction – certainly contributed to the emergence and growth of property bubbles, and bear a large degree of responsibility for the economic disaster that followed when property bubbles burst (see Chapter 13). But in addition to these short-term dynamics between states and markets, policy shifts a generation earlier during the 1980s and 1990s helped to foster changing conventions and expectations of home ownership and asset-based financial security among non-elite actors. These social changes produced new middle-class 'investment cultures' that also played an important role in stimulating and sustaining residential property booms during the 2000s (Schwarz and Seabrooke 2009). A focus on everyday actors in IPE can therefore help to reorient how the 'inputs' and 'outputs' of economic policies are understood. In doing so, it is necessary to extend time horizons beyond a short-term focus on the relative institutional capacities and economic performance of individual countries, and to look beyond market failures, crisis responses and institutional reforms that occur within narrow 'windows of opportunity' for policy change created by exogenous shocks. This can help to account for how the rules that govern market processes also shape intergenerational dynamics of wealth creation, saving and consumption, which have important long-term effects on everyday actors' normative beliefs, political preferences and economic expectations.

The everyday politics of economic crises

Everyday actors perform important roles in determining governance outcomes and shaping dynamics of change in the global political economy. In particular, everyday actions play an important part in how the 'meanings' of economic crises are defined and understood, and whether elite interpretations of a crisis are supported or contested by the wider population (Widmaier *et al.* 2007). A co-constitutive relationship therefore exists between the wants, beliefs and belief-driven actions of elite actors and those of non-elite actors, yet conventional accounts of the dynamics of economic change within IPE typically discount the reasons behind non-elites' everyday actions. In doing so, conventional accounts disregard an important dimension of economic relations that links formal policy change to macro-level outcomes. This goes beyond the assumption that non-elites' everyday actions conform to 'rational expectations' theories of market behaviour (Chwieroth 2009: 79), which can obscure how elite anxieties and populist resentment shape political contests over alternate policy paradigms (Widmaier 2010). By taking a closer look at how micro-level political economies interact with and shape meso-level (mid-range) and macro-level processes in the global political economy, IPE scholars can expand the range of actors that are conceived as consequential for understanding how economies work, as well as how actions taken by non-elites within and across states can potentially exert a transformative influence over global processes.

The dynamic interplay between what elite actors want and what they are capable of doing as economic managers and the everyday actions of non-elites is particularly important in shaping how policy-makers respond to the build-up of economic pressures and resulting economic shocks, and how effective they are in doing so. Prior to the onset of global financial crisis, for instance, non-elite actors in several OECD economies responded to rapid increases in capital gains in residential property markets by taking on far greater levels of debt in order to avoid being excluded from the rising wealth effects of house price booms. This complicated the role of governments in guarding against the risk of property booms transforming into busts, by incentivizing them to continue to stoke overheated asset bubbles to reap electoral rewards (Seabrooke and Tsingou 2009: 459).

The interplay between elite and non-elite actors also shapes how policy-makers handle economic crises. This can be briefly illustrated by the example of the Northern Rock 'bank run' in the UK in September 2007. The run on Northern Rock by everyday savers (retail depositors) was the UK's first bank run since 1866. Textbook theories of bank runs assume that 'mutually reinforcing anxiety' among a bank's depositors will lead them to panic and to collectively withdraw their credit to the institution by cleaning out their accounts when there are widespread public expectations of financial insolvency, a scenario epitomized in films such as *It's a Wonderful Life*. Avoiding the problem of bank runs is one of the main motivations behind governments extending guarantees and establishing systems of insurance for retail deposits in different countries, such as the US Federal Deposit Insurance Corporation, which aim to guard against panic withdrawal of deposits when a bank faces solvency issues by protecting the interests of the bank's depositors. In the case of Northern Rock, however, a relatively small proportion of its funding came from retail deposits (23 per cent in 2007), with the rest sourced from a mix of long-term borrowing and short-term loans through capital markets (Shin 2009: 102). Northern Rock therefore faced a maturity mismatch problem that stemmed from using short-term debt through capital markets to fund long-term lending to expand its mortgage assets, which jeopardized the bank's balance sheet when short-term money markets and inter-bank lending seized up in August 2007.

The bank run by everyday savers who had deposited funds with Northern Rock did not cause the bank's cash flow problems, which resulted from systemic changes in market conditions and the bank's relatively greater reliance than other UK financial institutions on non-retail funding sources (Shin 2009: 104). However, the actions by everyday savers that led to the bank run provided a political impulse that informed the UK government's policy response to the emerging global financial crisis, and challenged the government's long-term focus on expanding a system of 'asset-based welfare' (Watson 2009: 50). In the aftermath of the Northern Rock bank run, the government's response to the global financial crisis shifted gradually from market-based solutions that were focused on encouraging bank mergers and takeovers to bank nationalization and the expansion of guarantees for retail deposits. Moreover, the Northern Rock bank run represented the single event that contributed most to destroying the UK Labour government's reputation for competent economic management (Gamble 2009a: 455–6), which set the scene for the Labour Party's subsequent loss at the 2010 general election after 13 years in power.

A further example of the everyday politics of economic crises can be found in how everyday actors shape processes of monetary integration and disintegration. Whether national currencies or currency unions are successful relies heavily on the everyday actions of non-elites, which are shaped by their 'beliefs about money and ideas about how monetary rules should be organized' (Broome 2009a: 6). When economies come under extreme stress during a crisis, everyday actors may challenge the legitimacy of monetary systems in ways that shape aggregate monetary outcomes. During the breakdown of the ruble zone among post-Soviet countries in the early 1990s, for example, everyday actors engaged in survival strategies in response to economic hardship produced by their rapidly changing material circumstances. These everyday actions contributed to processes of dollarization as foreign currencies were used to protect savings against hyperinflation, as well as leading to demonetization, a lack of trust in the banking system, and the growth of barter economies to secure essential household goods. Collectively, these actions provided some everyday actors with an informal safety net to mitigate economic hardship based on social strategies of reciprocity and circuits of mutual obligation, epitomized in the Russian proverb 'Better a hundred friends than a hundred rubles'. Yet everyday actions also undermined the capacity of policy-makers to achieve macroeconomic goals such as sustaining tax revenues, reversing demonetization, maintaining consumer demand and achieving price stability, at the same time as producing monetary conditions that encouraged damaging forms of inter-state rivalry via competitive credit creation (Broome 2009a).

As these examples of economic crises suggest, understanding the roles that everyday actors play in the dynamics that shape the global political economy requires a broad range of conceptual tools as well as analytic flexibility in order to interpret the complex relations that link different economic and political processes and categories of action. Non-elite actors do not simply respond passively to economic stimuli, nor should their interests and ideas in a given situation be assumed in advance based on theoretical constructs. Moreover, 'everyday actions do not have to "win" to be meaningful' (Hobson and Seabrooke 2007: 14). The agency exercised by everyday actors can have both productive effects and limiting effects on the legitimate exercise of public and private authority in the global political economy. Everyday non-elite actors do not only constrain what states and market actors can do, whether through open forms of contestation such as resistance and public protest, or subtle forms of non-compliance and hidden defiance expressed in everyday social and economic actions that alter the effects of government policies and economic rules. Rather, non-elites can also have a generative effect on the power of states and other actors, through expressing economic and social norms that enable governments to intervene in economic processes and construct the rules that govern how markets work by conferring legitimacy and public support on their actions.

Avenues for further research in everyday IPE include the everyday dynamics of policy change, the creation and expansion of alternative economic spaces, the political economy of housing and the household and how cultural norms shape the constitution of economic rationalities. In each of these areas an everyday IPE approach can help to overcome the ontological limits that serve as a brake on conceptual innovation within the main theoretical perspectives in IPE. For example, the emergence (or absence) of widespread societal pressures for radical policy reforms in the aftermath of the global financial crisis is linked to how non-elite actors rationalize or resist changes in the redistributive role of the state (Stanley 2014). By expanding how actors, action, structures and change are conceived in IPE, everyday approaches can help to push out the analytic and empirical boundaries of the field.

Summary

Studying the roles of everyday actors in IPE is not simply a matter of taking a microscope to examine the localized effects of global processes of change and structures that are assumed to be controlled by elite actors. Nor is everyday IPE an attempt to ontologically substitute the study of everyday actors and the political economy of everyday life for the study of elite actors and broader patterns and dynamics of historical change, such as the rise of global finance in the latter half of the twentieth century. Rather, the focus on everyday actors involves an effort to understand how the beliefs, behaviour and preferences of non-elite actors connect with 'big structures and large processes' in contingent circumstances

(Tilly 1989), and how micro-, meso- and macro-processes of change in the global political economy interact and evolve over time.

Discussion questions

1. How do different concepts of agency shape dynamics of change in the world economy?
2. How do the identities of everyday actors constitute limits/possibilities for economic policy?
3. How do everyday actions influence government responses to economic crises?
4. How did everyday actors' changing economic expectations shape the emergence of residential property bubbles prior to 2007?
5. Why does domestic legitimacy matter for states in an era of economic globalization?
6. What other issue areas in IPE could be enhanced by incorporating the role of everyday actors?

Further reading

Amoore, Louise. 2002. *Globalization Contested: An International Political Economy of Work*. Manchester: Manchester University Press.

Hobson, John M. and Leonard Seabrooke (eds). 2007. *Everyday Politics of the World Economy*. Cambridge: Cambridge University Press.

Langley, Paul. 2008. *The Everyday Life of Global Finance: Saving and Borrowing in Anglo-America*. Oxford: Oxford University Press.

Muñoz, Carolina Bank. 2008. *Transnational Tortillas: Race, Gender, and Shop-Floor Politics in Mexico and the United States*. Ithaca, NY: Cornell University Press.

Nevins, Joseph and Nancy Lee Peluso. 2008. *Taking Southeast Asia to Market: Commodities, Nature and People in the Neoliberal Age*. Ithaca, NY: Cornell University Press.

Seabrooke, Leonard. 2006. *The Social Sources of Financial Power: Domestic Legitimacy and International Financial Orders*. Ithaca, NY: Cornell University Press.

PART II

Issues in the Global Political Economy

Global Trade

Introduction

The establishment of a common set of global trade rules is widely believed to be an important driver of growth in economic output and trade flows between countries. This is based on the theory of comparative advantage, which refers to the ability of a country to produce a particular good or service relatively more efficiently than others. This chapter examines the actors responsible for making – and breaking – global trade rules, and provides an overview of how the system of global trade rules has evolved over time. This discussion is linked to the establishment of the GATT among capitalist market economies after World War II, which led to the establishment of the WTO nearly half a century later in 1995. The chapter provides an overview of the evolution of trade politics from serving primarily as an instrument of state power, grand strategy and foreign policy by many of the world's largest and most powerful economies to the legalization of trade rules at the global level, which today both augment state power and constrain it. Contemporary trade politics among the majority of the world's economies is conducted by diplomats and affiliated trade experts who are instructed by their governments to seek national advantages through common rules and formalized processes, rather than being driven by military imperatives, territorial expansion and colonial conquest. This chapter surveys these broad historical changes in trade politics, as well as discussing the prospects for the evolution of global trade rules in the twenty-first century.

Background

The economic history of the twentieth century is to a large extent a history of enormous increases in global trade flows. These sweeping economic processes have driven changes in the role of the state in managing and regulating domestic and international economic activity, as well as reconfiguring the nature of public authority and political responsiveness to domestic economic interests and social groups. Cross-border exchange of goods and services increased markedly in the twentieth century, and especially in the decades following World War II. As Figure 10.1 illustrates using indicative historical data from the United Nations Statistics Division, the value of world merchandise exports (trade in goods) was over 12 times greater in 1960 than in 1900, with the greatest increase occurring in the postwar era.

In the contemporary era, growth in global trade flows has constituted a key driver of economic globalization. Trade growth has been stimulated by greater economic openness and the reduction of trade tariffs among many of the world's major economies. From 1964 to 2010, world merchandise exports have increased substantially year-on-year in percentage terms, with very few exceptions such as notable dips in

Figure 10.1   *Growth in world merchandise exports, 1900–60*

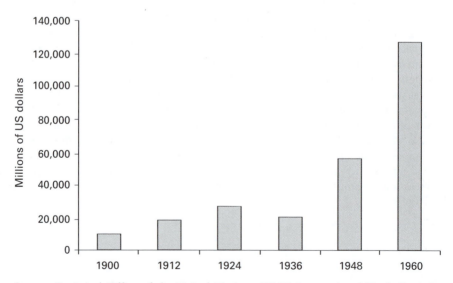

Source: Statistical Office of the United Nations (1962) *International Trade Statistics: 1900–1960*. New York: United Nations (http://unstats.un.org/unsd/trade/imts/Historical%20data%201900-1960.pdf).

Figure 10.2   *Growth in world merchandise exports, 1964–2010*

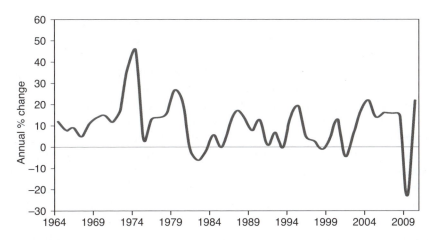

Source: World Trade Organization (2011) *International Trade Statistics 2011, Appendix: Historical Trends*. Geneva: WTO (http://www.wto.org/english/res_e/ statis_e/its2011_e/its11_appendix_e.pdf).

global merchandise trade during the oil price shocks and the breakdown of the Bretton Woods exchange rate system in the early 1970s, the early-1980s recession and debt crisis, the aftermath of the Asian financial crisis in 1997–98, and with the 2000 Dotcom crash and the terrorist attacks of 11 September 2001. The only time world trade in goods has shrunk sharply in the post-World War II era was during the global financial crisis of 2008–09, when trade in goods decreased globally by some 23 per cent in 2009 compared with 2008. Much of this was made up in 2010, when global trade in goods increased by a further 22 per cent (see Figure 10.2).

In broad terms, growth in global trade in goods has gone hand-in-hand with the greater legalization of global trade rules. After the end of World War II, the principles of the GATT gradually gained greater authority through successive rounds of trade negotiations. This led to the establishment of the WTO after the eighth round of multilateral trade negotiations through the GATT (the Uruguay Round) was concluded in 1994. Progressive legalization of international trade increased the stability of actors' expectations in how cross-border trade in goods and services are transacted, the procedures that govern how imports and exports are taxed and paid for, and the principles and rules that limit government support for domestic industries in relation to competition from foreign firms. The development of the postwar liberal multilateral trade system enabled the rapid growth of cross-border economic transactions, and served to integrate national markets for production and trade in goods and services.

The principle of free trade lies at the heart of the contemporary system of global trade rules in theory, if not always in practice. This has assumed a status within the field of the IPE equivalent to 'democratic peace theory' in IR. In its simplest form, democratic peace theory assumes that states with entrenched democratic political systems are less likely to engage in armed conflict with other democracies. As the IPE equivalent of a 'commercial peace theory', many proponents of global free trade argue countries which internationally integrate their manufacturing and service industries to increase trade with each other are less likely to go to war as a means to resolve international economic disputes. As economic links between countries expand and deepen through trade, so the theory goes, the likelihood of governments engaging in inter-state warfare is significantly reduced.

Under a liberal multilateral trade system, the prospect of armed conflict between states can entail high costs due to increased economic openness and interdependence. Businesses risk their access being blocked to critical imports for domestic consumption, or for components that will be re-exported as finished goods. Governments face economic costs in lost tax revenue and economic productivity, higher unemployment and the risk of reduced inward investment and increased capital outflows. Households may face supermarket shelves empty of many of their favourite products from abroad, or replaced with more expensive locally sourced substitute goods. In short, war is not good for (most) business (Kirshner 2007). To put this chestnut of contemporary IPE in historical context, rather than sending gunships to a country when inter-state economic relationships turn sour, as occurred at the start of the twentieth century, under a system of global trade rules states may instead take one another to 'court' through the WTO's dispute settlement process.

Every rule has its exceptions. When it comes to global trade rules, the WTO, despite its near-universal membership, has fewer member states than the IMF or the United Nations, while democratic states have continued to go to war with non-democracies they previously had significant trade links with. The use of economic coercion through trade sanctions also remains a common tool for powerful states to exercise leverage over weaker states in pursuit of foreign policy goals. This can entail devastating consequences for the domestic populations of those states that are the target of economic coercion, and can also prove highly costly to states that impose sanctions through lost export income (Drezner 2003: 643).

Trade, state power and the evolution of the multilateral trade system

The mid-nineteenth-century European free trade movement was centred on the role of Britain as a world economic power, as well as the 'civilizing mission' of the British Empire. This came to an end with the onset of trade protectionism during the Great Depression of the 1870s (Pigman 2006a; see Box 10.2). The global political economy of trade relations evolved in the century following World War I from mercantilist policies that were designed to boost the capacity of states to wage war, to the beggar-thy-neighbour protectionism that worsened many of the effects of the 1930s Great Depression, to the emergence of a voluntarist multilateral trade system after World War II under the GATT. In the middle of the 1990s the GATT principles became a more legalized framework with the establishment of the WTO (Mortensen 2012; Zangl 2008).

The route from mercantilist zero-sum trade policies to a more liberal multilateral trade system with firmer international legal obligations under the WTO has not been a smooth one. In the late 1940s, the US Senate failed to ratify the charter of the International Trade Organization (ITO), which was intended to be the third pillar of the postwar international economic order alongside the IMF and the World Bank. This resulted in the postwar multilateral trade framework being organized under the voluntarist GATT regime, rather than the more autonomous global umpire of international trade among capitalist market economies which had been envisaged as the ITO's role. The GATT was originally established in 1947 as a temporary bridge for establishing a multilateral trade framework until the ITO was fully established, and comprised a set of common trade principles that were designed to reduce trade restrictions between countries and to ensure that reductions in trade tariffs were not simply replaced with non-tariff barriers to trade (Simmons 2006).

The GATT enshrined the ideal of multilateralism at the heart of global trade relations through the most-favoured nation (MFN) principle. The MFN principle requires contracting parties to the GATT to extend any preferential treatment given to one country to all GATT signatories, in order to avoid the bilateral trade politics of the 1930s through eliminating discrimination in trade policies. Similar to the IMF's Article VIII rules (see Chapter 11), the principle of non-discrimination in the postwar multilateral trade system sought to defuse the potential for economic disputes between countries to escalate into armed conflict, or to result in beggar-thy-neighbour economic competition, by embedding the norm of multilateralism in states' macroeconomic policies.

Through successive rounds of GATT negotiations, from the Annecy Round (1949) to the Uruguay Round (1986–94), the number of

Figure 10.3   *G20 economy exports, 2011*

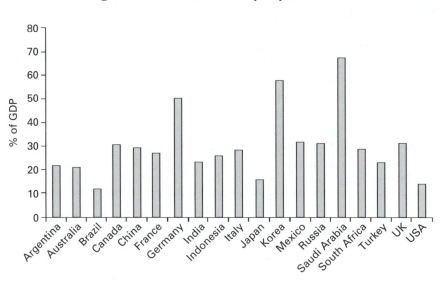

Source: UNCTADstat (www.unctadstat.unctad.org).

countries participating in GATT negotiations expanded from 13 to 123. GATT signatories reached agreements on trade liberalization through reductions in tariffs, controls on the spread of non-tariff barriers to trade and the expansion of market access through liberalizing trade in highly sensitive sectors such as agriculture. Since the establishment of the WTO in 1995 the organization's membership has expanded to 159 countries, while over two dozen countries are currently negotiating membership terms. In addition to maintaining a common set of trade rules and principles, the WTO has expanded the scope of its jurisdiction from merchandise trade to include other economic sectors such as trade in services and intellectual property rights (Mortensen 2012; May 2010).

In the globalized economy of the twenty-first century, states that are major exporters exercise a high degree of leverage on global trade rules through their influence over large domestic markets (Drezner 2007). At the same time, exporters also depend upon favourable global economic conditions to maintain demand for their products. As Figure 10.3 illustrates, some of the world's most successful exporters rely on trade for over half of their gross domestic product. For countries where non-resource exports make up a high proportion of GDP, such as Germany (51 per cent) and South Korea (58 per cent), national economic growth is tightly connected with the health of the world economy and the economic performance of their trading partners. One of the potential strengths of the US economy is that exports account for only 14 per cent

Figure 10.4 *World trade in goods and services, 2011*

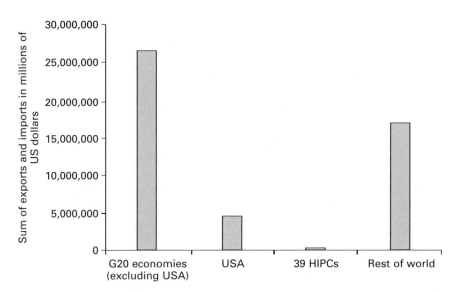

Source: UNCTADstat (www.unctadstat.unctad.org).

of GDP. This affords the USA a degree of insulation from volatility in global demand for its exports that is not available to many other large economies. At the same time, the US contribution to global trade remains high, with the combined sum of US exports and imports accounting for nearly 11 per cent of global trade flows in 2011. As Figure 10.4 makes clear, the USA maintains a pre-eminent position as a global trading power, and the G20 economies as a whole account for over 70 per cent of global exports and imports. In contrast, the combined imports and exports of the 39 HIPCs (see Chapter 14) account for less than 1 per cent of global trade.

Compared with the dominant position of G20 economies in global trade flows, many developing countries have struggled to influence the evolution of global trade rules and trade negotiations to their advantage. When developing countries have had some success in shaping processes of change in global trade rules, this has usually been associated with the formation of bargaining coalitions among developing countries to increase their collective leverage over trade negotiations through the GATT/WTO (Narlikar 2003). Among developing countries, small developing states in particular are often viewed as possessing only weak influence, if any, over the development of global trade rules that are typically assumed to constrain their policy autonomy to a far higher degree than larger economies. Such assumptions of weakness can mask the sources of state influence and the strategies through which even 'weak' actors can exercise leverage in the world economy (see Chapter 4). Small-state activism in the WTO, for example, has been identified as an important factor that has delayed the completion of the Doha 'Development' Round of WTO negotiations. Small states have augmented their low levels of influence and bargaining power through forming alliances with other small and middle power economies, notably in negotiations over liberalization in cotton trade (Lee and Smith 2008).

Contemporary challenges and sources of change

The expansion of the scope of the WTO's policy responsibilities across economic sectors has not gone unchallenged. In the aftermath of the apparent 'triumph' of economic liberalism with the end of the Cold War in the late 1980s and the post-communist 'transition' to market-based economies in the 1990s, the social legitimacy of the WTO came under sustained criticism in the late 1990s and 2000s from developing country policy-makers, journalists, trade unions and left-wing political parties and a diverse range of social activists. In 1999, the now infamous 'Battle in Seattle' saw the annual WTO Ministerial Conference disrupted and brought to a premature conclusion through direct action protests on-site and large-scale cooperation among a range of social groups that were fiercely critical of WTO rules and policies. Public protest and developing country activism gradually led to greater concessions to developing country interests. Meanwhile, subsequent WTO meetings have tended to geographically exclude the potential for public protests and have some-times involved heavy-handed police action by country hosts, further diminishing the legitimacy of the WTO in the eyes of many critics.

Public opposition to the WTO has sometimes been described as the 'alterglobalization' movement (Pigman 2006a). In particular, many left-wing social activists and community groups have criticized the WTO for entrenching iniquitous global trade relations and policy standards through the legalization of trade rules, which are seen to privilege the interests of larger developed economies over those of emerging, develop-ing and low-income economies. The WTO has also been criticized for protecting the interests of wealthy elites over the interests of non-elite actors in both developing and developed countries, such as workers in local industries. The fair trade movement (see Box 10.1) has strongly crit-icized WTO rules for privileging free trade principles to the detriment of fairness in trade relations between countries.

Commentators, activists and politicians on the right of the political spectrum have criticized the WTO for imposing external constraints on

Box 10.1 Free trade versus fair trade

Free trade is defined as the absence of government restrictions on either the price or supply of imported and exported goods. Countries which operate few restrictions on trade in most goods and services usually maintain some forms of trade restrictions, most notably on trade in agriculture, but also on trade in defence products.

The 'fair trade' social movement aims to use market-based processes to improve trade conditions and economic sustainability for producers in developing countries. Fair trade can be defined as: 'a trading partnership, based on dialogue, transparency and respect, that seeks greater equity in international trade. It contributes to sustainable development by offering better trading conditions to, and securing the rights of, marginalized producers and workers – especially in the South. Fair Trade organisations (backed by consumers) are engaged actively in supporting producers, awareness raising and in campaigning for changes in the rules and practice of conventional international trade' (European Fair Trade Association 2006).

the sovereign responsibilities of national governments. In this respect, the success of the WTO in legalizing global trade rules has come at a significant cost in terms of the perceived public legitimacy of its role in the global political economy. IPE scholars have criticized WTO policies on each of these fronts, as well as on the grounds that the organization serves to constrain economic strategies that are crucial for kick-starting development in poorer economies, while granting industrialized economies the space to pursue state sponsorship of high-value technology-intensive industries and partnerships with private sector actors (Weiss 2005).

Contemporary challenges for the future of global trade rules include the rise of emerging market economies – notably China and India. China's entry to the WTO in 2001 has been associated with a rapid expansion of China's trade surplus with the USA, as well as far higher levels of US investment in China (Zeng and Liang 2010). As Figure 10.5 illustrates, the USA has benefited from China's entry into the WTO's system of global trade rules, with US goods exported to China increasing by a factor of six from 2000 to 2011. China's exports to the USA have increased fourfold from approximately US$100 billion in 2000 to nearly US$400 billion in 2011. Representing a US trade deficit with China to the tune of nearly US$300 billion in 2011, the imbalance of trade between the two economies has become one of the most charged issues in global trade politics. This has given rise to substantial economic tensions between the two countries, with US policy-makers accusing China of

Figure 10.5   *US–China trade in goods, 2000–11*

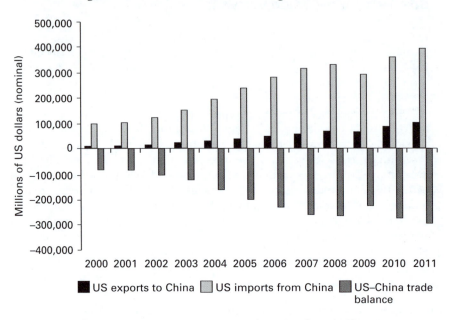

Source: United States Census Bureau (2012) *Trade in Goods with China* (www.census. gov/foreign-trade/balance/c5700.html).

unfair trade practices and currency manipulation to artificially boost its exports to the USA. Countries such as China and India are not yet able to call the shots over developed economies in global trade negotiations. However, their rapidly increasing importance to global trade flows and growing economic muscle have gained India and China greater leverage to veto changes to trade rules that do not match their interests (Narlikar 2007).

In addition to the substantial criticism the organization has attracted for promoting trade liberalization, since its establishment the WTO has struggled to achieve the degree of consensus on new multilateral trade negotiations that was painstakingly achieved with earlier rounds of negotiations under the GATT. This is in part due to the larger number of member states involved in WTO negotiations – which can be expected to make reaching consensus more challenging in any international organization – as well as WTO processes that formally rely on a one-state, one-vote principle (unlike the weighted-voting systems of the IMF and the World Bank, see Chapter 5). This enables weaker economies to cooperate through bargaining coalitions to alter, block, or slow down the pace of new initiatives. For example, the heavily criticized Doha 'Development' Round of WTO negotiations, which began two months

Box 10.2   The politics of trade protectionism

Trade protectionism is an economic policy of regulating or restraining cross-border trade to protect domestic firms and workers from foreign competition. Protectionist policies can include trade taxes, trade subsidies and supply restrictions. In addition to percentage taxes levied on imports (tariffs), direct fiscal transfers to domestic producers and import quotas, protectionist policies include non-tariff barriers to trade such as import quotas and licences, as well as product and safety standards, rules of origin, import bans, intellectual property laws and 'buy national' policies. Protectionist policies can also include indirect support for domestic producers through multiple exchange rate practices or other forms of exchange rate manipulation (see Chapter 11).

Example 1: Trade policies and political support for a government are sometimes closely connected. In March 2002, the George W. Bush administration in the USA introduced temporary steel tariffs of 8–30 per cent to protect the US steel industry from a perceived increase in steel imports which had been associated with a number of steel-makers declaring bankruptcy. Many observers viewed this trade policy as an attempt to gain electoral support from the 'Rust Belt' states of Pennsylvania and West Virginia in the 2004 US presidential election. Despite the WTO's DSB ruling against the legality of the steel tariffs, the Bush administration initially committed itself to maintaining them, which led the European Union to threaten retaliatory tariffs on US imports such as oranges and cars that were designed to hurt the President's electoral support in key states (including Florida and Michigan). In response to the threat of retaliatory tariffs, the George W. Bush administration removed the temporary steel tariffs in December 2003 (Zangl 2008: 837–8).

Example 2: In a contrasting example of the politics of trade protectionism, the government of Uzbekistan under President Islam Karimov introduced a multiple exchange rates regime by decree in January 1997, which redistributed foreign exchange earnings from cotton exports to importers of basic food goods, raw materials and capital goods through a preferential rate of foreign exchange for an approved list of importers. These foreign exchange measures, which were accompanied by a tightening of trade tariffs, aimed at strengthening the government's legitimacy through ensuring the cost of essential household goods remained low, while simultaneously shoring up a patronage system that enabled political and economic elites to extract rents from the banking system and from foreign exchange earnings. While the Uzbek government formally abandoned the multiple exchange rates regime in 2003, IMF estimates from 2000 put the total net transfer of financial resources from exporters to importers through the government's trade and exchange rate policies as equalling 16 per cent of GDP (Broome 2010a: 175–7).

after the terrorist attacks in the USA in September 2001, has repeatedly stalled, with negotiations deadlocked over agricultural trade issues in particular. More than 12 years after talks commenced, the Doha Round shows little sign of moving to a successful conclusion in the near future. In the absence of success in negotiating a new multilateral trade agreement, many WTO members have moved instead to negotiate bilateral or multi-party free trade agreements to secure common rules and market access for trade with key economic partners.

A further challenge for the contemporary multilateral trade regime is the growth of illicit trade flows. Among other things, this includes the illegal trade in drugs, environmental resource crimes such as illegal logging and trade in endangered species, trade in 'blood diamonds' and human trafficking (see Chapter 17; Andreas and Greenhill 2010; Quirk

---

Box 10.3   Selected actors in the multilateral trade system

- **Everyday actors**
  Through their consumption choices everyday actors influence trade links between countries as well as the corporate reputations of major firms engaged in global trade, such as preferences for fair trade products, locally produced products, or global consumer brands. In both democratic and undemocratic states, political leaders may use changes in trade policy to gain electoral or public support from particular segments of the population, usually through protecting domestic industries and workers from foreign competition.

- **International organizations**
  The WTO is the main organization charged with responsibility for upholding the current rules of the multilateral trade system. Through its DSB, the WTO has played a major role in the evolution of legal precedents to decide disputes between member states, and is able to authorize the use of retaliatory trade measures by successful complainants against countries that have lost a DSB case, in order to induce compliance with its rulings.

- **Market actors**
  Large domestic and multinational firms and producer associations can exert a high degree of leverage over a government's trade policies through corporate lobbying, as well as the potential threat to 'exit' a country when policies are deemed unfavourable to business. Firm influence over global trade rules may be aimed at gaining greater protection for domestic industries to compete with foreign competition, or may be targeted at greater trade liberalization to gain new market access abroad.   ➡

2011). Illicit international trade consists of trade in goods and services 'that are criminalized by states in importing or exporting countries' (Friman and Andreas 1999). Illicit cross-border economic transactions have emerged as a critical issue for IPE scholarship, while the 'globalization of crime' has also gained increased attention from IOs such as the UN (UNODC 2010). Although many observers have pointed to 'illicit globalization' as further proof that states are losing control of cross-border economic activities, illicit trade and capital flows have long formed an integral part of the global political economy. In some cases, states have either tolerated or have been complicit in the growth of illicit economic flows. In this respect, 'States are not simply being pushed aside by the globalization of illicit markets but are essential to their creation and perpetuation' (Andreas 2011: 423).

→

- **Non-governmental organizations**
  NGOs, including trade unions, advocacy networks such as Eurodad, non-state aid providers and development organizations, and international coalitions such as Jubilee 2000 have played an important role in public campaigns to shift the agenda in global trade negotiations towards the interests of poorer and developing countries through promoting pro-poor and sustainable development policies in trade.

- **Regional institutions**
  The European Union negotiates 'with a single voice' in WTO negotiations, while numerous regional bodies such as the Asia-Pacific Economic Cooperation forum, the Caribbean Community, the Pacific Alliance and the Union of South American Nations seek to foster regional economic interdependence through the promotion of free trade and economic cooperation between member states.

- **States**
  States are an importance source of change in the multilateral trade system, where leverage in global trade negotiations is commonly seen as being tilted towards the world's largest economies, such as the G20.

- **Trade ministries**
  Trade ministries and foreign diplomats commonly engage in economic diplomacy as 'trade ambassadors' to gain access to new markets for exports, facilitate trade partnerships, negotiate bilateral and multilateral trade agreements and maximize the benefits of state support for trade such as export credit and insurance.

In the process of making and breaking global trade rules states are key actors but they are not the only relevant players, nor are they always the most decisive ones. As Box 10.3 indicates a range of other actors either directly or indirectly shape global trade flows and the evolution of the rules governing the multilateral trade system, including firms, everyday actors, regional institutions and the WTO itself. While trade politics among developed economies is still heavily influenced by the maintenance and expansion of state power, the global trade rules that have evolved throughout the twentieth century and early twenty-first century have constituted a multilateral trade system that is not solely subject to the changing interests and political priorities of individual states.

One measure of the role of the WTO in restraining state actions when it comes to trade policies is how readily governments resort to trade protectionism in a global economic crisis. Despite the global financial crisis of 2008–09 representing the most damaging global economic disaster since the Great Depression of the 1930s, and notwithstanding WTO concerns about the rise of protectionist measures (WTO 2011b), the introduction of new trade protections and restrictions has not come close to the types of policies that sparked trade and currency wars between national economies in the decade preceding the onset of World War II. This indicates the importance of the WTO's role in restraining states' 'room to move' on trade policy and helping to maintain the benefits of cross-border economic exchange, as well as providing a legal channel for resolving international economic disputes without applying unsanctioned forms of bilateral economic coercion.

Summary

Understanding how the global political economy of trade has evolved is an important issue area within the study of contemporary IPE. In addition to being a speciality subject area in its own right, global trade is intimately connected to currency and exchange rate practices, the use of state power to gain national advantages in the world economy, a country's broader foreign policy agenda, revenue-raising and fiscal transfers, as well as issues of global economic justice. Trade politics is not a rarefied focus of study that centres solely on legal precedents and the small print of multilateral trade agreements. It revolves instead around the changing role of the state as an economic manager, how strong(er) and weak(er) states balance their interests and form alliances in the global political economy, and how governments strive to build or sustain social legitimacy for their rule. By taking into account the broad range of related issues that trade politics touches upon, and how those issues in turn may inform a government's trade policies, students can better understand the complexity of global trade relations in an era of economic globalization. In doing so, it is not enough to ask the question of whether 'free' trade is simply good or bad across the board, or whether the WTO benefits developed countries as a group and constrains the policy space of developing countries. The more challenging questions for IPE students to tackle centre on understanding who benefits from different choices for national trade policies and global trade rules, how they benefit and what the key sources of change are in global trade in the twenty-first century.

Discussion questions

1. Who are the winners and losers from a liberal multilateral trade system?
2. In what ways do different sets of actors gain and lose from the current system, and why?
3. How can developing economies exercise agency within the constraints of global trade rules?
4. How might existing global trade rules be reformed, and for whose benefit?
5. What factors will shape the future evolution of the multilateral trade system?
6. How does the behaviour of everyday actors shape trade policies and politics?

Further reading

Drahos, Peter and Ruth Mayne (eds). 2002. *Global Intellectual Property Rights: Knowledge Access and Development*. Basingstoke: Palgrave Macmillan.

Eagleton-Pierce, Matthew. 2012. *Symbolic Power in the World Trade Organization*. Oxford: Oxford University Press.

Hoekman, Bernard M. and Petros C. Mavroidis. 2007. *World Trade Organization: Law, Economics, and Politics*. London: Routledge.

Lee, Donna and Rorden Wilkinson (eds). 2007. *The WTO after Hong Kong: Progress in, and Prospects for, the Doha Development Agenda*. London: Routledge.

Narlikar, Amrita. 2003. *International Trade and Developing Countries: Bargaining Coalitions in the GATT and WTO*. London: Routledge.

Odell, John S. 2000. *Negotiating the World Economy*. Ithaca, NY: Cornell University Press.

Chapter 11

Global Money and National Currencies

Introduction

The role of money in a given society – and the effectiveness of a government's monetary policy tools – rests upon a general acceptance that the nominal value of a currency can readily be exchanged for material goods and services, both now and in the future. Key international currencies such as the US dollar bestow enormous political and economic benefits on the issuing state, while the structure of the international monetary system both shapes and is shaped by how different countries organize and govern their currencies. Currency exchange rates are one of the most important mechanisms through which broader changes in the global economic weather are transmitted between countries. Monetary integration between countries constrains the policy autonomy of participating states, and can dramatically increase the domestic costs of adjustment during episodes of economic crisis. This chapter examines the evolution of the international monetary system, focusing on how states exercise monetary power in the global political economy as well as the domestic politics of money. This discussion is linked to the emergence of global monetary norms such as current account convertibility after World War II, which set the scene for growth in global trade flows and subsequent moves towards greater capital freedom. The chapter provides an overview of the transition during the twentieth century from the Gold Standard, to the Gold–Dollar Standard, to the post-Bretton Woods 'Information Standard', and discusses the potential future development of the international monetary system in the twenty-first century.

Background

Money is a fundamental element of all modern economic activity for households, small businesses, states, transnational firms and a host of other actors. It functions as a medium of exchange for purchases, a unit of account for measuring value and a store of value for savings. For currencies which enjoy high levels of stability among domestic populations, the value of banknotes used at a local supermarket or personal savings in a bank account is often treated as a 'real' and concrete stock of wealth. Despite its critical importance in most societies today, however, money is not an objective fact of the global political economy. Money is, rather, a socially constructed fact of economic life, and the value of any currency depends on the beliefs and perceptions different actors share about it (ranging from everyday consumers to governments to currency traders), and the deliberate actions they take on the basis of these beliefs and perceptions. As a consequence, issues relating to the value and governance of money 'are *always* and *everywhere political*' (Kirshner 2003: 3, emphasis original).

With the notable exception of monetary unions such as the Eurozone, currencies are often presumed to correspond with national territories – what Cohen (1998: 1) refers to as the 'One Nation/One Money myth' – whether the currency in question is the British pound, the Chinese renmimbi, the Mexican peso, or the US dollar. However, the use of individual national currencies is seldom limited to the geographical territory of the countries that issue them. Many small states and self-governing territories officially use national currencies controlled by other states, such as the South African rand (used in Lesotho, Namibia and Swaziland), the Australian dollar (used in Kiribati, Nauru and Tuvalu) and the New Zealand dollar (used in the Cook Islands, Niue, Pitcairn Islands and Tokelau).

In other cases, one country's currency can be legally accepted as a means of payment in territories or regions that also use their own banknotes branded with different names and local symbols of identity, such as the Danish krone in the Faroe Islands and Greenland, or Bank of England notes in Scotland and Northern Ireland. The US dollar is used in a large number of territories as the official currency – and is often used unofficially in national territories where the local currency is unstable, lacks credibility, or is subject to stringent currency controls (such as the use of the US dollar in Zimbabwe prior to the abandonment of the Zimbabwean dollar in January 2009). In the everyday use of money for buying and selling, accounting and saving, individual currencies are not strictly limited to the geographical territory or the administrative jurisdiction of the issuing state.

In addition to the everyday use of one country's money by non-residents, the international status of a currency potentially bestows enormous economic and political benefits on the issuing state, and can provide an important source of state power in the global political economy. International monetary power is the ability of a state to manipulate international monetary relations in order to influence the preferences or actions of other states. Jonathan Kirshner (1995: 8) has defined three primary ways in which states may exercise international monetary power. These include: (1) manipulating the exchange rate value of their currency; (2) exploiting the dependence of other, more vulnerable countries on monetary conditions in the home state; and (3) deliberately disrupting the workings of the international monetary system (or threatening systemic disruption). How monetary arrangements in a particular country are governed can enhance the capacity of a state to influence domestic economic activity and shape the behaviour of actors such as firms, households, trade unions, commercial banks and others, as well as potentially enabling a state to exercise international monetary power over other countries.

Money therefore connects a state's role as an economic manager both to its own population and to the world economy. The price at which one country's currency is exchanged into another's – the exchange rate – is of crucial importance for the strength of the domestic economy and the welfare of a country's population, and ties the fortunes of national economies to broader changes in conditions in the world economy. Among other things, the rate at which one currency is exchanged for others impacts upon a country's international trade, the level of FDI, the servicing of public and private debt denominated in foreign currencies and the rate of inflation, as well as the overall balance of payments position. The cost of personal debt such as a foreign currency mortgage can skyrocket if the national currency depreciates against the currency in which the mortgage is denominated (or if the foreign interest rate rises above local interest rates). Conversely, a country's exports may become more competitive with the depreciation of the national currency. Upward or downward shifts in a country's exchange rate create both domestic winners and losers, and may be either advantageous or disadvantageous for national economic performance.

The evolution of the international monetary system

The international monetary system has evolved in tandem with the evolution of national currencies and exchange rate regimes. Defined as a set of common rules, principles and norms for making international payments across territorial borders, three different international monetary systems have been in operation during the last century: the Gold Standard; the Gold–Dollar Standard; and the contemporary market-based system of floating exchange rates, which is sometimes described as an 'Information Standard'. During the operation of each of these international monetary systems, the 'rules of the game' governing monetary relations between countries both shaped, and in turn were shaped by, the domestic politics of money and the economic role of the state in different societies.

The 'Gold Standard' was in place from the 1870s until World War I, and was briefly re-established in a modified form as the 'Gold Exchange Standard' from the mid-1920s until the mid-1930s. Under the Gold Standard key states such as Britain, France and Germany maintained the convertibility of their currencies at a fixed price in gold in the absence of controls on capital movements, with liquidity maintained by cooperation between central banks via loans and gold shipments (Oliver 2006: 109). The Gold Standard operated in theory, if not always in practice, as a self-regulating international monetary system. Embodying the ideas of economic liberalism, trade deficits under the Gold Standard were dealt with through domestic deflation and tighter monetary conditions rather than counteracted or mitigated through policy activism, which often imposed severe social and economic costs on domestic populations. The Gold Exchange Standard that was resurrected during the 1920s proved short-lived in large part because of changing political dynamics driven by new beliefs about the role of the state as an economic manager among social movements and the mass public in major economies (Seabrooke 2007: 803–4). The Gold Exchange Standard fell apart in the face of the high unemployment, the retreat from an open international economic order into closed currency and trade blocs and the nationalist politics generated by the global economic crisis of the Great Depression in the 1930s. From the searing experience of the failure of the Gold Standard and the inadequacy of orthodox responses to the economic challenges of the 1930s, policy-makers in leading states drew a series of lessons about domestic and international economic management that informed subsequent negotiations on a new postwar international economic order during World War II.

Following the political and economic chaos associated with the breakdown of the interwar Gold Standard in the 1930s and the Great Depression, a new international monetary system was created at the end of World War II with the 1944 Bretton Woods agreement, which included the establishment of the IMF and the World Bank (see Chapter 5). In stark contrast to the earlier Gold Standard, the Bretton Woods system incorporated international acceptance of national controls on capital flows, while maintaining the commitment to an open international trade system (Helleiner 1994: 25). The IMF was established as the formal institutional linchpin of the new international monetary system, in contrast to informal cooperation between national central banks under the Gold Standard. It was charged with fostering policy coordination and multilateral decision-making over currency relations between member states. While many countries did not join the IMF immediately following its creation – including centrally planned economies, most of which refused to join the IMF during the Cold War (Broome 2010a: 58) – membership quickly became standard for market economies in the aftermath of World War II.

Because it combined a liberal international economic order in trade and monetary relations with national capital controls to create space for domestic policy autonomy and the development of welfare states, the Bretton Woods system has been described by Ruggie (1982: 393) as the 'compromise of embedded liberalism'. There were three principal components of the Bretton Woods system. First, a legal commitment among member states to maintain fixed but adjustable 'par value' exchange rates, with the exchange rate of the US dollar fixed at $35 per ounce of gold and other countries fixing their exchange rates to the dollar. Second, the use of capital controls to mitigate currency speculation and harmful capital flows; and, third, the establishment of current account convertibility. Current account convertibility involves the liberalization of access to foreign exchange to pay for trade in goods and services, overseas travel and interest and dividend payments. Unlike the Gold Standard, international liquidity under the 'Gold–Dollar Standard' of the Bretton Woods system was to be maintained by states acting in cooperation with the IMF. Of these three main components of the system, the establishment of current account convertibility took far longer to achieve than was originally envisaged at the Bretton Woods conference, with Western European economies establishing dollar convertibility in the late 1950s and Japan restoring current account convertibility in 1964 (Helleiner 1994: 71, 75). As a consequence, the Bretton Woods system was only fully operational for roughly a decade from the late 1950s to the late 1960s, although the period from 1945 to 1971 is generally referred to as the 'Bretton Woods era'.

With the restoration of convertibility in most major economies from the late 1950s, the rapid growth of the 'Euromarkets' served to expand the international money supply and increased pressure on the system of fixed exchange rates (Seabrooke 2001: 61–6). The term 'Euromarkets' does not refer to either Europe or the euro currency. Rather, it refers to 'offshore' currency markets that enable currency transactions which are free from domestic interest rate regulations and other capital controls.

Because states had become reluctant to adhere to the spirit of the Bretton Woods system through making periodic adjustments in their par value exchange rates (in the expectation this would contribute to a loss of confidence in their currency), necessary exchange rate adjustments were often postponed, which allowed speculators to bet against 'overvalued' currencies through the Euromarkets while evading capital controls. Following substantial capital outflows from the USA during 1970 and 1971, radical economic measures were announced by US President Richard Nixon in August 1971. The 'Nixon Shocks' suspended the convertibility of the dollar into gold and imposed a 90-day wage, rent and price freeze as well as a 10 per cent import surcharge. These events effectively brought the Bretton Woods system to an end (Gowa 1983: 149–50).

With the demise of the Bretton Woods international monetary system, many states moved towards 'floating' market-determined exchange rates, which Harold James (1996: 612) has described as constituting a new Information Standard based on knowledge to replace the Gold–Dollar Standard of the Bretton Woods era. However, the contemporary international monetary system is characterized by a wide variety of national exchange rate regimes. As Table 11.1 illustrates, these range from 'floating' regimes, without an explicit target zone for central bank intervention in the value of the exchange rate, to 'intermediate' regimes, with an explicit target zone for the exchange value of a currency, to an institutional commitment to maintain a fixed or 'pegged' rate (such as currency boards, monetary unions and official dollarization).

An exchange rate regime is the institutional architecture and rules that govern how a currency is exchanged for foreign currencies. The choice of exchange rate regime in the contemporary era has an important influence on a country's macroeconomic performance by influencing trade patterns, the rate of inflation, domestic consumption, susceptibility to exogenous shocks and currency crises, as well as the ease with which an economy adjusts to changes to global economic conditions. In particular, the choice of exchange rate regime serves to shape actors' expectations regarding future inflation rates and economic stability. For example, pegged exchange rate regimes provide a nominal 'anchor' for inflationary expectations by reducing economic uncertainty, while both pegged and intermediate regimes contribute to trade integration through mitigating actors' expectations of 'currency risk' (whereby profits from imports or exports can quickly be eroded by exchange rate volatility). In contrast, floating exchange rate regimes are considered to be less susceptible to currency crises than pegged or intermediate regimes, due to their greater flexibility in enabling the domestic economy to adjust to changes in external economic conditions (Ghosh *et al.* 2010: 3).

Table 11.1   *Varieties of exchange rate regimes*

Pegged regimes	Intermediate regimes	Floating regimes
Hard pegs	Basket pegs Pegged within bands	
Conventional pegs	Floats with rule-based intervention Floats with discretionary intervention	Independent floats

Source: Ghosh *et al.* (2010: 38).

Individual exchange rate regimes can also be classified according to either the *de jure* regime in place (based on the officially declared system) or how the *de facto* regime operates in practice (based on an assessment of the actions of the central bank and exchange rate developments). These two forms of classification can cause countries' exchange rate regimes to be defined under different categories. As Figure 11.1 shows, most of the world's exchange rate regimes during the period from 2000 to 2007 were either pegged or intermediate regimes, regardless of whether a *de jure* or *de facto* classification is used. The evolution of the international monetary system from the Gold Standard to the postwar Gold–Dollar Standard to the post-Bretton Woods Information Standard can be understood in broad terms as a shift from a widespread belief in market solutions to foster stable international monetary relations in the late nineteenth and early twentieth centuries, to a preference for multilateral solutions (underwritten by US power) during the postwar era until the 1970s, to a hybrid system of market–state solutions from the early 1970s onwards. The development of the contemporary hybrid system has been based on increasing financial market discipline, combined with the reassertion of state control over monetary relations and exchange rate decisions. This has taken place within a multilateral system that is aimed at increasing transparency and greater exchange of economic information.

Following the demise of the Bretton Woods system, the global monetary role of the IMF has changed considerably from its original mandate as a multilateral forum to oversee and approve adjustments in the par value of member states' exchange rates. This had established a formal constraint on states' domestic policies by committing governments to maintaining a fixed exchange rate (James 1996: 588). In its place, the IMF gradually assumed a much weaker policy surveillance function that was sanctioned by an IMF Executive Board decision on surveillance

Figure 11.1 *Classification of exchange rate regimes, 2000–07*

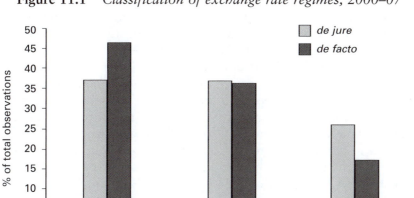

Source: Ghosh *et al*. (2010: 38).

principles in 1977 and the second amendment to the organization's founding charter – the Articles of Agreement – which became effective in 1978. Apart from emergency balance of payments lending, the IMF's primary role in the post-Bretton Woods international monetary system has been to encourage voluntary policy coordination among its member states through regular policy surveillance and consultations. Multilateral surveillance through the IMF is 'based on the principle that states are *accountable* to one another for the external implications of their internal policy decisions' (Pauly 1997: 141, emphasis original). States are therefore still expected to take the IMF's surveillance responsibilities seriously, but they are not formally bound to accept its policy advice in practice.

Contemporary challenges and sources of change

During the nineteenth and twentieth centuries the establishment of exclusive and more homogeneous national currencies became intricately tied to national sovereignty and the emergence of nation-states (Gilbert and Helleiner 1999: 5). The historical evolution of the politics of money is therefore linked to the capacity of states to exercise monetary power within and beyond their territorial borders, as well as the domestic, regional and global distributional consequences of alternative ways of regulating national money and foreign exchange. Today, much of the contemporary debate in IPE is focused on two main issues with respect to international monetary relations: (1) whether a shift away from independent national currencies towards monetary integration is inevitable in an era of financial globalization; and (2) the changing dynamics of currency competition among the world's leading economies.

The two most significant developments in international monetary relations in recent years have been the trend in many countries towards greater monetary integration and the challenge to the US dollar as the world's key international currency. The EU established the Eurozone monetary union in cash currency from 2002, with the euro previously launched in non-physical form from 1999 for banking and electronic transfers. This replaced the national currencies of participating EU member states with a new single currency. The countries now in the Eurozone comprise the initial group of 12 members that includes Austria, Belgium, Finland, France, Germany, Greece, Ireland, Luxembourg, the Netherlands, Italy, Portugal and Spain, with Slovenia joining in 2007, Cyprus and Malta in 2008, Slovakia in 2009 and Estonia in 2011. These 17 countries have made the political decision to relinquish their national monetary autonomy (which was already rather limited in several cases) in favour of the potential benefits to be gained from a common currency. Other examples of contemporary monetary unions outside developed industrial economies include the CFA Franc Zone in West Africa and Central Africa and the Multilateral Monetary Area in Southern Africa.

Based on the theory of 'optimum currency areas' (Mundell 1961), achieving monetary integration through the creation of a monetary union can provide a range of important benefits for national economies. Potential advantages can include greater trade integration, lower currency risk, cheaper external credit, higher rates of foreign investment and lower rates of inflation. More broadly, common currencies can help to stabilize actors' expectations about future economic developments, thereby reducing uncertainty and fostering a more secure environment for both personal and corporate economic decision-making. Monetary integration also comes with a serious potential downside (see Box 11.1): that is, less room for individual states to manoeuvre in the event of an economic crisis, such as the recent case of Greece. This requires core states to stand ready to shoulder a heavy burden in terms of the political and economic costs that may be necessary for sustaining monetary integration in the long term. '

A key currency is the preferred monetary unit used internationally for the purposes of global exchange, accounting and savings. As Benjamin Cohen (1998: 60) suggests, 'currency hegemony is a privilege of the few'. The US dollar, the dominant international currency since the end of World War II, has afforded US policy-makers the capacity to exercise a

---

Box 11.1   The costs of monetary disintegration

The Eurozone sovereign debt crisis that followed the global financial crisis of 2008–09 illustrates the need for political will and the commitment of significant economic resources to fund transfers between member states if a monetary union is to survive. As a core Eurozone state, Germany initially contributed €22.4 billion to a three-year financial rescue plan for Greece, and assumed a commitment for nearly €120 billion in guarantees for bonds that could be issued by the new European Financial Stability Facility (now managed by the European Stability Mechanism) to extend emergency loans to other Eurozone countries in severe economic distress. In contrast, the example of the breakdown of the rublezone during 1992–93 demonstrates the enormous social, political and economic costs involved when core states (in this case post-Soviet Russia) are not willing to fully commit to maintaining monetary integration. When common currencies fail, the economic costs can include rapid *demonetization* if everyday actors shift to conducting economic transactions via barter rather than using money as a medium of exchange, *dollarization* as people resort to using other 'hard' currencies with a more stable value, *hyperinflation* when prices for basic goods and services change rapidly on a daily (or hourly) basis, a rapid increase in *unemployment* as consumer demand weakens and the banking system freezes up, as well as ballooning private and public *debt* if households and firms lack the capacity to make repayments or deliberately refuse to do so and governments' tax revenues fall. Such dire economic conditions can also cause widespread civil unrest, rapid increases in poverty rates and a sharp decline in political legitimacy (Broome 2009a).

---

systemic influence over international monetary relations. While the official link between the US dollar and gold that was at the centre of the Bretton Woods system has not been re-established since the system broke down in the early 1970s, during the last four decades the dollar has continued to play the role of the world's key currency for trade and foreign exchange transactions, official foreign exchange reserves, international bank deposits and debt securities and as an 'anchor' for countries with pegged or intermediate exchange rate regimes (Helleiner 2009: 356). The pre-eminent role of the dollar in the world economy creates unique political and economic benefits for the USA. On the one hand, the need for other states to hold dollars as foreign exchange reserves provides strong incentives for central banks to buy US government debt, thereby lowering US interest rates. On the other hand, the USA is in a privileged position with its ability to exercise international monetary power through currency manipulation, the dependence of the rest of the world's economies on changes in US monetary conditions and the ability

Figure 11.2   *Top five countries with a US trade surplus, 2000–09*

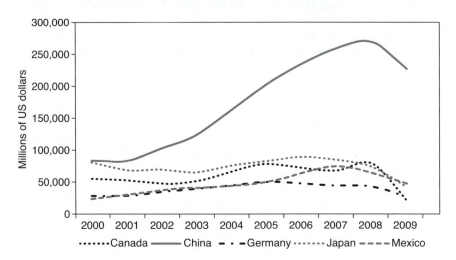

Source: US Census Bureau, Foreign Trade Statistics, various years (www.census.gov).

of the USA to disrupt the international monetary system (as US President Richard Nixon did in 1971).

Recent developments have raised doubts about the future role of the dollar as the world's key currency. Increasing global trade imbalances in the last decade have led to growing interdependence between the USA, as the world's greatest debtor, and its creditors. Especially significant is the changing relationship between the USA and emerging market economies such as China, which has rapidly increased its trade surplus with the USA from approximately US$84 billion in 2000 to US$227 billion in 2009 (see Figure 11.2). In addition to increasing trade imbalances, observers have pointed to the growing international status of the euro as presenting a major challenge to the future role of the dollar as the key international currency.

Despite the global importance of the Eurozone, there is little available evidence that suggests that the dollar will be rapidly supplanted by the euro as the world's primary currency for global exchange, accounting purposes and as a store of value any time soon. While the euro exhibits some of the features of a key currency given the size of the Eurozone's internal market, the euro also currently lacks the distinct social and political conditions that are deemed to be essential for the emergence of a new key international currency (Helleiner 2008a; McNamara 2008), with the EU as yet unable to exercise much geopolitical clout to rival the USA. Furthermore, financial market reactions to events that have threatened to worsen global macroeconomic stability – including the downgrading of the US credit rating by Standard & Poor's in 2011 – strengthened the value of the dollar rather than weakening it (Eichengreen 2012: 180–1). As Figures 11.3 and 11.4 illustrate, the dollar continues to dominate in the currency composition of foreign exchange transactions and official exchange reserves. The 2010 Triennial Central Bank Survey compiled by the Bank for International Settlements suggests the dollar was used on one side of between 85 and 90 per cent of all foreign exchange transactions throughout the last decade, while data on international reserves reported to the IMF shows that it remains far ahead of the euro as the reserve currency of choice for the world's central banks.

While the dollar is likely to continue to function as the key international currency for the foreseeable future, persistent US trade deficits – and China's growing trade surplus with the USA in particular – may lead to a new era of increasing tensions in international monetary relations, both in the short and the longer term. One example of rising tensions in international monetary relations was the push by the USA in 2007 to change the IMF's rules on its exchange rate surveillance. This was intended to harden the definition of 'exchange rate manipulation' and to prompt the IMF to pay greater attention to the potential links between currency manipulation and global trade imbalances, a move that was strongly resisted by China.

Recent evidence also suggests that financial elites in emerging economies increasingly perceive the dollar as a 'negotiated' currency, the international use of which is supported by a series of fragile political

Figure 11.3   *Currency composition of foreign exchange transactions*

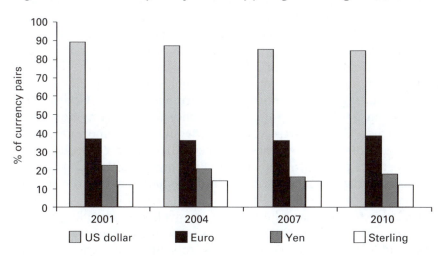

Source: Bank for International Settlements (2010).

Figure 11.4   *Share of national currencies in total official holdings of foreign exchange (end of year)*

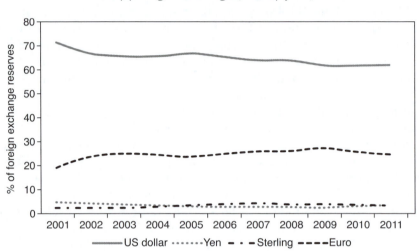

Note: Data on currency composition is available for approximately 55 per cent of total global reserves.
Source: IMF (2012) *Annual Report: Working Together to Support Global Recovery. Appendix 1: International Reserves*. Washington, DC: IMF (http://www.imf.org/external/pubs/ft/ar/2012/eng/pdf/a1.pdf).

bargains (Otero-Inglesias and Steinberg 2012; Helleiner 2008a). On several fronts, the strategic rationale for other countries to use the US dollar as the key reserve currency has diminished. In comparison to the Cold War era, for example, many of the states that hold large volumes of US dollars in their official reserves today are not locked into security alliances with the USA. The future status of the US dollar as the key international reserve currency depends on the willingness of other countries to continue to hold most of their official foreign exchange reserves in dollars, and there are signs that the international monetary order is slowly evolving into a fragmented 'multipolar' currency system (Cohen 2011; Eichengreen 2012). At the same time, a concerted shift away from the US dollar as the world's key reserve currency would involve enormous adjustment costs for many countries (Drezner 2010). As a consequence, the dollar benefits greatly from what Barry Eichengreen (2012: 124) describes as 'the advantages of incumbency'. The combination of the lack of a clear alternative currency to the dollar, the attractiveness of US Treasury debt to official investors and the adjustment costs involved in switching to a new international reserve currency have thus far served to encourage both US allies and 'contender' states to continue to support the centrality of the dollar in the international monetary system (Stokes 2013).

Box 11.2   Selected actors in international monetary relations

- **Everyday actors**
  Non-elite actors shape the fortunes of national currencies and international monetary relations through everyday choices over spending, saving, investment and borrowing.

- **Central banks**
  National and regional central banks perform influential roles that include issuing currency and managing foreign exchange reserves, acting as a lender of last resort, regulating the financial system, controlling the day-to-day operation of monetary policy and international policy coordination.

- **International organizations**
  The IMF remains an important institutional fulcrum for the international monetary system through its functions of surveillance, emergency lending and monitoring of states' formal monetary obligations. Other organizations such as the Bank for International Settlements and the Financial Stability Board also play significant roles in fostering international cooperation and policy coordination, and shaping the 'rules of the game' with respect to international monetary relations.

- **Market actors**
  In the contemporary era of international monetary relations, financial markets have come to play an important function through increasing the incentives for states to maintain open markets and liberal exchange rate regimes, as well as constraining the range of governments' economic policy choices.

- **States**
  States remain a key driver of change in the international monetary system, especially those countries able to use international monetary relations to exercise power against other countries or to effect systemic change.

The high politics of international monetary relations is likely to remain limited to a small number of regionally or globally important states (or groups of states in the case of monetary unions). Compared with other levers of power in the global political economy such as aid, trade, or credit, monetary relations between states tend to be more strictly hierarchical, and fewer states are capable of effectively using international monetary power as a source of coercion over others (Kirshner 1995: 22–3). The small number of viable monetary powers in the global political economy notwithstanding, an important characteristic of the post-Cold War international monetary system is the greater complexity of global monetary relations. Whereas Britain during the era of the Gold Standard and the USA during the Bretton Woods era could more often than not get their own way in political struggles over international monetary change, a broader range of actors impact upon the workings of today's international monetary system and the politics of money within individual states. The creation of the euro and the emergence of China as a rising economic power are likely to continue the trend towards a gradual dispersion of international monetary power.

Summary

Understanding monetary power and the evolution of the international monetary system is simultaneously about studying 'power politics' at the global or regional level and the everyday politics of money at the domestic level. The politics of monetary power in the global political economy is not simply determined by the relative economic resources commanded by different states, but also depends upon the social and political conditions that support different forms of money and international monetary systems. Nor is the politics of money the preserve of elite actors such as national governments, economic institutions such as central banks, or big business and major commercial banks. What non-elite actors believe about a currency, and how they behave on the basis of these beliefs, is an important source of strength (or weakness) which influences a state's domestic monetary capacity and its ability to project international monetary power.

Discussion questions

1. Why is the capacity to exercise monetary power a viable option for only a few states?
2. How does China's trade surplus with the USA impact upon international monetary relations?
3. Do the political and economic advantages of the euro outweigh the potential disadvantages?
4. How might the euro challenge the dollar as the world's key currency in the future?
5. What factors will shape the future evolution of the international monetary system?
6. How does the everyday behaviour of non-elite actors impact upon the politics of money?

Further reading

Cohen, Benjamin J. 2006. *The Future of Money*. Princeton, NJ: Princeton University Press.

Davies, Howard and David Green. 2010. *Banking on the Future: The Fall and Rise of Central Banking*. Princeton, NJ: Princeton University Press.

Helleiner, Eric and Jonathan Kirshner (ed.). 2009. *The Future of the Dollar*. Ithaca, NY: Cornell University Press.

James, Harold. 1996. *International Monetary Cooperation Since Bretton Woods*. Washington, DC: IMF and Oxford University Press.

Kirshner, Jonathan (ed.). 2003. *Monetary Orders: Ambiguous Economics, Ubiquitous Politics*. Ithaca, NY: Cornell University Press.

McNamara, Kathleen R. 1999. *The Currency of Ideas: Monetary Politics in the European Union*. Ithaca, NY: Cornell University Press.

Chapter 12

Global Capital Mobility

Introduction

International capital movements were subject to tight national controls in many states during the post-World War II era until the early 1970s, and in some countries until much later. Today, however, capital movements between many countries are largely free from policy restrictions. The contemporary global political economy is characterized by large capital flows between particular subsets of countries. Most capital flows travel between developed economies and emerging market economies, rather than less-developed economies. The expansion of cross-border capital mobility has been facilitated by a series of national, regional and global changes in rules, principles and policy practices during the last three decades.

Capital controls restrict access to foreign exchange for capital account transactions, which may target either capital inflows or outflows, or both. Various types of capital flows can be distinguished based on the different time horizons of investors. Short-term debt flows and flows of 'hot money' are invested in a particular jurisdiction for a brief period to earn quick profits from arbitrage, through taking advantage of interest rate differences or anticipated shifts in the value of exchange rates. Medium- or long-term capital flows include FDI and debt flows that have a maturity of more than one year. This chapter examines the politics of capital freedom, and identifies the main dynamics through which the governance of capital flows has changed from national restrictions on capital movements to international agreements to liberalize capital movements between economies.

Background

In the post-World War II era, the global political economy has been transformed from one where most states maintained some form of control on capital flows in order to preserve a higher degree of domestic policy autonomy and flexibility under the Bretton Woods system, to one where most developed economies and many developing economies have now removed almost all restrictions on capital movements. This radical shift from capital controls to capital mobility has substantially boosted the significance of private financial actors, and has increased the collective power of financial markets as 'disciplinary' forces that constrain the scope of governments' economic policy choices. This has restricted their 'room to move' in terms of policy options (Mosley 2000), while imposing severe economic consequences on countries whose governments are deemed by private actors to have lost 'policy credibility' (Grabel 2000). In September 1992, for example, the UK was forced out of the European ERM by financial speculation against the pound on 'black Wednesday' (Hassdorf 2005). This illustrates that the significance of financial markets in shaping the 'art of the possible' for states is not a constraint that applies only to weaker states or developing economies. The increasing volume and significance of global capital flows has reconfigured the autonomy and policy choice-set of all states. For states that are attractive destinations for inward capital flows, the increasing size and liberalization of international financial markets has provided substantial advantages in terms of diversifying their sources of external finance and deepening local financial markets, while simultaneously increasing the risks of a crisis leading to capital flight.

Foreign direct investment (FDI) is direct investment in production in a country, whereby overseas companies invest in existing firms or establish new subsidiaries. Most investment flows are exported from developed economies. For example, OECD investors accounted for approximately 83 per cent of global FDI flows in 2011, while 55 per cent of global FDI inflows were also received by OECD economies in the first quarter of 2012 (OECD 2012a). Only a select group of developing countries have been able to successfully take advantage of greater capital mobility, however. Most global capital flows are between a small group of emerging markets and wealthy developed countries. As Figure 12.1 illustrates, the volume of capital flows to all developing countries during the period from 2005 to 2010 was concentrated in particular regions (especially East Asia and the Pacific, and Europe and Central Asia). In recent years East Asian countries have received the lion's share of net capital flows, with comparatively low net inflows of capital going to regions such as the Middle East and North Africa, or to Sub-Saharan Africa.

Figure 12.1   *Net capital flows to developing regions, 2005–10*

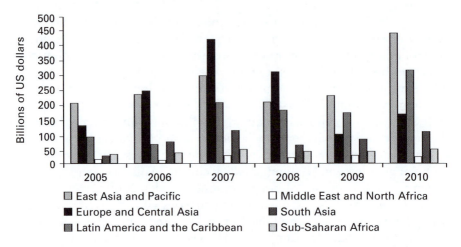

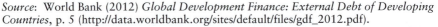

Source: World Bank (2012) *Global Development Finance: External Debt of Developing Countries*, p. 5 (http://data.worldbank.org/sites/default/files/gdf_2012.pdf).

When it comes to the liberalization of investment flows, even for countries that maintain relatively few restrictions on capital movements economic openness is a matter of degree rather than an absolute category. The OECD's FDI Regulatory Restrictiveness Index, for example, measures countries' legal restrictions on FDI to assign an overall openness score ranging from 0 (open) to 1 (closed). The index is compiled based on assessments of states' foreign equity restrictions, screening and prior approval requirements, rules for key personnel and other restrictions on the operation of foreign enterprises in host states, covering 22 economic sectors which are averaged to produce overall country scores. According to the 2012 OECD index, China, India, Japan and, to a lesser extent, Russia maintain some levels of restrictions on FDI in their economies. Based on index scores, these countries are far more restrictive than European states such as the UK, France and Germany and remain above the OECD average, but still fall well short of reaching the half-way point between the OECD's classification of 'closed' and 'open' economies in terms of FDI (Figure 12.2).

With respect to the evolution of policy norms regarding capital mobility in the global political economy after World War II, an important distinction exists between ideas about the appropriateness and types of restrictions on long-term capital flows in the form of FDI and short-term 'hot money' flows which enable currency speculation and opportunities to make profits through arbitrage. Arbitrage involves seeking profits through exploiting price differences between two or more markets.

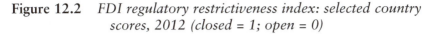

Figure 12.2   *FDI regulatory restrictiveness index: selected country scores, 2012 (closed = 1; open = 0)*

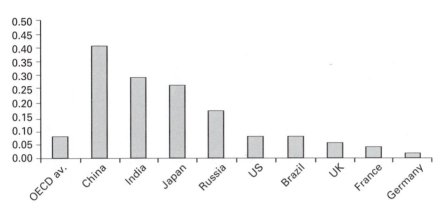

Source: OECD (2012) (http://www.oecd.org.investment/index).

Developed economies have long been supporters of capital freedom with respect to long-term flows, with OECD member states adopting the Declaration on International Investment and Multinational Enterprises in 1976. The 1976 Declaration by OECD countries, which was updated in 1979, 1984, 1991, 2000 and 2011, can be boiled down to three main elements. This first is guidelines for the appropriate conduct of multinational corporations in host countries. The second is the principle of 'national treatment', which entitles foreign direct investors to the same legal rights as local businesses. The third is an agreement for states to engage in international cooperation to avoid imposing conflicting requirements on multinational corporations, to make state policies that act as incentives or disincentives for FDI as transparent as possible and to continue to engage in consultation to improve cooperation on international investment issues (OECD 2012b).

   In contrast to long-term capital flows, the consensus among developed countries on the benefits of liberalizing restrictions on short-term capital movements is a far more recent development (discussed further below). Among developing countries, many states remain sceptical about the benefits of fully liberalizing capital account restrictions for short-term capital flows, which can impact upon the ownership structure of local businesses and whether profits are reinvested locally or flow overseas. They instead view short-term capital flows as a source of instability. This may include surges of capital inflows as well as the potential for rapid outflows and 'capital flight'. During the Asian financial crisis, for example, Malaysia contradicted the advice of the IMF, the US Treasury, and other international and regional economic organizations by introducing

Figure 12.3   *Foreign exchange turnover by currency, 2010*

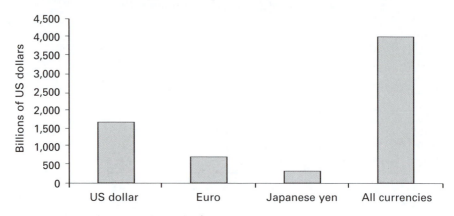

Source: King and Rime (2010) 'The $4 Trillion Question: What Explains FX Growth Since the 2007 Survey?', *BIS Quarterly Review*, December, p. 38 (http://www.bis.org/publ/qtrpdf/r_qt1012e.pdf).

capital controls on both inflows and outflows of capital to guard against financial contagion from crisis-affected economies. As the lessons from Malaysia's use of capital controls during the Asian financial crisis illustrate, the costs of introducing capital controls are high – even if the controls themselves ultimately prove to be effective in preventing capital flight. Malaysia's reputation in the international financial community was dented, with the major credit rating agencies Fitch, Moody's and Standard & Poor's each downgrading the country's sovereign risk rating (Abdelal and Alfaro 2003).

For all but the very largest economies, the volume of global capital flows relative to the size of their domestic economies is like comparing the size of an elephant to that of a mouse. The overall volume of capital flows has increased at a rapid pace in the four decades since the breakdown of the Bretton Woods system. Average turnover in global foreign exchange markets increased by 72 per cent between 2004 and 2007, and continued to grow by a further 20 per cent between 2007 and 2010 during the global financial crisis. By April 2010 global foreign exchange turnover had increased to US$4 trillion, approximately 41 per cent of which was in US dollars (Figure 12.3). The largest volume of foreign exchange transactions in 2010 were located in the UK, which accounted for 48 per cent of the global total according to the Triennial Banking Survey of the Bank for International Settlements. As Figure 12.4 illustrates, the UK, the USA and Japan alone accounted in 2010 for 61 per cent of global foreign exchange turnover. Markets

Figure 12.4　*Foreign exchange turnover by location, 2010*

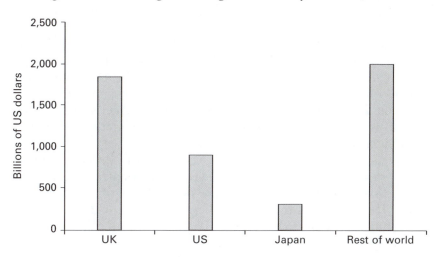

Source: King and Rime (2010) 'The $4 Trillion Question: What Explains FX Growth Since the 2007 Survey?', *BIS Quarterly Review*, December, p. 38 (http://www.bis.org/publ/qtrpdf/r_qt1012e.pdf).

for foreign exchange transactions therefore remain concentrated in a few select large developed countries.

The expansion of capital mobility

Currency convertibility is defined as 'the right to convert freely a national currency at the going exchange rate into any other currency' (Guitián 1994: 22). The concept of 'convertibility' can be defined in a number of ways. Different degrees of convertibility define who is legally permitted to exchange a country's currency, and the economic purposes for which a currency is permitted to be exchanged. Full, unrestricted currency convertibility encompasses both current account convertibility and capital account convertibility. Current account convertibility permits individuals and firms within a country to access foreign exchange in order to pay for external trade transactions, including goods, services, interest payments, share dividends and overseas travel. Capital account convertibility permits a country's residents to access foreign exchange to pay for financial assets abroad, and allows non-residents to repatriate their capital overseas (Cooper 1999: 89–90).

The two main architects of the Bretton Woods exchange rates system in 1944, Harry Dexter White and John Maynard Keynes, both viewed unbridled international capital flows as having a harmful impact on national economic performance and state policy autonomy. The objective of the postwar international monetary system was not to prevent all flows of capital across territorial borders, however. For example, Harry Dexter White's earlier view, which was formed during his doctoral research in the early 1930s, was not that capital flows should be stopped, but that they should be channelled and regulated through 'intelligent control' of the volume and direction of such flows (White, cited in Boughton 2002: 9). Keynes, in contrast, had a firmer view of capital controls as being essential for the creation and maintenance of international financial stability (Boughton 2002: 10).

National controls on capital flows were prevalent during the Bretton Woods era among both developed and developing countries. Nevertheless, cross-border capital movements were not fully regulated during this period. The creation of the 'Euromarkets' in 1957 provided a means for private financial actors to buy and sell US dollars in unregulated 'offshore' markets to get around national exchange restrictions (Helleiner 1994: 71–2; see Chapter 11). Even without resorting to offshore financial markets, private actors could find means to evade national capital controls, especially in countries where current account transactions for trade in goods and services were not subject to tight restrictions. A common method to evade capital controls is by either under-charging or over-charging for trade in goods and services in order to export or import capital through creative invoicing. This enables capital movements to be hidden in current account transactions. As a result, the line between what is defined as a capital account transaction and what is a current account transaction is sometimes blurred. Under its Articles of Agreement, the IMF maintains the formal right to determine what transactions should be counted in the capital account or the current account (Broome 2010c).

The rules and norms that characterized the global political economy during the Bretton Woods era were subsequently transformed by structural changes in the world economy and the policy decisions taken by states in response to these developments during the 1970s and 1980s. The breakdown of the Bretton Woods system in the early 1970s and the emergence of 'stagflation', where capitalist economies experienced historically high inflation rates at the same time as high unemployment, precipitated a shift away from the postwar monetary norms of the 'embedded liberal compromise' (Ruggie 1982). Until the 1970s the postwar era had been characterized by national capital controls to allow for variation in domestic policy settings, combined with open current accounts and exchange rate coordination to provide a hospitable international environment for the expansion of world trade and economic growth. In contrast, the post-Bretton Woods international monetary order was characterized by the deregulation of capital controls.

Box 12.1　Capital mobility and Thailand's financial crisis

In East Asia, the rapid growth of loans denominated in foreign currencies following the liberalization of capital accounts during the 1990s increased the risks that were associated with any depreciation of East Asian currencies, which would inflate repayments in domestic currencies and induce a greater likelihood of non-repayment to foreign lenders. In May 1997 when the Thai baht came under speculative attack, investors began pulling out as much of their capital as possible based on the conclusion that 'it was time to get out and to get out fast' (Bello 1998: 428). Foreign lenders discovered their heavy exposure to companies with high debt to equity ratios, and realized that currency falls would create a burgeoning loan burden that would increase the risks of default. As a consequence, international banks cut credit to all borrowers, including otherwise profitable export-oriented firms with relatively low debt to equity ratios that would benefit from currency depreciation. With 'too many baht chasing too few dollars' as capital was pulled out this placed a great strain on the value of the currency, creating pressure on the Thai government to officially devalue the exchange rate peg to the US dollar.

Because of investors' expectations that the baht would have to be allowed to depreciate against the US dollar, as well as the exacerbation of this pressure on the baht by the activities of currency speculators, the Bank of Thailand's attempts to maintain the currency's value at 25 baht to US$1 by selling large quantities of its dollar reserves were largely ineffective. When faced with a shock to the financial system, financial market participants lack information on which to form assumptions about the future levels of interest rates and exchange rates, with the result that 'expectations are prone to become more elastic' (Rogers 1989: 290–2). Under conditions of heightened economic uncertainty and volatility in exchange rates, currency speculators are able to exploit the 'elasticity of expectations' in order to make short-term gains. As well as currency speculation and the withdrawal of capital by foreign investors, domestic investors and firms in Thailand began to sell local currency, to ensure that they would have sufficient US dollars to meet necessary import costs and to service existing dollar-denominated debt. The aggregate effects of these individual actions caused the Thai currency to continue to depreciate, because individual investors acted pre-emptively on the shared expectation that its value would decline.

Although capital account liberalization continues to remain more controversial than current account convertibility, an increasing number of governments have been willing to liberalize their capital accounts in recent decades (Chwieroth 2009; Abdelal 2007; Leiteritz and Moschella 2010). For example, many countries in East Asia partially liberalized controls on capital flows during the late 1980s and early 1990s. This facilitated an enormous increase in capital inflows to the region, especially short-term portfolio investment flows (Noble and Ravenhill 2000: 4–5). The rapid increase in short-term capital inflows comprised one of the critical factors that led to the emergence of the Asian financial crisis in 1997, and enabled the rapid transmission of the crisis from Thailand to other countries in the region (see Box 12.1). The Asian crisis presented a stark example of the negative effects liberalized capital flows can have on national economies when things go wrong.

How the meanings of crises are narrated by elite actors has an important influence over the selection of crisis management strategies, as well as initiatives for structural economic reform. For example, the IMF's initial overview of the Asian financial crisis, in the December 1997 edition of its *World Economic Outlook* report, stressed the role of domestic factors rather than international capital mobility as the direct cause of the crisis. The IMF's analysis emphasized three causes of the crisis. The first of these was that governments in the region failed to mitigate the effects of the rapid growth of domestic demand, which resulted in unsustainable property and stock market bubbles and growing current account deficits in some countries. Second, the IMF argued that the pegged exchange rate regimes were maintained 'for too long', thereby exacerbating the growth of speculative activities. Third, because of the failure of governments to institute adequate prudential rules and regulatory oversight, banks provided loans that funded high-risk projects on the basis of borrowers' collateral rather than projected profit margins. Many foreign currency loans were invested in industries that faced overcapacity and slow export growth, or in domestic projects that did not earn foreign exchange and further contributed to the expansion of speculative bubbles which emerged in real estate and stock markets (IMF 1997: 40). These three broad points were repeated on numerous occasions by IMF officials, which established a preliminary explanation of the crisis as the result of domestic policy errors, rather than structural economic conditions such as the impact of globalized capital markets (Stiglitz 2000). This diagnosis of the causes of the crisis shaped the IMF's prescriptions for crisis management and structural economic reforms in East Asian economies, which centred on liberalizing domestic markets and adopting open economy models of economic governance and prudential financial regulation (Lai 2012).

Contemporary challenges and sources of change

The contemporary challenges posed by capital movements in the global political economy are manifold. Some states face substantial challenges in managing the problems associated with either surges in capital inflows or rapid capital outflows. Others are net capital importers, which struggle to attract international investment because they do not offer the same rate of returns as fast-growing emerging economies in Asia. In addition to the problem of attracting, managing and retaining capital inflows, further contemporary challenges from capital movements include the problem of illicit cross-border capital flows. These are flows of funds that most states and IOs treat as a policy problem because they result from the proceeds of criminal business, such as illicit trade in drugs, arms, humans and protected environmental resources, or are intended to finance criminal activities, such as terrorist financing and government corruption (Tsingou 2010).

While money laundered through domestic transactions to disguise the source (or destination) of funds has long posed a serious problem for many countries, in recent years the issue of international money laundering has gained greater salience for many policy-makers. States have sought to establish and diffuse an anti-money laundering regime to regulate illicit capital flows, operating through bodies such as the OECD and the Financial Action Task Force. This has the aim of regulating the laundering of funds gained from illicit activities such as corruption and drug trafficking ('proceeds of crime'), as well as flows of money used to finance illicit activities such as terrorism ('proceeds for crime') (Tsingou 2010). Efforts to diffuse a standard set of anti-money laundering policies have been highly successful, with common policies being adopted by over 180 states. However, recent research suggests that such policies are ineffective at achieving their intended purpose of regulating illicit financial transactions while imposing high compliance costs, a problem which is especially acute for low-income countries (Sharman 2011).

A further factor that may undermine the effectiveness of policies designed to combat cross-border illicit capital flows is the difficulty involved for regulators in distinguishing between legitimate financial transfers and criminal financial transactions that take place outside the formal international financial system. Informal fund transfer (IFT) systems enable the flow of funds between parties in different countries outside of formal financial channels, making it easier for the sender and recipient of funds to remain anonymous. As well as offering financial secrecy, IFTs can be faster and cheaper compared with formal international fund transfers (El Qorchi *et al.* 2003). Despite their informal status, IFT processes are commonly used for transferring migrant workers' remittances to their home state, and in some countries handle a higher volume of financial flows than the formal banking sector. In the aftermath of the terrorist attacks in the USA on 11 September 2001, however, informal financial practices have been subject to increasing regulatory intervention from policy-makers. This is because they have been viewed with suspicion as representing flows of 'underground money' that could be used to fund criminal activities, with the potential for IFT systems to be used as terrorist financing networks representing a particular concern for some countries (de Goede 2007).

As these points highlight, capital freedom is not a value-neutral policy choice, nor is it simply a matter of the potential advantages and disadvantages of unrestricted capital flows for macroeconomic stability in different countries. Rather, the politics of capital freedom is a highly sensitive topic that touches upon the high finance of currency speculation and investment, the everyday finance of migrant workers' remittances, state security and transnational crime. Seen in this light, it is perhaps surprising that support for the liberalization of (most) capital restrictions among developed countries is today as strong as it is. This continuing support stems in part from the roles played by three international bodies in developing, supporting and diffusing the idea of capital mobility as a global norm: the OECD, the European Commission and the IMF.

After a change in the position of the French government on the issue of capital mobility, which had long opposed the liberalization of capital flows in Europe, the European Council of Ministers issued a directive in 1988 that required all members to liberalize restrictions on capital flows (including between members and non-members). The initiative was driven by the role of the European Commission (EC), and especially the influence of the EC President Jacques Delors, as well as French and German national policy-makers, as part of a compromise between capital freedom and European monetary union. In the OECD, the organization's Code of Liberalization of Capital Movements was expanded in 1989 to include short-term capital flows. For OECD members such as the UK and Germany, the championing of open capital accounts among OECD members was a logical extension of the organization's early role in agreeing the liberalization of restrictions on long-term (FDI) capital flows between its member states. These institutional changes obliged members of both the OECD and the European Community/EU to remove most restrictions on capital movements between each other and with non-member countries. As a result, the countries that made up the lion's share of global trade and FDI flows formally embraced capital freedom not only as a policy choice but also as a formal multilateral rule that bound the hands of national policy-makers in the future (Abdelal 2007: 10–12).

For its part, the IMF promoted the liberalization of capital accounts as a long-term goal for all countries in three primary ways. The first was pursued informally through policy dialogue and surveillance processes with its member states. The emphasis on capital liberalization increased

---

Box 12.2   Selected actors and global capital mobility

- **Everyday actors**
  Everyday actors engage in capital movements through the financial system, as well outside formal financial channels through informal fund transfers.

- **International organizations**
  IOs have been important actors in the liberalization of restrictions on capital mobility in recent decades, especially the OECD and the IMF. In particular, IOs such as the OECD (and the EU) have played a critical role in codifying the obligation to maintain open capital accounts among their member states.

- **Market actors**
  Market actors collectively exercise influence through the aggregate effects of their investment decisions. Capital flows have increased to such a magnitude that rapid capital outflows now have detrimental consequences, at least in the short term, for all countries.

- **Regional institutions**
  The European Union has been the most prominent regional organization that has embraced capital account convertibility as a key economic norm among its member states. EU states must maintain fully open capital accounts with each other, as well as with non-EU members. While several EU members have a long commitment to capital mobility, such as the UK and Germany, others such as France embraced the principle of capital freedom in the second half of the 1980s.

- **States**
  States have been instrumental in removing restrictions on international capital movements. An increasing number of states have also negotiated bilateral investment treaties to remove restrictions on bilateral investment flows (Gallagher 2011).

---

during the 1980s and 1990s despite Article VI, Section 3, of the IMF's Articles of Agreement including the formal right of members to use controls to regulate international capital movements, so long as capital controls do not interfere with payments for current account transactions. The second way in which the IMF came to play a major role in the promotion of capital mobility as a global economic norm was through internal norm advocacy by a new generation of professional economists who entered the organization and rose through its ranks of seniority during the 1970s and 1980s in the post-Bretton Woods era (Chwieroth

2009). Closely related to this was the IMF's role in providing policy training to officials from developing countries through the IMF Institute and, from the 1990s onwards, for post-communist officials through the JVI and other regional training bodies affiliated to the IMF. International policy training may involve the transfer of knowledge about how to achieve economic objectives that individual states set themselves, but also socializes officials into common ways of thinking about the role of the state in the economy, as well as appropriate economic policy instruments and economic goals (Broome 2010b).

The third way the IMF promoted capital account liberalization during the 1990s was through a proposal to amend its Articles of Agreement to make the removal of restrictions on capital movements an obligation for all IMF member states, similar to the obligation to maintain current account convertibility (see Chapter 11). This proposal for a constitutional change was championed by the IMF despite being received with either ambivalence or opposition from the US Treasury and from private financial actors. The push to redefine members' formal obligations to include capital freedom was based upon a normative definition of capital liberalization as not only desirable but also an inevitable response to economic globalization, which the IMF saw as undermining the effectiveness of national capital controls (Moschella 2010a: 43–4). Despite receiving strong support from several European member states and the IMF's senior officials, led by IMF Managing Director Michel Camdessus, this controversial proposal was rejected in the aftermath of the Asian financial crisis in 1997–98 and the Russian financial crisis in 1998. Many observers outside the IMF, and some within it, interpreted these crises as a demonstration of the perils of enshrining a blanket commitment to capital freedom for all countries in all circumstances. After an intellectual case for the change to the IMF's mandate was first proposed to its Executive Board in 1994, the amendment fell by the wayside after it received strong opposition from the US Congress during negotiations over a funding increase for the IMF in 1998, which brought pressure to bear on the US Treasury to withdraw its lukewarm support for the change (Abdelal 2007: 138–59).

In the decade following the Asian financial crisis the IMF suffered a severe and, at the time, seemingly permanent dent to its institutional legitimacy, which partly contributed to a sharp decline in borrowing from the organization after 2002. When countries turned again to the IMF for emergency financing during the global financial crisis, the organization proceeded more cautiously on the issue of capital movements, and in some cases has supported the temporary use of capital controls by states to combat financial instability (Broome 2011). The IMF has since re-evaluated the appropriateness of policy tools to help manage inflows of capital. Recent IMF research has suggested that 'capital flow management measures' (capital controls) may help to guard against macroeconomic risks resulting from sharp increases in capital inflows, and may serve to safeguard financial stability. The IMF's focus has also shifted towards the potential policy problems in developed countries that are the main exporters of capital, rather than only focusing on capital importers. This has drawn attention to how monetary policy activism in developed countries, including historically low official interest rates, has served to encourage even greater capital flows into emerging market economies (IMF 2011: 25). Despite this greater flexibility on the part of the IMF towards restrictions on capital movements, global capital flows remain a major policy challenge for states, including those which may benefit most from access to pools of capital from other countries. The large net global capital flows during the 2000s have been identified as one of the main preconditions of the global financial crisis in 2008–09 (see Chapter 13), which created financial channels that rapidly transmitted financial liquidity shocks throughout the world (Speller *et al.* 2011).

One idea for reforming global financial governance which re-emerged during the global financial crisis was the proposal for a small tax on international financial transactions or foreign exchange transactions, a 'Tobin tax' to put some sand in the wheels of global finance. This was proposed by economist James Tobin in 1972, and was envisaged as a small percentage tax on foreign exchange transactions between different currencies to reduce volatility in exchange rates caused by currency speculation as opposed to exchange rate transactions to pay for trade (Brassett 2010). The introduction of some form of a Tobin tax to reduce or at least slow down short-term capital flows, as well as to potentially raise revenues as insurance against future financial sector bailouts, has recently been supported by some G20 states, as well as in principle by a number of EU members. The idea remains highly controversial, however. Most observers agree that, in order to be effective, a financial transactions tax would have be introduced by all major economies at the same time to avoid the problem of regulatory arbitrage.

Summary

Global capital flows now dwarf the size of most countries' economies, and have changed both the role and the capacities of state actors as financial regulators. Capital flows are a potential policy problem not only for states experiencing sharp capital outflows, but also for those which attract a surge in capital inflows. Despite the enormous increase in cross-border capital movements in the four decades since the Bretton Woods system collapsed, a large number of developing countries struggle to access global capital markets and find they are in a highly asymmetrical relationship when facing the collective influence of financial markets. In the post-World War II era, global economic norms have changed from acceptance of capital controls as legitimate and desirable tools of economic policy-making to enhance macroeconomic stability, stable financial relations and domestic policy autonomy, to a legal obligation on OECD and EU member states to remove restrictions on capital movements. More recently, the consensus on capital mobility among national policy-makers in developed states and IOs such as the IMF has become more flexible, at least in the case of developing countries and smaller developed states facing the prospect of capital flight. This has created policy space for the temporary use of capital controls during crisis episodes, and for the longer-term use of selective restrictions on capital inflows to guard against short-term spikes in 'hot money' flows.

Discussion questions

1. What are the main factors that have driven processes of increased capital mobility?
2. Who are the winners and losers from greater capital freedom?
3. How does capital mobility impact upon the management of financial crises?
4. Should states use capital controls to increase economic stability?
5. How does international economic integration reduce the effectiveness of capital controls?
6. What are the merits of the case for an international tax on capital movements?

Further reading

Abdelal, Rawi. 2007. *Capital Rules: The Construction of Global Finance.* Cambridge, MA: Harvard University Press.

Brassett, James. 2010. *Cosmopolitanism and Global Financial Reform: A Pragmatic Approach to the Tobin Tax.* London: Routledge.

Chwieroth, Jeffrey M. 2009. *Capital Ideas: The IMF and the Rise of Financial Liberalization.* Princeton, NJ: Princeton University Press.

Moschella, Manuela. 2010a. *Governing Risk: The IMF and Global Financial Crises.* Basingstoke: Palgrave Macmillan.

Swank, Duane. 2002. *Global Capital, Political Institutions, and Policy Change in Developed Welfare States.* Cambridge: Cambridge University Press.

Watson, Matthew. 2007. *The Political Economy of International Capital Mobility.* Basingstoke: Palgrave Macmillan.

Chapter 13

Financial Crises

Introduction

From today's vantage point, the recent history of the global political economy could be characterized as an 'age of crises'. Between the onset of the Latin American debt crisis in 1982 and the global financial crisis of 2008–09, the era of economic globalization discussed in previous chapters on trade, money and capital mobility was punctuated by recurrent financial shocks and crises. Although headline-grabbing financial events such as a bank run, a financial institution declaring bankruptcy, the freezing of bank deposits, or the sudden imposition of controls on capital outflows might worsen a crisis episode, they usually represent the surface symptoms of a financial crisis rather than the underlying cause. Throughout the last three decades, the sudden emergence of financial shocks drove many governments to seek sovereign bailouts from multilateral and bilateral creditors, and to sharply alter their economic policy settings in response to financial distress.

Greater levels of international economic integration have enabled the 'contagion' effects of financial crises to be swiftly transmitted across different countries and regions. As the financial crisis of the late 2000s demonstrated, economic interconnectedness has made it harder for financial shocks in systemically important economies to be effectively contained. The global financial crisis has challenged orthodox economic policy beliefs about the benefits of liberalized financial markets, and has led to renewed debate over how countries can achieve a balance between finance-led growth and financial stability. This chapter provides an introduction to financial crises, and examines both the causes of the global financial crisis and its consequences for the global political economy.

Background

Contemporary financial crises are multidimensional events that result from sudden changes in market conditions, and how these changes inform the expectations of financial market participants. Immediate causes include rapid changes in asset prices and the availability and price of credit, or a breakdown in the system of financial intermediation between lenders and borrowers. Other drivers of financial crisis include severe balance sheet problems, when firms, households, financial institutions, or states are unable to meet their current payment obligations due to revenue shortfalls or the liquidity structure of their assets. Financial crises can also emerge in response to the extension of large-scale government support, such as the emergency provision of funds to boost a financial institution's liquidity or to reorganize its capital structure through recapitalization (Claessens and Kose 2013). Recapitalization involves the reorganization of a corporation's capital structure through exchanging debt for equity, while liquidity refers to the ease with which assets can be converted into money, which determines the ability of an institution to meet its payment obligations.

Financial crises are typically 'preceded by asset and credit booms that turn into busts', during which financial market participants and policy-makers fail to recognize – or fail to act upon – the emergence of systemic financial risks (Claessens and Kose 2013: 4–5). The sudden onset of financial turmoil is widely understood to be a consequence of 'irrational' market actions, whereby unchecked financial speculation inflates asset prices to unsustainable levels. This is driven by what John Maynard Keynes (1936) termed 'animal spirits', or what former US Federal Reserve Chairman Alan Greenspan (1996) called 'irrational exuberance'. Such actions may be considered rational at an individual level if investors are responding to decisions by other financial market participants who are assumed to have access to better-quality information, a pattern of financial behaviour termed 'rational herding' (Devenow and Welch 1996).

The euphoria associated with financial booms has historically been a driver of increased speculation, leading to economic disaster. For John Kenneth Galbraith (1990: 12, 18), financial euphoria represents a 'mass escape from reality, that excludes any serious contemplation of the true nature of what is taking place'. Instead, the inflation of financial bubbles is driven by a shared assumption among market participants 'that there is something new in the world', a novel and infallible financial instrument or set of circumstances that will continue to drive the creation of financial wealth through capital gains. Although financial booms often follow hard on the heels of financial busts, what Galbraith (1990: 3–4)

terms 'the extreme brevity of financial memory' among market participants obscures the ability of investors to recognize in time that markets
are overheating and could be heading for a systemic collapse. Other
observers have described this pattern of market behaviour as the 'this-
time-is-different syndrome' (Reinhart and Rogoff 2009). The lessons of
previous episodes of financial disaster are quickly forgotten when new
financial bubbles emerge because market participants focus on continuing to increase profits through speculation, while governments reap
political rewards from the wealth effects of rising asset prices.

Globalization and the late-2000s financial crisis

The frequency and severity of financial crises during the last three
decades is often linked to economic globalization, but financial crises are
not a new phenomenon. The history of market-based economies over the
past three centuries suggests that 'Financial crashes are endemic to capitalism' (Gamble 2009b: 6). As the infamous Dutch example of 'Tulip
mania' in the seventeenth century illustrates, speculative episodes –
where asset prices skyrocket before crashing when the bubble bursts –
regularly punctuate cycles of economic booms with financial busts
(Galbraith 1990). Driven by the international integration of markets for
trade in goods, services and capital, the dynamics of globalization have
nonetheless had a profound effect on both the speed with which financial
systems can be placed under severe stress and the scale of the financial
disaster that ensues.

Over the course of the last four decades, many governments stepped
back from using discretionary intervention tools to shape the processes
and outcomes of economic decision-making, while at the same time
national economic borders were opened with the reduction of controls
on trade, capital and currency movements. After the breakdown of the
Bretton Woods exchange rate system in the early 1970s, greater international capital mobility went hand-in-hand with a shift towards financial
market deregulation (Nesvetailova 2007: 12–14). The dismantling of
interventionist economic controls means that governments are less able
to influence how capital inflows are invested and how quickly they can
be withdrawn from an economy. As the Asian financial crisis of 1997–98
demonstrated (see Chapter 12), this increases the potential for speculative asset bubbles to emerge that are financed by short-term foreign
currency loans provided by investors seeking high immediate returns.
These dynamics expand a country's vulnerability to financial shocks by
increasing reliance on short-term loans denominated in foreign currency,
debt which can rapidly inflate in value as a consequence of exchange rate

depreciation. Short-term loans can be quickly recalled in a market down-turn, which may push otherwise solvent borrowers into bankruptcy when alternative sources of finance dry up. Capital mobility also makes it easy for investors to pull their money out of a country quickly if their expectations of future profits change, compounding the financial problems that a country in the midst of a crisis already faces. These financial market dynamics contributed to the emergence and the scale of the Asian financial crisis, as well as enabling the effects of the crisis to be rapidly transmitted across countries in the region and beyond (Bello 1998; Wade and Veneroso 1998; Noble and Ravenhill 2000).

In the late-2000s financial crisis, the effects of globalization in escalating the speed and the scale of financial distress were illustrated by the example of two small states that sought to carve out a competitive advantage as offshore banking centres, Iceland and Cyprus. Both countries used their proximity to large markets and the advantages of capital mobility to develop financial sectors that far outstripped the size of their domestic economies. Prior to the collapse of the three main Icelandic banks within the space of a single week in October 2008 and the joint IMF–EU bailout for Cyprus in March 2013, the size of the banking sector in each country was over eight times the size of national GDP (Broome 2011; IMF 2013). In addition to domestic policy changes that encouraged a shift towards finance-led growth models prior to the crisis, international capital mobility enabled the unbalanced expansion of the banking sector in Iceland and Cyprus through large volumes of foreign deposits. This increased the systemic risks associated with financial distress, and amplified the severity of the resulting disaster in both cases. Systemic risk refers to the risk of the collapse of an entire financial system, rather than the collapse of an institution or group of institutions.

The global financial crisis of 2008–09 emerged from the US subprime crisis in 2007, and was driven by a sharp turnaround in financial expectations. Subprime mortgages involve a higher risk of default than 'prime' mortgage lending, which is calculated on the basis of a borrower's level of disposable income and judgements of their ability to repay mortgage debt. The conventional definition of a subprime borrower is someone who spends more than one third of their after-tax income servicing personal debt (Seabrooke 2009: 55). From 2003 onwards, a subprime mortgage bubble in the USA was inflated by the belief that house prices would continue to rise indefinitely, combined with the use of complex mathematical models for pricing asset-backed securities, such as collateralized debt obligations (CDOs). CDOs are asset-backed securities that are structured in multiple 'tranches', with varying degrees of risk. These pricing models relied on historical data for subprime mortgage default rates from the 1990s. In the previous decade, however, subprime lending only accounted for a small proportion of the US mortgage market, while rising house prices enabled subprime borrowers to refinance their mortgages at lower interest rates. During the 1990s US banks also remained cautious in how they assessed borrowers' creditworthiness and mortgage eligibility, in order to minimize the risk of loan defaults (Schwartz 2009: 188–9).

Each of these factors changed over the course of the 2000s. After the end of the dotcom internet bubble in 2000, expansionary monetary policy in the USA drove a recovery in stock prices, which quickly reached new highs (Carmassi *et al.* 2009). In an environment of cheap credit fuelled by low interest rates, subprime mortgage loans tripled between 2000 and 2006 to reach a total of US$1.17 trillion, close to 12 per cent of the US mortgage market (IOSCO 2008: 2). Rather than banks carefully screening subprime mortgage applicants and holding mortgages to term, mortgage brokers used an 'originate to distribute' model to create mortgage loans and then distribute the risk of default through 'pooling' mortgages as asset-backed securities that were sold to investors. Rapid growth of the market in mortgage-backed securities shortened the time horizons of mortgage lenders to a 'synchronic outlook', which focused on generating short-term profits by selling mortgage loans as securitized financial products (Rethel and Sinclair 2012: 2). This created a moral hazard problem whereby brokers and lenders faced powerful incentives to increase revenues by originating high volumes of subprime mortgages, which in turn reduced lenders' incentives to screen subprime borrowers rigorously for credit risk. In order for new subprime borrowers to continue to refinance their loans on more favourable terms as many were able to do in the 1990s, steady increases in residential property prices were required (Schwartz 2009: 189).

With US property values faltering by the mid-2000s, subprime mortgages that were in foreclosure or where payments were 60 days overdue nearly doubled from the end of 2005 to the end of 2006 to 10 per cent. When highly leveraged institutional investors in subprime mortgage-backed securities began suffering losses in the middle of 2007, several factors collided to exacerbate financial uncertainty. First, investors who sought to offload their investments in CDOs struggled to find new buyers as doubts about the quality of mortgage-backed securities and collateralized debt obligations rose. Second, credit rating agencies started to downgrade the risk rating of CDOs, which further reduced the willingness of investors to purchase mortgage-backed securities (see Chapter 7). Finally, faced with the need to repay their own shareholders and lenders, enough institutional investors moved at around the same time to sell their more liquid stock shares that it had the effect of sharply lowering stock market share prices across the board (IOSCO 2008: 4–5).

The subprime mortgage crisis transformed into a global credit crunch and financial crisis over the course of 15 months after June 2007, when hedge funds exposed to the subprime securities market first reported losses. The liquidity crisis in financial markets hit with severity at the start of August 2007 when the global banking group BNP Paribas cut off withdrawals from three hedge funds that were heavily exposed to subprime mortgage investments. Substantial losses by hedge funds triggered a 'fire sale' of financial assets at discounted prices, which drove up inter-bank lending rates before effectively freezing overnight lending between banks on 9 August 2007. Despite injections of liquidity into overnight credit markets coordinated by the European Central Bank (€95 billion) and the US Federal Reserve (US$24 billion), the credit crunch in inter-bank lending signalled the near-collapse of the international financial system, which led to the first bank run in the UK since the nineteenth century when Northern Rock suffered a liquidity crisis in September 2007 (Brunnermeier 2008: 13–14; Shin 2009). Twelve months later, on 15 September 2008, US investment bank Lehman Brothers filed for bankruptcy after losing nearly three-quarters of its share value in the first six months of the year due to enormous investment losses in subprime mortgages. The collapse of Lehman Brothers is widely recognized as the trigger that transformed financial liquidity problems into a systemic crisis of the global financial system.

The mortgage crisis escalated into a full-blown financial crisis through four interrelated financial mechanisms: (1) balance sheet effects; (2) lending channel effects; (3) runs on financial institutions; and (4) network effects. A balance sheet is a summary of an organization's assets, equity and liabilities at a specific point in time. Falling asset prices caused the deterioration of borrowers' balance sheets, which eroded the liquidity of financial institutions while simultaneously prompting a tightening of lending criteria for credit access. Financial institutions began to hoard funds rather than lending in retail or wholesale credit markets in response to uncertainty about their own future credit access. The capital base of financial institutions was further eroded by bank runs as investors' and depositors' trust in their solvency collapsed. In addition, the growth of financial securitization and the liberalization of controls on financial institutions' activities over the 1990s and 2000s created network effects because many banks acted simultaneously as both borrowers and lenders in the mortgage market, with the risk of mortgage defaults hedged through credit default swaps (CDSs). A CDS is a financial agreement that insures the buyer of a CDS against the risk of a loan default or other credit risk. This produced counter-party credit risks that threatened the solvency of major financial services institutions such as insurer AIG, which was heavily exposed to the declining value of CDOs through CDSs. In September 2008 AIG was forced to seek the largest government bailout of a private company in US history (Brunnermeier 2008: 3).

The consequences of the global financial crisis

For many countries – especially the European and North American economies that were at the heart of the financial turmoil – the effects of the global financial crisis were more severe than any previous crisis episode since the Great Depression of the 1930s. At a global level, the crisis sharply reduced world trade volumes and capital flows (see Chapters 10, 12 and 14). As Table 13.1 illustrates, economic output flat-lined in 2008 and fell steeply the following year in the USA and Europe, which generated negative spill-over effects on economic growth rates in countries which relied on trade and investment with the USA, the UK and Eurozone economies, such as Mexico, Brazil, Canada, Russia, Japan and non-Eurozone countries in Central and Eastern Europe. For the first time in the post-World War II era, the volume of world trade in goods and services shrunk substantially in 2009 by 11 per cent, with the volume of imports and exports in advanced economies decreasing more sharply than imports and exports in emerging and developing economies (see Figure 13.1). Since the peak of the global financial crisis in late 2008 and 2009, growth rates in many developed countries have remained anaemic. This is most notable in the case of the UK, while several Eurozone countries have faced sovereign debt problems since 2010 as the private sector debt crisis transformed into a public sector fiscal crisis. For emerging economies such as the ASEAN-5, and in regions such as Sub-Saharan Africa and the Middle East and North Africa, growth rates fell significantly in 2009 but remained positive. In contrast, official statistics indicate that growth rates in India and China continued to remain stable throughout 2009 and 2010.

At a domestic level, the countries that were at the heart of the crisis experienced falling house prices, sharp increases in house repossession and foreclosure rates and a financial crunch that had a catastrophic impact on the volume of credit available for mortgages, business loans and trade credit and inter-bank lending. For example, the collapse in the US housing market after 2006 produced a 35 per cent average drop in house prices, while the aggregate number of forced house sales by mortgage lenders through foreclosures increased from approximately 750,000 in 2006 to well over 2.5 million foreclosures in 2009 (Mian *et al.* 2011). Despite indicators of US economic recovery in some areas in 2012–13, financial distress remained a severe problem for many households five

Table 13.1 *Economic output (% change), 2008–14*

	2008	2009	2010	2011	2012	2013*	2014*
USA	0.0	-3.5	2.4	1.8	2.2	1.9	3.0
Euro Area	0.5	-4.3	2.0	1.4	-0.6	-0.3	1.1
Japan	-1.2	-6.3	4.5	-0.6	2.0	1.6	1.4
UK	-0.1	-4.9	1.8	0.9	0.2	0.7	1.5
Canada	0.5	-2.8	3.2	2.6	1.8	1.5	2.4
Central and Eastern Europe	3.0	-3.6	4.6	5.2	1.6	2.2	2.8
Russia	5.2	-7.8	4.3	4.3	3.4	3.4	3.8
China	9.6	9.2	10.4	9.3	7.8	8.0	8.2
India	6.4	6.8	10.1	7.7	4.0	5.7	6.2
ASEAN-5**	4.7	1.7	7.0	4.5	6.1	5.9	5.5
Brazil	5.1	-0.6	7.5	2.7	0.9	3.0	4.0
Mexico	1.5	-6.2	5.6	3.9	3.9	3.4	3.4
Middle East and North Africa	5.0	2.6	5.0	3.9	4.7	3.1	3.7
Sub-Saharan Africa	5.5	2.8	5.3	5.3	4.8	5.6	6.1

Note: * Projected change. ** Indonesia, Malaysia, Philippines, Thailand and Vietnam.
Source: International Monetary Fund, *World Economic Outlook*, various years. Washington, DC: IMF (http://www.imf.org/external/ns/cs.aspx?id=29).

Figure 13.1 *World trade in goods and services (% change), 2008–14*

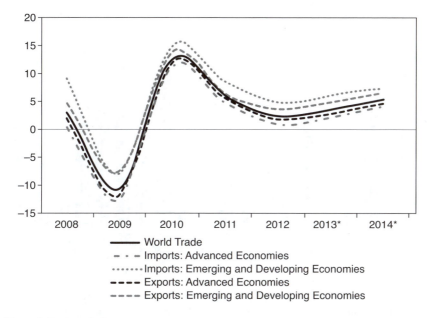

Legend:
— World Trade
– · – Imports: Advanced Economies
········· Imports: Emerging and Developing Economies
– – – – Exports: Advanced Economies
– – – – Exports: Emerging and Developing Economies

Note: * Projected change.
Source: International Monetary Fund, *World Economic Outlook*, various years. Washington, DC: IMF (http://www.imf.org/external/ns/cs.aspx?id=29).

years after the emergence of the subprime crisis. In 2012 the rate of US foreclosures remained high compared with pre-crisis levels, with over 1.8 million houses foreclosed and a further 1.5 million houses in the foreclosure process due to the inability of home-owners to service their mortgage payments (Moore 2013).

Governments around the world responded to the onset of the financial crisis with a mix of fiscal stimulus, monetary activism and bank recapitalization. Fiscal stimulus policies included temporary cuts in taxes on business, consumption and personal income, as well as new fiscal transfers to inject money directly into people's pocketbooks, to support struggling industries and to maintain capital investment. The size and form of stimulus packages varied significantly across countries. In response to a sharp drop in exports in late 2008 as the scope of the financial crisis in the USA and Europe became apparent, China's central government announced plans for a stimulus package of RMB4 trillion (approximately US$600 billion, a figure which balloons if fiscal stimulus pledges by China's local governments are added). New bank loans in China subsequently expanded to RMB9.6 trillion in 2009 (approximately US$1.4 trillion), around half of which were invested in infrastructure

Figure 13.2   *Fiscal stimulus in G20 countries (% of GDP), 2009–10*

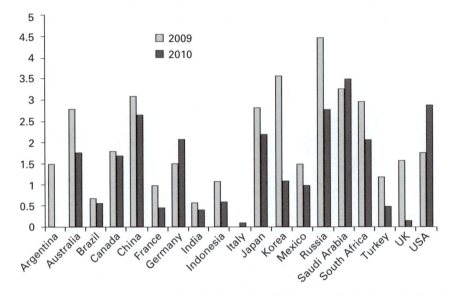

Source: International Monetary Fund (2010) *Fiscal Monitor: Navigating the Fiscal Challenges Ahead*, May. Washington, DC: IMF (http://www.imf.org/external/pubs/ft/fm/2010/fm1001.pdf).

projects (Breslin 2011). As Figure 13.2 indicates, fiscal stimulus packages introduced in 2009 and 2010 were higher as a proportion of GDP in China, Russia and other emerging economies compared with the level of fiscal stimulus in major developed economies such as the UK, Germany, France and the USA.

In developed economies, governments moved to inject liquidity into the financial system through recapitalizing distressed financial institutions, including the provision of new emergency credit lines. For troubled banks such as Lloyds, Royal Bank of Scotland and Northern Rock in the UK, policy-makers responded first with recapitalization, then nationalization. This meant that the government effectively became a majority shareholder in these financial institutions. To combat the severe economic downturn governments adopted aggressive monetary policies, including lowering short-term nominal interest rates close to zero (Mishkin 2009). Among major central banks, the US Federal Reserve moved faster and more aggressively to cut central bank interest rates as the crisis deepened over the course of 2008 and early 2009 in comparison with the Bank of England (BoE) and the European Central Bank (ECB) (see Figure 13.3). However, commercial banks responded by tightening lending criteria and hoarding capital in order to boost their reserves. In an attempt to expand the impact of monetary stimulus when

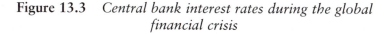

Figure 13.3   *Central bank interest rates during the global financial crisis*

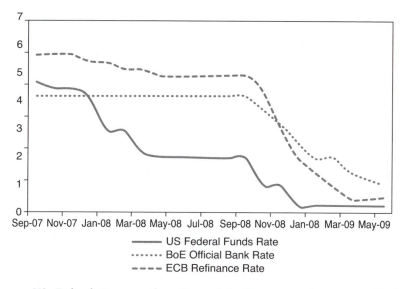

Source: US Federal Reserve (http://www.federalreserve.gov/monetarypolicy/open market.htm). European Central Bank (http://www.ecb.europa.eu/stats/monetary/rates/ html/index.en.html). Bank of England (http://www.bankofengland.co.uk/boeapps/iadb/ repo.asp).

cuts in short-term official interest rates failed to overcome weaknesses in credit markets, the BoE and the Federal Reserve introduced unorthodox 'quantitative easing' programmes. Quantitative easing is an increase in the money supply which is created by a central bank purchasing bonds and other debt instruments. Both central banks purchased large volumes of long-term government bonds, while the Federal Reserve also purchased mortgage-backed securities and bank debt. These measures were aimed at lowering long-term market interest rates and expanding the funds available to private sector financial institutions to increase their lending volumes (Christensen and Rudebusch 2012).

Restoring financial stability in an age of austerity

Some seven years after the emergence of the crisis, the question of 'Who is to blame?' for the financial disasters of the late 2000s remains the subject of fierce political debate. A common response is to blame the bankers. Banks' financial innovation activities generated systemic risks on a global scale, for which governments and their citizens are continuing to pay a hefty social and economic cost. The major credit rating agencies, which enabled the growth of speculation in the mortgage market through assigning low-risk ratings to securitized financial products, comprise another group of 'usual suspects' (Sinclair 2010). One response has been to blame borrowers in the USA, the UK and other countries who purchased houses on mortgage terms they could not afford to repay when market conditions changed. This pattern of behaviour was in part driven by the goal of gaining a foothold on the housing ladder in order to build assets over a life cycle, and to avoid being excluded from the wealth effects created by rising capital gains in housing (Seabrooke 2010b: 56). A substantial portion of blame can also be attributed to the generation of politicians and financial regulators who failed to alter pro-cyclical policy settings in order to safeguard financial stability. In the UK and the USA, 'light touch' regulatory regimes permitted financial market participants to engage in increasingly risky behaviour, much of which would have been illegal in an earlier era (McPhilemy 2013). The liberalization of financial activities over several decades also produced private financial institutions that in many cases were 'too big to fail', given the systemic impact of large bank failures on the economy and the international financial system.

The scale of the private sector financial crisis of the late 2000s caused many governments to stretch public sector balance sheets, which in some countries transformed the consequences of the credit crunch into sovereign debt problems. In Europe and North America, governments in 2009 and 2010 switched rapidly from promoting fiscal stimulus to fiscal austerity programmes in an effort to regain stability in public finances and to maintain their sovereign credit ratings. Austerity programmes involve cutting public expenditures with the aim of reducing a government's budget deficit and the level of public debt in the short-term, while alleviating the growth of public spending pressures over time. In practice, austerity typically centres on trimming the public sector wage bill; downsizing, outsourcing, or privatizing public services; and reducing the size of, or restricting access to, public entitlements such as childcare benefits, accommodation payments and pensions.

Austerity is therefore 'a form of voluntary deflation in which the economy adjusts through the reduction of wages, prices, and public spending to restore competitiveness, which is (supposedly) best achieved by cutting the state's budget, debts, and deficits' (Blyth 2013: 2). As a response to the consequences of the global financial crisis, austerity policies obscure the causes of most countries' immediate problems, and distort how fiscal sustainability is understood by equating household budgets with national budgets. Unlike those crises that are driven by fiscal profligacy when the level of public spending stretches far beyond a government's means, in most countries the financial crisis of the late 2000s comprised a private sector banking crisis. The increased stress on public finances resulted from efforts to bail out banks and other financial institutions, rather than as a consequence of loose fiscal policies.

The idea that running budget deficits in a recession and high levels of sovereign debt as a proportion of GDP constitute a fiscal crisis – requiring immediate public spending cuts – is highly dubious when countries' recent economic track records are taken into account. As Mark Blyth (2013: 5) points out in the case of Italy: 'public-sector debt in 2002 was 105.7 percent of GDP and no one cared. In 2009, it was almost exactly the same figure and everyone cared.' In the UK, the dynamics of fiscal austerity were driven by a political choice by the government to respond to the costs of the financial crisis by slashing discretionary public spending and benefit entitlements. For several other European countries, spikes in government bond yields have combined with existing fiscal pressures to force national policy-makers to seek external financial assistance through international bailouts. Among Eurozone economies, these pressures became acute from 2010 onwards. Eurozone governments in extreme financial distress were left with few alternative options to negotiating with the 'troika' of the EC, the ECB and the IMF for bailout funds in exchange for the introduction of austerity policies that shifted the burden of macroeconomic adjustment onto their populations.

Eurozone bailouts co-financed by the EU, European creditor states and the IMF have included large loans for Greece (€245.6 billion), Ireland (€67.5 billion), Portugal (€78 billion) and Cyprus (€10 billion). In addition, Spanish banks were recapitalized with a €41.4 billion loan from the European Stability Mechanism. The conditions attached to these bailouts led to widespread public protests and, in some cases, riots, while borrowing governments that faced voters at the ballot box were quickly shown the door. The political economy of Eurozone bailouts produced a high degree of policy uncertainty with regard to the effectiveness of the EU's crisis management strategy, whether EU institutions, large EU creditor states, or the IMF were calling the shots in bailout negotiations, and how great a 'haircut' bondholders would be forced to accept in sovereign debt restructuring. The 2013 bailout for Cyprus, for example, included unorthodox policies such as a tax on retail bank deposits, the introduction of capital controls and a temporary freeze on bank deposit withdrawals and electronic transactions, alongside other financial restrictions. The unprecedented proposal to tax retail bank deposits was widely criticized, and risked undermining social trust in financial institutions across other struggling Eurozone economies. The economic fallout from the financial disaster of 2008–09 created three mutually reinforcing crises that threaten the future of the euro: (1) a continuing liquidity crisis in the banking sector; (2) a deterioration of the terms on which many governments are able to access credit; and (3) weak economic growth (Shambaugh 2012). A negative feedback loop has linked together these problems in financial liquidity, sovereign credit-worthiness and fragile growth, with each problem worsening the effects of the others.

In these circumstances, much of the initial enthusiasm among policy-makers for engaging in root and branch reform of the rules, processes and safeguards of global financial governance quickly dissipated. The onset of the financial crisis in Europe and the USA produced a short-lived consensus in late 2008 around the need for coordinated policy activism among governments to stimulate global demand. It also prompted calls for a rewriting of global financial rules based on a 'new Bretton Woods' grand compromise between economic openness and stability, including the introduction of taxes on international financial transactions and other systemic reforms (Helleiner 2010; Helleiner and Pagliari 2009). Rather than transforming the architecture of global economic gover-nance, however, the initial effects of the crisis produced 'Twelve-month Keynesians' – policy-makers who briefly embraced economic stimulus policies in 2008–09 before becoming champions of fiscal austerity in 2009–10 (Blyth 2013: 54–6, 60–1).

Crises are narrated events, and the lessons that are drawn from crisis episodes are shaped by repeated practices of representation that, in turn, influence the scope for political action and policy change (Samman 2012). The catchwords of earlier crisis episodes include 'stagflation' in the economic crises that followed the breakdown of the Bretton Woods international monetary system in the 1970s, 'structural adjustment' in the 1980s Latin American debt crisis, 'market transition' in centrally planned economies in the early 1990s and 'crony capitalism' in the Asian financial crisis of 1997–98. While substantive changes are still unfolding in the aftermath of the global financial crisis, the widespread hope that policy-makers might capitalize on the opportunities provided by the crisis to quickly introduce structural reforms in the architecture of global financial governance were not fulfilled (Helleiner 2010). These initial 'great expectations' have instead been translated into 'slow transforma-tions' in post-crisis financial regulation (Moschella and Tsingou 2013).

One of the dominant reform themes to emerge during the global financial crisis centred on the benefits of adopting new instruments of macro-prudential regulation. In contrast to micro-prudential forms of financial regulation that are aimed at maintaining the solvency of indi-vidual financial institutions, macro-prudential regulation proposals are targeted at safeguarding stability at a systemic level. The gradual devel-opment of a consensus around the advantages of macro-prudential

---

> # Box 13.1   Selected actors in financial crises
>
> - **Club forums**
>   Clubs such as the G8 and the G20 serve as forums for political leaders to negotiate policy coordination and international regime changes in response to systemic financial crises.
>
> - **Everyday actors**
>   Non-elite actors often bear the burden of economic adjustment during financial crises, especially in a context of fiscal austerity. Collective responses by everyday actors to financial distress can prompt bank runs when financial institutions face liquidity problems, as well as capital outflows when depositors shift their savings offshore.
>
> - **International organizations**
>   The IMF continues to play a significant role in international crisis management through coordinating sovereign bailout loans for governments in exchange for the implementation of an agreed list of policy conditions. Other organizations such as the FSB and the BIS have also shaped the design of new international financial rules.
>
> - **Market actors**
>   Financial market euphoria during a boom creates pro-cyclical effects that further inflate financial bubbles, which also worsens the economic consequences of financial shocks. During the global financial crisis, financial institutions hoarded capital and tightened lending criteria to safeguard their own liquidity, which undermined the effectiveness of monetary stimulus and fiscal austerity policies.
>
> - **States**
>   National policy responses shape both the aggregate economic effects and the distributional effects of financial crises, and can influence the speed and quality of economy recovery. In cases where countries experiencing severe financial distress request a sovereign bailout from the IMF, regional institutions such as the EU and bilateral creditors, the extent of a government's policy discretion is constrained by conditions stipulated in loan agreements.

regulation potentially represents a direct challenge to the policy orthodoxy that prevailed prior to the global financial crisis.

Pre-crisis modes of regulation rested in large part on the assumption that financial markets were inherently efficient, and therefore sound financial regulation should concentrate on increasing transparency through disclosure requirements and the creation of risk management systems based on market prices. In contrast, macro-prudential regulation initiatives are grounded in the recognition that 'herding effects' make financial markets inherently pro-cyclical, with securitization techniques increasing the scope for volatility and financial shocks. Rather than relying on market discipline and transparency measures to govern financial risk, macro-prudential regulation might include the use of policy instruments such as limits on bank leverage and loan-to-value ratios, counter-cyclical capital requirements (increasing the capital reserves financial institutions must retain in boom periods) and controls on capital inflows to reduce the potential for international speculation to inflate financial bubbles (Baker 2013: 116–17, 131). Whether this shift in the focus of financial governance away from micro-prudential risk management techniques and towards macro-prudential regulatory responses will, in practice, constitute a definitive break with long-held assumptions about how financial risks emerge and how they should be regulated remains to be seen. As the economic history of the 1930s and 1940s suggests, translating ideational shifts into national policy reforms and structural changes in international economic governance after a systemic crisis can prove to be a lengthy process.

Summary

The financial crisis of the late 2000s was a systemic shock for the global political economy of the twenty-first century. The economic fallout from the crisis threw orthodox economic policy beliefs about the benefits of liberalized financial markets into doubt, and challenged policy-makers around the world to devise new methods for regulating financial risks in order to safeguard financial stability. In many developed economies the crisis led to a prolonged period of fiscal austerity, accompanied by weak growth, high unemployment and depressed demand as wages either stagnated or decreased in real terms. For some governments the introduction of austerity policies was a price they had to pay to access external financial assistance from the EU, bilateral creditors and the IMF. For others, the costs of domestic adjustment through austerity were self-inflicted as governments attempted to maintain sovereign creditworthiness and policy credibility with financial markets by contracting the economy through public spending cuts, at the same time as trying to inflate the economy through monetary stimulus.

An important consequence of the crisis was the demonstration effect it provided of the potential for market failure, especially in the context of financial liberalization. This created opportunities for political leaders in China and other emerging economies to sharpen their criticisms of the liberal principles underpinning market-based growth models and the contemporary architecture of global economic governance. On the one hand, the crisis served to accelerate existing trends in the shifting balance between developed economies in North America and Europe and rising economic powers in Asia. Emerging economies nonetheless remain in an interdependent relationship with developed economies, which suggests that contemporary predictions of the imminent demise of US structural power in the global political economy are, at best, exaggerating the short-term consequences of the crisis. On the other hand, many developed economies continue to struggle with weak growth, reduced fiscal space due to high sovereign debt, financial volatility and uneven rates of recovery across economic sectors and household income groups. These conditions suggest the continuing effects of the crisis still have a long way to run before the features of the post-crisis international financial system become clear.

Discussion questions

1. What were the causes of the global financial crisis in 2008–09?
2. Why did the global financial crisis lead to sovereign debt crises in the Eurozone?
3. How might financial regulation be reformed to foster greater financial stability?
4. How should governments change their economic policies in a recession, and why?
5. How do fiscal austerity programmes affect income distribution?
6. How should the architecture of international crisis management be reformed, and why?

Further reading

Blyth, Mark. 2013. *Austerity: The History of a Dangerous Idea*. Oxford: Oxford University Press.

Gamble, Andrew. 2009b. *The Spectre at the Feast: Capitalist Crisis and the Politics of Recession*. Basingstoke: Palgrave Macmillan.

Moschella, Manuela and Eleni Tsingou (eds). 2013. *Great Expectations, Slow Transformations: Incremental Change in Post-Crisis Regulation*. Colchester: ECPR Press.

Reinhart, Carmen M. and Kenneth S. Rogoff. 2009. *This Time is Different: Eight Centuries of Financial Folly*. Princeton, NJ: Princeton University Press.

Schwartz, Herman M. 2009. *Subprime Nation: American Power, Global Capital, and the Housing Bubble*. Ithaca, NY: Cornell University Press.

Underhill, Geoffrey R.D., Jasper Blom and Daniel Mügge. 2010. *Global Financial Integration Thirty Years On: From Reform to Crisis*. Cambridge: Cambridge University Press.

Chapter 14

Sovereign Debt

Introduction

Access to external sources of finance for domestic investment is widely agreed to be a critical ingredient for successful economic development and growth. Excluding official development assistance (ODA) and remittances by foreign workers to their home countries, for much of the post-World War II era official creditors provided the lion's share of external finance to developing countries in the form of debt flows from creditor governments and publicly guaranteed agencies as well as IOs such as the World Bank and the IMF. In recent decades the private sector has replaced official creditors as the largest source of external finance for many developing countries. FDI and access to private sources of finance now play a much greater role in national economic growth than at any previous time in history. However, countries which rely on high net debt inflows may run a greater risk of macroeconomic instability and financial distress, especially if they face adverse global economic conditions. The second half of the twentieth century and the first decade of the twenty-first century have been characterized by a succession of sovereign debt crises around the world. The IMF and the World Bank have both played a central role in coordinating the response to sovereign debt crises during the last 30 years. The outcomes of sovereign debt renegotiations determine the level of a debtor's repayment burden, and the distribution of financial losses that is sustained by official or private creditors. This chapter examines the causes and consequences of sovereign debt crises, and identifies the main drivers of change in the international sovereign debt regime.

Background

The process of developing international rules to protect the property rights of foreign capital owners developed initially among industrialized countries, and was later extended to less-developed countries in Africa, Asia, Latin America and elsewhere through a combination of diplomatic intervention, bargaining and coercion (Lipson 1985; Centano 1997). In the post-World War II era, the principle that interest payments due on sovereign debts must be maintained, even if the timetables for loan repayments are rescheduled or maturing debt is refinanced, was widely diffused around the world by the IMF and the World Bank. For example, in an attempt to establish credibility with the international financial community, when the World Bank was established it refused to lend to any state that had defaulted on loans during the Great Depression of the 1930s until these outstanding claims were settled (Lipson 1985: 169–70). While many developing countries have benefited in recent years from their ability to access both private and official sources of credit from external lenders, the current structure of the international sovereign debt regime is widely viewed as sustaining an unequal distribution of benefits and costs between developed countries, multilateral lenders and private lenders on the one hand, and developing country borrowers, on the other. The unequal nature of this relationship is especially stark in the case of low-income developing countries.

In addition to the potential for debt flows to have a positive effect on a country's economic development and growth through enabling individuals, firms and governments to access greater financial resources for investment, high debt flows may increase a country's economic vulnerability in several ways. For example, approximately 30 per cent of developing countries remain unable to raise public debt in their own currency, and must instead issue bonds that are denominated in foreign currency to attract foreign investors. This adds greater 'currency risk' to sovereign debt, whereby the capacity of a government to service its debt decreases if foreign exchange earnings from exports drop or the exchange rate sharply depreciates. Governments are also unable to 'monetize' debts through expanding the domestic money supply in the case of foreign currency debt obligations. Meanwhile, foreign currency debt which is put to non-productive uses, such as political patronage or subsidizing household consumption, may increase a country's ratio of debt service obligations to the value of earnings from exports and other foreign income, precipitating a debt crisis. A debt crisis can be defined as 'rescheduling under duress'. This occurs when a country's contractual debt obligations with creditor governments, private lenders, or multilateral lenders have to be rescheduled because a debtor government is either

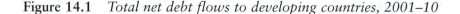

Figure 14.1   *Total net debt flows to developing countries, 2001–10*

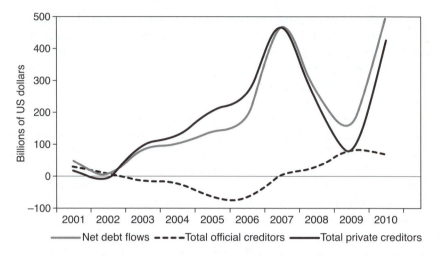

Source: World Bank (2012) *Global Development Finance: External Debt of Developing Countries*, p. 3 (http://data.worldbank.org/sites/default/files/gdt_2012.pdf).

unable or unwilling to meet its current payment obligations (Kapstein 1994: 84).

Major debt crises can potentially undermine the integrity of the international financial system. When faced with the risk of a sovereign debt default, for example, the IMF's reputation as a credible 'commitment mechanism' is also on the line. This helps to provide confidence to external creditors that sovereign debtors will meet their obligations (Broome 2008). The crisis management role of the IMF is often complicated by the involvement of 'supplementary financiers' who part-fund sovereign bailout packages for distressed economies. Recently, this role has been played by the EC and EU creditor states that have provided substantial contributions to IMF-sponsored bailout packages for Eurozone economies (see Chapter 13). The need to negotiate not only with debtor governments but also with other regional and multilateral organizations as well as creditor states makes it harder for the parties involved to gain mutually beneficial outcomes, as well as drawing multilateral lenders such as the IMF more closely into domestic politics in both creditor and debtor states (Hodson 2011: 103–6).

In previous episodes characterized by high levels of sovereign borrowing, much of the lending to developing countries was done by creditor governments, often through publicly guaranteed export credit and insurance agencies to help boost their own exports to debtor countries. However, as Figure 14.1 illustrates, in the past decade private

Figure 14.2   *Net official debt flows to developing countries, 2001–10*

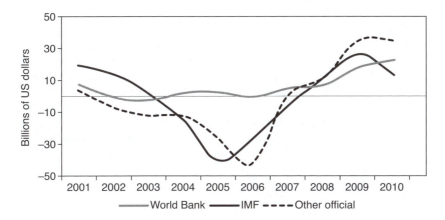

Source: World Bank (2012) *Global Development Finance: External Debt of Developing Countries*, p. 3 (http://data.worldbank.org/sites/default/files/gdf_2012.pdf).

Figure 14.3   Net private debt flows to developing countries, 2001–10

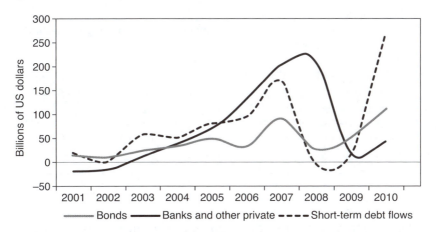

Source: World Bank (2012) *Global Development Finance: External Debt of Developing Countries*, p. 3 (http://data.worldbank.org/sites/default/files/gdf_2012.pdf).

sector lending has come to dwarf the amount of total official lending to developing countries. For the period from 2003–07 net debt flows to developing countries from official creditors decreased overall. This was due in part to reduced borrowing from multilateral lenders such as the IMF prior to 2008, as well as large repayments on bilateral loans from middle-income developing countries to Paris Club creditors (see Box 14.2).

Box 14.1   Key debt terms

- **Debt default**
  Debt is defined as outstanding financial liabilities arising from past borrowing, which may be owed to external or domestic creditors and is typically in the form of loans or bonds. Debt default occurs when a party is unwilling or unable to pay their debt obligations.

- **Debt rescheduling and debt relief**
  Agreements by creditors to lessen the debt burden of countries by either rescheduling interest and principal payments, sometimes on a concessional basis, or by partially or fully cancelling debt service payments falling due during a specific period of time.

- **Debt service to exports**
  The ratio of the sum of repayments on the principal and interest on total long-term debt (including public and publicly guaranteed debt and private non-guaranteed debt) to the value of exports of goods and services and receipts of income from abroad.

- **Debt service**
  Scheduled interest and principal repayments due on public and publicly guaranteed debt outstanding during a year.

- **Debt stocks and debt flows**
  External debt stocks are the accumulated amount of outstanding debt owed by a country to external creditors at a specific point in time. External debt flows refer to changes in the level of debt owed to external creditors over an interval of time (such as within one year).   →

The volume of official lending expanded significantly with the onset of the global financial crisis, which saw a sharp increase in the number of countries requesting IMF loans (see Figure 14.2). Part of the recent increase in bilateral official lending was due not to loans from traditional developed country creditors but rather to the emergence of a new group of developing country creditors. China alone accounted for nearly one third of the US$135 billion in new bilateral loans agreed between 2007 and 2010 (World Bank 2012: 5–6). In addition to a far greater reliance on private sources of external credit relative to official lenders, major developing country debtors have increasingly turned to short-term debt with a maturity date of less than 12 months as a key

➜

- **Grace period and maturity date**
  A 'grace period' is the time between when a loan is committed and when the first principal payment is due. A 'maturity' date is when the final principal payment on a loan falls due (the sum of the grace period and the repayment period).

- **Short-term and long-term external debt**
  External debt is owed to non-residents by residents of an economy and is repayable in foreign currency, goods, or services. Short-term debt is defined as debt that is due to mature within one year. Long-term debt has an original or extended maturity date of more than one year.

- **Official and private creditors**
  Official creditors are governments or other bilateral public agencies (such as export credit agencies) and multilateral institutions such as the World Bank and the IMF. Private creditors include bondholders, commercial banks, and other trade-related lenders.

- **Private non-guaranteed debt**
  Debt owed by private sector borrowers to external creditors on loans that do not benefit from a public sector guarantee by the debtor country.

- **Public and publicly guaranteed external debt**
  Public debt is the sum of external obligations of a public borrower, such as a national or local government or agency, or an autonomous public body. Publicly guaranteed external debt consists of external obligations on a private debtor, the repayment of which is guaranteed by a public entity such as a national government or agency.

source of external finance. This is illustrated in Figure 14.3, which demonstrates a significant increase in short-term debt as a proportion of total net debt flows to developing countries since 2009. The contemporary dynamics of global debt flows to developing countries have therefore shifted markedly over the course of the last ten years. Key changes include a greater dependence on private sources of external finance, the rise of a select group of developing countries as bilateral creditors and a rapid increase in short-term private debt in the aftermath of the global financial crisis.

The evolution of the international sovereign debt regime

Although some of the principles at the heart of the international sovereign debt regime can be traced back across several centuries, the contemporary evolution of the debt regime is usually dated from the 1970s, when developing countries faced higher oil import costs in the aftermath of the oil price shocks (see Chapter 17). This led to fears among developed country exporters that developing countries would be forced to cut their imports of manufactured goods in order to pay for the higher cost of oil. In these circumstances, large commercial banks in developed economies were encouraged to 'recycle' the petrodollar deposits they received from oil-exporting countries – which gained a foreign currency windfall after the oil price shocks – through lending to developing country oil importers in order to alleviate balance of payments shortfalls as well as to enable developing countries to maintain infrastructure spending. In addition, developed country governments aggressively promoted their own exports to developing countries through export credit and insurance agencies (Kapstein 1994: 58–80). These policies encouraged developing country governments to fund balance of payments shortfalls through borrowing from both official and private creditors, rather than adjusting economic policies in response to changes in global economic conditions.

In the early 1980s, developing country debtors faced additional economic challenges following the second oil price shocks, increases in international interest rates and reduced demand for their exports caused by a world recession. As a consequence of these exogenous conditions, developing country borrowers faced a heavy external debt burden in terms of both the stock of public and publicly guaranteed external debt. At the same time, many countries' debt service to exports ratios increased dramatically. In Brazil and Argentina, for instance, the ratio of debt service payments to export earnings doubled between 1973 and 1978, while Mexico's debt service to exports ratio increased from 30.3 per cent to 74.1 per cent. In August 1982 Mexico announced a debt moratorium on forthcoming interest payments on external debt. This led to the 1980s Latin American debt crisis, with a further 20 developing countries forced to reschedule their external debt obligations during 1983 (Kapstein 1994: 70–1, 88–9). The debt crisis resulted in a 'lost decade' for much of the region as economic growth stalled, incomes fell in real terms, unemployment skyrocketed and high rates of inflation eroded household purchasing power, while public revenue was diverted from social and education expenditures and infrastructure investment in order to meet debt repayments.

Throughout the 1980s, it was widely assumed that the solution for countries struggling with external debt was to balance the rescheduling of repayment obligations through the Paris Club with refinancing to safe-guard the integrity of the international financial system and, in particular, to uphold the principle of the sanctity of contracts. Debtor governments had argued strongly for sovereign debt relief, special treatment for low-income debtors and a move away from case-by-case debt rescheduling in order to shelter debt renegotiations from strategic politics, as key demands in the New International Economic Order negotiations during the 1970s and early 1980s (Callaghy 2004: 5). However, developed country governments and IOs such as the IMF and the World Bank resisted changing the principles at the heart of the international sovereign debt regime, and presented a 'moral hazard' counterargument against proposals to provide debt relief through reducing sovereign debt stocks. This maintained that debtor governments must honour previous loan agreements, even if these were to be paid off over an extended period of time, to avoid creating perverse incentives in the future for countries to increase their borrowing to unsustainable levels in order to secure a debt write-off (Easterly 2002a: 1679–81).

In contrast to middle-income developing countries that had borrowed heavily from private creditors as well as official creditors, the bulk of the debt owed by many low-income developing countries stemmed from trade credits or credit guarantees that had been extended by developing countries' export credit and insurance agencies in order to support their overseas exports. As a result, low-income country debtors in the 1980s faced the prospect a prolonged period shut out from private sources of external finance, as most had restricted access to private financing even during the bank lending boom of the mid-1970s. With their economic growth rates and terms of trade continuing to deteriorate during the 1980s, the non-concessional debt rescheduling conditions available to low-income countries through the Paris Club process only served to increase the overall stock of their outstanding debts throughout the course of the decade. This prompted widespread criticisms and challenges to the legitimacy of the international sovereign debt regime from policy-makers in both developed and developing economies, as well as international public campaigns to boost political support for changing the sovereign debt regime by coalitions of NGOs.

The advocacy role of NGOs in particular has played a critical part in shaping the evolution of the sovereign debt agenda during the last two decades (Busby 2007). Although the international sovereign debt regime had previously revolved around state interests and inter-state bargaining, during the 1990s and 2000s networks of NGOs led a concerted push for the governments of official creditors and multilateral lenders such as the IMF and the World Bank to accept the principle of debt reduction for the world's poorest and most indebted countries. This focused on altering the terms that were used to describe and to interpret the issue of low-income developing country debt, in order to build public support for a narrative that rich countries had an obligation to assist poorer countries through debt forgiveness. Public campaigns against developing country debt problems also challenged the legitimacy of 'odious debt' that had been contracted by previous governments in some developing countries. Odious debt is an concept that refers to sovereign debt incurred by 'illegitimate' regimes for purposes that do not serve the public interest, such as the purchase of military hardware for domestic repression, or the appropriation of debt funds for personal enrichment and corruption (Wong 2012).

The combined debt levels of countries that were given the HIPC label by the IMF and the World Bank during the 1990s rose from US$55 billion in 1980 to US$183 billion in 1990 and US$215 billion in 1995. In response, NGO networks focusing on debt issues such as Jubilee 2000, Oxfam International and Eurodad sought to persuade richer countries to reduce debt obligations in order to alleviate extreme poverty in HIPCs. While the transformative potential of civil society actors in the global political economy has sometimes been overstated in recent years, in this case NGOs played an important role in helping to shift the terms through which the international debt debate was framed, thereby altering the criteria on which appropriate policy solutions were evaluated (Callaghy 2004: 6, 44).

Reforming the international sovereign debt regime for HIPCs was a drawn-out process that evolved haphazardly from the late 1980s. Beginning in 1988 with agreement on the Toronto Terms (which allowed for a maximum 33 per cent reduction in official debt), Paris Club creditors gradually accepted that substantively addressing the chronic debt problems of low-income countries would require debt rescheduling on concessional terms. Initial proposals were limited to extending more generous 'grace periods' and a partial reduction in the stock of debt (see Box 14.1). When these changes to debt servicing agreements failed to make a significant improvement in the debt stocks and debt service ratios of many low-income countries, the process continued to evolve over the course of the 1990s and early 2000s.

The terms of debt renegotiations gradually became more favourable to sovereign debtors as Paris Club creditors subsequently agreed the Houston Terms in 1990 (enabling more generous rescheduling terms for middle-income debtors), the London Terms in 1991 (allowing for up to 50 per cent debt reduction for low-income countries) and the Naples Terms in 1994 (which increased debt reduction to a maximum of 67 per cent for the poorest countries that were eligible to borrow on concessional terms from the World Bank's International Development

> **Box 14.2   Club governance in the international sovereign debt regime**
>
> In the post-World War II era, renegotiations of sovereign debt owed to other governments have usually been dealt with on a case-by-case basis through the Paris Club, an ad-hoc grouping of official lenders first convened in Paris in 1956 as a forum for Argentina to renegotiate its outstanding debts with creditor governments. States seeking to reschedule the timetable for repaying official loans must have an IMF programme in place in order to assure creditors that the new terms for repaying loans will be observed. In order for a country to gain a debt rescheduling agreement through the Paris Club, three principles must be met: imminent default; policy conditionality; and burden sharing. First, countries must be able to demonstrate that sovereign default is imminent without a rescheduling agreement, a diagnosis which relies on the IMF's short-term balance of payments projections for a country. Second, creditor governments insist that a debtor country agree to a programme of reforms to national policy settings in order to resolve the causes of payment difficulties through an IMF loan agreement. Third, the costs of rescheduling debt must be shared among creditors according to the level of their exposure, with debtor countries unable to grant a particular creditor more favourable terms than others. Because of the importance that creditors have attached to upholding these principles and the ad-hoc nature of the Paris Club, the process has served to isolate debtors while helping to ensure solidarity among creditors (Rieffel 1985).

Association). This led to the establishment of the HIPC Initiative under the auspices of the World Bank and the IMF in 1996 on the Paris Club's Lyon Terms, which increased the level of debt reduction to 80 per cent for the world's poorest countries with high ratios of external debt to export earnings. The goal of the HIPC Initiative was for heavily indebted low-income countries to make an exit from the continual process of debt rescheduling by achieving 'debt sustainability'.

The debt debate progressed to proposals for 100 per cent cancellation of the external debts owed by HIPCs to developed country governments and multilateral lenders in the late 1990s. The Enhanced HIPC Initiative was created in 1999 following a review by the IMF and the World Bank of the initial outcomes of the 1996 HIPC Initiative. This incorporated the Cologne Terms, which extended up to 90 per cent debt reduction for HIPCs. This became available once eligible countries underwent an intensive process of policy surveillance and structural reform through the design of Poverty Reduction Strategy Papers (see Chapter 16). The international sovereign debt regime for HIPCs was further fine-tuned with the decision at the G8 Gleneagles Summit in July 2005 to accept 100 per cent cancellation of HIPC sovereign debts that were owed to the IMF and the World Bank through the Multilateral Debt Relief Initiative (Helleiner and Cameron 2006; Momani 2010).

A key change in the treatment of sovereign debt by bilateral official creditors and multilateral institutions that developed during the last two decades was the weakening of *pact sunt servanda* – the principle that 'pacts must be respected'. This was applied first on sovereign debt owed to other governments, and later in the case of debt owed to the IMF and the World Bank, which had sought to protect their preferred creditor status by ensuring that multilateral debts were repaid in full. Securing the protection of external creditors' property rights in their dealings with sovereign governments has been a central concern of international economic rule-making throughout the last two centuries (Tomz 2007). These changes therefore represent a significant shift in the treatment of sovereign debt contracts for a selective group of low-income countries.

Despite these changes in the international sovereign debt regime for HIPCs, more far-reaching initiatives to reform international debt restructuring processes have been unsuccessful. In response to the weaknesses inherent in the ad-hoc process of debt restructuring through the Paris Club, for example, IMF Deputy Managing Director Anne Krueger led proposals for the creation of a new SDRM in 2001–03. Eric Helleiner (2008b) has identified three reasons why a series of historical and contemporary proposals for formal SDRMs have failed to build a sufficient policy consensus to overcome opposition. First, both sovereign debtors and private creditors face strong collective action problems, resulting in a lack of support from both borrower states and private lenders. Second, the uncertain distributional consequences of establishing an SDRM tends to undermine support from creditors, who fear it would benefit debtors, while debtors fear the opposite. Third, private creditors' states have been unwilling to support SDRM proposals. In some cases the lack of state support for SDRM initiatives was a response to investor lobbying, while in other instances states sought to distance themselves from investor interests.

Contemporary challenges and sources of change

Developed country sovereign debt has re-emerged as a critical issue in the study of contemporary IPE, against the backdrop of continuing debt problems in the Eurozone and uncertainty over the growth of US trade and budget deficits. As Carmen Reinhart and Kenneth Rogoff (2009: 73) have observed, international banking crises have 'historically been associated with a high incidence of sovereign defaults on external debt'.

When banking crises result in a slowdown or contraction in world economic growth this reduces countries' export earnings and their capacity to service external debt, and can produce a credit crunch in periphery countries as investors engage in a 'flight to safety'. Meanwhile, the contagion effects of a banking crisis encourage investors to become more risk-averse in their investment strategies, at the same time as financial liquidity problems in one country may cause a loss of confidence in other financial systems (Reinhart and Rogoff 2009: 73–5). In Europe, the sovereign debt crisis which emerged in 2010 continues to threaten the future of the euro. Sovereign bailouts for distressed European economies have been provided by the EC and other creditors, including the IMF. This has involved large-scale financial assistance for Eurozone members such as Cyprus, Greece, Ireland, Portugal and Spain, as well as non-euro countries such as Hungary, Latvia and Romania. By 2013, the total size of the bailouts for EU states had reached nearly 500 billion euros (see Chapter 13).

Among developed country borrowers, the USA is by far the world's largest debtor in absolute terms, with much of its public debt in US Treasury bonds held by Japan and China. This has flow-on effects for the future maintenance of US military power and the size of the US defence budget, as well as the growing economic interdependence between the USA and China (Thompson 2007: 307–8). The rapidly growing stock of US public debt held by China is a critical dimension of the two countries' changing relationship, which is linked to the US–China trade deficit as well as frictions over China's exchange rate practices (see Chapters 10 and 11). China's total holdings of US Treasury securities have risen from US$92 billion in March 2000 to US$340 billion in June 2004, US$1,205 billion in June 2008 and US$1,726 billion in June 2011 (US Treasury 2012). China's trade surplus with the USA is viewed by many US policy-makers as the result of currency manipulation practices, which have facilitated the increasing rate of China's investment in US Treasury bonds (Foot and Walter 2011: 123–5). This in turn has boosted the capacity of the US government to maintain domestic spending and investment in a period of large budget deficits, at the same time as continuing to run large trade deficits.

With respect to global debt flows to developing countries, two of the most significant trends during the last decade include the enormous increase in private lending to developing countries, and a recent spike in short-term debt flows. The accumulated stock of external debt owed by developing countries with a maturity date of less than 12 months more than doubled from US$500 billion in 2005 to US$1,036 billion in 2010 (World Bank 2012: 2). Such a rapid increase in the stock of short-term external debt might typically be a cause for concern about the prospects for the stability of debt flows to developing country borrowers in the event of further global economic instability. Sharp increases in short-term debt flows to East Asian economies both preceded and partly precipitated the Asian financial crisis in 1997–98 (Noble and Ravenhill 2000: 4–5). Today, however, many of the top developing country debtors have created a buffer against the risks of non-renewal of short-term debt contracts and other systemic risks by substantially boosting their foreign exchange reserves. For the 129 developing countries covered in the World Bank's *Global Development Finance* annual report, the aggregate ratio of foreign exchange reserves to outstanding external debt rose each year from 2005 to 2010. From a foreign reserves-to-debt stock ratio of 77 per cent in 2005, this increased to 117 per cent in 2008 and to 131 per cent in 2010 (World Bank 2012: 2). Growth in the foreign exchange reserves of the largest developing country debtors means that borrowers may be able to sustain significant increases in the level of short-term debt, without the increase in sovereign credit risks that might normally be associated with these changes in the composition and maturity rates of external debt.

Despite dropping sharply in 2008 and 2009 in the middle of the global financial crisis, private debt flows to developing countries resurged

Table 14.1   *Top-ten borrowers, 2010*

Country	External debt stock (US$ billions)	External debt stock (percentage of total)	Percentage of total net flow
China	548.6	13.5	29.9
Russia	384.7	9.4	4.6
Brazil	347	8.5	14.6
Turkey	293.9	7.2	3.6
India	290.3	7.1	9.1
Mexico	200.1	4.9	4.3
Indonesia	179.1	4.4	2.6
Argentina	127.9	3.1	2.1
Romania	121.5	3	1.2
Kazakhstan	118.7	2.9	1.6
Total top-10 borrowers	2611.8	64.1	73.5
Other developing countries	1464.5	35.9	26.5
All developing countries	4076.3	100	100

Source: World Bank (2012) *Global Development Finance: External Debt of Developing Countries*, p. 4 (http://data.worldbank.org/sites/default/files/gdf_2012.pdf).

Box 14.3 Selected actors in the international sovereign debt regime

- **Club forums**
  The Paris Club is a group of official creditors from developing countries which meets to renegotiate the terms of sovereign debt contracts. Debtor countries negotiate with private creditors through the London Club to refinance debt owed to commercial banks.

- **International organizations**
  The IMF and the World Bank are major players in the international sovereign debt regime. To gain Paris Club agreements which reschedule countries' sovereign debt, the IMF must first agree a loan programme with debtor governments. The IMF, the World Bank and the regional development banks remain important sources of multilateral loans for many developing countries.

- **Market actors**
  Internationally active commercial banks are an important source of private loans to developing and developed countries, and can collectively influence both sovereign debt renegotiations and the terms of bailouts for distressed economies. Bondholders are lenders who invest in public or private debt (bonds), which helps to finance long-term investments and current expenditure. Bondholders may include institutional investors, governments, traders and individual investors. When bondholders opt to sell their assets en masse (effectively decreasing the value of sovereign bonds and increasing interest rates) this can constrain the policy flexibility available to governments, and may result in the need for a sovereign bailout.

- **Non-governmental organizations**
  NGOs, including advocacy networks such as Eurodad and international coalitions such as Jubilee 2000, have played an important role in public campaigns to change the international sovereign debt regime to better reflect the balance of interests between developed country public and private creditors and developing country debtors.

- **States**
  Debtor states typically find themselves in a weak negotiating position when faced with a debt crisis. The current structure of the international sovereign debt regime is widely viewed as encouraging solidarity among creditors while preventing collective action among debtors.

strongly in 2010. International capital flows to developing countries increased by some 68 per cent from the 2009 total to return to the 2007 level of US$1.1 trillion (World Bank 2012: 1). Much of this resurgence in capital flows to developing countries in 2010 represented a surge in short-term debt stocks, which rose in 2010 by 34 per cent compared with a 6 per cent increase in the stock of long-term external debt from 2009. The lion's share of net debt flows to developing countries continues to remain concentrated in a small group of middle-income countries. For example, 30 per cent of total net capital inflows in 2010 went to China, while the top-ten borrowers accounted for over 73 per cent of debt flows to 129 developing countries in 2010 (see Table 14.1).

The largest developing country debtors therefore rely heavily on private lending as a key source of external finance. At the same time, many other developing countries remain dependant on access to official bilateral credit as well as multilateral credit from the IMF, the World Bank and regional development banks. When private capital flows dried up during the global financial crisis, many borrowers turned once again to the IMF for emergency financial assistance. This provided a stark reminder that private lenders cannot substitute for public organizations that are able to provide lender of last resort functions during financial turmoil, however imperfect their design.

Summary

In the aftermath of the global financial crisis of 2008–09 sovereign debt issues have returned to the top of the political agenda in both developing and developed economies. The financing options that shape creditor–debtor relations in the global political economy have become segmented by debtor type in recent decades. Middle-income developing countries that are the largest borrowers can readily access private lending, although this may mean relying on short-term external debt contracts with a maturity date of less than 12 months. This is a select group, with the ten largest developing country debtors accounting for over 73 per cent of all debt flows to developing countries in 2010. A 'second tier' group of developing country borrowers are more likely to rely on a mix of private and official bilateral and multilateral lending for investment and current expenditure. Both the 'top tier' of largest developing country borrowers and 'second tier' debtors can – if faced with a debt crisis – potentially reschedule their debt repayments over a longer time horizon through the Paris Club and London Club processes, but are not eligible to access existing forms of debt relief from creditors that would reduce their total debt stocks. In contrast, the HIPC group remain dependent on debt relief on previous loans and new lending from official creditors, and are unable to access most private sources of external finance.

Discussion questions

1. Who drives change in the international sovereign debt regime, and why?
2. Who are the winners and losers from the contemporary sovereign debt regime?
3. How do sovereign debt crises differ between developed and developing economies, and why?
4. How should the system for restructuring sovereign debt be reformed, and for whose benefit?
5. What factors will shape the future evolution of the international sovereign debt regime?
6. Should 'odious debt' be repaid? If so, why? If not, why not?

Further reading

Aggarwal, Vinod K. and Brigitte Granville (eds). 2003. *Sovereign Debt: Origins, Crises, and Restructuring*. London: Royal Institute of International Affairs.

Hardie, Iain. 2012. *Financialization and Government Borrowing Capacity in Emerging Markets*. Basingstoke: Palgrave Macmillan.

Ocampo, José Antonio, Jan Kregel and Stephany Griffith-Jones (eds). 2013. *International Finance and Development*. London: Zed/United Nations.

Rieffel, Lex. 2003. *Restructuring Sovereign Debt: The Case for Ad Hoc Machinery*. Washington, DC: Brookings Institution Press.

Tomz, Michael. 2007. *Reputation and International Cooperation: Sovereign Debt across Three Centuries*. Princeton, NJ: Princeton University Press.

Wong, Yvonne. 2012. *Sovereign Finance and the Poverty of Nations: Odious Debt in International Law*. Cheltenham: Edward Elgar.

Chapter 15

Tax and Welfare

Introduction

The ability of governments to levy taxes is one of the defining features of state power. Taxes determine the volume of public revenue and therefore a state's capacity to spend money. Moreover, tax policies are a potent tool for governments to shape economic behaviour, and can be used as a form of business regulation. How governments raise revenue, what they spend it on and the exogenous factors that influence national fiscal policies underwent radical changes during the course of the twentieth century. Today, different countries rely on a wide variety of fiscal policies for raising government revenue, which reflect their different economic and developmental trajectories, ideas about the appropriateness of different forms and levels of taxation and the policy objectives of national governments. The development of tax policies has traditionally gone hand-in-hand with an expansion of the role of the state in providing public welfare services and greater administrative capacity to intervene in economic processes. In the contemporary global political economy a series of interrelated transformations in the external environment governments now face has impacted upon their capacity to levy taxes, which has altered the scope of national fiscal autonomy. These processes have affected all states despite their vastly different sizes and capacities, from small island states to major powers. This chapter puts these broad processes in context through explaining how the rise of global tax competition has shaped processes of change at the global, regional and national level, which have altered the political dynamics of welfare across many societies.

Background

The capacities of different states to extract revenue through taxes to fund public spending has been transformed in recent decades through changes in the global political economy that are associated with the international integration of markets for goods, services and capital. Increasing global trade flows between countries and the legalization of global rules to govern trade in goods and services have reduced the ability of individual states to gain revenue through trade tariffs and import charges, while increasing the potential for companies to relocate their business operations overseas to take advantage of lower production costs. At the same time, greater capital mobility has been stimulated by the liberalization of restrictions on cross-border capital flows, thereby enabling larger inward and outward flows of FDI as well as short-term 'hot money' flows for financial speculation and arbitrage (see Chapter 12). A number of countries have also been able to take advantage of increased access to international debt flows to finance public spending from external sources of finance rather than domestic revenue (see Chapter 14). The cumulative effect of these broader transformations in the external economic environment states face has constrained some of the means through which governments have traditionally raised public revenue through taxes, and has altered the parameters of modern welfare systems.

The amount of government revenue that is raised from taxes, the relative size of a country's total tax revenue as a proportion of GDP and how much revenue is raised through different types of taxes has tended

---

Box 15.1   Taxes

Taxes are compulsory financial charges levied by state authorities upon individuals or legal entities such as organizations and businesses. Taxes can be differentiated by: (1) whether they are paid *directly* by taxpayers to the government or are paid *indirectly* through intermediaries; and (2) whether they are based on the *value* or *quantity* of a particular good. Direct taxes are those which are levied directly on individuals (such as personal income tax) or businesses (such as corporate income tax). In contrast, indirect taxes are collected by intermediaries, and include consumption taxes (such as value-added tax) that are passed on to consumers by retail stores, with the tax proceeds subsequently paid to the government. An '*ad valorem* tax' is a financial charge based on the value of real estate or personal property (such as stamp duty on house sales, or inheritance tax), while a 'specific tax' is a financial charge that is based on a specific quantity of units regardless of value (such as excise taxes on fuel, tobacco and alcohol).

to change over time as economies have developed. Many developing countries continue to rely heavily on revenues gained from trade tariffs and export taxes that are generally easier to collect than other taxes, although IOs have encouraged developing countries to increase government revenue from income taxes and domestic consumption taxes in order to broaden their tax base and to reduce the effects of taxes on international trade (Seabrooke 2010a). Developed countries, in contrast, now draw the bulk of public revenue from income, business and consumption taxes (see Box 15.1), whereas in the past they also relied heavily on trade tariffs and customs duties to finance government expenditures.

The historical development of changes in taxation in developed countries can be illustrated through the case of the USA. As Figure 15.1 shows, during the past century property taxes have substantially reduced as a percentage of total US government revenues, which in the post-World War II era have been funded primarily through taxes on personal income. Compared with the period from 1915–45, the proportion of total revenue from excise taxes has also markedly declined while revenue from sales taxes has increased. Figure 15.1 highlights how the balance between government revenue that is drawn from personal income taxes compared with corporate income taxes has altered in the post-World War II era in the USA. Whereas personal and corporate income taxes respectively accounted for around 28 and 25 per cent of US public revenue in 1945, by 1970 these proportions had changed to 32 per cent and 11 per cent, while in 2009 personal income taxes accounted for 32 per cent of US public revenue while corporate income taxes made up only 5 per cent of revenue. These changes in the relative shares of personal income taxes and corporate income taxes in total US public revenue, along with other fiscal policy changes, have reduced the level of 'progressivity' in the US tax system over time. The relatively lower level of progressivity in the US tax system today compared with the 1960s or 1970s is not a phenomenon that is unique to the USA, but rather is part of a trend that has been identified to varying degrees in many developed economies (Piketty and Saez 2007).

A progressive tax system 'is one in which the share of income paid in taxes rises with income'. This can be contrasted with a regressive tax system 'in which the share of income paid in taxes falls with income'. More specifically, tax systems are usually defined as progressive when 'after-tax income is more equally distributed than before-tax income' (Piketty and Saez 2007: 4–5). Progressive taxation is often associated with the rise of centre-left political parties and the expansion of voting rights during the twentieth century. However, some states took steps to make their tax systems more redistributive in the early twentieth century

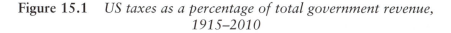

Figure 15.1   *US taxes as a percentage of total government revenue, 1915–2010*

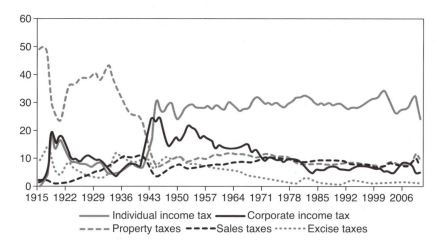

Source: Data compiled from www.usgovernmentrevenue.com.

as a response to participation in, and mobilization for, mass warfare (Scheve and Stasavage 2010).

In general, high levels of indirect taxation such as consumption taxes are deemed to have regressive effects because they are not based on progressively higher levels related to individual wealth or earnings. For example, the standard rate of the Value-Added Tax (VAT) was introduced in the UK in 1973 at 10 per cent, and in 2011 was increased from a rate of 17.5 per cent to 20 per cent on most goods and services sold domestically. The importance of VAT for UK public revenue has increased substantially since it was introduced, and it is now the third largest source of UK public revenue after income tax and National Insurance contributions (Adam and Browne 2011). However, the single rate of standard VAT means that lower-income households inevitably pay a far higher proportion of their after-tax income in VAT on basic goods such as groceries than that paid by higher-income households.

As these examples from the USA and the UK suggest, understanding the economic and social consequences of different tax policies requires look-ing at differences in marginal tax rates and types of taxes, as well as how different taxes contribute to overall public revenue in a particular country, how fiscal policies alter the after-tax distribution of wealth and how tax systems reflect social conceptions of fairness about who should shoulder the greatest share of the burden for public revenue and spending. How states extract revenue through taxes is fundamentally about the distribu-tion of economic resources both within a society and internationally, as well as the evolution of ideas about the legitimate role of governments in influencing economic processes and outcomes. In this respect, the social and economic consequences of tax policy decisions are not limited to the short-term, but can potentially influence the direction of policy change and the distribution of wealth across generations. Decisions over a state's tax policies at one point in time shape the social, political and economic context 'in which future tax policy choices are made' (Steinmo 2003: 229). In the contemporary era, many governments have found out the hard way that the pocketbook politics of taxation continue to be subject to a far higher degree of direct contestation by domestic social groups and businesses than other areas of economic governance such as monetary or trade policies.

Globalization and the welfare state

A state-based welfare system can be defined as the cluster of institutional processes through which governments redistribute income 'either through insurance schemes that mitigate risk or through spending on basic social services' (Haggard and Kaufman 2008: 3). These connected roles can be distinguished between: (1) the 'Robin Hood' function of a welfare system, which involves the redistribution of wealth and income between social groups; and (2) the 'piggy bank' function of a welfare system, which provides insurance and redistributes wealth and income over time (Barr 2012: 3). The term 'welfare state' is commonly used to refer to welfare systems in developed countries, and generally incorporates a state's activities in providing: (1) cash benefits; (2) healthcare; (3) education; and (4) food, housing and other welfare services (Barr 2012: 8).

A common theme in the globalization literature in the 1990s and 2000s was that international economic integration had stimulated a 'race to the bottom' between countries in terms of tax policies. Many observers suggested that highly mobile investors and businesses were exerting stronger pressure on governments to reduce corporate and income taxes or risk losing investment and jobs to countries that maintained lower tax regimes. This raised the prospect that downward pressure on tax rates would reduce the fiscal capacities of developed country governments to continue to fund their national welfare systems with existing levels of social expenditure. Based on the available data, however, increasing processes of economic globalization over the last four decades have gone hand-in-hand with gradual but significant increases in social spending by governments.

Overall, social spending in developed OECD countries has increased markedly in the last five decades from an average of slightly above 10 per

Figure 15.2   *Average OECD public social expenditure, 1980–2012*

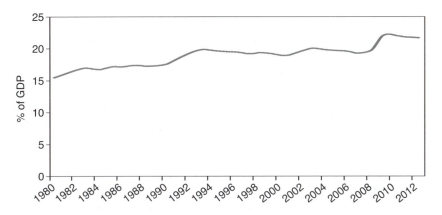

Source: OECD (2013) *Social Expenditure Database*. Paris: OECD (http://www.oecd.
org/els/soc/socialexpendituredatabasesocx.htm).

cent of GDP in 1960 (Castles 2007: 1) (see Figure 15.2).
Notwithstanding substantial national variation among developed countries in public spending, average social expenditure has tended to
increase rapidly during periods of economic crisis and to only decrease
slowly, if at all, in the aftermath of major crises. During recessions in the
early 1980s and early 1990s, for example, average OECD public social
spending as a proportion of GDP increased by around 2.5 percentage
points, without a substantial decline in social spending when economic
performance subsequently improved. In the recent global financial crisis
average OECD public social spending increased from 19 per cent of GDP
in 2007 to 22 per cent of GDP in 2009, and has since remained relatively
stable at this higher level (OECD 2012c). As Figure 15.2 illustrates, average social spending relative to GDP in developed OECD countries has
increased over the last three decades from 15.5 per cent of GDP in 1980
to around 22 per cent today.

   If economic globalization has not simply led to a 'race to the bottom',
this raises the question of what effects globalization has had on the fiscal
capacities of governments to fund social spending, and how processes of
international economic integration are linked to changing dynamics in
social spending. One of the most commonly identified effects of
economic globalization on national fiscal policies is the rise of global tax
competition, which has increased in tandem with the liberalization of
restrictions on cross-border capital flows (see Chapter 12). Tax competition refers to the pressures governments may face to either reduce rates of
taxation in order to avoid losing tax revenue to other countries with
lower tax rates, or the deliberate attempt to undercut the taxes of other

countries to lure 'tax-sensitive capital' away from foreign markets (Dehejia and Genschel 1999). Based on this line of reasoning, international tax competition between countries is assumed to increase when governments liberalize restrictions on capital movements. Greater capital mobility expands opportunities for actors to transfer capital between different jurisdictions in order to reduce their tax liabilities, as well as increasing the material incentives for doing so. This is expected to generate greater incentives for governments to reduce taxes on mobile capital, while maintaining or increasing taxes on immobile individuals and domestic transactions, such as personal income taxes and consumption taxes.

Research based on the experiences of over 100 countries during the period from 1970 to 1995 found no evidence that either maintaining open capital accounts or removing capital controls had a significant impact on public spending (Garrett 2001: 4). Studies suggest instead that higher levels of economic insecurity in developed countries has prompted changes in public expectations about the appropriate role of states in 'protecting' or 'compensating' different social groups for the negative welfare effects of international integration (Walter 2010). Other research has indicated that developing countries with democratic political systems tend to increase public spending on welfare policies in response to economic liberalization, while developing countries with non-democratic political systems are more likely to cut welfare expenditures (Nooruddin and Simmons 2009). How the dynamics of economic globalization are translated into national economic policy reforms is therefore strongly influenced by how responsive different political systems are to pressure 'from below', and to changing public expectations about the role of the state as an economic manager.

Globalization and taxation

Economic globalization is often associated with four dynamics of change in national taxation regimes. The first is the relatively greater ease with which many corporate actors can structure their business activities in order to minimize their tax obligations to a particular government. For example, many international companies use internal cross-border transfer prices to ensure that profits are effectively transferred from a high-tax jurisdiction to a low-tax jurisdiction 'with only an artificial connection to the real economic activity that should be the target of taxation' (Rixen 2011: 208–9). In addition to companies, such tax minimization arrangements are also used by some high-income individuals, who are able to establish a series of legal corporate entities on paper whose sole purpose is the transfer of wealth and income to avoid paying high taxes in their home state. The increasing use of this type of practice by businesses and high-income individuals has led many observers to conclude that the constraints on national governments' degree of fiscal autonomy have tightened as a result of economic globalization. However, the evidence suggests that countries are not involved in an all-out race to the bottom on fiscal policies, and that tax competition can serve to maintain diversity in different tax systems rather than driving convergence (Plümper *et al.* 2009). At the same time, some governments which have cut overall corporate tax rates have also reduced tax exemptions, allowances and credits for businesses in order to make the effects of corporate tax cuts neutral in terms of overall public revenue (Swank 1998).

The second international tax policy trend that has occurred during the last three decades is the shift towards a greater reliance on gaining public revenue from indirect taxes on consumption rather than direct income and corporate taxes. Taxing consumption is sometimes seen by both governments and taxpayers as a legitimate means to shape behaviour through increasing the cost of 'harmful' goods (such as alcohol and tobacco), while the trend in many countries away from multiple categories of sales taxes towards a unified consumption tax regime is seen as offering efficiency benefits in terms of tax administration, compliance and simplicity (such as VAT in the UK, or Goods and Services Tax – GST – in Australia and New Zealand). The move towards taxing consumption has accompanied a shift towards consumption-led economic growth models in some countries. Prior to the onset of the global financial crisis in 2008, this enabled public revenue to expand through growth in domestic consumption and residential property bubbles rather than through growth in manufacturing and exports (Schwartz and Seabrooke 2009). Organizations such as the EU, the OECD and the IMF have been instrumental over recent decades in championing a shift towards broadening consumption taxes in order to allow governments to simplify and reduce marginal tax rates on personal income (Broome and Seabrooke 2007).

The third international tax policy trend is a change in how governments use tax policies to shape patterns of economic behaviour. In developed countries in particular, a number of governments have shifted away from using tax policy to regulate what businesses do or to differentiate between domestic and foreign investment. In contrast, there has been a greater acceptance by many governments that market processes should determine investment allocation decisions through the creation of a market-conforming 'level playing field', rather than using taxes on business income as policy tools to foster certain kinds of corporate activities or to influence investment decisions (Swank 1998).

The final and more recent international tax policy trend is an increase in international cooperation on tax matters between governments, and especially between OECD member states. The level of international tax cooperation remains far lower than in other policy areas such as trade or monetary policy, and political sensitivities over tax issues with respect to both national governments and their broader populations limit the scope for international tax cooperation to areas where there are clear mutual advantages for different states, such as bilateral 'double taxation' agreements and policies that aim to avoid taxing business income twice in different tax jurisdictions. Double taxation agreements are bilateral or multilateral treaties between countries that aim to mitigate the effects of double taxation through defining which types of taxes can be levied in different tax jurisdictions, which organizations or individuals are exempt from the agreement and how the agreement will be enforced. The international double taxation avoidance regime emerged in the 1920s, and is geared towards enabling 'active' business income to be taxed in the source country where it is earned through sales of goods or services, while granting the country where businesses are resident (the home country) the right to tax 'passive' business income such as interests, dividends and royalties (Rixen 2011).

Notwithstanding the growth of bilateral double taxation agreements, which have increased from 35 treaties in 1928 to over 2,000 today (Rixen 2011: 207), international tax cooperation has usually been constrained by the domestic political and economic interests of national governments. As Dehejia and Genschel (1999: 404) suggest, 'tax competition ... is a particularly intractable problem for international cooperation'. The primary motivation today for some governments to cooperate with each other on tax policy to a greater extent than in the past is the material costs they face from the rise of 'tax havens'. In contrast to larger states, small state tax havens potentially stand to benefit the most from global tax competition, which can help to improve their individual revenue positions (Dehejia and Genschel 1999). As the discussion in the following section shows, tax havens pose a classic collective action problem for many governments. All governments that lose potential revenue to low-tax jurisdictions would benefit from greater international tax cooperation, because the costs involved for individual governments prohibit unilateral action. The nature of the problem potentially renders ineffective any unilateral attempts by a government to reduce revenue losses to tax havens, while even a collective effort by a sub-set of governments may fail if non-cooperating tax havens continue to attract tax-sensitive capital. Initiatives in the late 1990s and early 2000s by organizations such as the OECD and the Financial Action Taskforce to foster international tax cooperation through 'blacklisting' countries that

enable tax evasion activities or remain non-cooperative in sharing information with foreign tax authorities were strongly challenged by target
countries on the basis of the double-standard involved. The practice of
blacklisting involves an actor 'deliberately trying to impose its demands
on countries that know full well they are being subject to coercion'
through compiling a list of states that are identified as violating particular international policy norms. Blacklisting of tax havens aims to create
'pressure to comply primarily by damaging the reputation of those countries listed among the international finance industry and secondarily
through creating fears of capital flight' (Sharman 2006: 99). OECD
member states were subsequently criticized for seeking to reduce tax
competition from tax havens, while permitting continued tax competition between themselves (Sharman 2006: 86–7).

For developing countries, the challenges of adapting tax policies to
balance domestic priorities and exogenous economic conditions tend to
be even more complex than for developed countries that have built up
greater fiscal capacities over time. For example, increasing levels of trade
openness in developing countries has sometimes been associated with
significant reductions in public spending on social security programmes
(Segura-Ubiergo 2007: 5). In particular, developing countries which have
internationally integrated their economies by liberalizing both trade policies and restrictions on capital movements have faced stronger pressures
to shift their tax base from relatively *easy to collect* taxes such as trade
tariffs to *hard to collect* taxes including income and consumption taxes.
The latter forms of taxes are considerably more difficult to collect
because they are not administered at centralized locations, but require
instead a far greater administrative infrastructure for tax collection,
monitoring tax evasion activities and enforcing tax compliance
(Aizenman and Jinjarak 2009). In addition to economic pressures for
changes in tax policies, tax reforms in developing countries have also
been strongly promoted by IOs, with tax reforms often stipulated as
policy conditions that borrowing states must implement in order to
access IMF loans (Seabrooke 2010a).

Despite these broad international trends, national tax policies have
not undergone the level of policy convergence that some observers
predicted during the 1990s and early 2000s in response to economic
globalization. Several factors might explain the lack of a greater degree
of fiscal policy convergence, including both domestic institutional
constraints and social constraints on governments' scope for enacting
wide-ranging tax reforms. For example, some countries' political
systems and institutional processes enable a greater range of 'veto players' to influence or constrain the policy-making process, which might be
more consequential when it comes to tax policy than in other areas of

public policy that are subject to a lower level of political contestation. In addition to the institutional architecture of different states, domestic social norms that comprise ideas about how tax fairness is defined can also act as a brake on the autonomy of governments to enact tax policy reforms, or may provide a political stimulus for governments to expand tax rates in order to broaden the provision of public services (Seabrooke 2007).

In the contemporary era the international and domestic dynamics of tax politics may have altered, but decisions about current and future tax policies remain fundamental to debates over the efficiency and efficacy of the role of governments in influencing the distribution of wealth and income within a particular society. Some observers have suggested that economic globalization is more likely to prompt governments to compensate for the higher levels of economic uncertainty that are associated with international integration by increasing public spending to install a stronger buffer between global market processes and their domestic workforce (Garrett and Mitchell 2001). Others have suggested that while economic globalization has not induced the race to the bottom in tax policies that some predicted, the conventional wisdom that international integration processes have constrained the scope of national fiscal autonomy is demonstrated through the greater reliance by many states on tax revenue from personal income and consumption, rather than taxes on business income or capital gains (Genschel 2002).

Contemporary challenges and sources of change

One of the primary fiscal challenges facing many governments today is how to deal with the problem of offshore finance and tax havens. The term offshore 'refers not to the geographical location of economic activities, but to the juridical status of a vast and expanding array of specialized realms' (Palan 2003b: 2). There are several problems that the emergence of offshore finance has posed for many countries and especially for relatively high-tax developed countries, which lose potential public revenue through tax avoidance and tax evasion practices by individuals and businesses. Tax *avoidance* involves artificial schemes that take advantage of legal loopholes or deliberate structuring of assets to reduce tax liabilities. Tax *evasion* involves explicitly criminal behaviour including concealing income or filing misleading tax returns. The main challenges offshore finance poses for governments include the following: (1) the principle of sovereign equality; (2) the administrative and transaction costs of monitoring tax avoidance and evasion and enforcing compliance; (3) the possibility that effective regulation of offshore financial activities would require new restrictions on capital movements; and (4) the disparity between the profits that can be gained through tax avoidance and evasion and the associated penalties for doing so.

The principle of sovereign equality formally grants all states the right under international law to arrange their own tax policies as they see fit. In this respect, 'Tax havens are financial conduits that, in exchange for a fee, use their one principal asset – their sovereignty – to serve a non-resident constituency of accounts and lawyers, bankers and financiers, who bring a demand for the privileges that tax havens can supply' (Palan *et al.* 2010). Tax havens are jurisdictions with low or non-existent personal and corporate income taxes for non-residents. Key characteristics of a tax haven include financial secrecy, non-cooperation with foreign tax authorities, no requirement for individuals or business to have a substantive local presence and the deliberate promotion of a jurisdiction as an offshore financial centre (Sharman 2010: 4). On the one hand, small state tax havens maintain the formal legal entitlement to lease their sovereignty 'for a fee' to tax avoiders and evaders, which may be one of few developmental strategies available to some states. On the other hand, the principle of sovereign equality complicates efforts by high-tax jurisdictions to effectively respond to the problems posed by individuals and companies who structure their business activities through tax havens in order to reduce tax payments in their home state.

The resources available to companies and high-income individuals who seek to minimize their tax obligations in a particular jurisdiction often greatly exceed the resources many states are able to devote to tax administration, collection and enforcement activities. As a result, efforts to tackle tax avoidance and evasion through expanding governments' tax collection infrastructure can prove prohibitively expensive. The costs involved with tackling tax evasion and avoidance are high because tax minimization activities represent a constantly 'moving target', with strategies to exploit legal loopholes or ambiguities in regulations within high-tax jurisdictions continuously evolving. However, if governments expand their institutional capacities to monitor and regulate offshore finance this could increase public revenue well above the level of extra funds that are spent on enforcing tax rules, while a proportion of the extra compliance costs would be borne by businesses and individuals rather than the state. Indeed, one area where OECD governments have tightened up on offshore financial activities is through clamping down on the extent to which resident individuals and companies can continue to take advantage of the financial secrecy that tax havens have traditionally offered. Recent examples include the 2008 amendment to the EU's Savings Tax Directive, which requires that the 'beneficial owners of entities located in tax havens must be known and identified, and be subject to tax because of their association with their normal country of residence' (Palan *et al*. 2010: 245). This was reinforced in 2013 by an agreement among G8 leaders 'to make information on who really owns and profits from companies and trusts available to tax collection and law enforcement agencies' (Group of Eight 2013: 1).

Proposals to increase the regulation of offshore financial activities – such as through policy measures that target offshore tax jurisdictions or which target businesses and individuals that engage in offshore activities – may require the reintroduction of restrictions on capital movements. This would run counter to the recent trend over the last three decades in developed countries towards reducing restrictions on capital mobility, while the reintroduction of restrictive policies, even if they are narrowly targeted, would have significant flow-on effects for the operation of other areas of economic governance, such as official interest rates, exchange rate regimes and trade policy. Of course, these flow-on effects might provide additional positive benefits. However, the collective action problem at the heart of the challenge posed by offshore financial activities would still remain. As long as some states continue to attract tax-sensitive capital through low taxes and financial secrecy, direct policy measures by high-tax jurisdictions to combat tax avoidance and evasion activities may simply prove to be counterproductive.

Finally, because the prospective punishments 'do not fit the crime', tax professionals face strong incentives to enable their clients to evade their legal tax obligations on a cost–benefit basis. Introducing the Stop Tax Haven Abuse Act on the floor of the US Senate in 2007, for example, US Senator Carl Levin (2007) criticized the low penalties levied on tax professionals who enable businesses to avoid their tax liabilities, suggesting that 'A $1,000 fine is like a jaywalking ticket for robbing a bank'. Given the comparatively low penalties associated with tax minimization activities, tax avoidance or evasion may therefore be seen as a rational strategy to increase profits, both for the individuals and businesses who seek to minimize their tax payments and for the tax professionals who help them to do so.

As these points indicate, the policy dilemma some governments face in attempting to collectively address the issue of tax revenue that is lost to offshore financial centres remains complex. Despite the intractable problems associated with global tax competition, several developed country governments have recently come under greater pressure to act unilaterally to shore up their tax bases. In the UK, for example, high-profile media campaigns have targeted the tax avoidance and evasion activities of major UK high street firms, as well as the low taxes paid by many foreign businesses operating in the UK relative to their sales volumes

Box 15.2   Selected actors and global tax competition

- **Everyday actors**
  Everyday actors pay the greatest costs from tax avoidance and tax evasion activities. Because their income and economic transactions are less mobile than those of high-income individuals and international companies they may effectively pay a higher rate of tax despite lower earnings, and may also be disproportionately affected if a state's revenue problems lead to reductions in public spending.

- **International organizations**
  A number of IOs conduct research on the emergence, activities and policy consequences of offshore financial centres. The main organizations that have sought to foster international cooperation to regulate tax havens include the OECD, through its Committee on Fiscal Affairs as well as the creation in 1999 of a Forum on Harmful Tax Practices, and the Financial Action Task Force, through the compilation in 2000 of a blacklist of 15 'Non-Cooperative Countries or Territories'.

- **Market actors**
  Market actors such as high-income individuals and corporate entities have increasingly taken advantage of opportunities for minimizing tax liabilities through legally restructuring their financial arrangements in ways that 'shelter' their taxable income in offshore financial centres.

- **States**
  Governments in both high-tax jurisdictions and low-tax jurisdictions have played a major role in the evolution of the global financial system which now permits high-income individuals and companies to minimize their tax liabilities by operating through tax havens. In particular, growth in the business of tax havens has been driven by the reduction or elimination of restrictions on capital mobility, the globalization of production networks and increasing global trade flows, as well as the expansion of double-taxation avoidance agreements between states.

(Neville 2012). Against the background of a new 'age of austerity' in many countries in the aftermath of the global financial crisis and the deterioration of budget deficits due to lower tax revenues from weaker economic activity and the costs of financial sector bailouts, public demands for states to take action on reforming corporate taxation in line with social conceptions of tax fairness and burden-sharing can be expected to strengthen.

Summary

How states levy taxes, the rate at which they are levied and who should pay what share of public revenue are questions that centre on the politics of wealth and income distribution, and social conceptions of the legitimate role of governments in shaping economic processes and outcomes. Global tax competition has altered the dynamics of domestic tax politics through constraining the fiscal autonomy of individual governments. Yet while the exogenous constraints on governments have changed, earlier predictions that states were facing the imminent prospect of a race to the bottom as a consequence of international economic integration have proven to be largely unfounded. Many states have retained substantial autonomy in the setting of tax rates on personal income and consumption, while public revenue from corporate taxation across developed countries as a group has not precipitously declined. At the same time, tax systems in a number of developed and developing countries have become less progressive as the tax rates paid by the very wealthy have reduced relative to the rest of the population, while rampant tax evasion and tax avoidance practices by some businesses and high-income earners risk undermining the broader social legitimacy of the tax system in some countries.

Discussion questions

1. Should tax competition be regulated at the global level and, if so, how?
2. Who are the winners and losers from global tax competition?
3. How has economic globalization impacted upon the fiscal capacities of different states?
4. How has global tax competition affected developing countries?
5. Why have many small states chosen to become tax havens?
6. How has economic globalization shaped changes in national welfare systems?

Further reading

Garrett, Geoffrey. 1998. *Partisan Politics in the Global Economy*. Cambridge: Cambridge University Press.

Palan, Ronen. 2003b. *The Offshore World: Sovereign Markets, Virtual Places, and Nomad Millionaires*. Ithaca, NY: Cornell University Press.

Palan, Ronen, Richard Murphy and Christian Chavagneux. 2010. *Tax Havens: How Globalization Really Works*. Ithaca, NY: Cornell University Press.

Rixen, Thomas. 2009. *The Political Economy of International Tax Governance.* Basingstoke: Palgrave Macmillan.

Sharman, J.C. 2006. *Havens in a Storm: The Struggle for Global Tax Regulation.* Ithaca, NY: Cornell University Press.

Vlcek, William. 2008. *Offshore Finance and Small States: Sovereignty, Size and Money.* Basingstoke: Palgrave Macmillan.

Chapter 16

<hr/>

Global Poverty and Development

Introduction

The problems associated with global poverty and the challenges of economic development are a fundamental concern for IPE. The emergence of development as a modern concept is closely associated with the Industrial Revolution in the second half of the eighteenth and early nineteenth centuries, and remains bound up with the role and power of modern nation-states. Both development goals and the idea of 'development' itself comprise highly controversial issues that cut cross politics at the local, national, regional and global levels, and are subject to intense contestation over competing conceptions of fairness and justice in the global political economy. In comparison, the concept of *underdevelopment* refers to a situation where the resources of a country or area are not used to achieve their economic and social potential. In the twenty-first century, comparative statistical indicators show that levels of extreme poverty in many countries around the globe remain high, while debates over the most efficient allocation and use of foreign aid to tackle poverty and address broader development issues are characterized by strong disagreements among scholars, development practitioners and policy experts and the staff of IOs, as well as aid donor and recipient governments. This chapter introduces the contemporary context of economic development and global poverty, the role of economic ideas in shaping the range of possibilities for global development policies and the contemporary challenges and sources of change in development and poverty in the global political economy.

Background

While the roots of the concept of development are located in the eighteenth century, if not earlier, the global diffusion of development as a cluster of political and policy aims gained prominence after the end of World War II. This process went hand-in-hand with broader social and political dynamics such as decolonization, changing conceptions of international aid (Lumsdaine 1993) and the establishment of new forms of international organization and global governance in the last six decades. Today, the concept of development remains hotly contested and is defined in a range of different ways. Broad definitions include: (1) an understanding of development as a coordinated process that is geared towards achieving broad goals associated with improvements in material well-being; (2) a more specific set of strategic developmental targets and intended outcomes; and (3) development as an ideological project that is underpinned by implicit assumptions about social and economic progress and stages of historical change in different societies (Payne and Phillips 2010: 5).

Development targets typically aim at achieving both quantitative and qualitative changes in an economy. These may include infrastructural development, capital accumulation, improvements in health, literacy and life expectancy, environmental sustainability and the development of human capital, among other goals. Development is often equated with the expansion of economic output and other indicators of improved economic performance, but the two are not synonymous. Rather 'economic growth is one aspect of the process of economic development' (Sen 1983: 748). A feature that is common to different conceptions of development is that development involves a deliberate attempt to stimulate processes of economic and social change. According to Amartya Sen (1983: 754), for example, 'the process of economic development has to be concerned with what people can or cannot do'. Development in this sense refers to a particular set of goals associated with changes in human agency and capabilities, whereas economic growth is understood as one of the possible means to achieve some of those goals, rather than an end in itself.

Understanding the main drivers of development across different countries and the causes of underdevelopment in others is a complicated business. The main drivers of developmental processes often emerge in historically contingent political, economic and social circumstances that cannot easily be replicated in other contexts. Moreover, factors that enable or impede development in one context may potentially constrain or aid development prospects in another. A widely held assumption during the post-World War II era was that the availability of agricultural resources and an abundant food supply was an important prerequisite for enhancing a country's broader development prospects. Taking a comparative historical view of development processes and outcomes, however, Ester Boserup (1983: 402) has shown that in some cases an abundant food supply constrained rather than aided development, while in others conditions of food scarcity did not impede rapid processes of development. As this example illustrates, similar economic and environmental conditions will not necessarily lead to the same development processes and outcomes across different countries.

One of the fallacies often associated with efforts to understand the drivers of economic development and growth is the erroneous assumption that economic growth is synonymous with organic growth. Unlike organic processes of growth, economic growth is less 'mechanical', and instead is characterized by 'elements of belief, choice and invention'. The dynamic processes of economic growth generate societal and political conflicts, through which the 'Rates and directions of change can depend on who wins and who loses' (Stretton 1999: 85). Rather than processes of development comprising a set of regular and predictable cause-and-effect relationships, economic development in different contexts necessarily constitutes an irregular process that can lead to unexpected outcomes. As Hugh Stretton (1999: 85) has observed: 'Putting (say) capital investment or international aid or free trade or neoclassical economic theory into a national economic system is not like putting fuel into an engine, fertiliser into a field, an acorn into the ground, or food into a child.'

The persistence of underdevelopment and poverty in many countries in the twenty-first century can be partly explained by the questionable assumptions that have underpinned the evolution of global development policies. Two of these assumptions are particularly worth highlighting. The first is that national and international bureaucracies with responsibilities for development policies 'know what actions achieve economic development'. The second is the assumption that the provision of advice and money from international donors 'will make those correct actions happen' (Easterly 2007: 328–9). A fundamental problem with these assumptions is that theoretical explanations of development and underdevelopment in the global political economy cannot be based around single-cause models of economic change. Instead, they require a nuanced understanding of the multiple causal factors at work and a degree of analytic flexibility to account for intrinsic irregularity in development processes, as well as contextualized and contingent explanations of how development processes have worked (or not) in the past.

In the past six decades different theories of development have emerged, gained prominence and subsequently declined in influence as new theories evolved. These range, for example, from the emergence of 'modernization theory' in the early post-World War II era to 'dependency' theories of development that were prominent during the 1960s and 1970s. Modernization theory concentrated on the domestic attributes of a country, and conceived of development as primarily a process of emulation to 'catch up' with the development successes of Western capitalist economies. In contrast, dependency theories understand the development of poorer 'peripheral' or 'semi-peripheral' countries in the world economy as being systematically conditioned by the economic fortunes and expansion of richer 'core' developed economies (Leftwich 2000; Frank 1966).

In addition to theoretical perspectives that aim to establish causal relationships linking the problems of development and underdevelopment to strategic policy solutions, development issues comprise a major focus of normative theories of global economic justice across the study of IPE (Kapstein 2006: 7). These theories differ based on the focal point for action (states, the international society of states, or individuals) as well as the explicit policy objectives, ranging from the goal of equality of opportunity, to greater convergence in the distribution of wealth and resources, to ameliorating and preventing conditions of extreme deprivation. A key sticking point that lies at the heart of issues relating to global economic justice is the problem of competing conceptions of fairness held by different actors. As Ethan Kapstein (2006: 26) suggests, at the global level 'where states bring their own domestic conceptualizations of distributive justice to the table ... the challenge of creating a system that each one views as being fair or of mutual advantage would seem overwhelming, and perhaps impossible to meet', without a hegemonic state that is able to impose and enforce its own rules on all others. Moving beyond normative theory to state practices relating to global poverty and development highlights the intractable – although not unsolvable – dimensions of the challenge. For these reasons, responses to the challenges of poverty and development have tended to develop in an ad-hoc manner through voluntary international agreements and overlapping responsibilities shared between existing IOs, rather than through a more coordinated or more centralized global strategy.

Global poverty today

Issues related to global poverty are intimately connected with contemporary conceptions of development. Whereas economic development generally refers to improvements in standards of living and welfare, poverty is defined as a condition of relative or absolute deprivation.

Relative poverty is commonly understood as a condition of income inequality within a particular society or location, while absolute or extreme poverty is defined as the deprivation of basic human needs such as access to clean water, food, adequate shelter, healthcare, education and sanitation.

In the twenty-first century global poverty is a persistent challenge for hundreds of millions of people who experience the conditions of poverty in their daily lives, and remains an intractable problem for policy-makers at the national and global level despite the availability of technology, knowledge and resources to alleviate or prevent the basic effects of poverty. Each day, on average, 'almost one billion people will go hungry, 20,000 children will die from easily preventable health problems, 1,400 women will die from causes associated with maternity that are easy to diagnose and treat, and more than 100 million primary age children will not attend school' (Hulme 2010: 1). The existence of global poverty is not a problem that is unsolvable due to inadequate information and knowledge, a lack of skills and technology, or – at least in theory – insufficient infrastructure and resources for tackling conditions of material deprivation. Nor is there a shortage of actors at the global level whose tasks centre on addressing, alleviating, or preventing poverty. If anything, the opposite is the case. Today tens of thousands of institutions are engaged in researching the dynamics and causes of poverty, as well as mobilizing resources and implementing policies designed to reduce poverty rates around the globe. They range from IOs to government agencies; and from philanthropic foundations to NGOs (Hulme 2010: 9).

From the 1990s onwards the majority of development strategies have incorporated an explicit focus on poverty reduction, especially those supported by foreign aid from bilateral and multilateral donors. Based on definitions constructed by the World Bank, 'headcount' measures of absolute poverty can be defined as the proportion of a country's population living on less than US$1.25 per day in purchasing power parity terms (at 2005 international prices), although individual countries use different official cut-off points to establish levels of absolute poverty. Taking the World Bank's slightly higher measure of moderate poverty at US$2 per day, Figure 16.1 illustrates that people living in either absolute or moderate poverty represent a high proportion of the overall population in many countries, and in some cases account for well over half the population.

Greater recognition of the problems posed by global poverty, and an increased willingness for governments to take action to foster economic development around the world, helped to stimulate the expansion of bilateral and multilateral foreign aid programmes in the aftermath of

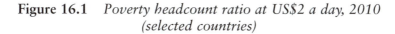

Figure 16.1 *Poverty headcount ratio at US$2 a day, 2010 (selected countries)*

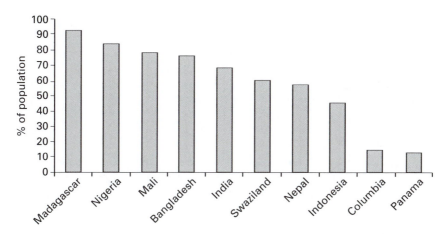

Note: Purchasing power parity exchange rates calculated at 2005 international prices.
Source: World Bank Data Catalog (http://data.worldbank.org/indicator/SLPOV.2DAY).

World War II (Lumsdaine 1993). Foreign aid is the voluntary transfer of economic resources from one country to another, with the objective – at least in part – of enhancing the welfare of the recipient country. The expansion of foreign aid transfers from some countries to others also reflected a desire to channel material capabilities towards strengthening strategic alliances and economic linkages between national markets, and to shape aid recipients' foreign and economic policies, especially during the East–West conflict of the Cold War era. As aid budgets and flows increased following the end of World War II, so did the size and scope of national and international bureaucracies charged with designing and implementing aid programmes and financial transfers. This led to a host of problems associated with the efficiency and effectiveness of foreign aid, including a focus on maximizing aid disbursements rather than the effectiveness of services delivered, as well as a focus on short-term time horizons with less investment in longer-term qualitative achievements and institutional learning. William Easterly (2002b) has described this as 'the cartel of good intentions'. Debate continues over the effectiveness of aid, as well as the problematic issue of whether aid should be allocated to poor countries or to poor persons. However, most observers agree that foreign aid transfers to expand education, healthcare and infrastructure in recipient countries tend to have a positive impact on economic development and poverty reduction (Kapstein 2006: 88).

The countries illustrated in Figure 16.1 that experience high rates of extreme and moderate poverty tend to also be characterized by high

Figure 16.2   *Income share held by highest 10% and lowest 10% of population, 2010 (selected countries)*

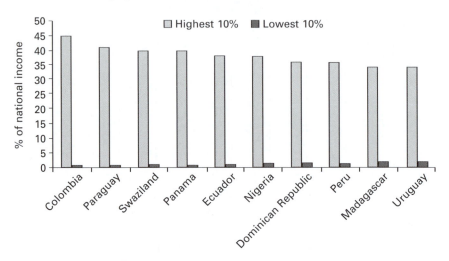

Source: World Bank Data Catalog (http://data.worldbank.org).

levels of income inequality between the richest 10 per cent of the population and the poorest 10 per cent of the population. As Figure 16.2 shows, the income held by the poorest 10 per cent of the population in these countries represents only a fraction of national income, while the income share of the richest 10 per cent stretches from over one third to almost 45 per cent of total national income. However startling such figures may be, rates of income inequality within developing economies generally receive far less attention and are less likely to lead to the mobilization of resources to reduce income inequality from the international donor community than the incidence and rate of extreme poverty among countries. Part of the explanation for this focus rests in the concept of 'poverty-efficient' aid allocation. This refers to the problem of 'how to get the greatest amount of poverty reduction from the smallest amount of aid' (Kapstein 2006: 91). The reduction of rates of extreme poverty is something that both bilateral and multilateral donors believe they can realistically address, at least in countries that are identified as maintaining 'good' economic policies.

Poverty reduction policies among the major IOs have expanded in tandem with efforts by donor states to monitor these organizations' activities, their performance and the effectiveness of different poverty-oriented schemes (Clegg 2010). This suggests that the greater attention paid to poverty reduction programmes at the global level has evolved, at least in part, because poverty-focused schemes provide a useful means for donor governments to monitor and control what IOs do. The effectiveness of schemes aimed at reducing extreme poverty rates can be quantified more easily and within more precise time frames than the activities of IOs in other areas of development policy, where outcomes are better assessed qualitatively and over longer time horizons. A related explanation factor is the ambiguous causal relationship between rates of relative poverty and extreme poverty in different societies. Many developed economies also maintain high rates of income inequality without comparable levels of extreme poverty, such as the USA (Hacker and Pierson 2010). For large sections of the population of many developed economies and their governments, global income inequality in itself may not be regarded as a pressing policy problem.

Additional reasons that might explain why the incidence of extreme poverty rather than relative poverty has become a central policy priority across much of the international donor community is that high levels of extreme poverty can be more readily cast in universal terms as a moral wrong, as well as being causally linked to other foreign policy concerns such as state security and transnational terrorism (Kapstein 2006: 176–7, 180). Global action programmes to address conditions of extreme poverty can potentially attract consensual support from disparate actors with a range of political motivations and policy preferences. Donor governments and aid recipient governments are more likely to hold competing conceptions of economic fairness when it comes to the issue of relative income inequality, which may also have a more tenuous link, if any, with donor states' broader foreign policy goals.

The data presented in Figures 16.1 and 16.2 shows the extent to which both extreme and relative poverty remain major challenges in some countries. Nonetheless, in recent decades a number of countries have had a high degree of success in reducing extreme poverty rates, achieving high levels of economic growth and realizing a broad range of additional development goals. Although the levels of success in economic development and poverty reduction vary significantly between individual countries, substantial regional variation in development outcomes can also be identified across the global political economy.

Figure 16.3 tracks changes in the proportion of the population living on less than the World Bank's official level of extreme poverty at US$1.25 a day across six regions every three years from 1981 to 2008. As the data illustrates, regions such as East Asia and the Pacific and South Asia have experienced enormous reductions in poverty headcount figures over the last three decades. The rate of change has been most pronounced in the East Asia and Pacific region, where the proportion of the regional population living below the World Bank's poverty line has fallen from 77 per cent of a total population of 1,492 million people in 1982 to 14 per cent

Figure 16.3   *Regional poverty headcount ratio at US$1.25 a day,*
1981–2008

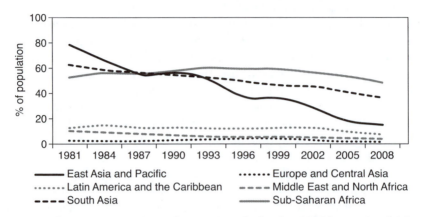

Note: Purchasing power parity exchange rates calculated at 2005 international prices.
Source: World Bank Data Catalog (http://iresearch.worldbank.org/PovcalNet/index.
htm?1).

of a total population of 1,983 million in 2008. In South Asia, poverty rates have also fallen sharply from 61 per cent in 1981 to 36 per cent in 2008. In contrast to these examples of development successes, Sub-Saharan Africa, which had the third highest poverty headcount in 1981, experienced an increase in poverty from 51 per cent of the population in 1981 to over 59 per cent in 1993, a figure which gradually decreased to 48 per cent in 2008. In other regions, the proportion of the population living below the World Bank's poverty line in the Middle East and North Africa is now less than one third of the level it was three decades ago, and the poverty headcount in Latin America and the Caribbean has nearly halved, a change which occurred rapidly between 2002 and 2008. Meanwhile, poverty in Europe and Central Asia is less than 0.5 per cent of the regional population, after rising substantially to nearly 4 per cent during the 1990s in the context of the post-communist transition in former centrally planned economies.

While poverty remains a major problem of global scope, different regions and different countries within those regions have experienced changing conditions and rates of poverty over the past three decades. Extreme poverty headcounts rose sharply in many countries during the 1980s and the 1990s. This was associated with economic liberalization processes that reduced income security and existing social safety nets for many of the world's poor, broader social and political changes brought about by the end of the Cold War (including changing priorities in global aid allocation) and economic and financial crises that further impoverished many people who were already below the poverty line, and pushed many more under it. Poverty headcounts at the regional level improved significantly across the globe in the decade preceding 2008. However, future World Bank headcount measures of extreme poverty that take into account the effects of the late-2000s financial crisis are likely to show new increases in several areas, including countries which did not directly experience a financial crisis but faced sharp reductions in global demand for their exports as well as reductions in aid and private capital flows (see Chapter 13).

Economic development strategies

Many of the theoretical and policy differences that have characterized competing approaches to economic development are located in debates over whether market-led or state-led strategies to foster development and poverty reduction are inherently superior. During the 1980s and 1990s 'heyday' of the Washington consensus (see Box 16.1), for example, the conventional wisdom within the IMF and the World Bank assumed that government-failure was a frequent, if not ubiquitous, characteristic of national development strategies. Critics of state-led approaches to development commonly pointed to the example of import-substitution industrialization (ISI) models, which aimed to reduce foreign imports through policies that favoured the growth of local industries and manufactured products as substitute goods in order to increase national self-sufficiency and build economies of scale. The term 'economies of scale' refers to the economic benefits firms gain through increasing the scale of production when greater size reduces the average production cost per unit. This was seen as a way to stimulate local employment in skilled and semi-skilled manufacturing jobs, and to expand the size of domestic markets. ISI approaches were commonly used by many developing countries from the 1950s until the 1980s, especially in Latin America. They were strongly criticized by advocates of market-oriented approaches to development on the grounds that, by insulating domestic industries from competition in international markets, nationalized industries grew less efficient and led to distortions in the allocation of domestic economic resources. Critics suggested these dynamics reduced productivity and impeded the development of economies of scale that might be achieved through international integration, while discouraging foreign investment due to restrictions on the repatriation of profits, barriers to entry and insufficient protections for international property rights.

The corollary of government-failure arguments against ISI models of development in the 1970s and 1980s was the assumption that instances of market failure only occurred in exceptional situations, and were often the result of misguided government actions (Chowdhury and Iyanatal 1993: 53). From this perspective, in order to improve the developmental performance of a country it was necessary to reduce the state's allocation role in economic processes. Meanwhile, the ability of governments to adopt sector-specific industrial policies that might improve upon or prevent market failure was assumed to be negligible. This view was partly based on the assumption that individual policy-makers (conceived as self-interested rational actors) were unlikely to be capable of refraining from using the power of government for personal gain and enrichment, which would inefficiently divert credit and profits from productive reinvestment in economic activities that would be likely to stimulate growth. It was also based on the assumption that private entrepreneurs would be more successful at identifying and exploiting economic opportunities because they were motivated by the pursuit of profits and possessed more accurate market knowledge, a lack of political constraints and greater exposure to market discipline in comparison with bureaucrats making investment decisions with public funds (Wade 1990: 13).

Advocates of a market-led approach to economic development argued that, in the long term, state-led development strategies such as ISI would result in serious distortions in the allocation of domestic resources, inhibit foreign investment and the development of economies of scale and, ultimately, would impair a country's development prospects. Proponents of markets rather than states as the primary agents of development during the 1980s and 1990s contended that the fundamental priority for enhancing economic development was for governments to get price signals right through market-based mechanisms (World Bank 1991: 4). It was assumed that governments could enable development by providing a favourable economic environment for growth and institutional conditions that would make it possible for private entrepreneurs to compete in world markets. As Cold War tensions reduced at the end of the 1980s and the start of the 1990s, centrally planned economies commenced reforms to adopt market-based methods of resource allocation and economic transformation. When the most prominent example of an alternative to market-based capitalism vanished with the disintegration of the Soviet Union at the end of 1991, advocates of market-oriented development strategies made the case that such policies should be followed universally as the right approach for all countries, regardless of their external economic environment or domestic context. In the 1991 *World Development Report* on 'The Challenge of Development', for example, the World Bank concluded that market-friendly policies embodied a new consensus that should be 'put into practice everywhere' (World Bank 1991: 157).

Box 16.1   The Washington consensus

The perception of a decline in the efficacy of demand-management policies and the demise of the Bretton Woods system from the mid-1960s to the early 1970s helped facilitate the dominance of neoclassical theoretical approaches within the International Monetary Fund and the World Bank from the 1980s (Bird 2001). Economic and political changes within and between developed countries also conditioned these theoretical and institutional transformations, including the relative decline of the economic capabilities of the USA, the shift to floating exchange rates and the oil price shocks of the 1970s (see Chapter 11). A broad area of agreement between the US Treasury and the main international organizations with their headquarters in Washington, DC, over economic ideas and 'best practice' policy prescriptions for development emerged during the 1980s. At a 1989 conference organized by the Institute for International Economics think-tank, John Williamson termed these ideas the 'Washington consensus'. Described as embodying shared conceptions of 'economic good sense' (Williamson 1990), the consensus comprised broadly defined policy goals for developing countries.

The key prescriptions of the Washington consensus included:

- fiscal discipline (small budget deficits);
- focusing public expenditure on health, education and infrastructure;
- reducing marginal tax rates and broadening the tax base to create greater economic incentives;
- financial liberalization, specifically with regard to allowing the market determination of interest rates;
- competitive and unified exchange rates;
- liberalization of government controls on trade;
- equal treatment for foreign and domestic businesses;
- privatization of state enterprises;
- deregulation of economic activities, with the partial exception of safety controls, environmental protection and the regulation of financial institutions; and
- legal protection of property rights.

While ISI policies in Latin America had been widely criticized by the early 1990s, alternative examples of state-led development strategies existed in the newly industrialized economies (NIEs) of East Asia, such as Japan, South Korea, Taiwan, Hong Kong and Singapore. The Asian 'Developmental State' model at its core comprised four main elements: (1) a highly competent and well-trained state bureaucracy; (2) a substantial degree of autonomy for state bureaucrats from the short-term interests of political decision-makers; (3) the principle that state policies to intervene in and regulate economic processes should be 'market-conforming' through close cooperation and coordination with business actors; and (4) the use of 'pilot agencies' to actively plan, design, coordinate and monitor how to use the power of the state to foster economic development (Johnson 1982). While the quantitative and qualitative successes of the developmental strategies of East Asian economies posed an apparent challenge in the early 1990s to advocates of market-led development strategies, these success stories quickly became framed as a triumph for market-based approaches and international integration. For example, prominent Johns Hopkins University economics professor and World Bank consultant Béla Balassa (1988: 288) concluded that economic growth in East Asia was driven for the most part by the establishment of policy frameworks that did not discriminate against exports (unlike ISI models). This enabled efficient resource allocation, economies of scale through exports and incentives for firms to continually upgrade their production technologies and expand their international market position. As Balassa (1988) noted, most of the East Asian NIEs made temporary use of import-substitution policy tools during the initial stages of kick-starting their developmental strategies, but did not maintain ISI methods over as long a period as Latin American economies had.

Figure 16.4   *East Asia and Pacific poverty headcount ratio at US$1.25 a day, 1981 and 2008**

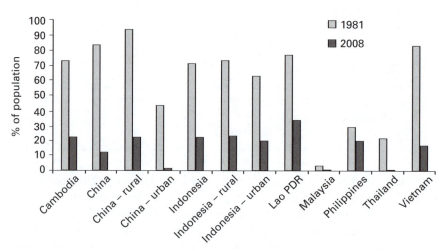

* Excludes Fiji, Micronesia, Papua New Guinea and Timor-Leste.
Note: Purchasing power parity exchange rates calculated at 2005 international prices.
Source: World Bank Data Catalog (http://iresearch.worldbank.org/PovcalNet/index. htm?1).

With respect to development in East Asia, much of the aggregate changes in income, poverty reduction and GDP in the last three decades are commonly attributed to China's remarkable economic growth rates. While the reduction in poverty headcount ratios in China between 1981 and 2008 is highly impressive, other economies in the region such as Indonesia, Thailand, Vietnam and Cambodia also recorded sharp drops in the proportion of their populations living on less than US$1.25 a day (see Figure 16.4). The data on urban versus rural poverty rates for large countries such as Indonesia and China illustrates that sharp reductions in rates of extreme poverty were not limited to urban populations, even if the gains of poverty reduction remain unevenly spread between rural and urban communities.

In response to the rapid development successes of East Asian economies, the World Bank initiated a formal study of the development experiences of eight countries in the early 1990s, sponsored by Japan, which was published in 1993 as a report on *The East Asian Miracle*. While this received numerous criticisms after it was released, the report recognized that in some cases governments' 'selective interventions' in resource allocation and shaping economic decision-making contributed to enhancing growth prospects. Nevertheless, the World Bank's earlier focus on the need for governments to 'get price signals right' was only partly amended in explaining East Asian economic development, to the requirement for governments to focus on 'getting the basics right' (World Bank 1993: 5). This enabled praise for the developmental state models applied in East Asian economies to be qualified as conforming – on the whole – with market-friendly policy settings.

The success of East Asian development strategies in fostering rapid processes of economic growth and poverty reduction provide a powerful example of what governments can achieve through policy activism. However, the legalization of global trade rules and the proliferation of bilateral trade and investment treaties since the 1990s locks governments into agreed policy parameters, which prohibit many of the policy tools previously used by East Asian governments to kick-start development. As Robert Wade (2003: 622) points out, the 'development space' for countries to chart innovative and actively state-led policy strategies in order to follow in the footsteps of the East Asian NIEs has shrunk over the last two decades.

A new example of successful and rapid state-led development has emerged with the 'rise of China', and the fostering through China's diplomacy of what some observers have termed a 'Beijing consensus' on the critical role of the state in development processes (Beeson 2009: 34). China's successes in achieving strong rates of economic growth and poverty reduction at the same time as maintaining a strong economic management role for the state has lent support to the strategies of other 'late developers' (such as Vietnam) that seek to avoid embracing programmes of across-the-board economic liberalization as the only development option available (Beeson and Pham 2012). Competition between alternative models of development is commonly framed as an evidence-based debate about policy effectiveness and economic efficiency in developmental strategies. However, claims over which model is superior, for which countries and at what stages of development are driven by a battle of political ideologies, which comprise competing conceptions of how markets and governments work, how they ought to work and for whose benefit (Ferchen 2013).

Contemporary challenges and sources of change

Economic development remains a dominant policy concern for IOs that are engaged in multilateral lending and concessional financial assistance. The IMF has resisted evolving into a global development institution, despite gradually refocusing much of its activities on concessional lending and poverty reduction over the last four decades (Clegg 2012). For the World Bank and the regional development banks, poverty reduction now forms a core part of their mandate. Through the construction of global policy norms, IOs can exercise substantial influence over how development is conceptualized at multiple levels of policy formation, design and implementation – as well as shaping benchmarks for how development outcomes are identified, measured and assessed. The policy advice emanating from IOs is not always favourably received, nor do IMF or World Bank pronouncements, reports and advice in a given issue area automatically succeed in shaping new normative standards. 'Best practice' policies that are successfully constructed as global policy norms by IOs may nonetheless influence what policies, in which circumstances, are defined as socially appropriate actions for governments and development practitioners to take (Park and Vetterlein 2010: 241).

The World Bank's conception of what poverty is, how it is measured and what steps should be taken to address it has changed substantially over the course of its history. Under Robert McNamara's presidency of the World Bank from 1968–81, for example, poverty reduction and economic growth were prioritized as representing two sides of the same coin. The World Bank's focus on poverty reduction largely shifted into the background during the 1980s, replaced with an almost exclusive focus on the achievement of economic growth in developing countries through externally financed programmes of structural adjustment. Over the course of the 1990s, the World Bank's thinking gradually shifted towards establishing the problem of global poverty as a fundamental concern for economic development, while the concept of poverty itself expanded and was redefined as a multidimensional problem in contrast to the narrower understanding of the experience and causes of poverty that characterized some of the organization's earlier approaches. These discursive and policy changes were not simply exercises in changing terminology and abstract principles, but had important implications for the types of policies the World Bank promoted, as well as the scope and purpose of its development lending programmes (Vetterlein 2012: 39–41).

The rise of the Washington consensus within the IMF and the World Bank during the 1980s and 1990s was challenged by the emergence of the Human Development paradigm. This was promoted by economists such as Mahbub ul-Haq, an advisor to the United Nations Development Programme (UNDP), who sought to broaden the global development agenda beyond the income-related aspects of poverty and the dominant focus on economic growth (Thomas 2001: 162–3). In collaboration with Amartya Sen and others, Mahbub ul-Haq launched the first UNDP Human Development Report (HDR) in 1990, which focused on rethinking the concept and measurement of development through the creation of the Human Development Index (HDI) (UNDP 1990). These reports provided a multidimensional approach to knowledge of development, which served to broaden the scope of policy debates beyond the narrower development focus of other flagship international publications such as the World Bank's World Development Report (WDR). The UNDP's search for alternative development indicators has been credited with being 'The UN system's most important contribution to directing attention away from a one-sided macroeconomic focus and back to the human and social aspects of development' (Stokke 2009: 344). The first HDR in 1990 defined the primary goal of development as the creation of 'an enabling environment for people to enjoy long, healthy and creative lives' (UNDP 1990). This redefined economic growth as one means (among many) to achieve the goal of development, rather than as an end in itself.

In the twenty-first century, global development priorities have been shaped by the agenda set by the Millennium Development Goals (MDGs). Established following the United Nations Millennium Summit in 2000, the MDGs comprise eight flagship development objectives that 191 member states of the UN and almost 30 IOs agreed to achieve within 15 years (see Box 16.2). The MDGs set a series of ambitious global targets for development and poverty reduction, many of which included quantifiable benchmarks for evaluating progress, and provided strong motivation for increasing aid flows from the international donor community.

Box 16.2   The Millennium Development Goals

1. **Eradicate extreme poverty and hunger:** to halve, between 1990 and 2015, the proportion of people whose income is less than US$1 per day; achieve full and productive employment and decent work for all, including women and young people; halve, between 1990 and 2015, the proportion of people who suffer from hunger.

2. **Universal education:** ensure that, by 2015, children everywhere, boys and girls alike, will be able to complete a full course of primary schooling.

3. **Gender equality:** eliminate gender disparity in primary and secondary education, preferably by 2005, and in all levels of education no later than 2015.

4. **Child health:** reduce by two-thirds, between 1990 and 2015, the under-five mortality rate.

5. **Maternal health:** reduce by three-quarters the maternal mortality ratio; achieve universal access to reproductive health.

6. **Combat HIV/AIDS:** have halted by 2015 and begun to reverse the spread of HIV/AIDS; achieve, by 2010, universal access to treatment for HIV/AIDS for all those who need it; have halted by 2015 and begun to reverse the incidence of malaria and other major diseases.

7. **Environmental sustainability:** integrate the principles of sustainable development into country policies and programmes and reverse the loss of environmental resources; reduce biodiversity loss, achieving, by 2010, a significant reduction in the rate of loss; halve, by 2015, the proportion of the population without sustainable access to safe drinking water and basic sanitation; by 2020, to have achieved a significant improvement in the lives of at least 100 million slum dwellers.

8. **Global partnership:** develop further an open, rule-based, predictable, non-discriminatory trading and financial system; address the special needs of least developed countries; address the special needs of landlocked developing countries and small island developing states; deal comprehensively with the debt problems of developing countries; in cooperation with pharmaceutical companies, provide access to affordable essential drugs in developing countries; in cooperation with the private sector, make available benefits of new technologies, especially information and communications.

Source: United Nations (www.un.org/millenniumgoals/bkgd.shtml).

Official reviews have indicated substantial progress in many areas of the eight priority objectives of the MDGs, with wide variation in the progress achieved across different development goals and in different regions (United Nations 2012a). Part of the blame for the uneven progress in reaching the MDG targets has been laid at the feet of donor governments. The 2012 MDG Gap Task Force Report identified a short-fall of US$167 billion between the volume of aid donor countries had committed towards achieving the MDGs and the amounts actually disbursed, with the volume of global foreign aid dropping nearly 3 per cent in 2011. Some developing countries have also faced greater trade barriers that have reduced their market access, because developed countries have maintained trade restrictions introduced as temporary measures in response to the global financial crisis in 2008 (United Nations 2012b).

Critics have also argued that the MDGs are either too ambitious or not ambitious enough, or have criticized the establishment of uniform global development goals rather than country- or region-specific targets (Feeney and Clarke 2009: 6–8). Some observers have argued that the focus on translating the principles behind the MDGs into quantitative performance measures for countries established uniform targets for assessing development progress that were unfair to many countries which were far less likely to achieve the MDGs due to unfavourable starting conditions. For example, achieving a 50 per cent reduction from 1990 to 2015 in the incidence of extreme poverty is a far higher hurdle in African countries than for many others. The same rates of economic growth across Africa and East Asia would result in smaller percentage reductions in poverty rates in the former because African countries as a group have the lowest per capita income of any region. Similarly, achieving a two-thirds reduction in child mortality rates is a far harder and more expensive task to achieve in countries that have very high mortality in comparison to other developing counties with lower child mortality rates (Easterly 2009). The uneven scale of the challenges faced by different countries and regions for attaining uniform development objectives suggests that using the MDGs as comparative indicators of development progress in different parts of the world during the period from 2000 to 2015 is highly problematic, and risks obscuring substantial developmental gains that may have been achieved despite countries not hitting the MDG targets. Other observers have raised concerns about the underlying motivations behind the MDG process. As David Hulme and Rorden Wilkinson (2012: 3) have noted, different countries and organizations lent support to the establishment of the MDGs for a complex variety of reasons, which ranged from 'wanting to do good' to simply 'wanting to appear to be doing good'.

Box 16.3   Selected actors and development

• **Everyday actors**
Everyday actors are both the targets and the agents of economic development. Non-elite actors in developing countries play a critical role in shaping development policy outcomes, while the political, financial and voluntary labour support of everyday actors in aid donor countries is closely connected to the maintenance and size of foreign aid programmes.

• **International organizations**
Many IOs play critical roles in different aspects of global development processes. The World Bank, as the pre-eminent development IO, exercises a significant degree of influence in shaping how development is conceived, as well as how measures of development and poverty are constructed, evaluated, transmitted and fed into policy formulation.

• **Non-governmental organizations**
NGOs may shape global development policies and norms through advocacy, research, public campaigning and lobbying activities, at the same time as playing a significant service-delivery function in designing, implementing and monitoring development programmes.

• **Market actors**
Transnational corporations impact on different countries' development prospects via their investment and production decisions, as well as through 'corporate social responsibility' practices. Sovereign ratings by credit rating agencies may influence the willingness of firms to invest in a country, as well as influencing the cost of a government's public debt to fund development programmes.

• **States**
States are key players in global development processes as aid donors and aid recipients, and in terms of their administrative capacities for negotiating, coordinating, designing and implementing development and poverty reduction projects.

There is little contention that the MDGs have served to reconstitute how global poverty is defined and understood. In particular, they have reinforced the acceptance of multidimensional understandings of poverty rather than narrow definitions that simply equate poverty with a lack of economic growth. At the same time, how poverty should be reduced and what developmental strategies should be pursued to achieve this end remain hotly disputed (Hulme and Wilkinson 2012: 3–4). Seventy years after the emergence of development as a global policy priority, sharp disagreements continue over the most effective policies for economic development and the normative goals towards which development strategies ought to be oriented.

Summary

The factors that shape global development policies comprise technical challenges as well as political questions over the appropriate normative goals of development. One of the main areas of debate among scholars, practitioners and policy experts is whether market-led or state-led policy strategies are better suited to realizing successful development outcomes. Some observers have suggested that changes in the architecture of global economic governance have reduced the space available for policy activism and an 'experimentalist' approach to development strategy. Others have pointed to rapid economic growth in China as evidence that the policy space for state-led development strategies remains negotiable. While the MDGs are often framed as representing universal moral imperatives for governments, strong disagreements persist over the appropriate means and ends of economic development and poverty reduction strategies.

Discussion questions

1. How should the concept of development be defined, and why?
2. What are the main policy differences between market-led and state-led development strategies?
3. What are the main causes of global poverty, and how might they be overcome?
4. How has economic globalization impacted upon national development strategies?
5. How do IOs shape development policies?
6. Is poverty reduction a prerequisite for successful economic development?

Further reading

Chang, Ha-Joon (ed.). 2007. *Institutional Change and Economic Development.* New York: UNU Press.

Hulme, David. 2010. *Global Poverty: How Global Governance is Failing the Poor.* London: Routledge.

Kapstein, Ethan B. 2006. *Economic Justice in an Unfair World: Toward a Level Playing Field.* Princeton, NJ: Princeton University Press.

Payne, Anthony and Nicola Phillips. 2010. *Development*. Cambridge: Polity Press.

Stokke, Olav. 2009. *The UN and Development: From Aid to Cooperation*. Bloomington: Indiana University Press.

Wilkinson, Rorden and David Hulme (eds). 2012. *The Millennium Development Goals and Beyond: Global Development after 2015*. London: Routledge.

Chapter 17

Resource Competition and Energy

Introduction

Access to natural resources (or 'raw' materials) is essential for economic growth, and especially for the development of manufacturing and agricultural industries. Non-renewable resources are by definition scarce, while the environmental issues related to resource competition do not respect national territorial boundaries, but rather are regional or global in scope. Key natural resources include energy materials (such as oil, natural gas and coal, as well as uranium for nuclear power), but also minerals and precious metals (gold, silver, iron, copper and so on), arable land (for farming), forests and plant life, wildlife and marine life and water. As well as providing important economic 'inputs' for industrial production, the quality and diversity of a country's natural environment may be a major source of income from international tourism.

In a number of key strategic regions, a new 'great game' has emerged between the existing and emerging major powers. This centres on achieving access to raw materials and energy supplies to fuel continued national and global economic growth, and to maintain long-term energy security in order to avoid implementing more radical changes in domestic economic activities and adjustment to a less carbon-intensive economy. Having an abundance of natural resources also presents both challenges and opportunities for different countries. This chapter examines the dynamics of global resource competition over energy supplies, and explores how resource-rich states have responded to the opportunities and constraints imposed by their natural resource wealth.

Background

The stock of natural resources in a particular country impacts upon economic production and the quality of life for the local population. For example, the availability of land for new building and construction impacts upon the quality and quantity of housing people can access, as well as influencing property prices and the development of housing finance systems (Schwartz and Seabrooke 2009). Meanwhile, decisions over how natural resources can be used have the potential to shape the livelihoods of entire communities, such as decisions over the location of large manufacturing plants, the regulation of waste management systems, or the construction of dams for hydroelectric power generation (Morton 2005).

Competition within and between states for control over natural resources is fierce. This can involve competition over access to land and the use of water supplies, as well as rights to exploit forests and plant life, wildlife, or marine life resources. In Southeast Asia, for example, both legal and illegal logging in countries such as the Philippines, Indonesia and Malaysia has led to rapid deforestation to satisfy demand for timber from Japan (Dauvergne 1997). Access to water has also become an important driver of political conflict (Conca 2005). The example of the Aral Sea in Central Asia provides a tragic example of the environmental consequences that can result from overuse and mismanagement of water resources. Formerly one of the four largest lakes in the world, the Aral Sea has steadily diminished following large-scale diversion of water for irrigation, and today has declined to around 10 per cent of its original size. The environmental consequences of the rapid decline in the size of the Aral Sea since the 1960s have included the destruction of local fishing industries, increasing temperatures and widespread public health problems stemming from pollution. Solutions to the Aral Sea crisis have proved elusive due to the difficulties in achieving regional political cooperation between bordering states (Weinthal 2002).

A series of key variables may influence the politics of resource competition between states. These can include: (1) whether individual states are net importers or net exporters of natural resources; (2) the level of national economic dependence on particular resources (such as water for agricultural production, or fiscal revenue from mineral exports); (3) the regulatory architecture for environmental management; (4) the level of state capacity to effectively implement and enforce environmental or resource policies; and (5) whether natural resources are largely under national control or whether they require international cooperation (either with bordering states or with international companies involved in the domestic resource sector). Whether states are net resource importers

Box 17.1   Resource nationalism

Resource nationalism involves domestic or state control of resource companies to ensure the maximum strategic benefit accrues to the home state. *Revolutionary resource nationalism* involves the consolidation of state power through control of natural resources, which can include the nationalization of privately owned assets or exploitation rights. *Economic resource nationalism* is aimed at increasing the state's fiscal revenue and share in natural resource wealth, rather than necessarily establishing political control over the resource sector. *Legacy resource nationalism* refers to the symbolic and cultural importance of maintaining national control of natural resources in many societies, while *soft resource nationalism* – practised in some OECD countries – aims at increasing revenue from raw materials without arbitrarily changing the existing regulatory framework (Bremmer and Johnston 2009: 150–1).

or exporters shapes how they engage in global resource competition. In particular, national dependence on the exploitation of natural resource wealth for fiscal revenue, economic growth and attracting investment provides both challenges and opportunities for economic development, including the danger of the 'resource curse'. This refers to the risk that a rich endowment of natural resources might impede rather than benefit a country's economic growth and development by increasing dependence on volatile global commodity prices, reducing the incentives for economic diversification and encouraging the emergence of a 'rentier state' in which revenues depend on selling or leasing resource assets rather than domestic revenue extraction (Cooley 2001: 165). Economic rents are income derived from the ownership of an asset where the price gained from the asset is significantly greater than the cost of production.

The domestic impact of a rich endowment of natural resources varies depending on whether states enjoy crop-based or energy- and mineral-based resource wealth. In Central Asia, following the demise of the Soviet Union, for example, Uzbekistan's crop-based resource wealth (cotton) was easier to exploit and to redirect to new markets in the early 1990s than Kazakhstan's oil, coal and mineral wealth, which shaped the reform strategies each state adopted for the transition from central planning to a market-based economy (Broome 2010a: 122–3). Some scholars have also found that oil and mineral wealth generate structural impediments for the development of democratic institutions (Ross 2001: 328).

Because of the scarcity of the world's raw materials, small states such as Kuwait (with oil), Sierra Leone (with diamonds) and the Kyrgyz Republic (with gold and hydroelectric energy) have found their resource wealth in high demand. At the same time, resource-rich countries often struggle to use their natural resource endowments to drive economic development and higher living standards. In some cases, resource wealth has become a contributing factor in causing or prolonging civil war (especially 'lootable wealth' such as diamonds) (Snyder and Bhavnani 2005: 564).

It is hardly surprising that relations between the 'haves' and the 'have-nots' with respect to natural resources often cause disputes between governments or contribute to internal conflict, as well as generating disputes between firms, NGOs, IOs, local communities and households. The ability to control access to natural resources, how the use of raw materials is governed and how the proceeds are distributed can provide an important source of state power and economic wealth. For this reason alone, international cooperation over the management and use of environmental resources is especially difficult to achieve, and may remain difficult to enforce even when agreements are reached.

Energy resources and the international political economy of oil

For more than a century, the development and growth of the world economy has relied upon access to fossil fuels as a key source of global energy supplies. While much of modern economic activity depends upon the use of natural resources for the production of goods and services, oil has long been an essential ingredient for economic growth and the success of national strategies of economic development. Among other things, oil is crucial for transport and for the functioning of firm distribution networks. Because of the fundamental role of oil in most societies, sudden changes in the price of oil create a ripple effect that can quickly spread to all sectors of a national economy and, potentially, the world economy. Due to the oligopolistic nature of the global oil industry, increases in the price of oil can cause a spike in domestic inflation rates due to the flow-on effects of higher transport costs for the domestic delivery of goods and services and international trade, as well as when petroleum is used for electricity generation. Cheap oil can also fuel increased rates of household consumption.

The control of energy resources is a major source of tension in the global political economy, while the diminishing stock of the world's oil reserves relative to likely future global demand has made the politics of energy a key driver of strategic competition among states (Kuzemko *et al.* 2012). The control of energy resources can be a potent source of political power. As a resurgent Russia has demonstrated in recent years to neighbouring states Ukraine and Belarus and to European energy consumers, the ability to cut off energy supplies simply through 'flipping a switch' can be an effective direct tool of economic coercion (Abdelal 2013). Likewise, the ability of a state to extract economic rents from the exploitation of natural resources provides an important source of domestic political power by increasing the opportunities for patronage through the allocation of wealth to regime supporters, as in the case of 'rentier states' such as Kazakhstan and Saudi Arabia.

As the extensive literature on the 'resource curse' illustrates, an endowment of significant resource wealth is not always beneficial for a country's broader economic development and overall living standards. Countries that are rich in minerals or fuels often experience lower rates of economic growth and development compared with resource-poor countries. This can be caused by a lack of diversification if economic activity is concentrated on the exploitation of raw materials, which may be further worsened if high export earnings from natural resources cause an appreciation in the exchange rate that harms agricultural and manufacturing trade. Meanwhile, dependence on fiscal revenue and export earnings from natural resources can make an economy particularly vulnerable to volatility in global commodity prices.

One strategy some governments have adopted in an attempt to avoid the effects of the resource curse has been the creation of sovereign wealth funds financed by the foreign exchange earnings of energy exports. Countries as varied as Norway and Kazakhstan have established oil funds in an effort to 'sterilize' the foreign exchange proceeds of energy exports and build up future financial resources (Kalyuzhnova 2011). Sovereign wealth funds can provide two kinds of benefits: fiscal benefits as a savings fund and broader macroeconomic benefits as a stabilization fund. Sovereign wealth funds therefore provide a pool of investment resources that can help to ensure a country's long-term fiscal sustainability. At the same time, investing a proportion of energy export earnings in a national oil fund, rather than using resource proceeds to finance public expenditure, can potentially help countries to 'self-insure' against macroeconomic volatility by stabilizing prices and lowering inflation rates (Shabsigh and Ilahi 2007).

The IPE of oil has changed markedly in the last half century. In the postwar era, the USA shifted from the position of the world's biggest oil producer to the world's biggest oil importer (see Figure 17.1). The USA is still the third largest oil producer, behind Saudi Arabia and Russia (see Figure 17.2). Unlike other large producers, US oil resources are used for domestic consumption, whereas Russia and Saudi Arabia occupy the positions of the world's first and second largest oil exporters, respectively.

Figure 17.1 *Top-ten oil importers and exporters, 2007*

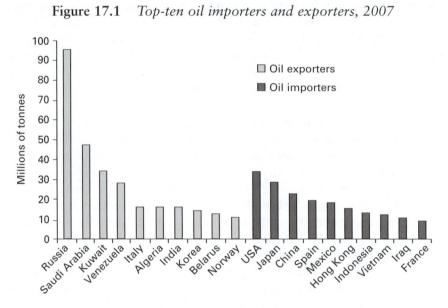

Source: Data from International Energy Agency (2009: 21).

Figure 17.2 *Top-ten oil producers, 2007*

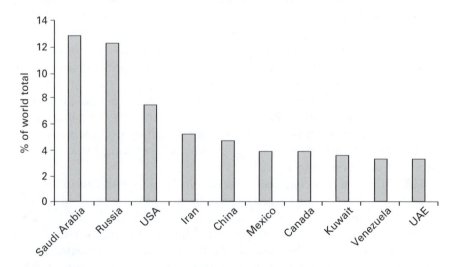

Source: Data from International Energy Agency (2009: 21).

Box 17.2   OPEC and the 1973 oil shocks

The Organization of the Petroleum Exporting Countries was formed in 1960 to exert pressure on major international oil companies to increase prices for producers, partly in response to restrictive US quotas on oil imports. The 1970s can be described as the 'OPEC decade', the period in which the organization was most influential in shaping the dynamics of global energy politics. An oil embargo on countries supporting Israel in the 1973 Arab–Israeli war was announced in October 1973, which lasted until March 1974, by the Organization of Arab Petroleum Exporting Countries (consisting of OPEC countries plus Egypt, Syria and Tunisia). The immediate economic effect of the 1973 oil shocks was the quadrupling of the price of oil, leading to a rapid increase in capital flows from importers to oil exporting countries as well as higher inflation in oil-importing countries. By cutting oil production and imposing an embargo producers were able to exercise a systemic form of power in the global political economy, known as the 'oil weapon', which was used to pursue a range of strategic aims. The political and economic goals of OPEC states included gaining a greater share of revenue from oil sales, influencing the foreign policies of major powers such as the USA in the Middle East, building up national military capabilities through arms purchases and increasing support for negotiations on a 'New International Economic Order' to rebalance the structure of the world economy. The use of the 'oil weapon' to achieve a change in the international economic order and to shift Western political support away from Israel was ultimately unsuccessful. However, the massive capital inflows experienced by OPEC members combined with the higher costs faced by developing country oil importers directly contributed to the economic conditions that resulted in the 1980s Latin American debt crisis (see Chapter 14).

One of the most significant episodes in the changing global political economy of the postwar era, in addition to the demise of the Bretton Woods international monetary system in the early 1970s, was the oil shocks of the 1970s, when the Organization of the Petroleum Exporting Countries (OPEC) suddenly increased the international price of oil in 1973 (see Box 17.2). This led directly to a quadruple increase in the domestic price of oil in the USA, which further stoked inflation at a time when the world economy was still recovering from the monetary uncertainty generated by the abandonment of the Bretton Woods system of fixed exchange rates. The consequences of the oil shocks and the emergence of 'resource nationalism' in OPEC countries in the early 1970s have continued to shape global resource competition over energy supplies long after the overwhelming dominance of OPEC producers in the international oil trade declined relative to non-OPEC producers during the 1980s. Among other things, the legacy of the oil shocks has driven the ongoing efforts of Western economies to develop renewable alternative energy sources to fossil fuels and has shaped the economic challenges facing oil-importing developing countries, as well as influencing the evolution of the foreign economic policies and strategic interests of major powers such as the USA.

The changing dynamics of resource nationalism

Prior to the 1970s, only Russia in 1917 and Mexico in 1938 had successfully nationalized domestic oil supplies. During the 1970s almost all oil supplies outside the USA were nationalized as oil-producing countries turned to resource nationalism to use oil price rises to increase economic rents and to influence the international distribution of wealth. Oil became a foreign economic policy instrument of exporting countries, such as the oil embargo placed on the USA and the Netherlands in October 1973 by OPEC for their support of Israel during the 1973 Arab–Israeli war. In response to the oil shocks, the USA founded the International Energy Agency (IEA) in 1974, which is affiliated to the OECD. The IEA was established to enhance cooperation in the distribution of oil among Western importers to blunt the impact of the 'oil weapon', to facilitate greater efficiency in oil production and the use of energy, and to encourage the expansion of 'strategic reserves' of oil (Morse 1999: 4–5). The effectiveness of changes by exporting countries in the price of oil through withholding production was further diminished by increases in taxes on oil products in major consuming countries. For example, Western European countries and Japan increased fuel taxes in the late 1970s to the point where crude oil imports were taxed at 100 per cent or more of the import price, which transferred a significant proportion of the economic rents generated by oil price rises from oil producers to oil importers (Morse 1999: 6). In the 1980s, the global political impact of resource nationalism began to decline compared with the 1970s as the USA formed a closer alliance with states in the Gulf region, and especially with Saudi Arabia. Several oil exporters in the Gulf subsequently moved towards greater cooperation with the USA on decisions over oil pricing and production in exchange for military security (Bromley 2005: 243–4).

More recent examples of *revolutionary resource nationalism* include the expropriation of private assets and the forced consolidation of state control over natural resources, as witnessed in Russia and Venezuela. Less extreme cases of *economic resource nationalism* include

Figure 17.3   *Annual US oil imports from OPEC and non-OPEC countries (thousands of barrels)*

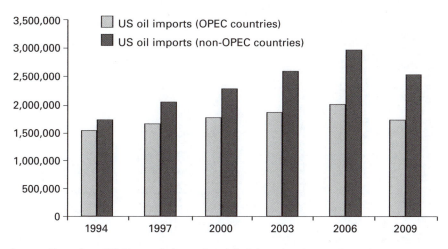

Source: Data from US Energy Information Administration (www.eia.gov).

Kazakhstan's efforts to increase fiscal revenue from oil exploitation and to expand the role of state-owned companies in extraction activities, but without challenging overall private foreign investment in the country's resource sector (Bremmer and Johnston 2009: 150–1). A new 'great game' has emerged in Central Asia between major powers for control of the region's natural resources (Cooley 2012). This is centred on the development of the physical infrastructure and exploitation rights for gas and oil reserves in the former Soviet republics, such as Kazakhstan, Turkmenistan and the Caucasus state Azerbaijan. In part, this has been driven by the US aim of expanding non-OPEC oil production to lessen its energy dependence on Middle Eastern oil (see Figure 17.3). The efforts of the USA during the 1990s and 2000s to entice Central Asian states to shift away from their traditional economic and political ties with Russia, and to reduce the latter's virtual monopoly over access to the region's natural resources, have met with mixed success. While Russia remains by far the dominant energy player in Central Asia and the Caucasus, the USA successfully persuaded several countries in the region to construct a new pipeline to pump oil from the Caspian Sea to Turkey (running from Azerbaijan and through Georgia), rather than via Russia (Bromley 2005: 246–7).

Central Asian energy supplies are substantial enough to matter politically and economically for the region and for the struggle between major energy consumers over security of supply, but are unlikely to rival those of the Middle East region (Nourzhanov 2006: 60). With the exception of

Figure 17.4   *Top-ten countries in proven oil reserves*

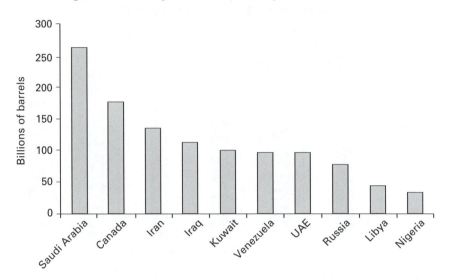

Source: Data from CIA, *The World Factbook*, 2009 estimates (www.cia.gov).

Russia, none of the post-Soviet states make it into the top-ten countries in terms of the world's proven oil reserves (see Figure 17.4). Kazakhstan is estimated to have the world's 11th largest reserves at 30 billion barrels, compared with Saudi Arabia's estimated 264 billion barrels or Canada's estimated 178 billion barrels of oil reserves. Because Russian companies such as Lukoil and Gazprom control large sections of Central Asia's energy infrastructure for oil, gas and electricity, US involvement in Central Asian energy politics is likely to increase the level of resource competition with its former Cold War foe.

Russia's resurgence as a potential 'energy superpower' in the last decade has led to heightened concerns about the country's newfound ability and willingness to exercise international clout through energy dominance. Russia's growing energy importance is based on its position as one of the largest producers of natural gas, its position as the second biggest oil producer and its leading position as an oil exporter (see Figures 17.1 and 17.2). An important characteristic of Russia's growing political muscle as a global energy supplier is the renationalization of energy resources through state-owned or state-controlled companies (Rutland 2008: 204–5). The wider political consequences of this form of 'state capitalism' were on full display in recent years during Russia's disputes with Ukraine over gas prices and the security of energy supplies to Europe. When Russian energy company Gazprom stopped gas deliveries to Ukraine in January 2006, the flow-on effects of the dispute led to severe shortfalls in gas supplies to European countries. This caused a 40 per cent reduction in gas supplies in Hungary and a 30 per cent fall in gas supplies in France, Austria, Slovakia and Romania (Abdelal 2013: 432). The 2006 dispute was resolved reasonably quickly, but this episode illustrates the potential long-term political problems that might develop if European countries increase their dependence on Russian energy supplies (Goldthau 2012).

Contemporary challenges and sources of change

Energy resources are of critical importance for global economic stability and national economic development and growth. Secure access to oil also remains an essential ingredient in the capacity of major states to project military power abroad. The total annual oil supplies used by the US military, for example, are roughly equal to the volume used by an entire national economy the size of Greece (Bridge 2010: 523). The challenges of global energy politics now go hand-in-hand with concerns in many societies about the problem of climate change and the wider environmental costs of dependence on carbon-based economic growth (see Chapter 18). Two of the most important developments in the changing dynamics of global resource competition include the continuing high level of dependence on oil for the world's energy supplies, despite efforts to develop alternative energy sources, and the rapidly growing energy needs of major emerging market economies.

Figure 17.5   *Composition of global primary energy supplies, 1973 and 2007*

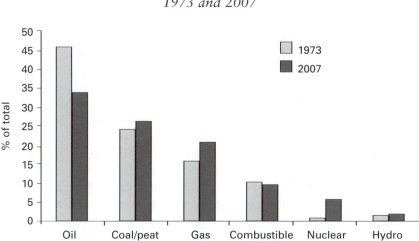

Source: Data from International Energy Agency (2009: 6).

Figure 17.6   *US oil prices, 2004–10*

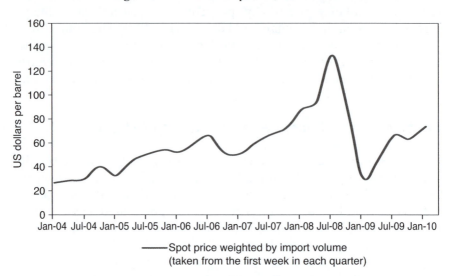

———Spot price weighted by import volume
(taken from the first week in each quarter)

Source: Data from US Energy Information Administration (www.eia.gov).

The composition of global energy supplies has gradually shifted in the four decades since the oil price shocks of 1973. Oil now forms a relatively smaller share of global energy supplies, having declined from roughly 46 per cent of total supplies in 1973 to 34 per cent in 2007, while the respective shares of nuclear energy and gas have significantly increased. Nonetheless, as Figure 17.5 illustrates, oil still remains by far the most important supply of global energy. The global importance of oil was starkly demonstrated in the energy crisis of 2007–08. Driven by financial market speculation, geostrategic concerns over conflicts in the Middle East and the publication of official reports with dire predictions of depleting oil reserves, the price of oil rapidly increased before falling sharply again in 2009 during the global financial crisis (see Figure 17.6). Among other things, the oil price spike significantly increased the importance attached to the goal of achieving 'energy independence' in US domestic politics (Goldthau and White 2009: 373).

The international dynamics of energy production have been transformed by the 'shale gas revolution' in the last decade and a half. This was made possible by the development of hydraulic fracturing, a controversial process of fracturing rock using highly pressurized liquid known as 'fracking', which enables the extraction of natural gas trapped in shale rock formations. This has led to the growth of unconventional methods of extracting oil and gas resources, which has transformed the geography of global energy production. The USA is now estimated to be sitting on

Box 17.3   Selected actors in global energy politics

- **Everyday actors**
  Everyday consumers of energy depend upon governments and firms to maintain secure energy supplies for commercial activity and household consumption. At the same time, everyday actors in many countries have increased pressure on their governments to develop renewable energy alternatives, through directly increasing the political salience of energy security and climate change issues at the national and local government level, as well as indirectly through changing preferences over recycling, solar power, more fuel-efficient automobiles and public transport options that generate lower greenhouse gas emissions.

- **International organizations**
  States cooperating through IOs impact upon global energy politics by increasing their collective leverage and ability to shape energy trends. Agreements on oil production targets among OPEC states continue to influence international oil prices, while Western energy consumers cooperate through the IEA to increase their capacity to respond to energy price shocks and to diversify their sources of energy supplies.

- **Market actors**
  Both international oil companies and national oil companies remain major players in the political economy of global resource competition, in particular through funding investment in oil and gas exploration and the development of the physical infrastructure for transporting energy supplies from producers to consumers. Market forces are now of greater importance in setting international oil and gas prices, following the liberalization of the international oil market as a consequence of the changing dynamics of the industry during the 'OPEC decade' of the 1970s (Goldthau and White 2009).

- **States**
  Major power states exercise influence by shaping the 'rules of the game' for the global energy market, and through providing financial, political and diplomatic, and sometimes military, support for their energy firms to gain access to new supplies of natural resources. The decisions made by major energy exporters continue to exert a significant impact on both energy prices and security of supply for energy consumers.

the equivalent of up to 90 years of recoverable shale gas (based on current consumption), with US shale gas production surpassing Russian gas production in 2009. These developments have enabled almost all domestic consumption of natural gas to be produced within the USA and Canada. US gas exports to Western Europe have also threatened to erode the market share of Russia's Gazprom, challenging Gazprom's market power as the main provider to 'a gas-hungry European market' (Goldthau 2012: 212–13).

The contemporary dynamics of global resource competition have become further complicated by the growing importance of a broader range of actors in global energy politics. These changes range from the growth of new major energy consumers to the 'scramble' for energy resources in Africa and Central Asia. The range of variables that influence changes in international energy prices has also expanded following the liberalization of international energy markets and the demise of the vertically integrated structure of international oil companies with the emergence of more aggressive resource nationalism in the 1970s (and again in the late 1990s and 2000s).

One of the greatest immediate challenges for global energy politics is the effect that the rise of emerging economies and their need for access to natural resources has had on ramping up competition for the world's remaining energy supplies. The US Energy Information Administration has predicted a gradual but steady long-term increase in the international price of oil in the next 25 years – with oil prices expected to double between 2010 and 2035 – which will have a significant impact on global energy politics through increasing existing pressures on governments to secure greater access to alternative energy supplies (such as renewable sources, as well as nuclear power). Based on the unexpected spike in energy prices during 2007 and 2008, however, these estimates of long-term price increases may be overly conservative, while it is difficult to predict how the growing demand for energy supplies from rising economic powers will impact upon future scenarios for global resource competition.

The rapid growth of China's economy in the last two decades has driven the objective of securing access to energy supplies to the top of China's foreign economic policy agenda. China's energy consumption is predicted to increase by 125 per cent by 2025. In response, the Chinese government has engaged in extensive 'resource diplomacy' during the last decade and a half, especially in Africa (Mohan and Power 2008: 30). Given the high concentration of the world's proven oil and gas supplies in a few geographical regions, the intensity of resource competition between the world's major energy consumers can be expected to increase further in the near future. This may involve greater risk of sudden disruptions in energy supplies, or slowly emerging supply gaps due to inadequate investment in transport infrastructure and new production capacity (Corelljé and Linde 2006: 533, 538). Rising energy demand will also hasten the point at which 'peak oil' is reached, after which the rate of global petroleum extraction and oil production is expected to sharply decline.

Summary

Global energy politics and resource competition between energy consumers and producers has had a transformative impact on the global political economy during the last four decades. This has driven important changes in capital flows from energy importers to energy exporters, with flow-on effects for global investment trends and sovereign debt, as well as influencing national development strategies and trade patterns. Markets, governments and firms all play important roles in shaping the evolution of global competition over access to raw materials, as well as determining the impact of national resource wealth in domestic processes of economic and political change. In the twenty-first century, the expansion of China's 'resource diplomacy' in Africa, Russia's more assertive resource nationalism and US efforts to secure access to the world's remaining energy resources have given added importance to the evolving dynamics of energy politics as a key source of change in the global political economy.

Discussion questions

1. Why is international cooperation over the management of natural resources hard to achieve?
2. Is resource nationalism an effective economic strategy for developing states?
3. How will declining oil supplies relative to demand shape the future international political economy of energy?
4. How might states avoid the potential constraints of the resource curse?
5. Who are the dominant actors in global resource competition, and why?
6. How does energy politics impact upon efforts to shift to a less carbon-intensive economy?

Further reading

Dunning, Thad. 2008. *Crude Democracy: Natural Resource Wealth and Political Regimes*. Cambridge: Cambridge University Press.

Jones Luong, Pauline and Erika Weinthal. 2010. *Oil is Not a Curse: Ownership Structure and Institutions in Soviet Successor States*. Cambridge: Cambridge University Press.

Richardson, Ben. 2009. *Sugar: Refined Power in a Global Regime*. Basingstoke: Palgrave Macmillan.

Shaffer, Brenda. 2009. *Energy Politics*. Philadelphia: University of Pennsylvania Press.

Wilson, Jeffrey D. 2013. *Governing Global Production: Resource Networks in the Asia-Pacific Steel Industry*. Basingstoke: Palgrave Macmillan.

Yergin, Daniel. 2009. *The Prize: The Epic Quest for Oil, Money and Power*. New York: Simon & Schuster.

Chapter 18

The Environment and Climate Change

Introduction

Contemporary environmental challenges are reshaping how the nature of the global political economy is understood. From conflicts over access to scarce resources and dependence on non-renewable fossil fuels for energy and transportation to the problems generated by climate change, increasing population size and density, natural disasters, transnational environmental crime, pollution and environmental degradation, the salience of environmental issues for IPE has significantly increased in recent years. The greater importance attached to environmental issues has driven a variety of new research agendas in the field that have challenged traditional conceptions of economic growth, development, wealth and public goods, on subjects such as sustainable development, the political economy of environmental governance at the national, regional, or global level and the emergence of low-carbon 'climate capitalism' models of industrial expansion (Newell and Paterson 2010).

The prospects for achieving international cooperation on environmental issues face many of the same collective action obstacles as other governance areas, where public or private actors can achieve few positive gains by acting alone but lack the short-term incentives that would increase their willingness for burden-sharing and common actions. Nevertheless, many observers have argued that the nature of environmental challenges remain distinct in several important ways from other global policy challenges, and may not be amenable to conventional state-based solutions such as multilateral treaties or expanding the responsibilities of existing IOs. This chapter discusses how changing environmental dynamics have impacted upon the global political economy, and how contemporary processes may shape the future evolution of environmental governance and models of development and growth.

Background

Environmental challenges are a defining feature of the contemporary global political economy. Numerous environment-related issues have gradually gained inclusion in global and regional policy agendas as warranting greater action from state and non-state actors, and have received increased scholarly attention in academic research on changing global political dynamics. Some of these issues have included transnational environmental crime and the illegal exploitation of natural resources (Elliott 2007), the problems associated with achieving international cooperation to mitigate environmental disasters resulting from mismanagement of natural resources (Weinthal 2002), the influence that environmentalist norm advocates have had on the policies of IOs (Park 2010b) and many others. Among the broad range of environmental issues that now receive more sustained attention in the study of IPE, however, it is climate change that has become widely accepted as being the highest ranked priority for global action.

The politics of achieving concerted action on climate change across national boundaries has proven to be a daunting task. For example, the notion of burden-sharing is more complex with respect to environmental challenges than in many other issue areas. This is because it refers not only to the distribution of the costs of mitigating and adapting to climate change across different societies and socio-economic groups, but also centres on intergenerational processes of burden-sharing – including the prospect of substantially increased future costs for present inaction (Page 2008). Meanwhile, the development of a political consensus on the causes of and solutions to climate change lags far behind the scientific consensus on the scale and scope of the problem, even when there is political agreement that climate change is an empirically quantifiable phenomenon (Oreskes 2004).

According to the Intergovernmental Panel on Climate Change (IPCC), which was created in 1988 by the World Meteorological Organization and the United Nations Environment Programme (UNEP), climate change is defined as 'a change in the state of the climate' that can be quantitatively measured and which 'persists for an extended period, typically decades or longer', whether this is 'due to natural variability or as a result of human activity' (IPCC 2007: 30). In this definition, climate change differs from the narrower usage referred to in the 1992 United Nations Framework Convention on Climate Change (UNFCCC), which specifically links changes in the planet's climate system to human activity. This is termed *anthropogenic* climate change, which refers to changes in the climate system resulting directly or indirectly from human activity rather than natural variability. As the Fourth Report of the IPCC observed in 2007, during the period from 1995 to 2006 the world experienced 11 of the 12 warmest years in average global surface temperatures since 1850, which occurred at the same time as substantial decreases in Artic sea ice and increases in the rate at which the global average sea level rose. Among other potential effects, the consequences of changes in the planet's climate system have been associated with the increasing frequency and intensity of extreme weather events in several regions, increases in heat-related mortality rates and the spread of infectious diseases in Europe, shifting seasonal cycles and changes in Arctic and Antarctic eco-systems. While the strength of the links that IPCC scientists have identified between climate change and observed ecological changes are explicitly stated with varying levels of confidence, the evidence on the overall direction of change in the world's climate system is overwhelming. Drawing from over 29,000 observational data series in 75 studies, IPCC scientists concluded in 2007 that 'more than 89% are consistent with the direction of change expected as a response to warming' of the climate (IPCC 2007: 33).

One of the key causes of changes in the planet's climate system is the rate of increase in greenhouse gas (GHG) emissions in the last two centuries. GHG emissions have grown substantially since the Industrial Revolution, but the rate of increase in GHG emissions has been especially pronounced during the past four decades, when global emissions increased by 70 per cent between 1970 and 2004. Despite a decrease in global energy intensity during this period, measured as declining carbon dioxide (CO_2) emissions per unit of energy, which reduced global emissions by one third, global income growth and population growth respectively contributed to increasing emissions by 77 per cent and 69 per cent (IPCC 2007: 36–7). In short, any environmental gains from a gradual shift towards less carbon-intensive use of energy during the period from 1970–2004 were more than wiped out by economic and demographic changes over the same period. These basic figures provide a snapshot of the scale of the policy challenges associated with climate change. At the same time, however, rapid changes in 'green technologies' have enabled the development of renewable energy sources, more efficient energy storage and transmission and low-carbon production processes.

Sustainable development and economic growth

Many observers have argued that one of the largest obstacles to meaningful and effective action to address climate change is the continuing dependence on the assumption that the pursuit of growth is an essential feature of modern economies. Growth is typically understood as an aggregate measure of the percentage change in the level of economic output in a given area, without taking into account the negative externalities that may be associated with existing modes of industrial production and consumption. Negative externalities are welfare costs such as social consequences and spill-over effects that are not incorporated within the price for a particular good. Advocates of environmentally friendly economic policies and production processes have argued that the global focus on growth should be replaced by the pursuit of the goal of sustainable development to avoid the 'tragedy of the commons', a situation in which common resources are over-exploited because individual actors lack the motivation to use them sustainably.

The concept of sustainability directly challenges how the economy is commonly understood by governments, businesses, media organizations, households and individuals alike. The 1987 Report of the World Commission on Environment and Development – known as the Brundtland Commission – defined sustainable development as 'meeting the needs of the present without compromising the ability of future generations to meet their own needs' (United Nations General Assembly 1987). Intended to become a central guiding principle for the UN, national governments and other actors, the Brundtland Commission's definition of sustainable development strongly influenced the subsequent UN Framework Convention on Climate Change which was agreed at the UN Conference on Environment and Development (UNCED) in Rio de Janeiro in 1992 (the 'Earth Summit'), and continues to be one of the most commonly used definitions of environmental sustainability.

While the concept of limits to economic growth can be traced back to the classical political economy of Adam Smith and John Stuart Mill, modern expressions of similar ideas are also found in theories of the 'steady-state economy'. Articulated by Herman Daly and other ecological economists from the 1970s onwards, this conception of sustainability requires a transition to an economy where total gross domestic product remains more or less constant (Daly 1973). As Daly (2005) has noted, economic growth is often assumed to be a panacea solution to wide variety of policy challenges such as poverty, unemployment and overpopulation. However, these common assumptions of the benefits of growth quickly break down when the economy is conceived as 'a subsystem of the finite biosphere that supports it', rather than as a sphere of human activity that operates independently of the limits of the natural world. Once the finite limits of the biosphere are reached, Daly argues, 'uneconomic growth' will quickly make societies poorer rather than richer as non-renewable resources are depleted at an accelerated rate. In contrast to this bleak scenario, proponents of a steady-state economy argue that policy-makers should shift from an obsession with quantitative increases in economic output (growth), towards qualitative improvements in economic processes and outcomes (development).

As a political term, 'sustainability' is frequently used to refer to a wide variety of different policies and political objectives, ranging from more radical proposals for a transition to a steady-state economy to less-ambitious proposals for adapting existing economic processes and growth models to reduce the effects on environmental resources and the climate system. In terms of market-based strategies for responding to the challenges of climate change and other environmental issues, numerous options are available in the existing scholarly and policy literature that could contribute to mediating the short- and longer-term consequences of environmental challenges. Effective policy solutions to environmental challenges are often assumed to depend upon successful cooperation at the global or regional level. As IPCC experts noted in 2007, the existing literature provides substantial evidence of policy options that can help to reduce global greenhouse gas emissions, and is also characterized by a high level of agreement on what actions will prove most effective (IPCC 2007: 62). As Table 18.1 illustrates, once the goals of economic development are recast to take into account their environmental impact and sustainability issues, there is no inherent reason why the objectives of addressing climate change considerations and fostering economic development must be seen as mutually exclusive.

The potential economic consequences of climate change are severe, and will increase markedly over the long term without effective action to mitigate the negative externalities of contemporary industrial processes and consumption patterns. The costs of climate change will nonetheless be distributed unevenly across the globe, with some geographic areas and economic sectors projected to make economic gains as temperatures rise, while other economic sectors and geographical areas will face substantial costs. At the global level, conservative estimates of the prospective costs of a 4°C rise in average temperatures range from 1 to 5 per cent of world GDP (IPCC 2007: 69).

One key area of contention is whether the effects of climate change are likely to increase or to decrease societal pressures in different countries for greater democratic accountability and responsiveness. Some observers have suggested that authoritarian regimes might have a comparative advantage that makes them better placed to impose necessary environmental adjustments on unwilling populations, who may face a trade-off between civil liberties and environmental sustainability (Beeson 2010). For countries that are engaged in continuing processes of democratization, the impact of climate change over time on national political systems that are in 'transition' is difficult to predict. As Peter Burnell (2012: 817) points out: 'In developing countries especially,

Table 18.1   *Integrating climate change considerations into development policies*

Selected sectors	Non-climate change policy instruments and options	Potentially affects
Macro-economy	Implement non-climate taxes/subsidies and/or other fiscal and regulatory policies that promote sustainable development	Total global greenhouse gas emissions
Forestry	Adoption of forest conservation and sustainable management practices	Greenhouse gas emissions from deforestation
Electricity	Adoption of cost-effective renewables, demand-side management programmes and transmission and distribution loss reduction	Electricity sector CO_2 emissions
Petroleum imports	Diversifying imported and domestic fuel mix and reducing economy's energy intensity to improve energy security	Emissions from crude oil and product imports
Insurance for building/transport sectors	Differentiated premiums, liability insurance exclusions, improved terms for green products	Transport and building sector greenhouse gas emissions
International finance	Country and sector strategies and project lending that reduces emissions	Emissions from developing countries

Source: IPCC (2007: 62).

competition for people's votes at election time places a premium on promises of economic progress, not reductions of GGEs [greenhouse gas emissions].' Despite strong public support for increased use of renewable energy technologies in many developed countries in principle, renewable energy initiatives such as solar energy and wind farms are often met with localized and organized opposition (Barry *et al.* 2008). Others have pointed to indicators of a global deliberative system emerging around environmental governance. While imperfect, this has produced a broad set of policy alternatives that might gradually result in an expansion of deliberative democratic processes at the global level to address the challenges of climate change (Dryzek and Stevenson 2011).

Global environmental governance

The dominant focus of much of the scholarship on environmental challenges and the global political economy has tended to follow a common thread, which has focused on the problems associated with designing, negotiating and enforcing common rules and institutions at the international level to manage or mitigate the effects of climate change. As Peter Newell (2008: 508, emphasis original) has observed, 'Debate continues to centre on how to motivate *self-interested states* to act in ways which protect and enhance the global commons' – the planet's un-owned natural resources. This starting point orients analysis towards many of the traditional problems that characterize the creation and enforcement of international policy regimes, such as how to manage the problem of free-riders, how to effectively sanction non-compliance and how to mitigate institutional fragility while avoiding bureaucratic pathologies (Newell 2008: 508–9). In contrast to this conventional approach, Newell (2008: 509) suggests that gaining a more comprehensive understanding of the evolution and causes of global environmental challenges and developing innovative strategies to address them is easier to achieve by asking the question: 'Which social relations make environmental degradation possible?'

Rather than focusing primarily on public actors such as states and intergovernmental organizations as the fulcrum of contemporary forms of global environmental governance, the evolving regulatory dynamics associated with the management or mitigation of environmental challenges can be viewed as expressions of multi-actor and multi-site governance processes. Contemporary forms of environmental governance often 'embody hybrid formations whose governance practices are only possible through cooperation and competition between each of the key "governance providers"', including states, market actors, and civil society organizations (Newell 2008: 520). Examining the changing pattern of environmental governance therefore involves studying the complex dynamics of public–private relations in the global political economy, rather than assuming that environmental governance is primarily a matter of either inter-state negotiations and agreements, on the one hand, or the privatization of responsibility for managing public goods, on the other (Falkner 2003: 84).

Figure 18.1   *Environmental Kuznets curve*

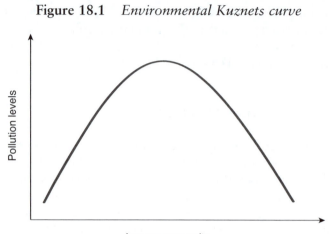

Income per capita

A number of existing IOs have been slow to adapt their activities and roles to take account of the increasing salience of environmental challenges for the dynamics of growth and development in the global political economy. In the case of the IMF, for example, environmental concerns have long been viewed as peripheral to the organization's primary macroeconomic responsibilities, or conceived as causally linked to the challenge of increasing growth and per capita income in particular countries based on an 'environmental Kuznets curve' (see Figure 18.1). The environmental Kuznets curve is the hypothesis that economic growth will increase pollution levels until per capita income reaches a certain threshold of development, after which environmental quality will improve. In 1990 the IMF initiated a policy of liaising more closely with those IOs undertaking analytical and empirical research on environmental issues, such as the World Bank, the United Nations, the OECD and the GATT, as well as consulting with selected environmental NGOs, such as the World Resources Institute and the Worldwide Fund for Nature, in order 'to gain a better understanding of the impact of macroeconomic policies on the environment' (IMF 1993: iii). While the organization views the achievement of macroeconomic stability and the removal of price distortions as generally beneficial for enhancing environmental protections, for at least the last two decades the IMF has recognized the problem of negative externalities resulting from market failures such as the over-exploitation of natural resources and the lack of accounting for social costs. More recently, the IMF has become engaged in advocating the use of fiscal policies to help countries mitigate the effects of climate change (de Mooij *et al.* 2012).

The World Bank has a longer history of being closely involved in environmental policy initiatives. In 1970 the World Bank established an

Office of Environmental and Health Affairs (subsequently renamed the Office of Environmental Affairs), which, despite a poorly defined mandate and weak institutionalization, marked the organization out as an early pioneer at the global level on environmental issues (Gutner 2002: 51–3). In the late 1980s under the presidency of Barber Conable, the World Bank significantly expanded and restructured its institutional resources and personnel to develop a stronger focus on incorporating environmental policies and safeguards across its lending operations and other activities, driven in part by pressures from the US Congress and the US Treasury, as well as by criticisms from environmental NGOs (Gutner 2002: 54–5). Since the start of these far-reaching reforms in its approach to environmental issues in 1987, the World Bank has cultivated a reputation as a global leader on environmental policies. It subsequently became a key Implementing Agency of the Global Environment Facility, established in 1991, which funds environmentally friendly development projects around the globe. Today, the five organizations that make up the World Bank Group commonly present an image of themselves as champions of sustainable development norms, although they continue to do so in uneven ways that communicate mixed environmental messages to other actors (Park 2007).

The United Nations has a strong track record going back over four decades in shaping global debates and thinking on environmental issues. The 1972 United Nations Conference on the Human Environment (the 'Stockholm Conference') helped to establish the agenda-setting role of the UN as a leading advocate of developing new strategies to respond to environmental issues. The Stockholm Conference led to the creation of the UNEP, which has responsibility for coordinating UN environmental activities and fostering the design and implementation of environmentally friendly policies and development projects around the world. One of the widely recognized successes in the UNEP's history was the negotiation of the 1987 Montreal Protocol on Substances that Deplete the Ozone Layer (the 'Montreal Protocol'), a protocol to the 1985 Vienna Convention for the Protection of the Ozone Layer. This established a Multilateral Fund to provide assistance to developing country parties to the agreement whose consumption and production of ozone-depleting substances fall below a set threshold, to help them comply with the treaty's control measures on chlorofluorocarbons (CFCs) and chlorinated hydrocarbons. The Montreal Protocol is recognized as a landmark success in terms of global environmental governance, both because it has since been ratified by all member states of the UN and because scientific evidence suggests that compliance with the treaty has been associated with a levelling-off or decrease in the atmospheric concentration of ozone-depleting substances.

Box 18.1　Selected actors and climate change

- **Everyday actors**
  Everyday actors contribute to anthropogenic climate change through the aggregate effects of carbon-intensive consumption habits and energy use, but may also mitigate these effects through adopting less carbon-intensive consumption practices and increasing demand for environmentally friendly goods and services.

- **International organizations**
  Many IOs now include a focus on environmental issues within their activities, while other institutions have been established with a mandate for coordinating policy across a range of environmental concerns (such as the UNEP) or to address specific environmental issues (such as the UNFCCC).

- **Market actors**
  Market actors play important roles in shaping the prospects for effective environmental governance through their lobbying activities, charitable donations, brand management activities, market power and environmental management practices. Some firms contribute to causing environmental damage as polluters, while others have developed less carbon-intensive technologies that may help reduce global greenhouse gas emissions.

- **Non-governmental organizations**
  Environmental NGOs act as lobbyists, social activists and norm advocates at local, national, regional and global governance levels, and may also be involved with service-delivery functions for environmentally friendly development projects.

- **States**
  States play a key role in the negotiation of international environmental treaties and shaping other public forms of global environmental governance, as well as through national policy settings which establish environmental standards and support for 'green' technologies and goods to foster collective changes in economic processes, or which may continue to favour the growth of 'dirty' industries.

Despite some notable areas of improvement in global environmental governance, more recent climate change negotiations have been less successful, either due to incomplete ratification among UN member states or because negotiations have ended in stalemate as a result of competing conceptions of national economic interests. With respect to inter-state cooperation to protect the environment, the Rio Declaration on Environment and Development, which was agreed at the 1992 'Earth Summit', established the principle that 'States have common but differentiated responsibilities' for addressing global environmental degradation (United Nations General Assembly 1992). Subsequent negotiations during the 1990s resulted in the signing of the Kyoto Protocol to the UNFCC in 1997, which set explicit targets for countries to limit or reduce GGEs from 1990 levels between 2008 and 2012. Despite being signed and ratified by over 190 UN member states, the USA failed to ratify the Kyoto Protocol on the basis of competitiveness issues in relation to developing countries and the implementation costs of the agreement. The withdrawal of the USA reduced the scope of the Kyoto Protocol by excluding the world's largest economy and one of the biggest producers of GGEs. Based on UN estimates, the USA accounted for some 23 per cent of global GGEs in 2002, and is currently second only to China in its contribution to global emissions (Vezirgiannidou 2010).

The Kyoto Protocol incorporated a political compromise between agreements to limit or modify GGEs while upholding the objective included in the UNFCC to maintain 'an open international economic system that would lead to sustainable economic growth and development in all Parties, especially developing country Parties, thus enabling them better to address the problems of climate change' (United Nations 1992). While continued support for economic growth was important for gaining agreement on reductions in GGEs, it also reaffirmed the assumption underlying the concept of the environmental Kuznets curve: that while growth increases environmental degradation and greenhouse gas emissions, continued growth will enhance countries' capacities to reduce or reverse environmental damage in the long term.

The creation of a normative framework linking market-led economic growth to action to tackle environmental problems is what Steven Bernstein has referred to as the compromise of 'liberal environmentalism'. This involves the promotion of market mechanisms (such as carbon trading) 'over 'command and control' methods (standards, bans, quotas, and so on) as the preferred method of environmental management' (Bernstein 2001: 7). Under this normative framework, 'a liberal international economic order, privatization of global commons, and market norms are not only perceived as compatible with environmental protection, but also necessary for the successful incorporation of concern for the environment in the practices of relevant state and non-state actors' (Bernstein 2001: 213).

Despite these weaknesses, the Kyoto Protocol provides an example of a climate change agreement that was successfully negotiated and received near-universal ratification in the face of intense political controversy.

More recent global efforts to negotiate a successor treaty to govern future limits on GGEs, in contrast, have ended in an effective stalemate. In December 2009, a UN Climate Change Conference was held in Copenhagen (the 'Copenhagen Summit') following two years of intense pre-conference negotiations over a new global climate change agreement. These efforts resulted in an ambiguous, non-binding Accord that was drafted towards the end of the conference by the USA, China, India, South Africa and Brazil, and which was rejected with strong criticisms from several other participating states on the grounds that it lacked democratic legitimacy. The events leading up to the conclusion of the Copenhagen Summit were described by one government delegate as representing a switch in priorities 'from saving the world to saving face' (Dimitrov 2010: 20). The failure at the Copenhagen Summit of governments to agree even a non-binding climate change declaration through the UN process has led some observers to suggest that future policy action on climate change is likely to be restricted to national, bilateral and regional initiatives. This might produce further fragmentation in the emerging architecture of global environmental governance, which could either lead to a set of complementary governance processes organized around common principles and norms or may result in conflicting mandates, processes and purposes across different institutional settings (Biermann *et al.* 2009: 19).

An important dimension of the challenge of adapting to climate change through creating a 'decarbonized' economy is highlighted in work by Peter Newell and Matthew Paterson (2010). Examples where governments and IOs have achieved some success in fostering environmentally friendly economic changes, including reductions in the production and consumption of ozone-depleting substances such as CFCs, relied on encouraging shifts in industrial inputs and consumer choices that were not structurally determined. In this case, 'Persuading people to by CFC-free deodorants may have worked in helping to address ozone depletion.' However, 'Persuading people to fly less in a world of cheap flights, to leave their cars at home when their nearest shops are out of town is harder because food, energy, and transport systems, currently organized, assume a world unconstrained by limits on carbon use' (Newell and Paterson 2010: 8). The comparison between ozone depletion through CFCs and climate change resulting from GGEs illustrates the policy dilemma faced by national decision-makers and their populations. When effectively regulating environmental 'bads' requires achieving broader structural changes in how economies and societies operate across-the-board – rather than reducing the use of environmentally harmful products for which substitute goods are readily available or are not prohibitively costly to develop – the scale of the challenge is far greater.

Summary

Environmental challenges have become a fundamental concern for the future of the global political economy. Climate change is now located at the forefront of a range of complex and interconnected environmental issues that are reshaping how the world economy works and the evolution of global processes of cooperation between state and non-state actors. The complex policy dilemmas created by a changing climate system are accompanied by uncertainty over how environmental shifts might impact upon the effectiveness of different systems of political representation and modes of governing, as well as by rising estimates of the long-term economic costs associated with ineffective action to mitigate the effects of climate change. Among advocates for action on climate change, disagreements persist between liberal environmentalists, who favour the use of market-based processes to alter economic behaviour through price mechanisms, and those who see contemporary environmental challenges as demanding a more fundamental process of structural change in the global political economy of the twenty-first century.

Discussion questions

1. Who are the winners and losers from existing forms of environmental governance?
2. What are the main factors contributing to deadlocks in global environmental negotiations?
3. How should the intergenerational costs of adjusting to climate change be distributed?
4. What are the merits and drawbacks of the concept of 'sustainable development'?
5. Are democratic or authoritarian political systems better suited to adapting to climate change?
6. How could global environmental governance be made more effective?

Further reading

Bernstein, Steven. 2001. *The Compromise of Liberal Environmentalism.* New York: Columbia University Press.

Biermann, Frank and Philipp Pattberg (eds). 2012. *Global Environmental Governance Reconsidered.* Cambridge: MIT Press.

Clapp, Jennifer and Peter Dauvergne. 2005. *Paths to a Green World: The Political Economy of the Global Environment.* Cambridge: MIT Press.

Elliott, Lorraine M. 2004. *The Global Politics of the Environment, Second Edition*. Basingstoke: Palgrave Macmillan.

Newell, Peter and Matthew Paterson. 2010. *Climate Capitalism: Global Warming and the Transformation of the Global Economy*. Cambridge: Cambridge University Press.

Park, Susan. 2010b. *World Bank Group Interactions with Environmentalists: Changing International Organisation Identities*. Manchester: Manchester University Press.

References

Abbott, Kenneth W. and Duncan Snidal. 1998. 'Why States Act through Formal International Organizations'. *Journal of Conflict Resolution* 42(1): 3–32.

Abbott, Kenneth W. and Duncan Snidal. 2000. 'Hard and Soft Law in International Governance'. *International Organization* 54(3): 421–56.

Abdelal, Rawi. 2001. *National Purpose in the World Economy: Post-Soviet States in Comparative Perspective*. Ithaca, NY: Cornell University Press.

Abdelal, Rawi. 2007. *Capital Rules: The Construction of Global Finance*. Cambridge, MA: Harvard University Press.

Abdelal, Rawi. 2013. 'The Profits of Power: Commerce and *Realpolitik* in Eurasia'. *Review of International Political Economy* 20(3): 421–56.

Abdelal, Rawi and Laura Alfaro. 2003. 'Capital and Control: Lessons from Malaysia'. *Challenge* 46(4): 36–53.

Abdelal, Rawi, Mark Blyth and Craig Parsons (eds). 2010. *Constructing the International Economy*. Ithaca, NY: Cornell University Press.

Abdelal, Rawi, Yoshiko M. Herrera, Alastair Iain Johnston and Rose McDermott. 2009. In *Measuring Identity: A Guide for Social Scientists*, edited by Rawi Abdelal, Yoshiko M. Herrera, Alastair Iain Johnston and Rose McDermott. New York: Cambridge University Press, 1–13.

Adam, Stuart and James Browne. 2011. 'A Survey of the UK Tax System'. *Briefing Notes* 9. London: Institute for Fiscal Studies. <www.ifs.org.uk/bns/bn09.pdf>

Aizenman, Joshua and Yothin Jinjarak. 2009. 'Globalisation and Developing Countries: A Shrinking Tax Base?'. *Journal of Development Studies* 45(5): 653–71.

Allison, Graham T. 1971. *Essence of Decision: Explaining the Cuban Missile Crisis*. New York: HarperCollins.

Amoore, Louise. 2002. *Globalization Contested: An International Political Economy of Work*. Manchester: Manchester University Press.

Andreas, Peter. 2011. 'Illicit Globalization: Myths, Misconceptions, and Historical Lessons'. *Political Science Quarterly* 126(3): 403–25.

Andreas, Peter and Kelly Greenhill (eds). 2010. *Sex, Drugs, and Body Counts: The Politics of Numbers in Global Crime and Conflict*. Ithaca, NY: Cornell University Press.

Archer, Candace and Stefan Fritsch. 2010. 'Global Fair Trade: Humanizing Globalization and Reintroducing the Normative to International Political Economy'. *Review of International Political Economy* 17(1): 103–28.

Avant, Deborah D., Martha Finnemore and Susan K. Sell (eds). 2010. *Who Governs the Globe?*. Cambridge: Cambridge University Press.

Babb, Sarah. 2012. 'The Washington Consensus as Transnational Policy Paradigm: Its Origins, Trajectory and Likely Successor'. *Review of International Political Economy* 20(2): 268-97.

285

Baker, Andrew. 2006. *The Group of Seven: Finance Ministries, Central Banks and Global Financial Governance*. London: Routledge.

Baker, Andrew. 2008. 'Global Monitor: The Group of Seven'. *New Political Economy* 13(1): 103–15.

Baker, Andrew. 2012. 'The "Public Interest" Agency of International Organizations? The Case of the OECD Principles of Corporate Governance'. *Review of International Political Economy* 19(3): 389–414.

Baker, Andrew. 2013. 'The New Political Economy of the Macroprudential Ideational Shift'. *New Political Economy* 18(1): 112–39.

Balassa, Béla. 1988. 'The Lessons of East Asian Development: An Overview'. *Economic Development and Cultural Change* 36(3): 273–90.

Bank for International Settlements. 2010. *Triennial Central Bank Survey of Foreign Exchange and Derivatives Market Activity in 2010: Final Results*. Basle: Bank for International Settlements.

Barber, William J. 1967. *A History of Economic Thought*. Harmondsworth: Penguin.

Barnett, Michael and Raymond Duvall. 2005. 'Power in International Politics'. *International Organization* 59(1): 39–75.

Barnett, Michael and Martha Finnemore. 2004. *Rules for the World: International Organizations in World Politics*. Ithaca, NY: Cornell University Press.

Barr, Nicholas. 2012. *Economics of the Welfare State*, 5th edn. Oxford: Oxford University Press.

Barry, John, Geraint Ellis and Clive Robinson. 2008. 'Cool Rationalities and Hot Air: A Rhetorical Approach to Understanding Debates on Renewable Energy'. *Global Environmental Politics* 8(2): 67–98.

Beckert, Jens. 1996. 'What is Sociological about Economic Sociology? Uncertainty and the Embeddedness of Economic Action'. *Theory and Society* 25(6): 803–40.

Beeson, Mark. 2009. 'Developmental States in East Asia: A Comparison of the Japanese and Chinese Experiences'. *Asian Perspective* 33(2): 5–39.

Beeson, Mark. 2010. 'The Coming of Environmental Authoritarianism'. *Environmental Politics* 19(2): 276–94.

Beeson, Mark and Stephen Bell. 2009. 'The G-20 and International Economic Governance: Hegemony, Collectivism, or Both?'. *Global Governance* 15(1): 67–86.

Beeson, Mark and André Broome. 2010. 'Hegemonic Instability and East Asia: Contradictions, Crises, and US Power'. *Globalizations* 7(4): 507–23.

Beeson, Mark and Hung Hung Pham. 2012. 'Developmentalism with Vietnamese Characteristics: The Persistence of State-led Development in East Asia'. *Journal of Contemporary Asia* 42(4): 539–59.

Bello, Walden. 1998. 'East Asia: On the Eve of the Great Transformation?'. *Review of International Political Economy* 5(3): 424–44.

Bello, Walden. 2009. 'States and Markets, States versus Markets: The Developmental State Debate as the Distinctive East Asian Contribution to International Political Economy'. In *Routledge Handbook of International Political Economy (IPE): IPE as a Global Conversation*, edited by Mark Blyth. London: Routledge, 180–200.

Berger, Suzanne. 1996. 'Introduction'. In *National Diversity and Global Capitalism*, edited by Suzanne Berger and Ronald Dore. Ithaca, NY: Cornell University Press, 1–25.

Bernard, Mitchell and John Ravenhill. 1996. 'Beyond Product Cycles and Flying Geese: Regionalization, Hierarchy, and the Industrialization of East Asia'. *World Politics* 47(2): 171–209.

Bernstein, Steven. 2001. *The Compromise of Liberal Environmentalism*. New York: Columbia University Press.

Bernstein, Steven. 2011. 'Legitimacy in Intergovernmental and Non-State Global Governance'. *Review of International Political Economy* 18(1): 17–51.

Best, Jacqueline. 2010. 'The Limits of Financial Risk Management: Or What We Didn't Learn from the Asian Crisis'. *New Political Economy* 15(1): 29–49.

Best, Jacqueline and Matthew Paterson (eds). 2009. *Cultural Political Economy*. London: Routledge.

Bieler, Andreas and Adam David Morton. 2008. 'The Deficits of Discourse in IPE: Turning Base Metal into Gold?'. *International Studies Quarterly* 52(1): 103–28.

Biermann, Frank, Philipp Pattberg, Harro van Asselt and Fariborz Zelli. 2009. 'The Fragmentation of Global Governance Architectures: A Framework for Analysis'. *Global Environmental Politics* 9(4): 14–40.

Biersteker, Thomas J. and Rodney Bruce Hall. 2002. 'Private Authority as Global Governance'. In *The Emergence of Private Authority in Global Governance*, edited by Rodney Bruce Hall and Thomas J. Biersteker. Cambridge: Cambridge University Press, 203–22.

Bird, Graham. 2001. 'What Happened to the Washington Consensus?'. *World Economics* 2(4): 33–51.

Bleiker, Roland. 2001. 'Forget IR Theory'. In *The Zen of International Relations: IR Theory from East to West*, edited by Stephan Chan, Peter Mandaville and Roland Bleiker. Hampshire, NY: Palgrave.

Blyth, Mark. 2002. *Great Transformations: Economic Ideas and Institutional Change in the Twentieth Century*. Cambridge: Cambridge University Press.

Blyth, Mark. 2003. 'Structures Do Not Come with an Instruction Sheet'. *Perspectives on Politics* 1(4): 695–706.

Blyth, Mark. 2013. *Austerity: The History of a Dangerous Idea*. Oxford: Oxford University Press.

Boserup, Ester. 1983. 'The Impact of Scarcity and Plenty on Development'. *The Journal of Interdisciplinary History* 14(2): 383–407.

Boughton, James M. 2002. 'Why White, Not Keynes? Inventing the Postwar International Monetary System'. *IMF Working Paper* WP/02/52. Washington, DC: IMF. <www.imf.org/external/pubs/ft/wp/2002/wp0252.pdf>

Brassett, James and Eleni Tsingou. 2011. 'The Politics of Legitimate Global Governance'. *Review of International Political Economy* 18(1): 1–16.

Bremmer, Ian and Robert Johnston. 2009. 'The Rise and Fall of Resource Nationalism'. *Survival* 51(2): 149–58.

Breslin, Shaun. 2011. 'China and the Crisis: Global Power, Domestic Caution, and Local Initiative'. *Contemporary Politics* 17(2): 185–200.

Breslin, Shaun. 2013. 'China and the Global Order: Signalling Threat or Friendship?'. *International Affairs* 89(3): 615–34.

Bridge, Gavin. 2010. 'Geographies of Peak Oil: The Other Carbon Problem'. *Geoforum* 41(4): 523–30.

Bromley, Simon. 2005. 'The United States and the Control of World Oil'. *Government and Opposition* 40(2): 225–55.

Broome, André. 2008. 'The Importance of Being Earnest: The IMF as a Reputational Intermediary'. *New Political Economy* 13(2): 125–51.

Broome, André. 2009a. 'Money for Nothing: Everyday Actors and Monetary Crises'. *Journal of International Relations and Development* 12(1): 3–30.

Broome, André. 2009b. 'When do NGOs Matter? Activist Organizations as a Source of Change in the International Debt Regime'. *Global Society* 23(1): 59–78.

Broome, André. 2010a. *The Currency of Power: The IMF and Monetary Reform in Central Asia*. Basingstoke: Palgrave Macmillan.

Broome, André. 2010b. 'Global Monitor: The Joint Vienna Institute'. *New Political Economy* 15(4): 609–24.

Broome, André. 2010c. 'Stabilizing Global Monetary Norms: The IMF and Current Account Convertibility'. In *Owning Development: Creating Policy Norms in the IMF and the World Bank*, edited by Susan Park and Antje Vetterlein. Cambridge: Cambridge University Press, 113–36.

Broome, André. 2011. 'Negotiating Crisis: The IMF and Disaster Capitalism in Small States'. *The Roundtable: The Commonwealth Journal of International Affairs* 100(413): 155–67.

Broome, André. 2012. 'Constructivism in International Political Economy'. In *Global Political Economy: Contemporary Theories*, 2nd edn, edited by Ronen Palan. London: Routledge, 211–22.

Broome, André and Leonard Seabrooke. 2007. 'Seeing Like the IMF: Institutional Change in Small Open Economies'. *Review of International Political Economy* 14(4): 576–601.

Broome, André and Leonard Seabrooke. 2012. 'Seeing Like an International Organisation'. *New Political Economy* 17(1): 1–16.

Brown, Vivienne. 1993. 'Decanonizing Discourses: Textual Analysis and the History of Economic Thought'. In *Economics and Language*, edited by Willie Henderson, Tony Dudley-Evans and Roger Backhouse. London: Routledge.

Browning, Christopher S. 2006. 'Small, Smart, and Resilient? Rethinking Identity in the Small States Literature'. *Cambridge Review of International Affairs* 19(4): 669–84.

Bruff, Ian. 2010. 'European Varieties of Capitalism and the International'. *European Journal of International Relations* 16(4): 615–38.

Bruff, Ian. 2011. 'Overcoming the State/Market Dichotomy'. In *Critical International Political Economy: Dialogue, Debate and Dissensus*, edited by Stuart Shields, Ian Bruff and Huw Macartney. Basingstoke: Palgrave Macmillan, 80–98.

Brunnermeier, Markus K. 2008. 'Deciphering the Liquidity and Credit Crunch 2007–08'. *NBER Working Paper Series* 14612. Cambridge: National Bureau of Economic Research. <www.nber.org/papers/w14612>

Brunsson, Nils and Johan P. Olsen. 1993. *The Reforming Organization*. London: Routledge.

Buchanen, Allen and Robert O. Keohane. 2006. 'The Legitimacy of Global Governance Institutions'. *Ethics and International Affairs* 20(4): 405–37.

Burggraf, Helen. 2012. 'World's Largest 1,000 Banks' Assets Grew, Challenges Remain, TheCityUK Says'. *International Advisor* 1 May. <www.international-adviser.com/news/uk/worlds-largest-1000-banks-assets-grew-cityuk-says>

Burnham, Peter. 1994. 'Open Marxism and Vulgar International Political Economy'. *Review of International Political Economy* 1(2): 221–31.

Burnell, Peter. 2012. 'Democracy, Democratization and Climate Change: Complex Relationships'. *Democratization* 19(5): 813–42.

Busby, Joshua William. 2007. 'Bono Made Jesse Helms Cry: Jubilee 2000, Debt Relief, and Moral Action in International Politics'. *International Studies Quarterly* 51(2): 247–75.

Cabrera, Luis. 2010. *The Practice of Global Citizenship*. Cambridge: Cambridge University Press.

Cabrera, Luis. 2011. 'Introduction: Global Institutional Visions'. In *Global Governance, Global Government: Institutional Visions for an Evolving World System*, edited by Luis Cabrera. New York: State University of New York Press.

Callaghy, Thomas M. 2004. *Innovations in the Sovereign Debt Regime: From the Paris Club to Enhanced HIPC and Beyond*. Washington, DC: World Bank Operations Evaluation Department.

Campbell, John L. 1998. 'Institutional Analysis and the Role of Ideas in Political Economy'. *Theory and Society* 27(3): 377–409.

Campbell, John L. 2004. *Institutional Change and Globalization*. Princeton, NJ: Princeton University Press.

Carmassi, Jacopo, Daniel Gros and Stefano Micossi. 2009. 'The Global Financial Crisis: Causes and Cures'. *Journal of Common Market Studies* 47(5): 977–96.

Carpenter, R. Charli. 2010. 'Governing the Global Agenda: 'Gatekeepers' and 'Issue Adoption' in Transnational Advocacy Networks'. In *Who Governs the Globe?*, edited by Deborah D. Avant, Martha Finnemore and Susan K. Sell. Cambridge: Cambridge University Press, 202–37.

Castles, Francis G. 2007. 'Introduction'. In *The Disappearing State? Retrenchment Realities in an Age of Globalisation*, edited by Francis G. Castles. Cheltenham: Edward Elgar, 1–18.

Centano, Miguel Angel. 1997. 'Blood and Debt: War and Taxation in Nineteenth-Century Latin America', *American Journal of Sociology* 102(6): 1565–605.

Cerny, Philip G. 1990. *The Changing Architecture of Politics: Structure, Agency, and the Future of the State*. London: Sage.

Cerny, Philip G. 2010. 'The Competition State Today: From *raison d'État* to *raison du Monde*'. *Policy Studies* 31(1): 5–21.

Checkel, Jeffrey T. 1998. 'The Constructivist Turn in International Relations Theory'. *World Politics* 50(2): 324–48.

Chowdhury, Anis, and Iyanatal Islam. 1993. *The Newly Industrialising Economies of East Asia*. London: Routledge.

Christensen, Jens H.E. and Glenn D. Rudebusch. 2012. 'The Response of Interest Rates to US and UK Quantitative Easing'. *The Economic Journal* 122(564): 385–414.

Chwieroth, Jeffrey M. 2009. *Capital Ideas: The IMF and the Rise of Financial Liberalization*. Princeton, NJ: Princeton University Press.

Claessens, Stijn and M. Ayhan Kose. 2013. 'Financial Crises: Explanations, Types, and Implications'. *IMF Working Paper* WP/13/28. Washington, DC: IMF. <www.imf.org/external/pubs/ft/wp/2013/wp1328.pdf>

Clegg, Liam. 2010. 'Our Dream is a World Full of Poverty Indicators: The US, the World Bank, and the Power of Numbers'. *New Political Economy* 15(4): 473–92.

Clegg, Liam. 2012. 'Post-Crisis Reform at the IMF: Learning to be (Seen to be) a Long-term Development Partner'. *Global Society* 26(1): 61–81.

Clift, Ben and Ben Rosamond. 2009. 'Lineages of a British International Political Economy'. In *Routledge Handbook of International Political Economy (IPE): IPE as a Global Conversation*, edited by Mark Blyth. London: Routledge, 95–111.

Clift, Ben and Cornelia Woll. 2012. 'Economic Patriotism: Reinventing Control over Open Markets'. *Journal of European Public Policy* 19(3): 307–23.

Coe, Neil M., Peter Dicken and Martin Hess. 2008. 'Global Production Networks: Realizing the Potential'. *Journal of Economic Geography* 8(3): 271–95.

Cohen, Benjamin J. 1998. *The Geography of Money*. Ithaca, NY: Cornell University Press.

Cohen, Benjamin J. 2007. 'The Transatlantic Divide: Why are American and British IPE so Different?'. *Review of International Political Economy* 14(2): 197–219.

Cohen, Benjamin J. 2008. *International Political Economy: An Intellectual History*. Princeton, NJ: Princeton University Press.

Cohen, Benjamin J. 2011. *The Future of Global Currency: The Euro Versus the Dollar*. Abingdon: Routledge.

Conca, Ken. 2005. *Governing Water: Contentious National Politics and Global Institution Building*. Cambridge: MIT Press.

Cooley, Alexander A. 2001. 'Booms and Busts: Theorizing Institutional Formation and Change in Oil States', *Review of International Political Economy* 8(1): 163–80.

Cooley, Alexander. 2009. 'Contested Contracts: Rationalist Theories of Institutions in American IPE'. In *Routledge Handbook of International Political Economy (IPE): IPE as a Global Conversation*, edited by Mark Blyth. London: Routledge, 48–61.

Cooley, Alexander. 2012. *Great Games, Local Rules: The New Great Power Contest in Central Asia*. New York: Oxford University Press.

Cooper, Andrew F. 2010a. 'Labels Matter: Interpreting Rising States through Acronyms'. In *Rising States, Rising Institutions: Challenges for Global Governance*, edited by Alan S. Alexandroff and Andrew F. Cooper. Washington, DC, and Waterloo: Brookings Institution Press and Centre for International Governance Innovation, 63–82.

Cooper, Andrew F. 2010b. 'The G20 as an Improvised Crisis Committee and/or a Contested "Steering Committee" for the World'. *International Affairs* 86(3): 741–57.

Cooper, Andrew F. 2013. 'Civil Society Relationships with the G20: An Extension of the G8 Template or a Distinctive Pattern of Engagement?'. *Global Society* 27(2): 179–200.

Cooper, Andrew F. and Ramesh Thakur. 2013. *The Group of Twenty*. London: Routledge.

Cooper, Richard N. 1999. 'Should Capital Controls be Banished?'. *Brookings Papers on Economic Activity* 1999(1): 89–141.

Corelljé, Aad and Coby van der Linde. 2006. 'Energy Supply Security and Geopolitics: A European Perspective'. *Energy Policy* 34(5): 532–43.

Cottarelli, Carlo. 2005. 'Efficiency and Legitimacy: Trade-Offs in IMF Governance'. *IMF Working Paper* WP/05/107. Washington, DC: IMF. <www.imf.org/external/pubs/ft/wp/2005/wp05107.pdf>

Cox, Robert. 1981. 'Social Forces, States and World Orders: Beyond International Relations Theory.' *Millennium: Journal of International Studies* 10(2): 126–55.

Craig, David and Doug Porter. 2003. 'Poverty Reduction Strategy Papers: A New Convergence'. *World Development* 31(1): 53–69.

Daly, Herman E. (ed.). 1973. *Toward a Steady-State Economy*. San Francisco: W.H. Freeman & Co.

Daly, Herman E. 2005. 'Economics in a Full World'. *Scientific American* 293(3): 100–7.

Daquila, Teofilo C. and Le Huu Huy. 2003. 'Singapore and ASEAN in the Global Economy: The Case of Free Trade Agreements'. *Asian Survey* 43(6): 908–29.

Dauvergne, Peter. 1997. *Shadows in the Forest: Japan and the Politics of Timber in Southeast Asia*. Cambridge: MIT Press.

Davies, Thomas Richard. 2008. 'The Rise and Fall of Transnational Civil Society: The Evolution of International Non-Governmental Organizations Since 1839'. *City University Working Papers on Transnational Politics* CUTP/003. London: City University. <www.staff.city.ac.uk/tom.davies/CUWPTP003.pdf>

Dawson, Thomas C. and Gita Bhatt. 2001. 'The IMF and Civil Society Organizations: Striking a Balance'. *IMF Policy Discussion Paper* PDP/01/2. Washington, DC: IMF. <www.imf.org/external/pubs/ft/pdp/2001/pdp02.pdf>

de Goede, Marieke. 2003. 'Beyond Economism in International Political Economy'. *Review of International Studies* 29(1): 79–97.

de Goede, Marieke (ed.). 2006. *International Political Economy and Poststructural Politics*. Basingstoke: Palgrave Macmillan.

de Goede, Marieke. 2007. 'Underground Money', *Cultural Critique* 65(1): 140–63.

de Mooij, Ruud A., Michael Keen and Ian W.H. Parry. 2012. *Fiscal Policy to Mitigate Climate Change: A Guide for Policymakers*. Washington, DC: IMF.

Dehejia, Vivek H. and Philipp Genschel. 1999. 'Tax Competition in the European Union'. *Politics and Society* 27(3): 403–30.

Devenow, Andrea and Ivo Welch. 1996. 'Rational Herding in Financial Economics'. *European Economic Review* 40(3–5): 603–15.

Dimitrov, Radoslav S. 2010. 'Inside Copenhagen: The State of Climate Governance'. *Global Environmental Politics* 10(2): 18–24.

Dixon, Martin. 2007. *Textbook on International Law*, 6th edn. Oxford: Oxford University Press.

Dreher, Axel and Martin Gassebner. 2012. 'Do IMF and World Bank Programs Induce Government Crises? An Empirical Analysis'. *International Organization* 66(2): 329–58.

Drezner, Daniel W. 1999. *The Sanctions Paradox: Economic Statecraft and International Relations*. Cambridge: Cambridge University Press.

Drezner, Daniel W. 2003. 'The Hidden Hand of Economic Coercion'. *International Organization* 57(3): 643–59.

Drezner, Daniel W. 2007. *All Politics is Global: Explaining International Regulatory Regimes*. Princeton, NJ: Princeton University Press.

Drezner, Daniel W. 2010. 'Will Currency Follow the Flag?'. *International Relations of the Asia-Pacific* 10(3): 389–414.

Dryzek, John S. and Hayley Stevenson. 2011. 'Global Democracy and Earth System Governance'. *Ecological Economics* 70(15): 1865–74.

Duffield, John. 2007. 'What are International Institutions?'. *International Studies Review* 9(1): 1–22.

Easterly, William. 2002a. 'How Did Heavily Indebted Poor Countries Become Heavily Indebted? Reviewing Two Decades of Debt Relief'. *World Development* 30(10): 1677–96.

Easterly, William. 2002b. 'The Cartel of Good Intentions: The Problem of Bureaucracy in Foreign Aid'. *The Journal of Policy Reform* 5(4): 223–50.

Easterly, William. 2007. 'Was Development Assistance a Mistake?'. *American Economic Review* 97(2): 328–32.

Easterly, William. 2009. 'How the Millennium Development Goals are Unfair to Africa'. *World Development* 37(1): 26–35.

Eichengreen, Barry. 2012. *Exorbitant Privilege: The Rise and Fall of the Dollar*. Oxford: Oxford University Press.

Elias, Juanita. 2010. 'Locating the 'Everyday' in International Political Economy: That Roar Which Lies on the Other Side of Silence'. *International Studies Review* 12(4): 603–9.

Elias, Juanita. 2011. 'Critical Feminist Scholarship and IPE'. In *Critical International Political Economy: Dialogue, Debate and Dissensus*, edited by Stuart Shields, Ian Bruff and Huw Macartney. Basingstoke: Palgrave Macmillan, 99–116.

Elias, Juanita. 2013. 'Davos Woman to the Rescue of Global Capitalism: Postfeminist Politics and Competitiveness Promotion at the World Economic Forum'. *International Political Sociology* 7(2): 152–69.

Elliott, Lorraine. 2007. 'Transnational Environmental Crime in the Asia Pacific: An 'Un(der)securitized' Security Problem?'. *The Pacific Review* 20(4): 499–522.

El Qorchi, Mohammed, Samuel Munzele Maimbo and John F. Wilson. 2003. 'Informal Fund Transfer Systems: An Analysis of the Informal Hawala System'. *IMF Occasional Paper* 222. Washington, DC: IMF.

European Fair Trade Association. 2006. *EFTA: Joining Fair Trade Forces*, February. <www.european-fair-trade-association.org/efta/Doc/What.pdf>

Falkner, Robert. 2003. 'Private Environmental Governance and International Relations: Exploring the Links'. *Global Environmental Politics* 3(2): 72–87.

Feeney, Simon and Matthew Clarke. 2009. *The Millennium Development Goals and Beyond: International Assistance to the Asia-Pacific.* Basingstoke: Palgrave Macmillan.

Ferchen, Matt. 2013. 'Whose China Model Is It Anyway? The Contentious Search for Consensus'. *Review of International Political Economy* 20(2): 390–420.

Finnemore, Martha. 2009. 'Legitimacy, Hypocrisy, and the Social Structure of Unipolarity: Why Being a Unipole Isn't All It's Cracked Up to Be'. *World Politics* 61(1): 58–85.

Finnemore, Martha and Kathryn Sikkink. 1998. 'International Norm Dynamics and Political Change'. *International Organization* 52(4): 887–917.

Foot, Rosemary and Andrew Walter. 2011. *China, The United States, and Global Order.* Cambridge: Cambridge University Press.

Ford, Michele and Nicola Piper. 2007. 'Southern Sites of Female Agency: Informal Regimes and Female Migrant Labour Resistance in East and Southeast Asia'. In *Everyday Politics of the World Economy*, edited by John Hobson and Leonard Seabrooke. Cambridge: Cambridge University Press, 63–79.

Foucault, Michel. 1991. *Discipline and Punish: The Birth of the Prison.* London: Penguin.

Frank, Andre Gunder. 1966. 'The Development of Underdevelopment'. *Monthly Review* 18(4): 17–30.

French, John R.P., Jr. and Bertram Raven. 1959. 'The Bases of Social Power'. In *Studies in Social Power*, edited by Dorwin Cartwright. Ann Arbor: University of Michigan Press, 150–67.

Friman, H. Richard and Peter Andreas (eds). 1999. *The Illicit Global Economy and State Power.* Lanham: Rowman & Littlefield.

Galbraith, John Kenneth. 1990. *A Short History of Financial Euphoria.* New York: Viking Press.

Gallagher, Kevin P. 2011. 'Losing Control: Policy Space to Prevent and Mitigate Financial Crises in Trade and Investment Treaties'. *Development Policy Review* 29(4): 387–413.

Gamble, Andrew. 2009a. 'British Politics and the Financial Crisis'. *British Politics* 4(4): 450–62.

Gamble, Andrew. 2009b. *The Spectre at the Feast: Capitalist Crisis and the Politics of Recession.* Basingstoke: Palgrave Macmillan.

Gammon, Earl. 2008. 'Affect and the Rise of the Self-Regulating Market'. *Millennium: Journal of International Studies* 37(2): 251–78.

Garrett, Geoffrey. 1998. *Partisan Politics in the Global Economy.* Cambridge: Cambridge University Press.

Garrett, Geoffrey. 2000. 'The Causes of Globalization'. *Comparative Political Studies* 33(6/7): 971–91.

Garrett, Geoffrey. 2001. 'Globalization and Government Spending around the World'. *Studies in Comparative Development* 35(4): 3–29.

Garrett, Geoffrey and Deborah Mitchell. 2001. 'Globalization, Government Spending and Taxation in the OECD'. *European Journal of Political Research* 39(2): 145–77.

Genschel, Philipp. 2002. 'Globalization, Tax Competition, and the Welfare State'. *Politics and Society* 30(2): 245–75.

George, Alexander L. and Andrew Bennett. 2005. *Case Studies and Theory Development in the Social Sciences*. Cambridge: MIT Press.

Germain, Randall. 2009. 'Of Margins, Traditions, and Engagements: A Brief Disciplinary History of IPE in Canada'. In *Routledge Handbook of International Political Economy(IPE): IPE as a Global Conversation*, edited by Mark Blyth. London: Routldge, 77–91.

Germain, Randall. 2011. 'New Marxism and the Problem of Subjectivity: Towards a Critical *and* Historical International Political Economy'. In *Critical International Political Economy: Dialogue, Debate and Dissensus*, edited by Stuart Shields, Ian Bruff and Huw Macartney. Basingstoke: Palgrave Macmillan, 61–79.

Germain, Randall. 2012. 'Governing Global Finance and Banking'. *Review of International Political Economy* 19(4): 530–5.

Gereffi, Gary, John Humphrey and Timothy Sturgeon. 2005. 'The Governance of Global Value Chains'. *Review of International Political Economy* 12(1): 78–104.

Gilbert, Emily and Eric Helleiner. 1999. 'Introduction: Nation-States and Money: Historical Contexts, Interdisciplinary Perspectives'. In *Nation-States and Money: The Past, Present and Future of National Currencies*, edited by Emily Gilbert and Eric Helleiner. London: Routledge, 1–21.

Gilpin, Robert. 2000. *The Challenge of Global Capitalism: The World Economy in the 21st Century*. Princeton, NJ: Princeton University Press.

Ghosh, Atish R., Jonathan D. Ostry and Charalambos Tsangarides. 2010. *Exchange Rate Regimes and the Stability of the International Monetary System*. IMF Occasional Paper 270. Washington, DC: IMF.

Goel, Ran. 2004. 'A Bargain Born of a Paradox: The Oil Industry's Role in American Domestic and Foreign Policy'. *New Political Economy* 9(4): 467–92.

Goldman, Michael. 2005. *Imperial Nature: The World Bank and Struggles for Social Justice in the Age of Globalization*. New Haven, CT: Yale University Press.

Goldthau, Andreas. 2012. 'Emerging Governance Challenges for Eurasian Gas Markets after the Shale Gas Revolution'. In *Dynamics of Energy Governance in Europe and Russia*, edited by Caroline Kuzemko, Andrei V. Belyi, Andreas Goldthau and Michael F. Keating. Basingstoke: Palgrave Macmillan, 210–26.

Goldthau, Andreas and Jan Martin White. 2009. 'Back to the Future or Forward to the Past? Strengthening Markets and Rules for Effective Global Energy Governance'. *International Affairs* 85(2): 373–90.

Gourevitch, Peter A. and James Shinn. 2005. *Political Power and Corporate Control: The New Global Politics of Corporate Governance*. Princeton, NJ: Princeton University Press.

Gowa, Joanne. 1983. *Closing the Gold Window: Domestic Politics and the End of Bretton Woods*. Ithaca, NY: Cornell University Press.

Grabel, Ilene. 2000. 'The Political Economy of "Policy Credibility": The New Classical Macroeconomics and the Remaking of Emerging Economies'. *Cambridge Journal of Economics* 24(1): 1–19.

Greenspan, Alan. 1996. *Remarks by Chairman Alan Greenspan at the Annual Dinner and Francis Boyer Lecture of The American Enterprise Institute for Public Policy Research*, 5 December. Washington, DC: The Federal Reserve Board. <www.federalreserve.gov/boarddocs/speeches/1996/19961205.htm>

Griffin, Penny. 2007. 'Refashioning IPE: What and How Gender Analysis Teaches International (Global) Political Economy'. *Review of International Political Economy* 14(4): 719–36.

Griffin, Penny. 2009. *Gendering the World Bank: Neoliberalism and the Gendered Foundations of Global Governance*. Basingstoke: Palgrave Macmillan.

Group of Eight. 2013. *G8 Leaders' Communiqué: The Lough Erne Summit*. <www.g8.utoronto.ca/summit/2013lougherne/Lough_Erne_2013_G8_Leaders_Communique_2.pdf>

Group of Twenty. 2009. *Leaders' Statement: The Pittsburgh Summit*. <www.pittsburghsummit.gov/mediacenter/129639.htm>

Gstöhl, Sieglinde. 2007. 'Governance through Government Networks: The G8 and International Organizations'. *Review of International Organizations* 2(1): 1–37.

Guitián, Manuel. 1994. 'The Choice of an Exchange Rate Regime'. In *Approaches to Exchange Rate Policy: Choices for Developing and Transition Economies*, edited by Richard C. Barth and Chorng-Huey Wong. Washington, DC: IMF, 13–36.

Gutner, Tamar L. 2002. *Banking on the Environment: Multilateral Development Banks and Their Environmental Performance in Central and Eastern Europe*. Cambridge: MIT Press.

Gutner, Tamar and Alexander Thompson. 2010. 'The Politics of IO Performance: A Framework'. *Review of International Organizations* 5(3): 227–48.

Hacker, Jacob S. and Paul Pierson. 2010. *Winner-Take-All Politics: How Washington Made the Rich Richer – And Turned Its Back on the Middle Class*. New York: Simon and Schuster.

Haggard, Stephan and Robert R. Kaufman. 2008. *Development, Democracy, and Welfare States: Latin America, East Asia, and Eastern Europe*. Princeton, NJ: Princeton University Press.

Hall, Peter A. and David Soskice. 2001. 'An Introduction to Varieties of Capitalism'. In *Varieties of Capitalism: The Institutional Foundations of Comparative Advantage*, edited by Peter A. Hall and David Soskice. New York: Oxford University Press, 1–68.

Hall, Rodney Bruce. 2008. *Central Banking as Global Governance: Constructing Financial Credibility*. Cambridge: Cambridge University Press.

Hall, Rodney Bruce and Thomas J. Biersteker. 2002. 'Introduction: Theorizing Private Authority'. In *The Emergence of Private Authority in Global Governance*, edited by Rodney Bruce Hall and Thomas J. Biersteker. Cambridge: Cambridge University Press, 3–22.

Handel, Michael I. 1990. *Weak States in the International System*, 2nd edn. New York: Frank Cass.

Hardie, Iain. 2012. *Financialization and Government Borrowing Capacity in Emerging Markets*. Basingstoke: Palgrave Macmillan.

Harman, Sophie. 2012. *Global Health Governance*. Abingdon: Routledge.

Hassdorf, Wolf. 2005. 'Emperor without Clothes: Financial Market Sentiment and the Limits of British Currency Machismo in the ERM Crisis'. *Millennium: Journal of International Studies* 33(3): 691–722.

Hawkins, Darren G., David A. Lake, Daniel L. Nielson and Michael J. Tierney (eds). 2006. *Delegation and Agency in International Organizations*. Cambridge: Cambridge University Press.

Hearl, Derek. 2006. 'The Luxembourg Presidency: Size Isn't Everything'. *Journal of Common Market Studies* 44(s1): 51–5.

Helleiner, Eric. 1994. *States and the Reemergence of Global Finance: From Bretton Woods to the 1990s*. Ithaca, NY: Cornell University Press.

Helleiner, Eric. 2002. 'Economic Nationalism as a Challenge to Economic Liberalism? Lessons from the 19th Century'. *International Studies Quarterly* 46(3): 307–29.

Helleiner, Eric. 2008a. 'Political Determinants of International Currencies: What Future for the US Dollar?'. *Review of International Political Economy* 15(3): 354–78.

Helleiner, Eric. 2008b. 'The Mystery of the Missing Sovereign Debt Restructuring Mechanism'. *Contributions to Political Economy* 27(1): 91–113.

Helleiner, Eric. 2010. 'A Bretton Woods Moment? The 2007–2008 Crisis and the Future of Global Finance'. *International Affairs* 86(3): 619–36.

Helleiner, Eric and Geoffrey Cameron. 2006. 'Another World Order? The Bush Administration and HIPC Debt Cancellation'. *New Political Economy* 11(1): 125–40.

Helleiner, Eric and Stefano Pagliari. 2009. 'Towards a New Bretton Woods? The First G20 Leaders Summit and the Regulation of Global Finance'. *New Political Economy* 14(2): 275–87.

Henry, Nicholas. 2011. 'Civil Society amid Civil War: Political Violence and Non-Violence in the Burmese Democracy Movement'. *Global Society* 25(1): 97–111.

Herbertsson, Tryggvi Thor and Gylfi Zoega. 2003. 'A Microstate with Scale Economies: The Case of Iceland'. *Working Paper* 1–2003. Reykjavik: Centre for Small State Studies, Institute of International Affairs, University of Iceland.

Higgott, Richard and Matthew Watson. 2008. 'All at Sea in a Barbed Wire Canoe: Professor Cohen's Transatlantic Voyage in IPE'. *Review of International Political Economy* 15(1): 1–17.

Hirschman, Albert O. 1982. 'Rival Interpretations of Market Society: Civilizing, Destructive, or Feeble?'. *Journal of Economic Literature* 20(4): 1463–84.

Hobson, John M. 2000. *The State and International Relations*. Cambridge: Cambridge University Press.

Hobson, John M. 2012. 'Part 2: Reconstructing the Non-Eurocentric Foundations of IPE: From Eurocentric "Open Economy Politics' to Inter-Civilizational Political Economy". *Review of International Political Economy* DOI:10.1080/09692290.2012.733498.

Hobson, John M. and Leonard Seabrooke. 2007. *Everyday Politics of the World Economy*. Cambridge: Cambridge University Press.

Hobson, John M. and Leonard Seabrooke. 2009. 'Everyday International Political Economy'. In *Routledge Handbook of International Political Economy (IPE): IPE as a Global Conversation*, edited by Mark Blyth. London: Routledge, 290–306.

Hodson, Dermot. 2011. *Governing the Euro Area in Good Times and Bad*. Oxford: Oxford University Press.

Hopf, Ted. 1998. 'The Promise of Constructivism in International Relations Theory'. *International Security* 23(1): 171–200.

Holmes, Christopher. 2012. 'Problems and Opportunities in Polanyian Analysis Today'. *Economy and Society* 41(3): 468–84.

Homolar, Alexandra. 2010. 'The Political Economy of National Security'. *Review of International Political Economy* 17(2): 410–23.

Homolar, Alexandra. 2012. 'Multilateralism in Crisis? The Character of US International Engagement under Obama'. *Global Society* 26(1): 103–22.

Hooper, Chalotte. 1999. 'Masculinities, IR and the "Gender Variable": A Cost–Benefit Analysis for (Sympathetic) Gender Sceptics'. *Review of International Studies* 25(3): 475–91.

Hulme, David. 2010. *Global Poverty: How Global Governance is Failing the Poor*. London: Routledge.

Hulme, David and Rorden Wilkinson. 2012. 'Introduction: Moving from MDGs to GDGs: Development Imperatives Beyond 2015'. In *The Millennium Development Goals and Beyond: Global Development after 2015*, edited by Rorden Wilkinson and David Hulme, 1–16.

Imam, Patrick. 2010. 'Exchange Rate Choices of Microstates'. *IMF Working Paper* WP/10/12. <www.imf.org/external/pubs/ft/wp/2010/wp1012.pdf>

IMF. 1993. 'The Fund and the Environment'. SM/93/251. Washington, DC: IMF.

IMF. 1997. *World Economic Outlook: Interim Assessment December 1997*. Washington, DC: IMF. <www.imf.org/external/pubs/ft/weo/weo1297/pdf/1297ch6.pdf>

IMF. 2000. 'Recovery from the Asian Crisis and the Role of the IMF'. *IMF Issues Brief* 00/05. Washington, DC: IMF. <www.imf.org/external/np/exr/ib/2000/062300.htm>

IMF. 2009a. *Annual Report of the Executive Board for the Financial Year Ended 30 April, 2009, Appendix I: International Reserves*. Washington, DC: International Monetary Fund.

IMF. 2009b. *World Economic Outlook : Sustaining the Recovery*, October 2009. Washington, DC: IMF. <www.imf.org/external/pubs/ft/weo/2009/02/pdf/text.pdf>

IMF. 2011. 'The Multilateral Aspects of Policies Affecting Capital Flows'. *IMF Policy Paper*. Washington, DC: IMF. <www.imf.org/external/np/pp/eng/2011/101311.pdf>

IMF. 2012. *Annual Report 2012: Working Together to Support Global Recovery*. Washington, DC: IMF. <www.imf.org/external/pubs/ft/ar/2012/eng/pdf/ar12_eng.pdf>

IMF. 2013. 'Cyprus: Request for Arrangement Under the Extended Fund Facility'. *IMF Country Report* No. 13/125. Washington, DC: IMF. <www.imf.org/external/pubs/ft/scr/2013/cr13125.pdf >

International Energy Agency. 2009. *Key World Energy Statistics 2009*. Paris: IEA.

IOSCO. 2003. *Report on the Activities of Credit Rating Agencies*. The Technical Committee of the International Organization of Securities Commissions. <www.iosco.org/library/pubdocs/pdf/IOSCOPD153.pdf>

IOSCO. 2008. *Report on the Subprime Crisis*. The Technical Committee of the International Organization of Securities Commissions. <www.iosco.org/library/pubdocs/pdf/IOSCOPD273.pdf>

IPCC. 2007. *Climate Change 2007: Synthesis Report*. An Assessment of the Intergovernmental Panel on Climate Change. <www.ipcc.ch/publications_and_data/publications_ipcc_fourth_assessment_report_synthesis_report.htm>

James, Harold. 1996. *International Monetary Cooperation Since Bretton Woods*. Washington, DC: IMF and Oxford University Press.

Jerven, Morten. 2013. *Poor Numbers: How We Are Misled by African Development Statistics and What to Do about It*. Ithaca, NY: Cornell University Press.

Jessop, Bob. 2008. *State Power*. Cambridge: Polity Press.

Johnson, Chalmers. 1982. *MITI and the Japanese Miracle: The Growth of Industrial Policy, 1925–1975*. Stanford: Stanford University Press.

Joyce, Joseph P. 2012. *The IMF and Global Financial Crises: Phoenix Rising?* Cambridge: Cambridge University Press.

Kalyuzhnova, Yelena. 2011. 'The National Fund of the Republic of Kazakhstan (NFRK): From Accumulation to Stress-Test to Global Future'. *Energy Policy* 39(10): 6650–7.

Kaplinsky, Raphael. 2005. *Globalization, Poverty and Inequality: Between a Rock and a Hard Place*. Cambridge: Polity.

Kapstein, Ethan B. 1994. *Governing the Global Economy: International Finance and the State*. Cambridge, MA: Harvard University Press.

Kapstein, Ethan B. 2006. *Economic Justice in an Unfair World: Toward a Level Playing Field*. Princeton, NJ: Princeton University Press.

Katzenstein, Peter J. 2003. 'Small States and Small States Revisited'. *New Political Economy* 8(1): 9–30.

Katzenstein, Peter J. 2005. *A World of Regions: Asia and Europe in the American Imperium*. Ithaca, NY: Cornell University Press.

Keohane, Robert O. 1983. 'The Demand for International Regimes'. In *International Regimes*, edited by Stephen D. Krasner. Ithaca, NY: Cornell University Press, 141–72.

Keohane, Robert O. and Joseph S. Nye, Jr. 2002. 'The Club Model of Multilateral Cooperation and Problems of Democratic Legitimacy'. In *Power and Governance in a Partially Globalized World*, edited by Robert O. Keohane. London: Routledge, 219–44.

Kerkvliet, Benedict J. Tria. 2005. *The Power of Everyday Politics: How Vietnamese Peasants Transformed National Policy*. Ithaca, NY: Cornell University Press.

Keynes, John Maynard. 1936. *The General Theory of Employment, Interest and Money*. London: Macmillan.

Kiff, John, Sylwia Nowak and Liliana Schumacher. 2012. 'Are Rating Agencies Powerful? An Investigation into the Impact and Accuracy of Sovereign Ratings'. *IMF Working Paper WP/12/23*. Washington, DC: IMF. <www.imf.org/external/pubs/ft/wp/2012/wp1223.pdf >

Kirshner, Jonathan. 1995. *Currency and Coercion: The Political Economy of International Monetary Power*. Princeton, NJ: Princeton University Press.

Kirshner, Jonathan (ed.). 2003. *Monetary Orders: Ambiguous Economics, Ubiquitous Politics*. Ithaca, NY: Cornell University Press.

Kirshner, Jonathan. 2007. *Appeasing Bankers: Financial Caution on the Road to War*. Princeton, NJ: Princeton University Press.

Kirshner, Jonathan. 2009. 'Realist Political Economy: Traditional Themes and Contemporary Challenges'. In *Routledge Handbook of International Political Economy (IPE): IPE as a Global Conversation*, edited by Mark Blyth. London: Routledge, 36–47.

Kirton, John, Jenilee Guebert and Shamir Tanna. 2010. 'G8 and G20 Summit Costs'. *G20 Information Centre: Fact Sheets*. Toronto: University of Toronto. <www.g8.utoronto.ca/evaluations/factsheet/factsheet_costs.pdf>

Koch, Martin. 2009. 'Autonomization of IGOs'. *International Political Sociology* 3(4): 431–48.

Krasner, Stephen D. 1984. 'Approaches to the State: Alternative Conceptions and Historical Dynamics'. *Comparative Politics* 16(2): 223–46.

Krätke, Michael R. and Geoffrey Underhill. 2005. 'Political Economy: The Revival of an 'Interdiscipline''. In *Political Economy and the Changing Global Order*, 3rd edn, edited by Richard Stubbs and Geoffrey R.D. Underhill. Oxford: Oxford University Press, 24–38.

Kratochwil, Friedrich. 2006. 'The Genealogy of Multilateralism: Reflections on an Organizational Form and Its Crisis'. In *Multilateralism under Challenge? Power, International Order, and Structural Change*, edited by Edward Newman, Ramesh Thakur and John Tirman. Tokyo: United Nations University Press, 139–59.

Kuzemko, Caroline, Andrei V. Belyi, Andreas Goldthau and Michael F. Keating (eds). 2012. *Dynamics of Energy Governance in Europe and Russia*. Basingstoke: Palgrave Macmillan.

Lai, Jikon. 2012. *Financial Crisis and Institutional Change in East Asia*. Basingstoke: Palgrave Macmillan.

Lake, David A. 2009. *Hierarchy in International Relations*. Ithaca, NY: Cornell University Press.

Lake, David A. 2011. 'Why "isms" are Evil: Theory, Epistemology, and Academic Sects as Impediments to Understanding and Progress'. *International Studies Quarterly* 55(2): 465–80.

Langley, Paul. 2008. *The Everyday Life of Global Finance: Saving and Borrowing in Anglo-America*. Oxford: Oxford University Press.

Langley, Paul. 2009. 'Power-Knowledge Estranged: From Susan Strange to Poststructuralism in British IPE'. In *Routledge Handbook of International Political Economy (IPE): IPE as a Global Conversation*, edited by Mark Blyth. London: Routledge, 48–61.

Lebow, Richard Ned. 2010. *Forbidden Fruit: Counterfactuals and International Relations*. Princeton, NJ: Princeton University Press.

Lee, Donna and Nicola J. Smith. 2008. 'The Political Economy of Small African States in the WTO', *The Roundtable: The Commonwealth Journal of International Affairs* 97(395): 259–71.

Leftwich, Adrian. 2000. *States of Development: On the Primacy of Politics in Development*. Cambridge: Polity.

Leiteritz, Ralf and Manuela Moschella. 2010. 'The IMF and Capital Account Liberalization: A Case of Failed Norm Institutionalization'. In *Owning Development: Creating Policy Norms in the IMF and the World Bank*, edited by Susan Park and Antje Vetterlein. Cambridge: Cambridge University Press, 163–80.

Levin, Carl. 2007. Statement of Senator Carl Levin on Introducing the Stop Tax Haven Act to the US Senate, Part II. 17 February. <www.levin.senate.gov/newsroom/press/release/?id=e73b9f29-425e-4472-8ec3-a3d062bf4122>

Lipson, Charles. 1985. *Standing Guard: Protecting Foreign Capital in the Nineteenth and Twentieth Centuries*. Berkeley and Los Angeles, CA: University of California Press.

Lumsdaine, David Halloran. 1993. *Moral Vision in International Politics: The Foreign Aid Regime, 1949–1989*. Princeton, NJ: Princeton University Press.

Lupovici, Amir. 2009. 'Constructivist Methods: A Plea and Manifesto for Pluralism'. *Review of International Studies* 35(1): 195–218.

Maass, Matthias. 2009. 'The Elusive Definition of the Small State'. *International Politics* 46(1): 65–83.

Martinez-Diaz, Leonardo. 2009. 'The G20 After Eight Years: How Effective a Vehicle for Developing-Country Influence?'. In *Networks of Influence? Developing Countries in a Networked Global Order*, edited by Leonardo Martinez-Diaz and Ngaire Woods. Oxford: Oxford University Press, 39–62.

Martinez-Diaz, Leonardo and Ngaire Woods (eds). 2009. *Networks of Influence? Developing Countries in a Networked Global Order*. Oxford: Oxford University Press.

Mastanduno, Michael. 2009. 'System Maker and Privilege Taker: US Power and the International Political Economy'. *World Politics* 61(1): 121–54.

Matten, Dirk and Andrew Cane. 2005. 'Corporate Citizenship: Toward an Extended Theoretical Conceptualization'. *Academy of Management Review* 30(1): 166–79.

Mattli, Walter (2001). 'The Politics and Economics of International Institutional Standards Setting: An Introduction'. *Journal of European Public Policy* 8(3): 328–44.

Mattli, Walter and Ngaire Woods. 2009. 'In Whose Benefit? Explaining Regulatory Change in Global Politics'. In *The Politics of Global Regulation*, edited by Walter Mattli and Ngaire Woods. Princeton, NJ: Princeton University Press, 1–43.

May, Christopher. 2010. *The Global Political Economy of Intellectual Property Rights*, 2nd edn. London: Routledge.

McDonald, Matt. 2008. 'Securitization and the Construction of Security'. *European Journal of International Relations* 14(4): 563–87.

McNamara, Kathleen R. 1999. *The Currency of Ideas: Monetary Politics in the European Union*. Ithaca, NY: Cornell University Press.

McNamara, Kathleen R. 2008. 'A Rivalry in the Making? The Euro and International Monetary Power'. *Review of International Political Economy* 15(3): 439–59.

McPhilemy, Samuel. 2013. 'Formal Rules versus Informal Relationships: Prudential Banking Supervision at the FSA Before the Crash'. *New Political Economy* 18(5): 748–67.

Mian, Atif, Amir Sufi and Francesco Trebbi. 2011. 'Foreclosures, House Prices, and the Real Economy'. *NBER Working Paper Series* 16685. Cambridge: National Bureau of Economic Research. <www.nber.org/papers/w16685>

Minoiu, Camelia and Javier A. Reyes. 2011. 'A Network Analysis of Global Banking: 1978–2009'. *IMF Working Paper WP/11/74*. Washington, DC: IMF. <www.imf.org/external/pubs/ft/wp/2011/wp1174.pdf >

Mishkin, Frederic S. 2009. 'Is Monetary Policy Effective During Financial Crises?'. *NBER Working Paper Series* 14678. Cambridge: National Bureau of Economic Research. <www.nber.org/papers/w14678>

Mohan, Giles and Marcus Power. 2008. 'New African Choices? The Politics of Chinese Engagement'. *Review of African Political Economy* 35(115): 23–42.

Momani, Bessma. 2010. 'Internal or External Norm Champions: The IMF and Multilateral Debt Relief'. In *Owning Development: Creating Policy Norms in the IMF and the World Bank*, edited by Susan Park and Antje Vetterlein. Cambridge: Cambridge University Press, 29–47.

Moore, Heidi. 2013. 'US Homebuilding is Booming – and so are Foreclosures for Struggling Owners'. *Guardian*, 17 January. <www.guardian.co.uk/business/2013/jan/17/us-homebuilding-booming-foreclosures>

Moravcsik, Andrew. 1997. 'Taking Preferences Seriously: A Liberal Theory of International Politics'. *International Organization* 51(4): 513–53.

Morgenthau, Hans J. 1952. 'Another 'Great Debate': The National Interest of the United States'. *American Political Science Review* 46(4): 961–88.

Morse, Edward L. 1999. 'A New Political Economy of Oil?'. *Journal of International Affairs* 53(1): 1–29.

Mortensen, Jens L. 2012. 'Seeing Like the WTO: Numbers, Frames and Trade Law'. *New Political Economy* 17(1): 77–95.

Morton, Adam David. 2011. *Revolution and the State in Modern Mexico: The Political Economy of Uneven Development*. Plymouth: Rowman & Littlefield.

Morton, Katherine. 2005. *International Aid and China's Environment: Taming the Yellow Dragon*. London: Routledge.

Moschella, Manuela. 2010a. *Governing Risk: The IMF and Global Financial Crises*. Basingstoke: Palgrave Macmillan.

Moschella, Manuela. 2010b. 'International Financial Governance in Hard Times: Tracing the Transformations'. *Contemporary Politics* 16(4): 421–36.

Moschella, Manuela. 2013. 'Designing the Financial Stability Board: A Theoretical Investigation of Mandate, Discretion, and Membership'. *Journal of International Relations and Development* 16: 380–405.

Moschella, Manuela and Eleni Tsingou (eds). 2013. *Great Expectations, Slow Transformations: Incremental Change in Post-Crisis Regulation*. Colchester: ECPR Press.

Mosley, Layna. 2000. 'Room to Move: International Financial Markets and National Welfare States'. *International Organization* 54(4): 737–73.

Mundell, Robert A. 1961. 'A Theory of Optimum Currency Areas'. *American Economic Review* 51(4): 657–65.

Murphy, Craig N. and Douglas R. Nelson. 2001. 'International Political Economy: A Tale of Two Heterodoxies'. *British Journal of Politics and International Relations* 3(3): 393–412.

Narlikar, Amrita. 2003. *International Trade and Developing Countries: Bargaining Coalitions in the GATT and WTO*. London: Routledge.

Narlikar, Amrita. 2007. 'All That Glitters is not Gold: India's Rise to Power', *Third World Quarterly* 28(5): 983–96.

Narlikar, Amrita. 2010a. 'India's Rise to Power: Where Does East Africa Fit In?'. *Review of African Political Economy* 37(126): 451–64.

Narlikar, Amrita. 2010b. *New Powers: How to Become One and How to Manage Them*. London: Hurst & Co.

Narlikar, Amrita. 2013. 'Introduction: Negotiating the Rise of New Powers'. *International Affairs* 89(3): 561–76.

Nesadurai, Helen E.S. 2009. 'Finance Ministers and Central Bankers in East Asian Financial Cooperation'. In *Networks of Influence? Developing Countries in a Networked Global Order*, edited by Leonardo Martinez-Diaz and Ngaire Woods. Oxford: Oxford University Press, 63–94.

Nesvetailova, Anastasia. 2007. *Fragile Finance: Debt, Speculation and Crisis in the Age of Global Credit*. Basingstoke: Palgrave Macmillan.

Neville, Simon. 2012. 'Starbucks Pays £8.6m Tax on £3bn Sales'. *Guardian*, 15 October. <www.guardian.co.uk/business/2012/oct/15/starbucks-tax-uk-sales>

Newell, Peter. 2008. 'The Political Economy of Global Environmental Governance'. *Review of International Studies* 34(3): 507–29.

Newell, Peter and Matthew Paterson. 2010. *Climate Capitalism: Global Warming and the Transformation of the Global Economy*. Cambridge: Cambridge University Press.

Nielson, Daniel L., Michael J. Tierney and Catherine E. Weaver. 2006. 'Bridging the Rationalist–Constructivist Divide: Re-engineering the Culture of the World Bank'. *Journal of International Relations and Development* 9(2): 107–39.

Noble, Gregory W. and John Ravenhill. 2000. 'Causes and Consequences of the Asian Financial Crisis'. In *The Asian Financial Crisis and the Architecture of Global Finance*, edited by Gregory W. Noble and John Ravenhill. Cambridge: Cambridge University Press, 1–35.

Nooruddin, Irfan and Joel W. Simmons. 2009. 'Openness, Uncertainty, and Social Spending: Implications for the Globalization–Welfare State Debate'. *International Studies Quarterly* 53(3): 841–66.

Nørgaard, Ole and Sally N. Cummings. 2004. 'Conceptualising State Capacity: Comparing Kazakhstan and Kyrgyzstan'. *Political Studies* 52(4): 685–708.

Norrlof, Carla. 2010. *America's Global Advantage: US Hegemony and International Cooperation*. Cambridge: Cambridge University Press.

Nourzhanov, Kirill. 2006. 'Caspian Oil: Geopolitical Dreams and Real Issues'. *Australian Journal of International Affairs* 60(1): 59–66.

O'Brien, Robert and Marc Williams. 2013. *Global Political Economy: Evolution and Dynamics*, 4th edn. Basingstoke: Palgrave Macmillan.

OECD. 2012a. *FDI in Figures*. Paris: OECD. <www.oecd.org/daf/international investment/investmentfordevelopment/statistics.htm>

OECD. 2012b. *Text of the OECD Declaration on International Investment and Multinational Enterprises*. Paris: OECD. <www.oecd.org/daf/international investment/investmentpolicy/oecddeclarationoninternationalinvestmentand multinationalenterprises.htm>

OECD. 2012c. *Social Spending After the Crisis: Social Expenditure (SOCX) Data Update 2012*. Paris: OECD. <www.oecd.org/els/soc/OECD%282012 %29_Social%20spending%20after%20the%20crisis_8pages.pdf>

Oliver, Michael J. 2006. 'Civilizing International Monetary Systems'. In *Global Standards of Market Civilization*, edited by Brett Bowden and Leonard Seabrooke. London: Routledge, 107–18.

Oreskes, Naomi. 2004. 'Beyond the Ivory Tower: The Scientific Consensus on Climate Change'. *Science* 306(5702): 1686.

Otero-Inglesias, Miguel and Federico Steinberg. 2012. 'Is the Dollar Becoming a Negotiated Currency? Evidence from the Emerging Markets'. *New Political Economy* 18(3): 309–36.

Overbeek, Henk. 2012. 'Transnational Historical Materialism: "Neo-Gramscian" Theories of Class Formation and World Order'. In *Global Political Economy: Contemporary Theories*, 2nd edn, ed. Ronen Palan. London: Routledge, 162–76.

Page, Edward A. 2008. 'Distributing the Burdens of Climate Change'. *Environmental Politics* 17(4): 556–75.

Palan, Ronen. 2003a. 'Tax Havens and the Commercialization of State Sovereignty'. *International Organization* 56(1): 151–76.

Palan, Ronen. 2003b. *The Offshore World: Sovereign Markets, Virtual Places, and Nomad Millionaires*. Ithaca, NY: Cornell University Press.

Palan, Ronen (ed.). 2012. *Global Political Economy: Contemporary Theories*, 2nd edn. London: Routledge.

Palan, Ronen, Richard Murphy and Christian Chavagneux. 2010. *Tax Havens: How Globalization Really Works*. Ithaca, NY: Cornell University Press.

Park, Susan. 2005. 'How Transnational Environmental Advocacy Networks Socialize International Financial Institutions: A Case Study of the International Finance Corporation'. *Global Environmental Politics* 5(4): 95–119.

Park, Susan. 2007. 'The World Bank Group: Championing Sustainable Development Norms?'. *Global Governance* 13(4): 535–56.

Park, Susan. 2010a. 'Designing Accountability, International Economic Organisations and the World Bank's Inspection Panel'. *Australian Journal of International Affairs* 64(1): 13–36.

Park, Susan. 2010b. *World Bank Group Interactions with Environmentalists: Changing International Organisation Identities*. Manchester: Manchester University Press.

Park, Susan and Antje Vetterlein (eds). 2010. *Owning Development: Creating Policy Norms in the IMF and the World Bank*. Cambridge: Cambridge University Press.

Pauly, Louis W. 1997. *Who Elected the Bankers? Surveillance and Control in the World Economy*. Ithaca, NY: Cornell University Press.

Payne, Anthony. 2008. 'After Bananas: The IMF and the Politics of Stabilisation and Diversification in Dominica'. *Bulletin of Latin American Research* 27(3): 317–32.

Payne, Anthony and Nicola Phillips. 2010. *Development*. Cambridge: Polity Press.

Peck, Jamie. 2010. *Constructions of Neoliberal Reason*. Oxford: Oxford University Press.

Phillips, Nicola (ed.). 2005. *Globalizing International Political Economy*. Basingstoke: Palgrave Macmillan.

Phillips, Nicola. 2009. 'The Slow Death of Pluralism'. *Review of International Political Economy* 16(1): 85–94.

Phillips, Nicola (ed.). 2011a. *Migration in the Global Political Economy*. Boulder: Lynne Rienner.

Phillips, Nicola. 2011b. 'Informality, Global Production Networks and the Dynamics of "Adverse Incorporation"'. *Global Networks* 11(3): 380–97.

Phillips, Nicola and Catherine E. Weaver (eds). 2010. *International Political Economy: Debating the Past, Present and Future*. London: Routledge.

Pigman, Geoffrey A. 2006a. 'Civilizing Global Trade: Alterglobalizers and the "Double Movement"'. In *Global Standards of Market Civilization*, edited by Brett Bowden and Leonard Seabrooke. London: Routledge, 188–204.

Pigman, Geoffrey Allen. 2006b. *The World Economic Forum: A Multi-Stakeholder Approach to Global Governance*. London: Routledge.

Pigman, Geoffrey Allen. 2010. *Contemporary Diplomacy*. Cambridge: Polity.

Piketty, Thomas and Emmanuel Saez. 2007. 'How Progressive is the US Federal Tax System? A Historical and International Perspective'. *Journal of Economic Perspectives* 21(1): 3–24.

Plümper, Thomas, Vera E. Troeger and Hannes Winner. 2009. 'Why is There No Race to the Bottom in Capital Taxation'. *International Studies Quarterly* 53(3): 761–86.

Poovey, Mary. 1998. *A History of the Modern Fact: Problems of Knowledge in the Sciences of Wealth and Society*. Chicago: Chicago University Press.

Quirk, Joel. 2011. *The Anti-Slavery Project: From the Slave Trade to Human Trafficking*. Philadelphia: University of Pennsylvania Press.

Quirk, Joel and Darshan Vigneswaran. 2005. 'The Construction of an Edifice: The Story of a First Great Debate'. *Review of International Studies* 31(1): 89–107.

Rai, Shirin. 2013. 'Gender and (International) Political Economy'. In *Oxford Handbook on Gender and Politics*, edited by Georgina Waylen, Karen Celis, Johanna Kantola and Laurel Weldon. Oxford: Oxford University Press, 263–88.

Ravenhill, John. 1998. 'Cycles of Middle Power Activism: Constraint and Choice in Australian and Canadian Foreign Policies'. *Australian Journal of International Affairs* 52(3): 309–27.

Ravenhill, John. 2008. 'In Search of the Missing Middle'. *Review of International Political Economy* 15(1): 18–29.

Ravenhill, John (ed.). 2011. *Global Political Economy*, 3rd edn. Oxford: Oxford University Press.

Reinhart, Carmen M. and Kenneth S. Rogoff. 2009. *This Time is Different: Eight Centuries of Financial Folly*. Princeton, NJ: Princeton University Press.

Rethel, Lena. 2011. 'Whose Legitimacy? Islamic Finance and the Global Financial Order'. *Review of International Political Economy* 18(1): 75–98.

Rethel, Lena. 2014. 'Bank Regulation after the Global Financial Crisis'. In *Financial Regulation after the Global Financial Crisis*, edited by Tony Porter. London: Routledge.

Rethel, Lena and Timothy J. Sinclair. 2012. *The Problem with Banks*. London: Zed.

Reus-Smit, Christian. 1997. 'The Constitutional Structure of International Society and the Nature of Fundamental Institutions'. *International Organization* 51(4): 555–89.

Reus-Smit, Christian. 2005. 'Liberal Hierarchy and the Licence to Use Force'. *Review of International Studies* 31(s1): 71–92.

Reus-Smit, Chrisian. 2007. 'International Crises of Legitimacy'. *International Politics* 44(2/3): 157–74.

Rieffel, Alexis. 1985. 'The Role of the Paris Club in Managing Debt Problems'. *Essays in International Finance* 161. Princeton, NJ: Princeton University Press.

Rixen, Thomas. 2011. 'From Double Tax Avoidance to Tax Competition: Explaining the Institutional Trajectory of International Tax Governance'. *Review of International Political Economy* 18(2): 197–227.

Rogers, Colin. 1989 *Money, Interest and Capital: A Study in the Foundations of Monetary Theory*. Cambridge: Cambridge University Press.

Ross, Michael L. 2001. 'Does Oil Hinder Democracy?'. *World Politics* 53(3): 325–61.

Ruggie, John Gerard. 1982. 'International Regimes, Transactions, and Change: Embedded Liberalism in the Postwar Economic Order'. *International Organization* 36(2): 379–415.

Ruggie, John Gerard. 1993. 'Multilateralism: The Anatomy of an Institution'. In *Multilateralism Matters: The Theory and Praxis of an Institution*, edited by John Gerard Ruggie. New York: Columbia University Press.

Rutland, Peter. 2008. 'Russia as an Energy Superpower'. *New Political Economy* 13(2): 203–10.

Samman, Amin. 2012. 'The 1930s as Black Mirror: Visions of Historical Repetition in the Global Financial Press, 2007–2009'. *Journal of Cultural Economy* 5(2): 213–29.

Samuels, Warren J. 1990. 'Introduction'. In *Economics as Discourse: An Analysis of the Language of Economics*, edited by Warren J. Samuels. Boston: Kluwer Academic.

Scherer, Andreas Georg, Guido Palazzo and Dorothée Baumann. 2006. 'Global Rules and Private Actors: Toward a New Role of the Transnational Corporation in Global Governance'. *Business Ethics Quarterly* 16(4): 505–32.

Scheve, Kenneth and David Stasavage. 2010. 'The Conscription of Wealth: Mass Warfare and the Demand for Progressive Taxation'. *International Organization* 64(4): 529–61.

Scholte, Jan Aart. 2008. 'Defining Globalisation'. *The World Economy* 31(11): 1471–502.

Scholte, Jan Aart (ed.). 2011. *Building Global Democracy? Civil Society and Accountable Global Governance*. Cambridge: Cambridge University Press.

Scholte, Jan Aart, Robert O'Brien and Marc Williams. 1999. 'The WTO and Civil Society'. *Journal of World Trade* 33(1): 107–24.

Schwartz, Herman M. 2009. *Subprime Nation: American Power, Global Capital, and the Housing Bubble*. Ithaca, NY: Cornell University Press.

Schwartz, Herman M. 2010. *States versus Markets: The Emergence of a Global Economy*, 3rd edn. Basingstoke: Palgrave Macmillan.

Schwartz, Herman M. and Leonard Seabrooke (eds). 2009. *The Politics of Housing Booms and Busts*. Basingstoke: Palgrave Macmillan.

Scott, James C. 1985. *Weapons of the Weak: Everyday Forms of Peasant Resistance*. New Haven, CT: Yale University Press.

Seabrooke, Leonard. 2001. *US Power in International Finance: The Victory of Dividends*. Basingstoke: Palgrave Macmillan.

Seabrooke, Leonard. 2004. 'The Economic Taproot of US Imperialism: The Bush *Rentier* Shift'. *International Politics* 41(3): 293–318.

Seabrooke, Leonard. 2006. *The Social Sources of Financial Power: Domestic Legitimacy and International Financial Orders*. Ithaca, NY: Cornell University Press.

Seabrooke, Leonard. 2007. 'The Everyday Sources of Economic Crises: From 'Great Frustrations' to 'Great Revelations' in Interwar Britain'. *International Studies Quarterly* 51(4): 795–810.

Seabrooke, Leonard. 2010a. 'Bitter Pills to Swallow: Legitimacy Gaps and Social Recognition of the IMF Tax Policy Norm in East Asia'. In *Owning Development: Creating Policy Norms in the IMF and the World Bank*, edited by Susan Park and Antje Vetterlein. Cambridge: Cambridge University Press, 137–59.

Seabrooke, Leonard. 2010b. 'What Do I Get? The Everyday Politics of Expectations and the Subprime Crisis'. *New Political Economy* 15(1): 51–70.

Seabrooke, Leonard and Eleni Tsingou. 2009. 'Power Elites and Everyday Politics in International Financial Reform'. *International Political Sociology* 3(4): 457–61.

Segura-Ubiergo, Alex. 2007. *The Political Economy of the Welfare State in Latin America: Globalization, Democracy, and Development*. Cambridge: Cambridge University Press.

Sen, Amartya. 1983. 'Development: Which Way Now?'. *The Economic Journal* 93(372): 745–62.

Shabsigh, Ghiath and Nadeem Ilahi. 2007. 'Looking Beyond the Fiscal: Do Oil Funds Bring Macroeconomic Stability?'. *IMF Working Paper* WP/07/96. <www.imf.org/external/pubs/ft/wp/2007/wp0796.pdf>

Shambaugh, Jay C. 2012. 'The Euro's Three Crises'. *Brookings Papers on Economic Activity*, Spring. <www.brookings.edu/~/media/Projects/BPEA/ .../2012a_Shambaugh.pdf>

Shapiro, Michael J. 1981. *Language and Political Understanding: The Politics of Discursive Practices*. New Haven, CT: Yale University Press.

Sharman, J.C. 2006. *Havens in a Storm: The Struggle for Global Tax Regulation*. Ithaca, NY: Cornell University Press.

Sharman, J.C. 2009. 'The Bark *is* the Bite: International Organizations and Blacklisting', *Review of International Political Economy* 16(4): 573–96.

Sharman, J.C. 2010. 'Offshore and the New International Political Economy'. *Review of International Political Economy* 17(1): 1–19.

Sharman, J.C. 2011. *The Money Laundry: Regulating Criminal Finance in the Global Economy*. Ithaca, NY: Cornell University Press.

Shin, Hyun Song. 2009. 'Reflections on Northern Rock: The Bank Run that Heralded the Global Financial Crisis'. *Journal of Economic Perspectives* 23(1): 101–19.

Sil, Rudra and Peter J. Katzenstein. 2010. *Beyond Paradigms: Analytic Eclecticism in the Study of World Politics*. Basingstoke: Palgrave Macmillan.

Sil, Rudra and Peter J. Katzenstein. 2011. 'De-Centering, Not Discarding, the 'Isms': Some Friendly Amendments'. *International Studies Quarterly* 55(2): 481–85.

Simmons, Beth A. 2006. 'From Unilateralism to Multilateralism: Challenges for the Multilateral Trade System'. In *Multilateralism under Challenge? Power, International Order, and Structural Change*, edited by Edward Newman, Ramesh Thakur and John Tirman. Tokyo: United Nations University Press, 441–59.

Sinclair, Timothy J. 2005. *The New Masters of Capital: American Bond Rating Agencies and the Politics of Creditworthiness*. Ithaca, NY: Cornell University Press.

Sinclair, Timothy J. 2010. 'Round Up the Usual Suspects: Blame and the Subprime Crisis'. *New Political Economy* 15(1): 91–107.

Singer, David Andrew. 2007. *Regulating Capital: Setting Standards for the International Financial System*. Ithaca, NY: Cornell University Press.

Slaughter, Anne-Marie. 2004. 'Everyday Global Governance'. *Daedalus* 132(1): 83–90.

Smith, Nicola J. 2011. 'The International Political Economy of Commercial Sex'. *Review of International Political Economy* 18(4): 530–49.

Smith, Roy C., Ingo Walter, and Gayle DeLong. 2012. *Global Banking*, 3rd edn. Oxford: Oxford University Press.

Smith, William and James Brassett. 2008. 'Deliberation and Global Governance: Liberal, Cosmopolitan, and Critical Perspectives'. *Ethics and International Affairs* 22(1): 69–92.

Snyder, Richard and Ravi Bhavnani. 2005. 'Diamonds, Blood, and Taxes: A Revenue-Centered Framework for Explaining Political Order'. *Journal of Conflict Resolution* 49(4): 563–97.

Speller, William, Gregory Thwaltes and Michelle Wright. 2011. 'The Future of International Capital Flows'. *Financial Stability Paper* 12. London: Bank of England. <www.bankofengland.co.uk/publications/Documents/fsr/fs_paper 12.pdf>

Springer, Simon. 2012. 'Neoliberalism as Discourse: Between Foucauldian Political Economy and Marxian Poststructuralism'. *Critical Discourse Studies* 9(2): 133–47.

Standing, Guy. 2010. 'Global Monitor: The International Labour Organization'. *New Political Economy* 15(2): 307–18.

Stanley, Liam. 2014. ' "We're Reaping What We Sowed": Everyday Crisis Narratives and Acquiescence to the Age of Austerity'. *New Political Economy* 19, forthcoming.

Statistical Office of the United Nations. 1962. *International Trade Statistics: 1900–1960*. New York: United Nations. <http://unstats.un.org/unsd/trade/imts/Historical%20data%201900-1960.pdf>

Steinmo, Sven. 2003. 'The Evolution of Policy Ideas: Tax Policy in the 20th Century'. *British Journal of Politics and International Relations* 5(2): 206–36.

Stiglitz, Joseph. 2000. 'The Insider: What I learned at the World Economic Crisis'. *The New Republic* 222 (16–17). <www.tnr.com/article/politics/the-insider#>

Stiglitz, Joseph, Amartya Sen and Jean-Paul Fitoussi. 2009. *Report of the Commission on the Measurement of Economic Performance and Social Progress*. <www.stiglitz-sen-fitoussi.fr/documents/rapport_anglais.pdf >

Stokes, Doug. 2013. 'Archilles' Deal: Dollar Decline and US Grand Strategy after the Crisis'. *Review of International Political Economy*. <http://dx.doi.org/10.1080/09692290.2013.779592>

Stokke, Olav. 2009. *The UN and Development: From Aid to Cooperation*. Bloomington: Indiana University Press.

Stone, Diane. 2008. 'Global Public Policy, Transnational Policy Communities, and Their Networks'. *The Policy Studies Journal* 36(1): 19–38.

Stopford, John and Susan Strange, with John S. Henley. 1991. *Rival States, Rival Firms: Competition for World Market Shares*. Cambridge: Cambridge University Press.

Strange, Susan. 1994. *States and Markets*, 2nd edn. London: Continuum.

Stretton, Hugh. 1999. *Economics: A New Introduction*. Sydney: University of New South Wales Press.

Swank, Duane. 1998. 'Funding the Welfare State: Globalization and the Taxation of Business in Advanced Market Economies'. *Political Studies* 46(4): 671–92.

Thirkell-White, Ben. 2004. 'The IMF and Civil Society'. *New Political Economy* 9(2): 251–70.

Thirkell-White, Ben. 2009. 'Dealing with the Banks: Populism and the Public Interest in the Global Financial Crisis'. *International Affairs* 85(4): 689–711.

Thomas, Caroline. 2001. 'Global Governance, Development and Human Security: Exploring the Links'. *Third World Quarterly* 22(2): 159–75.

Thompson, Helen. 2007. 'Debt and Power: The United States' Debt in Historical Perspective'. *International Relations* 21(3): 305–23.

Thorhallsson, Baldur and Anders Wivel. 2006. 'Small States in the European Union: What Do We Know and What Would We Like to Know?'. *Cambridge Review of International Affairs* 19(4): 651–68.

Tiberghien, Yves. 2007. *Entrepreneurial Stats: Reforming Corporate Governance in France, Japan, and Korea*. Ithaca, NY: Cornell University Press.

Tilly, Charles. 1989. *Big Structures, Large Processes, Huge Comparisons*. New York: Russell Sage Foundation.

Tomz, Michael. 2007. *Reputation and International Cooperation: Sovereign Debt across Three Centuries*. Princeton, NJ: Princeton University Press.

Tooze, Roger and Craig N. Murphy. 1996. 'The Epistemology of Poverty and the Poverty of Epistemology in IPE: Mystery, Blindness, and Invisibility'. *Millennium: Journal of International Studies* 25(3): 671–707.

Tribe, Keith. 1999. 'Adam Smith: Critical Theorist?'. *Journal of Economic Literature* 37(2): 609–32.

True, Jacqui. 2012. *The Political Economy of Violence against Women*. Oxford: Oxford University Press.

Trumbull, Gunnar. 2006. *Consumer Capitalism: Politics, Product Markets, and Firm Strategy in France and Germany*. Ithaca, NY: Cornell University Press.

Tsai, Kellee S. 2007. *Capitalism without Democracy: The Private Sector in Contemporary China*. Ithaca, NY: Cornell University Press.

Tsingou, Eleni. 2010. 'Global Financial Governance and the Developing Anti-Money Laundering Regime: What Lessons for International Political Economy?'. *International Politics* 47(6): 617–37.

Tsingou, Eleni. 2012. 'Club Model Politics and Global Financial Governance: The Case of the Group of Thirty'. PhD dissertation, Amsterdam University.

UNCTAD. 2007. *The Universe of the Largest Transnational Corporations*. Geneva: UNCTAD. <www.unctad.org/en/Docs/iteiia20072_en.pdf>

UNCTAD. 2012. *World Investment Report 2012: Towards a New Generation of Investment Policies*. Geneva: UNCTAD. <www.unctad-docs.org/UNCTAD-WIR2012-Full-en.pdf>

UNDP. 1990. *Human Development Report 1990: Concept and Measurement of Human Development*. Oxford: Oxford University Press. <http://hdr.undp.org/en/reports/global/hdr1990/chapters/>

Underhill, Geoffrey. 2000. 'State, Market, and Global Political Economy: Genealogy of an (Inter-?) Discipline'. *International Affairs* 76(4): 805–24.

Underhill, Geoffrey. 2005. 'Conceptualizing the Changing Global Order'. In *Political Economy and the Changing Global Order*, 3rd edn, edited by Richard Stubbs and Geoffrey R.D. Underhill. Oxford: Oxford University Press, 3–23.

Union of International Associations. 2012. *Yearbook of International Organizations 2012–2013*. <www.uia.be/yearbook>

United Nations. 1992. *United Nations Framework Convention on Climate Change*. <http://unfccc.int/files/essential_background/background_publications_htmlpdf/application/pdf/conveng.pdf>

United Nations. 2012a. 'Millennium Development Goals: 2012 Progress Chart'. New York: UN. <www.un.org/millenniumgoals/pdf/2012_Progress_ E.pdf>

United Nations. 2012b. 'Press Release: Significant MDG Gains Risk Slowing Under Declining Aid'. New York: UN. <www.un.org/millenniumgoals/2012_Gap_Report/Press_Release.pdf>

United Nations General Assembly. 1987. *Report of the World Commission on Environment and Development*. General Assembly Resolution 42/187. <www.un.org/documents/ga/res/42/ares42-187.htm>

United Nations General Assembly. 1992. *Report of the United Nations Conference on Environment and Development. Annex I: Rio Declaration on Environment and Development*. A/CONF.151/26 (Vol. I). <www.un.org/documents/ga/conf151/aconf15126-1annex1.htm>

United Nations General Assembly. 1994. *Report of the Global Conference on the Sustainable Development of Small Island Developing States*. A/CONF.167/9, 25 April–6 May, 1994. Bridgetown, Barbados: United Nations. <www.un.org/esa/dsd/dsd_aofw_sids/sids_pdfs/BPOA.pdf>

UNODC. 2010. *The Globalization of Crime: A Transnational Organized Crime Threat Assessment*. New York: United Nations. <www.unodc.org/documents/data-and-analysis/tocta/TOCTA_ Report_2010_ low_res.pdf?>

US Treasury. 2012. *Securities (b): Special Data Series*, Part A: US Securities, Annual Surveys. <www.treasury.gov/resource-center/data-chart-center/tic/Documents/shlhistdat.html>

Vakil, Anna C. 1997. 'Confronting the Classification Problem: Toward a Taxonomy of NGOs'. *World Development* 25(12): 2057–70.

Van Rooy, Alison. 2004. *The Global Legitimacy Game: Civil Society, Globalization, and Protest*. Basingstoke: Palgrave Macmillan.

Vezirgiannidou, Sevasti-Eleni. 2010. 'Entering the Zone of Agreement: The United States in Climate Change Negotiations'. In *Deadlocks in Multilateral Negotiations: Causes and Solutions*, edited by Amrita Narlikar. Cambridge: Cambridge University Press, 164–87.

Vetterlein, Antje. 2012. 'Seeing Like the World Bank on Poverty'. *New Political Economy* 17(1): 35-58.

Vlcek, William. 2008. *Offshore Finance and Small States: Sovereignty, Size and Money*. Basingstoke: Palgrave Macmillan.

Wade, Robert. 1990. *Governing the Market: Economic Theory and the Role of Government in East Asian Industrialization*. Princeton, NJ: Princeton University Press.

Wade, Robert Hunter. 2003. 'What Strategies are Available for Developing Countries Today? The World Trade Organization and the Shrinking of "Development Space"'. *Review of International Political Economy* 10(4): 621–44.

Wade, Robert H. 2012. 'The Politics behind World Bank Statistics: The Case of China's Income'. *Economic and Political Weekly* 47(25): 17–18.

Wade, Robert and Frank Veneroso. 1998. 'The Asian Crisis: The High Debt Model versus the Wall Street–Treasury–IMF Complex'. *New Left Review* 228: 3–22.

Walter, Andrew and Gautam Sen. 2009. *Analyzing the Global Political Economy*. Princeton, NJ: Princeton University Press.

Walter, Ryan. 2011. *A Critical History of the Economy: On the Birth of the National and International Economies*. London: Routledge.

Walter, Stefanie. 2010. 'Globalization and the Welfare State: Testing the Microfoundations of the Compensation Hypothesis'. *International Studies Quarterly* 54(2): 403–26.

Ward, Michael. 2004. *Quantifying the World: UN Ideas and Statistics*. Bloomington: Indiana University Press.

Warwick Commission on International Financial Reform. 2009. *The Warwick Commission on International Financial Reform: In Praise of Unlevel Playing Fields*. Coventry: University of Warwick. <http://www2.warwick.ac.uk/research/warwickcommission/financialreform/report/uw_warcomm_intfinreform_09.pdf>

Watson, Matthew. 2005. *Foundations of International Political Economy*. Basingstoke: Palgrave Macmillan.

Watson, Matthew. 2009. 'Planning for a Future of Asset-Based Welfare? New Labour, Financialized Economic Agency and the Housing Market'. *Planning, Practice and Research* 24(1): 41–56.

Watson, Matthew. 2010. 'The Historical Roots of Theoretical Traditions in Global Political Economy'. In *Global Political Economy*, edited by John Ravenhill. Oxford: Oxford University Press, 29–66.

Watson, Matthew. 2011. 'Competing Models of Socially Constructed Economic Man: Differentiating Defoe's Crusoe from the Robinson of Neoclassical Economics'. *New Political Economy* 16(5): 609–26.

Watson, Matthew. 2012. 'Desperately Seeking Social Approval: Adam Smith, Thorsten Veblen and the Moral Limits of Capitalist Culture'. *British Journal of Sociology* 63(3): 491–512.

Weaver, Catherine. 2008. *Hypocrisy Trap: The World Bank and the Poverty of Reform*. Princeton, NJ: Princeton University Press.

Webb, Michael C. and Stephen D. Krasner. 1989. 'Hegemonic Stability Theory: An Empirical Assessment'. *Review of International Studies* 15(2): 183–98.

Weinthal, Erika. 2002. *Statemaking and Environmental Cooperation: Linking Domestic and International Politics in Central Asia*. Cambridge: MIT Press.

Weiss, Linda. 2005. 'Global Governance, National Strategies: How Industrialized States Make Room to Move under the WTO'. *Review of International Political Economy* 12(5): 723–49.

Widmaier, Wesley W. 2004. 'Theory as a Factor and the Theorist as an Actor: The 'Pragmatist Constructivist' Lessons of John Dewey and John Kenneth Galbraith'. *International Studies Review* 6(3): 427–45.

Widmaier, Wesley W. 2010. 'Emotions Before Paradigms: Elite Anxiety and Populist Resentment from the Asian to the Subprime Crises'. *Millennium: Journal of International Studies*. 39(1): 127–44.

Widmaier, Wesley W., Mark Blyth and Leonard Seabrooke. 2007. 'Exogenous Shocks or Endogenous Constructions? The Meanings of Wars and Crises'. *International Studies Quarterly* 51(4): 747–59.

Willetts, Peter. 2011. *Non-Governmental Organisations in World Politics: The Construction of Global Governance*. London: Routledge.

Williamson, John. 1990. *Latin American Adjustment: How Much Has Happened?*. Washington, DC: Institute for International Economics.

Wilson, Patrick. 1983. *Second-Hand Knowledge: An Inquiry into Cognitive Authority*. Westport, CT: Greenwood Press.

Woll, Cornelia. 2008. *Firm Interests: How Governments Shape Business Lobbying on Global Trade*. Ithaca, NY: Cornell University Press.

Wong, Yvonne. 2012. *Sovereign Finance and the Poverty of Nations: Odious Debt in International Law*. Cheltenham: Edward Elgar.

Woods, Ngaire. 2006. *The Globalizers: The IMF, the World Bank, and Their Borrowers*. Ithaca, NY: Cornell University Press.

World Bank. 1991. *World Development Report 1991: The Challenge of Development*. Washington, DC: Oxford University Press.

World Bank. 1993. *The East Asian Miracle: Economic Growth and Public Policy*. New York: Oxford University Press.

World Bank. 2012. *Global Development Finance: External Debt of Developing Countries*. Washington, DC: World Bank. <http://data.worldbank.org/sites/default/files/gdf_2012.pdf>

WTO. 2011a. *International Trade Statistics 2011, Appendix: Historical Trends*. Geneva: WTO. <http://www.wto.org/english/res_e/statis_e/its2011_e/its11_appendix_e.pdf>

WTO. 2011b. *Director-General's Report on Trade-Related Developments (Mid-October 2011 to Mid-May 2012)*. Geneva: WTO. <www.wto.org/english/news_e/news12_e/dgreportsum_e.pdf>

Young, Kevin L. 2012. 'Transnational Regulatory Capture? An Empirical Examination of the Transnational Lobbying of the Basel Committee on Banking Supervision'. *Review of International Political Economy* 19(4): 663–88.

Young, Oran R. 1989. *International Cooperation: Building Regimes for Natural Resources and the Environment*. Ithaca, NY: Cornell University Press.

Zangl, Bernhard. 2008. 'Judicialization Matters! A Comparison of Dispute Settlement Under GATT and the WTO', *International Studies Quarterly* 52(4): 825–54.

Zeng, Ka and Wei Liang. 2010. 'US Antidumping Actions against China: The Impact of China's Entry into the World Trade Organization', *Review of International Political Economy* 17(3): 562–88.

Index